BOOKS BY BERNARD A. WEISBERGER

Reporters for the Union
They Gathered at the River
The American Newspaperman
The Age of Steam and Steel
Reaching for Empire
The District of Columbia
The New Industrial Society
The American Heritage History of the American People
The Impact of Our Past
Pathways to the Present
The Dream Maker: William C. Durant, Founder of General Motors

FOR CHILDREN

Captains of Industry
Illustrious Americans: Samuel Gompers
Booker T. Washington

THE
DREAM
MAKER

THE DREAM MAKER

William C. Durant,
Founder of General Motors

by Bernard A. Weisberger

LITTLE, BROWN AND COMPANY   Boston   Toronto

B-Du/

Second Printing

Unless otherwise indicated, photographs are used through
the courtesy of the General Motors Institute, Alumni Foundation's Collection of Industrial History, Flint, Michigan.

The author is grateful to the following publishers and
individuals for permission to quote material as noted: Mr.
James J. Storrow, Jr., for excerpts from *Son of New England*
by Henry Greenleaf Pearson. Wm. B. Eerdmans Publishing
Company for excerpts from *Billy Durant: Creator of General
Motors,* 1973, by Lawrence R. Gustin. Used by permission.
Wayne State University Press for excerpts from *Lumber-
man from Flint,* by Martin D. Lewis.

LIBRARY OF CONGRESS CATALOG CARD NO. 79-90456

MV

Designed by Janis Capone

*Published simultaneously in Canada
by Little, Brown & Company (Canada) Limited*

PRINTED IN THE UNITED STATES OF AMERICA

To Joan, *with love*
for good and sufficient reasons

Willy was a salesman. And for a salesman, there is
no rock bottom to the life. He don't put a bolt to a
nut, he don't tell you the law or give you medicine.
He's a man way out there in the blue, riding on a
smile and a shoeshine. And when they start not smiling back—that's an earthquake. And then you get
yourself a couple of spots on your hat, and you're
finished. Nobody dast blame this man. A salesman is
got to dream, boy. It comes with the territory.

—Arthur Miller, *Death of a Salesman*

Contents

Illustrations

THE MATRIX: FLINT FACES AND PEOPLE

THE FAMILY

THE BUICK YEARS

Preface

The man is almost entirely forgotten now, even in towns that once delighted to do him honor. His own generation sleeps with its fathers. Some men and women ripe in years frown for a moment when his name is mentioned and say oh, yes, wasn't there a car of that name, I think my uncle had one? Among the young, except for perhaps a handful of automotive history enthusiasts, mention of him stirs no flicker of recognition.

The thoroughness, the depth of that forgetting cannot be measured until one knows what the man did. He founded the General Motors Corporation. And to grasp the magnitude of that statement, to encompass all its echoes, it is necessary to think for a moment about what General Motors is to the automobile industry, and what the automobile is to the United States of America.

No one needs to be told that we are a nation on wheels, bound to wheels, fused with wheels. In the two hundredth year of American independence, there were registered in the states of the Union a total of 137,287,000 passenger automobiles, trucks, and buses. Since the total enumerated population was 216,817,000, that amounts to better than one motor vehicle for every other American, taking all ages indiscriminately together. Close to one for every adult, virtually a second population of transportation machines, surging back and forth over three million miles of paved street and roadway, converting into motion the energy contained in 115,173,-739,000 gallons of liquid hydrocarbon fuel in that single year of 1976. And this mechanical populace, like the human one to which it was fastened, discarded and renewed part of itself annually, through deaths in the junkyard, births in the factory. In 1976 the production of passenger cars alone amounted to 8,497,893. Two years later the total was still growing. Preliminary estimates yielded 1978 production figures of 9,175,836 such automobiles.

To build, operate, and service these legions of machines annually requires, some economists calculate, one-fifth of the nation's steel, over half of its rubber, one-fourth of its glass, large percentages of its lead, copper, zinc, and aluminum, and millions of man-hours of labor. It is estimated that one American worker in six depends, directly or indirectly, on the health of automobile manufacturing for livelihood.

The astonishing thing is that this state of affairs was created in less than a single generous lifetime. The commercial production of autos in significant numbers did not begin until the twentieth century began. It took only seventy-odd years for the auto to rework the social and geographic landscape like taffy, create and condemn communities like a capricious sovereign, tilt the balance between Man and Nature throughout the great globe itself.

The industry rose and grew through a competitive carnage remarkable even in the iron annals of modern business history. Over time, some fifteen hundred would-be manufacturing firms in the United States announced their intention to market cars. Many got no further than accumulating a sheaf of drawings and patent applications, a demonstration model, portfolios of letterhead stationery and stock certificates, a few hundred square feet of office and plant space, leased in hope and quickly lost. But hundreds did manage to achieve at least some level of function witnessed by cars with their names on the road.

And of them all, four alone remain. Within them are the digested remains of others, a few flying the old flags as "divisions." But there are only four firms, however conglomerated, sending forth all but an infinitesimal fraction of each year's new domestically produced vehicles. They are the General Motors Corporation, the Ford Motor Corporation, the Chrysler Corporation, and American Motors Corporation.

And of these four, General Motors is the largest. It made 5,284,498 of those 9.1 million 1978 automobiles, more than one-third again as many as the other three put together. More than twice Ford's total of 2,557,197, more than four and one half times Chrysler's 1,126,168, and better than thirty-two times American's modest 163,554.

Nor was that all. For General Motors was more than an auto-making concern. In the American republic's two hundredth year and its own sixty-eighth it also manufactured trucks, buses, locomotives, automotive parts, accessories and components for marine, aviation, and stationary engines, electric and electronic switching, measuring, relaying and recording equipment for military and civilian use, air conditioners, tape recorders, washers and dryers, freezers, refrigerators, microwave ovens, and trash compactors. Its 29 major operating divisions in the United States accounted for 117 plants in 73 cities. It ran 7 factories in Canada, and had assembly and manufacturing facilities in 21 other countries. Its average number of employees for the twelve months was 681,000. In 1975, which had not been a good automobile year, its net sales were some $35 billion, its net income over one-and-one-quarter billion dollars. It paid nearly $3.5 billion in various local, state, national, and foreign taxes.

This was what the man had begun.

When he created General Motors in 1908 it was simply a holding company, its assets the capital stock of two auto-making firms. But the germs of its future development were in his imagination. Its gargantuan proportions, its protean diversity are a natural flowering of the conception which ruled his planting. The memory of his name may have faded into illegibility in the records, but even now, if the supercorporation should be divested of those divisions that he directly sired, it would virtually cease to exist.

Consider this genealogy. The five passenger-car divisions of General Motors are Chevrolet, Pontiac, Buick, Oldsmobile, and Cadillac.

What was once the Buick Motor Company was begun by an inventor, David Buick, who hoped to market a car carrying his name and certain engine improvements of his own devising, which he believed would be irresistible. Inside two years, he found himself drowning in frustration and debt, dragging a number of backers with him. At that point, the man was invited to step in and take over. He did, and four years later, Buick was at the top of the national sales charts.

Then the man organized General Motors and used its stock to buy out the stock of the Buick Motor Company, and of the Olds Motor Company, whose merry Oldsmobile had already become a catchword in the national mind for the pleasures of mobility. Then he bought the Oakland Motor Company, whose cars would later take the name of its headquarters in Pontiac, Michigan. Then he bought the Cadillac Motor Company, whose products even then were celebrated for luxury and quality workmanship. And in all these purchases, he was consciously aiming at the goal of having automobiles of many different purposes, sizes, styles, and prices made and sold under one corporate roof.

Chevrolet, the best-selling car to fly the General Motors flag, was entirely of the man's begetting. He commissioned the designing and building of the first models, raised the funds, and stitched together the factory and sales organizations. He named the line for Louis Chevrolet, who was a widely known test and race driver of Buicks, in order to pick up the marketable connotations of speed and skill in what would otherwise have been some unfamiliar French syllables.

Two other divisions of General Motors, responsible for its enormous array of electrical gear, also bear the imprint of the man.

There is a collection of factories on the General Motors organization chart under the heading of A.C. Those are the initials of Albert Champion, Parisian-born, who developed a high-quality spark plug for gasoline engines in 1908. The man was shown the plug, liked what he saw, and set up the inventor as his partner in a new company that eventually became a part of General Motors.

Then there are the plants that operate under the general heading of Delco. The name is a combination of acronym and abbreviation, standing for the Dayton Engineering Laboratories, Incorporated. Originally it was an independent company that designed and manufactured batteries, starters, and other electrical elements of automobile power plants. The man enfolded it in General Motors in 1916. With it came Charles F. Kettering, an engineering genius who was nested at the center of the automobile's technological improvement, like a radiant energy cell, for more than three decades thereafter.

And Frigidaire, whose cooling and cleaning and preserving and cooking apparatus is known in millions of homes — Frigidaire began life as a tiny concern, thrashing and staggering in its efforts to market the invention of one of its partners, something that he called a "Frigerator." The man stumbled onto it when it was at the point of expiration, and was kindled. He refinanced it out of his own pocket, reorganized it, gave it its modern name, which he had made up, nursed it like a plaything, and then sold it to the directors of General Motors at a price that probably did not equal his own investment.

This does not exhaust the list. Some readers who have got this far may think that they have identified the man. They will guess Alfred P. Sloan, the powerful and acute administrator who directed the corporation's fortunes for much of its modern history, as president from 1923 until 1946, and chairman of the board from 1937 until 1956. Their guess will be wrong. Sloan came into the General Motors picture eight years after its beginning, when the roller-bearing factory that he headed was bought — by the man, of course.

Even the three rival auto-making enterprises that have lasted until now have direct historical connections with General Motors and its founder. He wanted Ford to be included in the original plan of combination that was in his mind, and he had got Ford's agreement, but the deal collapsed, punctured by Ford's demand for more cash down than the man had or the banks would lend. A year later it happened again. The price and the terms were set that would have rewritten automobile history by making Ford a constituent company of General Motors. But for a second time, no lender would furnish the hard up-front dollars needed to close the bargain.

The Chrysler Corporation had its origin in 1924, when Walter Chrysler finally renamed for himself a nearly defunct motor firm that he had already reorganized, refinanced, and revived. Walter Chrysler had entered the auto business, however, as a hired executive of General Motors. He had intended to leave it in 1916, but was persuaded to stay on when the man offered him a small fortune in annual salary. The two of them had a stormy three-and-one-half-year relationship, at the end of which Chrysler quit to walk the path to independence and competition.

American Motors Corporation had its incarnation in a merger of several organizations in 1954. Its backbone was the Nash Motor Company, named for Charles W. Nash. Nash went to work in 1890 as an ordinary laborer for the man who began General Motors, when the man was already rich, Nash was poor, and neither of them had ever seen an automobile. Twenty-two years later, they were still friends, and Nash had risen to become General Motors' president. Then circumstances arose that made it impossible for them to work together any longer. Nash then left to head his own concern, which was also created by taking over the assets of one of the many casualties of the trade. In a sense, then, both the Chrysler Corporation and American Motors Corporation are spinoffs from General Motors, formed by men to whom the founder was a patron.

How could such a man topple into obscurity so bottomless? Because he lost control of his creation. The father of fortune in others, he himself died without a cent he could call his own. His trail was a dizzying parabola of success and disaster, of treasures won and then swept away.

He created corporations as men of other times had discovered new lands or founded kingdoms. Some of those men lost out, too, and died in exile, in dungeons, or at the executioner's hand. He shared with them the failed dreamer's end. Obscurity is the twentieth-century American version of execution. Monuments are reserved for those who wed victory and die in her embrace, not for those who enjoy her favors transiently and then forsake them.

How could such a plummet follow such a climb? How could such vision miss snares underfoot? A partial answer is that he unwittingly pitted himself against forces whose power to undo him he could not or would not comprehend. But that is only another way of saying that his nature embodied a fatal fearlessness, a trust in his stars that obliterated caution—a faith that is the plunger's asset and his doom. His life illustrated yet another time the aphorism that character is destiny. And to understand how his destiny unfolded, it is necessary to go back to the beginning.

THE
DREAM
MAKER

1)

Drummer from

Flint

I When Rebecca Durant moved for good to Flint, Michigan, in 1872, she
was in the position that women of her time dreaded above almost all
things. She was nearly forty years old, her marriage had failed, and it had
failed because of her own unwise choice. It only underscored her plight
that she was settling in temporarily with her sister Rhoda, for Rhoda's
husband was a prize acquisition—a doctor and an outstanding citizen
—whereas Rebecca's had been a drunkard, an idler, a wastrel, and a
failure, who had capped matters by leaving her, so that she was unmated,
yet not free, and with two children to raise. There was a fifteen-year-old
daughter, christened Rebecca but known as "Rosa," and a ten-year-old boy,
"Willie."

Her situation was painful but not desperate. Her standing in Flint was

1.
"Willie" Durant, just emerging from his teens

2.
The earnest, boutonniered young executives of the Durant-Dort Carriage Company. Durant at far left, A. B. C. Hardy just in front of him and to his left, J. Dallas Dort, with moustache, in center

3.
William A. Paterson, wagonmaker and patriarch of Flint

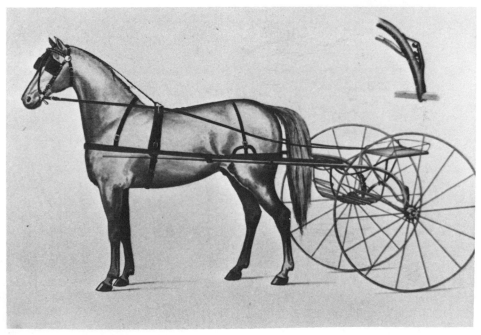

4.
A late model Flint Road Cart, the start of it all

5.
An idealized Flint Road Cart factory, bursting with energy, like the passing trains

6.
Flint's main artery, Saginaw Street, around 1903, with not an automobile in sight

secure in spite of everything. Her father, dead just three years, had been its premier businessman, then its mayor, and finally governor of Michigan. Thanks to his success, her position could not be taken away from her, and money was no problem. What was more, the responsibility that had been thrust on her was possibly a disguised blessing, and she was a woman wont to look for blessings in adversity. Whatever her griefs, she was not rudderless. She must raise her children properly. Her son, especially, must be compensated for his fatherless state, and given the advantages and the strength to resist the temptations that had destroyed his sire. To that mission she would unstintingly give the remainder of her life.

Actually there would be no lack of male role models for the child, whose full name, as recorded at his birth in Boston on December 8, 1861, was William Crapo Durant. Foremost would be the source of his middle name, the maternal grandfather, the merchant and mayor and governor, Henry Howland Crapo. His influence was palpable in Flint still. One of its manifestations was in the presence of several sons-in-law, husbands to some of his nine daughters. While some of these were cut to ordinary measure — men like Lucy's spouse, Humphrey H. Smith, or Aunt Emma's, Harlan P. Christy, both employed at the family lumber mill — Uncle James Willson, with whom Willie and Rosa would live at first, was something different.[1] Not yet forty, he was already a bearded, patriarchal figure with a busy lifetime half behind him. At sixteen, he had left his parents' farm in Canada, seeking the main chance in the gold fields of California. Illness forced him back at Olean, New York. Later, he returned there and earned his bread in the young field of photography. From freezing local worthies on glass plates he had gone to teaching school, though he himself had only attended a village academy for a single year. Finally, he had found his vocation in the medical department of the University of Michigan, from whence he came in 1857, still only twenty-three, to begin a practice in Flint. When the Tenth Michigan, a regiment almost entirely of Flint boys, marched off to the Civil War under a colonel who had twice been their mayor, it seemed only natural that Dr. Willson, too, should go along as their surgeon.

In 1872 he was a respected figure as he drove his high-wheeled "shay" around town on house calls. His surplus energies were poured into his chosen community. He was an organizer of the Genesee County Savings Bank, a member of the Genesee County Agricultural Society, a trustee of the Presbyterian church. In all, a formidable presence for a small boy newly settled under his rooftree.[2]

Uncle James was matched in stature by Uncle William Wallace Crapo, the governor's one son. He lived in New Bedford, Massachusetts, the family's original home, where he had an active career of his own in law, politics, and business. But because he took his responsibilities to his sisters with profound seriousness, he also continued to manage the Crapo properties in Michigan. Henry H. Crapo, dying, had fretted that his estate was not adequate for his widow and nine daughters. He had asked William, therefore, not to divide it immediately, but to manage and enlarge it until its multiplication was respectable in New England eyes. And William remained faithful to the charge for forty-eight years before he finally closed matters out, piling an executor's cares atop his other burdens as if nothing could please him more than being harnessed to duty.[3]

Uncle William's distant example, like Uncle James's immediate presence, would be a powerful magnetizing force for Willie. But his life was influenced most deeply, if unconsciously, by the endowments he received from his dead grandfather and his vanished father. Both these unseen architects of his being were Yankees, each vastly different from the other, and totally unlike the cheeseparing, flinthearted stereotype of the rural New Englander who strode the comic stage.

II Rebecca saved some of the letters that her father wrote to "Willie" during his grandson's baby years in Boston. Driven by love, the old man plunged and floundered gamely in unfamiliar waters of playfulness. In June of 1864 he addressed a plea to "Master Willie."

"Grand Pa" would say very briefly in this letter that he wants to have a visit from him *very, very* much. Grand Pa knows that "Willie" is a very fine boy, and he is very proud of him, and I suppose his mother is equally so. But, "Willie," "Grand Pa" is very busy and has a great deal of work on his hands, and he wants "Willie" very much to help him. Now, "Willie," I want him to ask his "mother" to take "Rosy" and "Pa Pa" and put themselves under his care, and then I want "Willie" to take them all out to Flint this summer to make "Grand Pa" a good long visit. That would be very nice — wouldn't it? And what good times we *would* have, *wouldn't* we![4]

By the following spring he seemed to think he had the hang of it a little better, and tried again from the Executive Mansion in Lansing. To "My Noble Boy" he confided that he had "been looking long time" for Willie and another grandson, Harry. He lamented that

Grand Pa's got *no boys* — only "*Tom-Boys*" and he wants Harry and Willie very much indeed. Why can't he and Harry come and stay long while with Grand Pa who is very busy and wants help — "Willie be Grand Pa's Private Secretary and Harry be Grand Pa's Military Secretary. . . ."

Grand Pa'll have *big time* with his Boys. Come, Willie, and make long visit to

"Grand Father."[5]

And there was another communication from the Executive Office laid away by Rebecca, too, this one an official-looking "General Orders No. 27," creating "a Military District . . . to include among other large and populous precincts the City of *Boston*," especially the territory around Springfield Street, which was to fall under the command of "that *noble* and *highly distinguished Veteran soldier as well as Heroic and Gallant Officer, Brevet Brig.-General 'Willie' Crapo Durant*," who was endowed with powers for the "*full, complete* and *absolute Government*" of said Military Department."[6]

Clumsy as they were, these verbal recreations were an uncharacteristic relaxation of Crapo's official rigor. Externally he showed the world the granite facade of a secure, hardworking moralist who had translated copybook precepts into worldly success. Within, there was a private human being consumed by anxiety, ambition, loneliness, and occasional self-pity. The price of the conflict was a hardening of Crapo's will to achieve that carried him into relentless overexertion and an eventual physical breakdown.

He was the son of a struggling Dartmouth, Massachusetts, farmer, who was too poor to give him any patrimony except the instinct for survival. He managed to teach himself enough to escape lifelong toil among the rocks and stones, becoming the village schoolmaster at seventeen. He married at twenty-one, but stayed in Dartmouth another eight years, apparently as a dutiful son, for as soon as his father died, he moved his family to New Bedford. Though a town of only 8,000 in 1833, it was a busy whaling port, ripe with opportunities for a business-minded hustler.

Crapo hustled for his brood, missing no opportunity and denying himself any leisure. He bought and sold real estate, farm produce, and general merchandise on commission. He worked as an accountant and as a gauger, checking the accuracy of the scales and barrels and flasks in which the men of New Bedford measured out their goods, their profits, and their lives, eyes narrowed for any fractional advantage. Though he disclaimed interest in politics, he accepted election as town clerk and tax collector in order to get the eight-hundred-dollar annual salary. There was no limit to the number of cards he played. He became secretary of an insurance company. He published a business directory. Even his one hobby, horticulture, was turned to useful account when he became sales agent for a plant nursery, then went into the business on his own hook.

This constant endeavor kept the Crapo family table supplied, but failed to satisfy Henry Crapo's deeper yearning to amass some real capital. With

whatever savings he could spare, he would launch small, hopeful investments. One of them was the purchase of land—for himself and for the
accounts of others—in Michigan. Acres in the new state were cheap for the
most part, because they were unsettled and still largely inaccessible. But
they were also covered with thick stands of pine, and Michigan was edging
into a long lumber boom that would succeed the fading fur trade as its
economic heartbeat. In December of 1854 a Detroit land speculator
dangled a bait before Crapo's nose in the form of a huge pineland tract for
$150,000. The sum was far beyond his means, but not out of reach of his
hunger. He was touched with that Yankee dualism that condemned
borrowing for personal consumption as sinful self-indulgence, but would
plunge giddily into the credit markets for some business purpose.

He sought out two New Bedford associates and talked them into going
thirds with him on the purchase, floating before them a lyrical prospectus
of a fortune in wood waiting for the saw. Simply by cutting the timber off the
tract, a net profit of $30,000 a year could be realized. At the end of five
years the cleared, now-arable land would still be worth more than a million.
What Crapo did not add was that he himself would have an excruciating
struggle to make regular payments on his own $50,000 assessment. And
what he did not know was that, when he volunteered to go out and set up
the lumbering operation as a token of earnestness, he was involving
himself, at fifty-one, in a complete change of life, with the specter of
bankruptcy to be constantly at his shoulder for at least half a dozen years.

Lumbering was a seasonal business. In the winter the loggers set up
their camps in the snowbound forests and violated the white silence with
the rasping, percussive noises of progress—the *thuck* of axes, the screech
of saws, falling limbs crackling and crashing in powdery white geysers. The
men would haul stripped tree-carcasses on ox-drawn sleds down to the
banks of frozen rivers. In the spring the logs—each marked with the
symbol of its owner—floated downstream, jostling each other like cattle in
the slaughterhouse chutes. They would finally be halted by booms strung
from bank to bank, and then the lumberjacks would dance over their wet,
slippery backs, fork them into separate clusters, and feed them to the mills
that turned them into boards that were sorted again, and stored, and
seasoned, and finally sold to become studs and flooring and siding and
frames and shingles and spokes—and profits. The whole process took
almost a year, from winter's beginning to next autumn's end. In all that time
the lumberman was paying sawyers and teamsters and cooks and firemen
and machinists and common laborers, and premium prices for real estate
and construction materials and insurance and credit, and not a cent was
coming in, especially if the business was new.

This was what Crapo, with almost no cash reserves, had gotten himself into. He had done so, moreover, at a time when the money markets were decentralized and unregulated, which meant that banknotes and commercial paper might have value one morning and be scrap the next, and that ready money might sometimes simply disappear altogether as it did in his second season of operation, 1856–1857. His letters home became a constant cry for cash. "I am in great want of every dollar I can raise." "I am harassed and perplexed to my very 'wits end' for want of means to pay men." "I shall be obliged to draw upon you tomorrow for funds for future expenses, as we cleaned out everything in the shape of money last night."[7]

Worse than the daily race with insolvency was the fatigue, and more bitter than that was the loneliness. He found a place to saw his logs in Flint, a small settlement that had sprung into being thirty years earlier as a fur-trading post. It was ideally suited to be a lumber center, for the Flint River, on its descent into Lake Huron, flowed straight through it from the pinelands, just before exploding into rapids. The town already had seven sawmills in 1855. Crapo bought one of them, and then, while struggling to keep it repaired and running, let speculative lust triumph over common sense, and bought another within a year. The end result was that he had to spend far more time than he had planned in the West, far too many solitary nights in boardinghouses and exhausting days in the still half-wild forests. Through his constant letters to William ran a litany of depression and mistrust.

"I am very well and have endured the cold and exposure far better than I anticipated," ran one report, but Crapo added immediately: "My mind and thoughts dwell constantly on home."[8] While he complained abundantly of "constant and almost daily rides in an open wagon over hard roads [in] this cold weather,"[9] it was the psychic, rather than the physical, toll that he felt most heavily.

I see everywhere around me such evidences of "hard times," *etc.* as to feel very little of that small share of courage left which I was permitted to take with me from Flint.[10]

Alone here and separated from all those influences of home and affection which have sustained me through many years of toil . . . few can tell or will ever know or realize how much of fortitude and resolution has been required to carry me through the last two years of my life.[11]

And the pressure was relentless; only by devoting "all [his] powers of body and mind" to business, he cried out in his loneliness, could he avoid "inevitably" losing everything acquired over "many years of care and anxiety."[12]

By 1858, it was too much. He decided to cut loose from his New England anchorage, commit himself to the new business completely, and bring his wife and unmarried daughters to Flint. He sold his interest in the pinelands (though he clung to scattered bits of real estate) and concentrated on the mills. His situation eased somewhat then, as rising lumber prices at the beginning of the Civil War kept Flint busy and prosperous, inhaling the sweet aroma of dollars with every whiff of sawdust. Yet now he could not break the risk-taking habit. He poured twelve thousand dollars into a hole in the ground—a well to bring up brine for conversion into salt. It was abandoned, dead, at 1,400 feet. He was luckier in organizing a company to build a railroad from Flint to nearby Holly, where it joined with a main line to give the town's lumber year-round access to markets. That was completed and paid for in cash, a quarter of a million of it raised in New Bedford and Boston through stock sales by Crapo and son. He became president of the tiny line, and later of the Flint and Pere Marquette, with which it merged.

As if time somehow hung on his hands, he took on political assignments. He insisted that it was merely a practical step, to make sure of a favorable tax and legal climate for his operations. William, by now worried about his father's stability, must have remonstrated, since Crapo wrote him: "Do not fear. I shall spend no more time than my interest will warrant. . . . I shall not let it interfere with my business in the slightest degree."[13] In actual fact, he did believe that whatever was not business-connected was not worthy of serious attention. The Civil War itself drew only an indifferent observation: "This war excitement for a period will engross the attention of everybody, yet just as sure as all the men and boys will return to their work again when the circus troup[e] is out of sight, so sure will all hands turn their attention to business again as soon as war is fairly inaugurated and its novelty has passed away."[14]

Notwithstanding this disdain, he accepted the Republican nomination for mayor in 1860, and his appetite grew by what it fed on. He went to the Michigan Senate in 1862, was named to run for the governorship in 1864, and won. He was reelected in 1866. At that time, therefore, he was managing his mills, his railroad, the company store that he had set up, some farms that he owned and leased, and the affairs of the state of Michigan. His tall, lean figure, "with shoulders slightly stooping from continual application in the counting room,"[15] as one reporter noted, was almost never seen in any nonworking setting.

By now, he seemed to recognize that he was in the grip of compulsion, but he could not wrestle free. In the spring of 1866 he promised William that he would sell out and retire. "I have worked very hard for years," he wrote, "and have done an amount of mental and other labor sufficient to break down any man."[16] But only a few weeks later a fire, the perennial nemesis of the lumber business, swept through one of his mills. His immediate reaction was that this reverse "forced" him to stay in business and recoup the loss. At once he began to build a replacement, one of the state's biggest.

Even so uncompromising a will, however, could not hold off physical deterioration. In 1861 he began to suffer spasms of the bladder, and in time they became a regularly recurring punishment that could be relieved only by frequent resort to the catheter. In 1865 he collapsed while on an inspection trip in Michigan's upper peninsula, and his new son-in-law, Dr. Willson, was hastily sent to his relief. In the winter of 1867 internal hemorrhages felled him like one of his trees. Then a blood clot in one eye made it temporarily useless. To recuperate, he went back to Flint, where he would have himself driven to the mills and yards in a "shay," a gaunt, half-blind figure, fretting and commanding. "The 'Boys,'" he told William, "think that I am not only cross, but rather uneasy for a sick man, and that I scold a great deal."[17] Yet he went on producing letters of exhortation, reproof, and lament. As soon as he returned to a fully active schedule, the ravages began anew — more hemorrhages, and morphine as the only barrier between himself and pain to the end of his term.

In the summer of 1869 he at last yielded to surgery for the bladder stone that the doctors had diagnosed. But it was too late for salvation by scalpel for a system so abused. On the twenty-third of July, at 5:30 A.M., Crapo relapsed from his postoperative convalescence and died.

Such was Willie's "Grand Pa." By the time of his death he had made the transition from New Englander to midwesterner. His roots were not in a soil, but in a system of behavior that could move with him. He came to share the midwestern faith that in the West lay the seeds of a dazzling future. "Its resources are immense," he wrote in 1862, "and although it has already reached a point of no small importance, these resources have hardly yet begun to be developed."[18] He had also absorbed the traditional western suspicion of the eastern moneyed interests who seemed to control credit and markets. Constantly at war with important lumber jobbers in Albany, a major distribution point for Michigan's output, he declared that he hated to send lumber eastward, "for it is too long a road, and is lined with too many who live by plundering the manufacturer of everything."[19]

His major disappointment in life was that he could not draw William out of New Bedford and into Flint and the web of speculative enthusiasms. There was a curiously inverted relationship between these two. It was the youthful son who exercised restraint on the plunging and rearing old man. In 1860 Crapo had almost gone under, unable to meet his payments on a number of notes in Massachusetts. William, then thirty, went into his own savings to pay off the most pressing creditors, and got other loans renewed by personally endorsing them. Then he wrote to his father:

I hope to see the great mountain of my life—your large indebtedness —removed some day. This will surely happen if you will stick with me to the doctrine of *selling* and not *buying*. This we must do. Let us get out of debt. We can do it. And then perhaps there will be some enjoyment to life.[20]

It was a gentle reproof, made in love and loyalty, but underlying it was William's determination to remain his own man, on his own native ground. So Crapo spent his last years with an unsatisfied hunger for a manchild at his side. That was the meaning of his mock-plaintive lament to little Willie, "Grand Pa's got *no boys*." The yearning was so sharp that it prompted him to the unusual step of expressing in his will the hope that William would be "blessed with worthy sons."[21]

This dynastic desire, as much as anything, marked Henry Howland Crapo, ostensibly a practical businessman, as someone possessed by urges beyond dollar signs—by a headstrong will to have his seed perpetuated. The result was a heavy emotional investment in the success of his sons-in-law, and it was under that freight of expectation that Willie's father collapsed. Even in proving unequal to his burden, however, he left another kind of powerful example for his little boy.

III William Clark Durant seemed to have the proper credentials when he first came calling on Rebecca. His family tree, like that of the Crapos, ran back to seventeenth-century New England. He was born in 1827, and when Crapo met him in 1854 he had moved from his hometown of Lempster, New Hampshire, to Boston and seemed to be another aggressive, energetic upcountry boy, arrived in the city to make his fortune. He was not. His father had been a tavern keeper, and he himself, at twenty-seven, was still only a clerk in the Webster National Bank, both facts sources of unease to an abstemious and ambitious potential father-in-law. But Durant seems to have had an appealing nature and a salesman's gift of power to paint his prospects in bright colors, and these overrode any early misgivings.[22]

It was through bank business that he and Crapo became acquainted, since Webster National was an agent for Michigan land companies from whom Crapo was buying. Social contact followed when Durant showed up on bank errands in New Bedford, and soon he was clearly wooing twenty-one-year-old Rebecca. The courtship was recognized, a subject for good-natured joking. His supervisor at the bank, Durant wrote after one visit to the Crapos, thought he was "improved much" in his looks. "He said 'laying off in these country places for two or three days . . . for instance, New Bedford'—was very beneficial to health."[23] A year and a half later, in the autumn of 1855, wedding preparations were in full flurry, Rebecca and her mother were visiting Durant in Boston, and Crapo was commenting on affairs from his frozen exile in Michigan. On November 29, Thanksgiving Day, New Bedford's city clerk formally recorded the marriage.[24]

For the first few years the marriage flowed along in the usual fashion, and the gossipy, smalltalking letters that passed among Durant and his father and brother-in-law might have been gathered from a William Dean Howells chronicle of sober Yankee mating. Durant bought more land warrants for Crapo, and likewise some greening and Baldwin apples in Boston when the New Bedford price of $2.75 a barrel seemed outrageous. Crapo nudged Durant for visits from "you and 'Becky.'" He stopped in on them once in Boston, and Durant advised William: "We had the pleasure of Father's company last evening. . . . He appears in good spirits—was glad to see him so well and lively." After a while, Durant was drawn into the labyrinth of Crapo's cash-flow problems, the older man asking him to pay off certain bills, and reimburse himself by collecting small debts due to the Crapo account in New Bedford. The letters ended with "Affectionatelys," and appeared to hint at a developing partnership among the kinsmen in Flint, New Bedford, and Boston, the kind of blood-and-money network through which many a New England mercantile family had prospered.

One surviving letter, however, indicated that Durant was made of different metal from his in-laws. Whereas both Crapos seemed to relish overwork, Durant did not.

I am very busy as Riddle has gone to the White Mountains on his vacation. Is to be gone two weeks. I have to stand at his desk and it takes all my time. After he returns . . . the paying teller goes for two weeks. So there is no leisure for me for *a month* certain. In September *Durant goes 3 weeks* in addition to what he has had to make up *for extra work.*[25]

Such an attitude could hardly have impressed in-laws as promising, but the first overt sign of trouble did not come until May of 1861. Rebecca was in Flint for a long visit, waiting for her husband to join her. Crapo sent him a letter with a list of goods to buy in Boston but explained that he was also furnishing a copy to William, and if William had any different directions, Durant should be "governed by them." Whether or not out of pique at a sense of demotion, Durant responded by canceling his plans for a trip to

Michigan, and demanding that his wife and year-and-a-half-old daughter return. "I am very sorry for this," was Crapo's answer, "but must be reconciled to the disappointment," though he did sign the letter "Yours most affectionately."[26]

Two years later, at the end of another visit, trouble was gross and palpable. William Durant stunned his father-in-law with the announcement that he was going to become a stockbroker. The decision was the result of a growing interest in the market, but more than that, Durant was apparently convinced that the brokerage business would lift him out of a job that was too confining for his pretensions. Crapo, however, as he told his son, was more than doubtful.

> When Durant was here I thought he was too much imbued with a mania for stock speculation, and my advice to him was to go back into the Bank and hold on to his place there, and be careful about committing himself wholly and entirely to the troubled and uncertain seas of stock speculation, which I regard like every other system of gambling when pursued as a profession.[27]

Crapo's fears were more than justified. Had Durant been a man to consult omens he, too, would have hesitated to press his luck. He came of an ill-starred tribe. His family was poor, and his father, a brother, and a sister had all died before he was ten; his mother before he was thirty. But he had scored some successes in part-time trading; the charm that had won him Rebecca seems to have attracted some backers as well, and he must have believed that the heavens were now ready to smile on him. His error was recorded in the reports of R. G. Dun & Co. (now Dun and Bradstreet), which, with surgical detachment, compressed six years of failure into six inches of entries.

July 21 '64 Durant and Hastings, Stockbrokers. Commenced a few months ago. D was previously in the Webster Bank and H in the Merchants Bank, and refer severally to Mr. Thomas & Mr. Heaven. We learn that they commence with a capital of about 50 million, the largest part being D's. He made money in the Petherick Corner. Their references speak of them as being perfectly reliable, some others think D rather too sharp. Are good at present, however.

May 19 '65 It is very difficult if not impossible to place them; are great speculators & do a risky business, have a good many friends, said to have 25,000 shares of Water Power (they & friends) at 40, plus a number of other dubious operations. May come out right.

March 31, '66 Dissolved; business continued by W. C. Durant.

June 1, '66 Advt. "I have this day admitted Jas. C. Durant [William's younger brother by two years] as partner in my business, which will be conducted under style of W. C. Durant & Co."

June 12 '66 Late firm lost good deal of money. J. C. D. is not known to bring any strength to the firm, considered quite weak and not reliable. Brokers would require collateral on any time transactions.

Nov. 26 '66 Same, and have a poor reputation. Weak in means but have friends that are [illegible]

June 15 '67 Just the same. Weak in Cr[edit] but seem to have money at command from some quarter.

Jan. 1 '68 Advt. Dissolved by mutual consent. The affairs will be settled and continued by W. C. Durant.

Feb. 29 '68 The retirement of J. C. is of no particular significance. Standing unchanged.

June 4 '70 No improvement and not entitled to credit.

Nov. 30 '70 Out of business.[28]

So, two, partners, six years and uncounted dollars after he began as a stockbroker, Durant was finished. He had lost his dream, his savings, and the respect of his in-laws. Thereafter he would be impaled, for the record, on the pens of others who were concerned but unforgiving. Almost nothing of his own side of the story survived—not even a picture from which one might try to judge his character.

Eighteen sixty-eight was the turning point, the year when it was impossible to deny how far apart were the Crapo and Durant trajectories. In 1857, the year of his wedding, Durant was still a young man of presence who might think of himself as a banker instead of a bank clerk, and Henry H. Crapo was still a middle-aged New Bedford businessman struggling to keep his footing in a new venture. But in 1868, Crapo was a success in every way, and Durant, forty-one, was sinking into the quicksand. And drinking.

In May of that year, the governor, Dr. Willson, and William Crapo put their heads together—probably not for the first time—on what to do about Rebecca's husband. Willson thought he had an answer. There was a dry goods emporium in Flint run by three local businessmen. One of them wanted to get out, and suggested to Willson that he induce the Crapos to buy his share for Durant. The unhappy father-in-law mulled it by letter. "I think there is a fine opening for Durant here if he wants it. . . . I do not want to see Durant drifting along. . . . Very soon he will be an old man with a son to be provided for and settled down with some kind of business." And yet he hesitated. "Durant can't bring his mind to any practical business point and to make money by small legitimate profits but must do it by reckless ventures, by wild speculations. . . . I would be glad to help Durant any way I can when he'll let [go] this foolish dabbling with stocks and go into some honest, legitimate business. How can I do it?"[29]

Apparently he could not or would not do it by making Durant a merchant of ribbons, calico, and buttons, for no more was said about the proposed deal. Then, at the end of June, the Durants came to Flint for what proved to be a climactic visit. For a week there was peace, while Durant traveled up to Lake Superior on business, still looking for the golden key, and "Grand Pa" happily took six-year-old Willie to watch sheep sheared on one of his farms, and on other diverting adventures. Then Durant returned for three weeks. He was broke and angry, his father-in-law dying piecemeal, and whatever happened in those hot days must have been very ugly. On the day before the Durants left — July 30 — Henry Crapo took Rebecca aside and handed her a hundred dollars, with the clear intention of keeping it out of William Durant's hands. Then, even while they were still en route homeward, Crapo wrote an eight-page letter to his son, a virtual outcry of pain, disappointment, anxiety, dogmatism, thwarted plans, and evil premonitions, its passion visible in blots, dashes, underlinings, crossings-out and interlineations.

My dear Son:

Durant, Rebecca and the children left here this morning for Boston. Since Rebecca and the children were here Durant has been "drifting about" — up to Lake Superior, down to Detroit, and any where else that he could find any pretext to drift. I have seen enough to satisfy me that he must *change his course at once*, or a short time will land him in the *gutter*. There is in fact nothing of him. He has a peculiar kind of smartness, but it is entirely without *judgment, principle* or even common sense, at least in his present state of mind. He has gambled in stocks and has traded with a class of men of as little principle as himself, but a great deal more ability and shrewdness than he possesses, until he has become lost to every principle of manhood. He has made some money by gambling in stocks — but having a mind without the least balance, he has permitted himself through flattery and whiskey, to be used by others as a mere tool, until he is now "used up" both in character and means. I had no idea that he had got so low. . . .

He has not mind enough to know what to do, and has apparently given himself up to intoxicating drinks. He can't get by a saloon or a drinking hole, no matter how low, without a "tip." The Dr. and myself have tried to find some place for him here where he could get into business and make a living, but his appetite for intoxicating drinks is so strong, I presume he had not been here a week before every business man in Flint knew that he was a *tippler*, and that he thought more of whiskey than any kind of business, and visited openly our saloons where no decent man is seen. He has been so intoxicated here as to have a regular drunken jab with Rebecca at the table before us all, so that we felt it the best course to leave the table one by one to avoid a scene. Poor Rebecca! Her visit was not half out, and has been spoiled by him, and she has gone home, almost broken hearted.

Crapo went on to explain that he had talked to Durant "very plainly and decidedly," adding a highly improbable reservation: "I have said nothing to him that was *angry*." What he wanted was a promise of reform, and a full disclosure of Durant's actual financial standing, so that something might be arranged. But even as his pen scratched its contemptuous way across the paper, he was struggling between hope that something might yet be done for "Becky's" sake, and his bitter conviction that Durant was beyond salvage:

Durant seems now to be penitent and "owns up" but he is even now, with all his smartness, more of a boy than a man; and if he comes to you as I presume he will, *you must be decided*. Let him know distinctly that he must change his course or expect nothing from me, for if I have ultimately to take care of his family I shall do so without any copartnership in the matter with him. . . .

P.S. I have somewhere the draft of my will; but I am unable to find it just now. If I can't find it I shall be obliged to trouble you for a copy, as I may wish to make some change so that Durant can not have the control of any thing I may be able to leave Rebecca.[30]

Within another two weeks he wrote again, relenting slightly. "When you see him, make the best of it and let me know."

He might make a good living here, and even lay up some money, if he would only cease to be a "Boy" and be a rational husband and father; and shape his course from the dictates of *duty*, and from the exercise of *reason* and *judgment* rather than from an entire abandonment of all these.[31]

Twelve months later, it no longer mattered for Henry Howland Crapo. He was dead. The family saga went on to its bitter conclusion without his participation. There was the obligatory family reunion at the funeral, and conversation between the brothers-in-law then was probably restricted and somber. But less than two months after, William had taken over his father's role and was lecturing Durant without skipping a beat of the measure the older Crapo had set.

Your case has worried me very much, and I was hoping that something promising a change would be indicated before I left [on a business trip]. It seems to me so clear that the longer you stay in Boston you harm

yourself and bring misery to your wife and children that I could not bear
to go away and know that you were among your old associations and
temptations. . . . You can break away from the temptations around you
but you seem not inclined to do it. Why you are so disinclined I cannot
imagine. There certainly can't be any pleasure to you in seeing an
unhappy wife and crying children. . . .

If you felt one hundredth part as sad about this as I do, you would
arouse to some measures to bring back again the happy days you once
enjoyed.

Do, I pray you, form some plan and act upon it at once.

Yours affectionately,[32]

Durant, his brokership already giving its death rattle, appears to have
been unable to act on this "affectionate" message, and may have separated
from his wife in that very year of 1869. "Things are *no* better," she confided
to a sister, "but fearfully worse. I know it's all just as you write. We must be
patient longer."[33] By 1872 they were incontrovertibly sundered. Once, at
least, in that year she had a letter from him which she passed on to William,
presumably for advice on how to reply. William's answer was crisp. He,
too, had had mail from Durant, "full of excuses—very humble and full of
the most solemn promises. It is hardly worth while to send it to you."[34]

For a few years more Durant knocked, humbly enough, at the Crapo
doors now forever barred to him. In November of 1875, when William was
serving in the House of Representatives, he received a letter from Willie's
father, asking if he could arrange a clerkship for him. In his negative reply,
he once more scolded his brother-in-law, this time without any pretensions
of kindness, and concluded: "I suppose you will make some arrangement
about the Life Ins. premium coming due."[35] No answer from Durant
survived, but two years later there was a final encounter, a concluding
rebuff. Durant, trying to buy some land for another party and earn an
agent's commission, approached William for information concerning mort-
gages on the tract that were held in New Bedford. A pathetic scene must
have occurred, for he wrote, soon after:

I am really anxious to get hold of the lands so as to make something,
as I need it. . . . [W]hile at Flint you seemed too busy when I saw you to
say anything. If you can assist me in this plan, please write at once.[36]

Willie was fifteen that October of 1877. Did his father see him "while at
Flint," being snubbed by his uncle? Or at all? And if he did, what passed
between them? There is no answer. From that point on, William Clark
Durant vanished from the official collective memory of the Crapos. He was
listed in a Detroit city directory for 1879. And in 1883 he died, according to
a tombstone put up over his grave in East Lempster. There is no record of
who brought the body back, or who paid for the stone.[37]

7., 8. & 9.

(Opposite, above) Rebecca Durant, beloved mother of "the Man"

(Opposite, below) Clara Pitt Durant, a young Flint business wife

(Above) Daughter Margery, loyally enthroned in a 1905 Model C Buick

10.
Catherine Lederer Durant married the rising "motor wizard" in 1908 after his divorce.

IV There is no way to tell, either, how much of this strife pierced through the protective curtain that the adults would naturally draw around the children. Rosa was older and more aware, and very possibly harmed by it—none the less so, perhaps, because of the attention lavished on her little brother. For him there would be the problem of growing up male with only memories of a father who had become an unmentionable subject among his only known relations, his mother's clan. But it was buried under waves of maternal cosseting. Already at four he was garbed like a little prince, in a suit with a round collar, buttoned at the throat, and buttons marching diagonally from midwaist to shoulder like a grenadier's, a suitable uniform to exercise his commission from Grand Pa. At seven, he was dressed in black velvet with a red cap, to be taken to a parade in Boston in honor of President Grant, and he was also given a drum and drumsticks. "He looked fine—a quick little chap," Rebecca noted on a piece of paper later, as she laid the drumsticks away to be saved. "He may never be President, but . . . he will always be his mother's good boy, I am sure."[38]

Adolescence in Flint was also, for him, an experience that enhanced security. He had a home of his own by the time he was fourteen. In 1875, the governor's widow died. There was a distribution of her share of the estate, and with money in hand, Rebecca was able to move into a house just around the corner from the Doctor and Rhoda. She made it one of those crowded nests that demonstrated the cultivation and respectability of middle- and upper-middle-class women, and the acquisitive virtues of the men, living or dead, who had provided for them. There were crystal chandeliers sprinkling bursts of light on heavy, carved chairs upholstered in brocade, on richly figured carpets, on solid and dark tables and highboys, on looped and drawn curtains, on urns and displayed china —all of it reflected and multiplied, to be enjoyed more, in gold-framed mirrors.

In and out of Rebecca's parlors flowed the best of Flint society, in cohesive currents of neighborliness and kinship. There were family assemblies, and the formal social calls of holiday routine, and meetings of the various societies sponsored by the First Presbyterian Church, of which Rebecca was a leading figure. And parties, too. Clubs of Flint's best people, such as the Kettle Drum Society and the Married People's Club, gave musicales and dances—hours from eight to eleven, with refreshments, and departure time signaled by the orchestra melting into "Home, Sweet Home." "Among those who had spacious homes for these brilliant affairs," a chronicle of Flint's organizational life reported, "were Dr. J. C. Willson and Mrs. R. C. Durant."[39]

Willie himself would enter this associational network as his birthdays ticked by. He was sent to Professor Van Der Velpen's class at the Flint

Conservatory of Music (it would have been unthinkable for a music teacher to have a lesser title), and he learned to play the cornet well enough there to become enrolled in a local band. There was also "Base Ball." Flint had two teams in 1877, and one of them, at least, the Flint Athletics, elected their pitcher, catcher, and manager. At sixteen, Willie was chosen manager. After a game at the Fair Grounds once, Rebecca gave a supper for both teams. Besides the players, there were fourteen guests, including her minister, the Reverend H. M. Curtis, table decorations of miniature gilded baseball bats (she called them "gold sticks"), and from the ceiling hung green vines and a banner with a motto on each side. One was congratulatory, and the winners were seated so as to face it; the other offered some appropriately uplifting consolation to "the sorry ones."[40]

In the fall of 1875 Willie entered the Flint High School, close to his home. The school building was brand new, and the city officials were inordinately proud of it and liked to point out that it cost $80,000, had its own external boiler-house and water supply, a 2,000-pound bell, a $650 belltower clock from Boston, and teachers' desks furnished by a local man, W. B. Colson, which were, a local history boasted, "a practical demonstration of the skill of our mechanics."[41] In this spired building, five teachers — one of them the principal — taught Flint's children the great fundamentals: algebra, physiology, spelling, penmanship, physical geography, rhetoric, United States history, general history, arithmetic, and geometry. Willie Durant also studied French and got his lowest grade in it, an 81. But his record was otherwise highly respectable, with a highest mark of 99 in United States history, and so it was not from a sense of failure that he announced, in the spring of his fourth year, that he had had enough of formal education, and would quit to go to work.[42]

If the decision caused any family conflict, it was not recorded, and actually not likely. Whatever informal class system Flint possessed did not yet require its elite to have diplomas, and in fact distrusted them. If Governor Crapo's grandson wanted to tackle the world instead of law, preaching, or medicine, it was an acceptable choice, one that a man of seventeen had a right to make. The fathers of Flint judged that three and a half years in their high school gave a youngster all the basic skills needed, and that most worthwhile education would be furnished by life in Flint itself, and they had some grounds for believing so.

Flint was, like many Michigan towns, an outpost of a great New England migration that had rolled across the country sowing uplift like wheat. A social register of Genesee County, of which Flint was the seat, expressed pride that nine-tenths of the original settlers came from New York State and New England, "and brought with them the advanced ideas of the favored communities from which they came upon the subjects of education and religious observances."[43] The consequence was that even at its most raw, even when its buildings still smelled of fresh sap, Flint did not entirely lack pretensions to culture. Material pursuits dominated its horizons for a certainty, but they were linked with mental and spiritual disciplines in a system of thought and action that was serenely self-justifying, and able to generate and direct powerful social energies.

In Willie's schooldays Flint, with a population of only four thousand, had four weekly newspapers, the *Republican*, the *Journal*, the *Globe*, and the *Wolverine Citizen*. (The *Journal* took and survived the risky modern step of going daily in 1883.) Flint had ten churches, too, one each for the Presbyterians, Episcopalians, Baptists, and Congregationalists and Adventists, two for the Methodists, one German Evangelical congregation, one Roman Catholic flock, and even a house of worship of the African Methodist Episcopal Church Zion. Mill owner and millhand, storekeeper and logger, matron and chambermaid, coachman and judge, black, white, alien and native, on Sunday all Flint worshipped, each family according to its fashion. And during the week, each church did those things that, by mutual agreement, were worthy of effort—taught and comforted and succored and corrected and buried and baptized, each denomination a little cell of the larger organism of community.[44]

A few blocks from the high school stood a library building that had cost nearly six thousand hard-raised dollars to build in 1866, some of the money being donated by Henry H. Crapo. And the women of Flint in 1876 supported an American history class that met once weekly, and, inspired by the Philadelphia Centennial Exposition, a club that would "undertake studies in art."[45]

In the high-school building was a "valuable cabinet illustrating the natural history of the county and State,"[46] its stones and fossils and skeletons and maps lovingly assembled by the Flint Scientific Institute, which had unfortunately foundered during the Civil War for lack of funds.

And Flint did not lack for music. The Harmonia Club, a singing society, held recitals around town; so did a later choral club, the Fuguenoids. More popular music was provided by Gardner's Flint City Band, which serenaded and enlivened political meetings and church festivals and steamboat excursions, and in fact nearly all the city's public gatherings. Flint was choked with pride in the band. In 1876 the ladies donated and the mayor presented to them a $300 gold E flat cornet imported from England, and two years later they justified the gift by beating out nineteen other cities in the State Band Tournament at Lansing, carrying off $100 and another gold cornet in prizes. The chronicle of these triumphs made it very clear that the players were

not a beer-drinking, junketing crowd in any sense, but [were] recruited from the ranks of the business men and the professions in the beautiful city of Flint, and constitute[d] a standing advertisement for that city which [was] worth ten times what it [cost] the citizens.[47]

Flint even had, for a time, one of the best Shakespeare collections in the country, the property of Edward H. Thomson, who was elected mayor in 1878. (It was given to the University of Michigan on his death.) Thomson zealously promoted Flint and had managed, while a state Senator in Lansing, to enlarge its academic establishment by securing for it the location of the Michigan School for the Deaf.[48]

The sum of all these institutions was not a Flint that resembled Boston or Concord. Culture could always be in danger of sinking to mere polish, the preserve of women; civic spirit was potentially a veneer for boosterism. Nonetheless, a boy of good family, simply by watching and imitating, learned quickly that the key to the whole system was self-improvement. All of these clustered, overlapping hives of activity made life confining, public, secure, and purposeful. The purpose was, as the Ladies Library Association put it, "securing avenues for wider views, for higher and nobler aspirations."[49]

Betterment was a law of life, and that this zeal for betterment could be easily transferred from the moral to the material sphere was an obvious conclusion from seeing merchants, manufacturers, bankers, and lawyers lend the weight of their endorsement and the power of their savings accounts to beneficial causes. Civilization advanced on the impetus of material success. A responsible male had a duty to accumulate, and then to found and foster — to do those things, in short, which Willie Durant's father had failed to do.

All of the uplifting activity flowered on the primary stem, money. The nurture of money was basic. It was how the money was made and used that set off one family, one town, one section from another. And the second lesson that an observant youngster in the Flint of the 1870s could not fail to learn was that Flint made its money by manufacturing. A few hours with a newspaper, a walk through the streets, almost any public function or social conversation made that clear.

Flint was in its second incarnation when Willie Durant moved there, the lumber town built on the ashes of fur traders' campfires. But even as he ripened physically, Michigan's forests were vanishing under the ax. Lumbering was like fishing, mining, or the other "extractive industries"; the more efficient it was, the faster it devoured its own foundations. "No living man," Henry Crapo observed late in life, "is, I am sensible, aware of the rapidity with which our pine forests in Northern Michigan . . . are disappearing."[50] In the year of his death Flint had nine sawmills going, producing some ninety million feet of boards. Ten years after that, the number of mills had dropped to three, the output to less than forty million feet.

What saved Flint from becoming a ghost town was that it managed, like its neighboring Genesee County hamlets, to shift part of its economic base into other activities. It is an economic truism that the profits of handling raw material lie largely in the final stages of processing. Flint's business-men discovered that for themselves. They had a goodly share of the manufacturing activity reported for the county by a state census of 1874. It included ten planing mills, which made sashes, doors, and blinds; six "stave, heading and hoop" factories, four that made finished barrels, kegs, pails and tubs, and two that turned out furniture and chairs. Some of the "factories" were tiny affairs, employing only a dozen or fewer hands. But among all of them they embraced a sizable collection of machines carefully and explicitly enumerated by the census-takers. There were lathes and molders; edging saws, relishers, and wedge-cutters; sash-mortisers, scroll saws, and stave-jointers; tenoning machines, panel-raising machines, scouring machines, resawing machines, boring machines, and boring-and-franking machines. And Flint therefore was well supplied with men who could build, mount, adapt, and repair these machines, who were proud of them, who could willingly turn them to any purpose that a capitalist's imagination might frame.

Second in number to the various woodworking plants in the county were fifteen mills for grinding flour. Flint had three of them.

Then came three woolen and cotton mills. Two were Flint's. Between them they were turning out 180,000 yards of "cassimeres" and 48,000 pounds of stocking yarn a year by 1879, some of it bought as far away as San Francisco.

Willie Durant could see, any time he chose, a working paper mill in town, producing two tons of wrapping each day, most of it for sale in Detroit.

Or he could watch the blacksmiths at work in Castree and Odell's agricultural implement shop, which made plows, drags, cultivators, and bobsleighs.

Or visit the works of the Flint Gas-Light Company, which piped more than four million cubic feet of gas a year to 260 customers through seven miles of main pipe, as evident a sign of Flint's keeping step with progress as anyone could ask.[51]

But of all the properties that made Flint "noted as an active, enterpris-ing, commercial and manufacturing center," those rising fastest in impor-tance when Durant finished school were the four that manufactured wagons and carriages. All were locally owned, as was a fifth that came along in 1882, and at least two of them vividly illustrated the continuous, interlocking nature of business leadership, social standing, and political power in the small city.

There were three modest establishments that would be familiar sights. One belonged to George Henry Sturt, an Englishman. He had arrived with his father in 1857, and they had immediately gone into the manufacture of "wagons, cutters and sleighs." It was a close family enterprise, and the story ran that George Henry's young bride had, with her own hands, upholstered the seat cushions for early models in cheerful stripes and patterns.

Not far away was the little ten-man workshop of Abner Randall, a migrant from New York. Randall, a trained machinist and metalworker, served Flint at various times as a member of its school board and an alderman. He had forged the square and compass that decorated the Masonic Temple, though in putting them up, in 1874, he had lost his footing on the scaffold and plunged to earth, breaking many bones, and was never quite healthy thereafter.

There were two brothers named Stewart in Flint, who were both skilled in vehicle work, and one of them, in 1879, had just begun making body parts on his own, but he was still so short of capital that he was renting space in other shops.[52]

The dean of wagonmakers, however, was William A. Paterson. His new three-story brick factory at the corner of Sixth and Saginaw, the town's main artery, was a showpiece and a testimonial to his own driving, imperious nature. He was born poor, like Henry H. Crapo, and Canadian, like Uncle James Willson, in 1838. Early in his Ontario rural childhood he was orphaned and farmed out to an uncle. The uncle, it was later recalled, "in slicing off the top of a boiled egg at breakfast would give Willie the top slice and that was all." At fourteen, the hungry boy was apprenticed to a carriage-builder. Five years later he set out with his tools on a journeyman's odyssey through New England, Kentucky, and Illinois. He finally came to rest in Pontiac, Michigan, a vehicle-making center. Then, in 1869, he heard of opportunities in Flint, and went there with a brother to help and five hundred dollars to invest. It had taken him nine years of sweat and calculation to arrive at the three-story factory, and he was determined to make the most of it.

At the start he had worked alongside his hired hands, but one day he pitched his sledgehammer through the window and roared at them: "From now on I'm going to be a businessman!" He began to put money into building enterprises, and was the leader in putting up several downtown hotels and office structures. He was also one of the founders of the Union Trust and Savings Bank. One day, rumors of a panic swept town; before long, lines were forming at the Union Trust withdrawal windows. Paterson rushed by train to Detroit, and borrowed large sums of cash on his personal note. Returning, he elbowed his way through the crowd, glared around him, summoned a clerk to the wicket, and in a voice that carried throughout the building ordered the recording of his own huge deposit. The crowd dispersed, and the run was over.

To go from artificer to investor to mayor (in 1890) was only natural. He was woven closely into the texture of Flint's social fabric — a Republican, a Presbyterian, a Mason, a Knight of Pythias, a Knight Templar on the record, and perhaps an Odd Fellow and a Knight of the Maccabees as well, since Flint had those organizations, too. It did not displease him, apparently, to recall his manual-labor beginnings from time to time. A Flint legend, unconfirmable, held that when his Episcopalian brethren needed an iron cross to top the steeple of their new church, he hammered it out with his own hands.[53]

Paterson's leadership was challenged by the emergence of the Flint Wagon Works, in 1882, and what made that firm unique was that it did not owe its creation to a blacksmith or wagonmaker. It was set up by members of the most successful lumber firm in town, next to Crapo's, a direct transfer of entrepreneurship and capital from a waning to a rising industry. The names of its begetters were Josiah Begole and George Walker. Along with a deceased partner, David Fox, they had operated a busy sawmill from 1865 onward. Walker was little known, but Begole, sixty-three years old, had a political career in the state Senate and the national House of Representatives behind him. Like Crapo, he was of French descent, kept a showplace farm, and reached the governorship, in that very year of 1882.

Begole and Walker sank the formidable sum of $100,000 into the Flint Wagon Works, and hired as its supervisor a publicity-shy Civil War veteran from Connecticut named James H. Whiting. It was not long before the firm was one of Flint's major economic props.[54]

V This was the city that imprinted itself on the imagination of a young boy given to dreams of glory. Its pool of skilled labor, capital, and management talent readied it for a possible takeoff into some dramatic future. The new and exciting things going on in town had to do with the greasy processes that involved smoke, the clang of metal on metal, the screech of teeth on wood, the hiss and pop of valved steam exerting its power on rods and levers and wheels that suddenly came alive and changed things. The honorables of Flint were the men who understood and controlled these cunning processes, and raised money and culture from them. Such men appeared strong, invulnerable to failings like drink and bad nerves that beset weak sons and brothers, sensitive wives and daughters. To enter their world was a natural prompting of ambition. As surely as pyramids and hieroglyphs told Egyptians that they were children of the sun, or totem poles reminded some Indians that they were brothers and sisters to turtles and eagles, the smokestacks of Flint informed its boys that they were a race of builders.

Willie Durant was probably a dreamer in his boyhood. His earliest photograph shows an adolescent with a large Adam's apple, neatly brushed hair, and already a somewhat distant focus of the eyes. If he confided his plans on dropping out of school to anyone, they were never repeated for the printed page. The only extant writing from Durant's own teenage pen is a joke in a chum's autograph book: "There is a happy time not far away (examinations.) Yours truly, W. C. Durant."[55]

Yet he clearly meant to go to work—there was no other choice, really—and to penetrate Flint's business world. For someone who had forsworn professional training, there were two gateways. One had to learn a mechanical skill, and rise from the shop, or show a talent for figures and salesmanship, and begin in an office or behind a counter. For young Durant, it would be that second path.

But first, either `by family tradition or someone's desire to impart a lesson, or out of a general Flint conviction that even the sons of first families should not be pampered, he had to begin in overalls, however briefly. Durant was not prepared for that. His first job was at the family lumber mill—that much nepotism seems to have been permissible—and he showed up in the uniform of the good citizen, a woolen suit that chastened his body in a tight, itchy clasp up to the very throat, and at the throat a shiny stiff collar. The foreman to whom he was referred examined this swaddled creature briefly, then told the boy to take off his coat, and sent him out to be introduced to his work, which was piling lumber at seventy-five cents a day. Egalitarianism was paid its official token.[56]

Durant did not remain at this muscular apprenticeship long. In a short while, he took a second, nighttime job, selling patent medicines made up by a town drugstore. It brought in another three dollars a week, and unveiled his true, shining gift, which was salesmanship. He was so apt at it that he presently found another sales job, this one with a Flint cigarmaking company owned by George T. Warren, leaving the mill behind forever, though some local historians later had an impression that he stayed there long enough to rise from stacker to supervisor.

He started work for Warren with a request for two dollars a day in travel expenses. His employer yielded experimentally, but was convinced that the cost of maintaining him on the road, in addition to paying his salary, would eat up any profits. In two days, Durant came back with a massive order for 22,000 cigars. He had simply gone straight to the nearest city of any size, Port Huron, and convinced storekeepers there to bypass the local wholesalers and order directly from the factory in Flint at lower prices. Grandfather, had he known, could not have been more approving. Neither could Mr. Warren. In a while, Durant was working for a $100-a-month salary, and had replaced three other salesmen.[57]

He was testing waters, piling up experience, feeling for the limits of his powers. He sold real estate. He took on work as a bookkeeper for the local water supply company, and then became involved in handling complaints and winning new customers. He may have had a job with the gas works as well. He was at so many things, in so many places, that after a long time people would remember him as holding positions that he never held, as if it were inconceivable that any Flint undertaking of the early 1880s could have prospered without his touch. It is incontrovertible that he went into the business of selling fire insurance, a lamentably profitable one in Flint, whose wooden workshops, lamplit and full of oily wastes, burned down with excruciating frequency. With a friend, I. Wixom Whitehead, he set up a partnership that soon gathered several agencies into one of the largest insurance firms in central Michigan. Behind all this early success were sleepless energies and irresistible persuasiveness.

He did not fit the conventional image of the salesman. It was about at the time of his youth that the "drummer" entered the popular mind as a stereotype, a man armored in brass, with a tongue as nimble as a cricket, fingers that could outline glories in the air and then seal the customer's lapel in their grasp — a joiner and backslapper at home, and on the road, the seducer of innumerable mythical farmers' daughters, dazzled by a man who ate daily in restaurants and had seen five-story buildings. And yet in no one's recollection does any part of this caricature resemble Durant.

He was, all who knew him agreed, soft-spoken and often the last to speak. He dressed neatly but not conspicuously, his smile was gentle and winning, his eyes serious. His power rested on an ability to project his own unswerving faith in the product. "Assume that the man you are talking to knows as much or more than you do," was his advice to other salesmen. "Do not talk too much. Give the customer time to think. In other words, let the customer sell himself. Look for a self-seller."[58] His art was to turn the eyes of the prospect inward, to give him a vision of himself as somehow improved, transmuted, assisted in worthy undertakings by the product, so that the salesman became a mere window through which the customer perceived vistas to which he had been previously blind. The end result was not merely an order signed, but a friend made.

The problem was to find things to sell that deserved this care. "Willie" grew into "young Mr. Durant," seeking, waiting, practicing. He smiled at a life that smiled on him. By the age of twenty-three he was living alone with Rebecca, enjoying the undivided fullness of the attention that she delighted to give him. Rosa was gone, married in 1878 to a local man, Dr. John

Willett. There was undoubtedly some surplus money, some for the bank, and some for small flyers of investment, like a roller-skating rink of which he was part owner, making a few dollars out of the squealing revels of Flint couples on Saturday nights. Or, more soberly, shares in the utilities companies. Above all, there had to be the satisfaction of the patent proof that he would not prove to be a copy of his flawed, shadowy father.

The open question was of what direction he would move in, what kind of career a bright and popular young Crapo male could be expected to raise on a foundation of insurance, water mains, and cigars.

All Flint would agree, however — even, it must be assumed, Rebecca — that a rising young man needed a wife. On New Year's eve of 1884, a local newspaper jocularly ran a story on *Flint's Young Bachelors. A List of Young Men of this City Who Have Not Yet Succumbed to Cupid's Darts. Something for the Young Ladies to Paste in their Hats.*

Inasmuch as tomorrow begins the Leap Year, when the young gentlemen are supposed to take a back seat and allow the young ladies to do the gallant — to take the young men to the theater and other places of amusement, to see them to the front gate of their residences at 2 A.M., to do the "proposing," *etc., etc.* . . . we publish below a partial list of the marriageable and desirable young men of this city, who have up to the present time successfully withstood the effects of the fair sex. . . . Some of the candidates are really "good catches" and cannot long remain in the matrimonial market unclaimed.

Among the list of names, "Wm. C. Durant" was identified as among the "very desirable victims, and should receive the especial attention of the fair sex."[59] A year and a half later, he disappeared from the list of eligibles. On June 17, 1885, Durant was married to Clara Pitt, the daughter of the ticket agent of the Flint and Pere Marquette railroad. If it was considered a match somewhat beneath the grandson of the road's former president, no one was indiscreet enough to say so, and perhaps no one thought so. Dynastic matches were not in fashion in little Flint, and even as the daughter of a minor official, Clara had respectability, which was the true god of the domestic hearth. Like all wives, she would assume her husband's status.

The couple was married by the Reverend Mr. Curtis, received the traditional gifts, including an upright piano from the bride's father, and dashed through the conventional shower of rice for the carriage that would take them to the railroad station and the first leg of a honeymoon that began in Detroit.

They returned to move into a house of their own at Fourth Avenue and Garland Street, a few moments' walk from Rebecca's. Within five and a half years there were two children, Margery, born in 1887, and Clifford, in

1890. Clara posed for a portrait with both of them on her lap when the son was still an infant. The camera did justice to her good looks, her hair in soft ringlets, her clear skin, her large eyes. Yet about her full, slightly pouted lips there was already a suggestion of reproachful resignation.

And so, as he passed his twenty-fourth birthday at the end of 1885, William Durant was "settled," at least in the social mind of Flint. But not in his own, which kept its secrets. It was within his grasp to become a successful head of an insurance firm, to sow his money locally and prudently, and to pick up whatever political and other rewards would grow in familiar soil. His imaginative reach, however, already exceeded that grasp. What he needed was an avenue to bigger things, an opening to dart through. A sporting chance. He found it, suddenly, under his nose, in an unpremeditated encounter in downtown Flint one September day in 1886.

2)

The Master

Carriage Maker

I He was walking down Saginaw Street to keep an appointment, just
prior to a board meeting of the water company, and he was in a hurry.
No one else seemed to be. The side avenue stretched ahead of him in
easygoing autumn fullness. Wagons were parked along its edges, horses
switching their tails and occasionally tossing their heads against the bri-
dles that held them fast to the hitching posts. Men came and went from
Veit and Perry's harness and leather shop, Ellis's bicycle store, the printing office of the *Wolverine Citizen*, the Bryant House, which was both
local hotel and meeting place of the Masonic Lodge and other orders.
Above the expanse of two-story-high roofs rose cruciform symbols — the
iron cross above St. Paul's, and the many wooden ones formed by the
crossbars and poles that carried Flint's recently installed telephone and

electric wires. At the major intersection of Kearsley and Saginaw, on opposite corners, stood the First National Bank of Flint and the Genesee County Savings Bank. Church, banks, printing office, hotel, markets — the elements of civilization, suspended in momentary tranquillity.

Durant's destiny was at the intersection, too. It was disguised as his friend, John Alger, who worked at Jim Bussey's hardware store. Destiny, in this unlikely manifestation, was waving at him from the seat of a two-wheeled cart, offering him a lift.

Gratefully, he climbed in. The cart was simple, little more than a modified sulky. Its four-foot wheels held between them a simple seat, barely twenty-four inches wide, a tight fit for two adult bottoms, surrounded by a low iron bar for hanging on. The passenger's and driver's feet rested on a curved, slatted footboard. The whole thing resembled a ferris wheel's chair, brought down to earth. But when Durant had squeezed himself in, and the horse was giddupped into a trot, he made a pleasant discovery. The seat swayed easily up and down and side to side, with none of the hard bouncing and shaking that usually went with a ride in a light vehicle.

When they dismounted, Durant made a quick examination, and discovered the secret in a beautifully simple idea. It was all in the mounting of the seat on the springs. They were half-elliptical, curving forward from the rear axle like old-fashioned pistols fastened by their butts. At the top of the "barrels" were horseshoe-shaped stirrups, through which the shafts ran. The seat was fastened by wooden arms to the tops of these stirrups. It rode up and down with the flexing steel, but the stirrups moved freely around the shafts, so that none of their vibration was felt.

Durant was entranced. The cart was slight, graceful-looking, smooth-riding, and, above all, so simple that it was clearly inexpensive to make. It would be an ideal form of individual personal transportation for short distances. In his mind was an idea that he had not yet put into words: the inspired salesman should look for a self-seller, and if he could not find one, *make* one. He saw himself selling the cart to young men of modest means, showing them at how little cost they could be borne swiftly, comfortably on necessary errands, or on the pursuit of legitimate relaxation. And he knew at that moment that the demand he could create for the cart would be so great that no one of lesser clairvoyance than himself could be trusted to take the risks necessary to fill it. He would be manufacturer as well as salesman.

He found out from John Alger that the cart had been made in Coldwater, some seventy-five miles away. His other affairs pushed aside, he got on the local train the very next day, spent the night at Coldwater's hotel, and on the following morning poked his head inside the door pointed out to him as belonging to the cart "factory" of William Schmedlin and Thomas O'Brien. He was comforted at once by the familiar smell of shavings. He was in the carpenter shop. Around him were unfinished spokes, shafts, and seat-boards. From another room in the back he could hear the clanking of hammers. That would be where the blacksmiths were working on bolts, springs, fittings. That was all. There was no office. The plant, he judged quickly, looked as if it might turn out two carts a day.

He found O'Brien, pleasant-faced and fiftyish, among the carpenters. To him he explained softly, quickly, why he was there. He had ridden in their cart, liked it "immensely," thought that it had a "wonderful future." He had very little money, but wanted to buy a small interest in the concern.

O'Brien listened thoughtfully, and answered. They did not need another partner, he was sure, but they might be willing to sell the whole outfit. But Schmedlin ought to be asked. He stepped back into the blacksmiths' room and returned with a young man whom Durant immediately found likable—alert and self-confident, like himself. Perched on a carpenter's bench, he chatted with them awhile, then asked: "If the business is for sale, what is the price?"

They were possibly surprised by the quickness of the question, but obviously required no elaborate accounting to come up with an answer. For $1,500 anyone could take away everything—finished and unfinished carts, lumber and parts on hand, dies and patterns. Schmedlin held the patent on the spring-and-stirrup combination, and wanted a royalty, but Durant said no to that, and got his way. Then he made his proposal, directly and without hesitation or bluff. He did not have the money. But he thought he could raise it, if they would give him a little time. Let them all step over to the office of Schmedlin and O'Brien's attorney and draw up a bill of sale and an assignment of patent, and deposit them in the partnership's bank. He would leave for Flint immediately. If the funds were not in the Schmedlin and O'Brien account in five days, the deal was off.

It was agreed. Less than twenty-four hours later, Durant found himself standing on Saginaw Street again, about to tackle the job of raising $1,500. Whatever savings he might have had before marriage had vanished into his new home and furnishings—had, in fact, been converted into $3,500 in debt. It was a large sum of money for the time and place. Lenders would be very skeptical about advancing more to a young man, even a popular and hardworking one, for a new business venture.

He mulled over the possibilities. There was Josiah Begole, his grandfa-ther's old, friendly competitor. But he frankly lacked the nerve to ask him.

And there was Uncle William, or any other Crapo relative, the most logical choice in one way. But there was an overpowering drawback for the son of William Clark Durant. "If I make a failure of this venture," he thought to himself, "I will never hear the last of it." That decision cut him off, unfortunately, from at least two banks. The Genesee County Savings Bank had been founded by Uncle James, and numbered among its directors cousin Will Orrell. The First National Bank of Flint had recently been headed by Uncle Ferris Hyatt. The same motive that barred approach to the seemingly innumerable husbands and sons of Crapo women also ruled out close friends of the family. At that moment, his connections seemed an absolute disadvantage.

That left the Citizens Bank of Flint, "not as pretentious as the others, but sound as a rock." Its president, Robert J. Whaley, looked the very model of a small-town banker. He had light hair, small ears, close-set eyes behind rimless glasses, and an expression, to judge by later photos, that might merely have been nearsighted but seemed kindly. Durant entered the bank and climbed a flight of steps to Whaley's office, an old-fashioned curiosity shop, furnished in simple pieces and dust. He explained himself quickly and appealingly.

"Do you think it is all right?" asked Whaley.

"I would not be here, Mr. Whaley, if I did not think so."

"Come with me," said Whaley, and marched him downstairs to the cashier, and ordered that a ninety-day note should be made out to Mr. Durant, and the proceeds put in an account for him. In a matter of minutes, he had put Durant on the road to becoming a manufacturer.

Durant walked over to his insurance office, sat down, and meditated on his next steps. His problems were far from solved. He had enough to pay O'Brien and Schmedlin, and another five hundred dollars to move the establishment to Flint, but not a cent of working capital.

At that moment, the door opened, and the youthful, moustached face of Josiah Dallas Dort looked in. "Hello, Billy," he said, using the nickname by which Durant was becoming known to close friends outside the family. "I've missed you — where have you been?"

"Over in Coldwater, Dallas. And by the way, I'm in the manufacturing business."

"What are you going to manufacture?"

"Road carts."

Dort's eyes widened. He was both a partner and a clerk in Bussey's store, and he knew exactly what Durant meant.

"Do you mean to say that you've gotten involved in making that road cart of Johnny Alger's?"

"Bought it lock, stock, and barrel, with the patent as well."

Dort weighed the implications of this for a moment; his friend's sudden announcement had set mental wheels of his own whirring. He was ten months older than Durant, another young businessman with his fortune to make. He came from Inkster, a town just outside of Detroit, and had gone to a nearby school where one of his classmates was a boy, two years younger, from Dearborn, named Henry Ford. He had attended the state's normal school at Ypsilanti, but found commerce a more attractive prospect than teaching. He had made his way eventually to Flint, and to James Bussey, who hired him to manage the hardware store on a salary-plus-profit-sharing basis, which now had four more months to run. He had met "Billy" earlier in the year, and they had hit it off at once.

Dort's ambition to be independent was no less sharp than Durant's. He was ready to jump at a chance to leave the second-class status of employee behind him. He now put to Durant, surprised and grateful, the one question above all that he needed to hear. "Will you sell me a half-interest?" Durant would, in fact, be delighted to do so for $1,000.

Dort immediately ran across the street for a conference with Bussey, and returned full of enthusiasm. Bussey was having a bad year, and was glad to release him from the contract with a $500 cash payoff in settlement of all accounts. The other $500, he told his new partner, would be no problem. He would be on the one o'clock train to Inkster, where his mother lived in what he called the old homestead. "I know she will let me have the money," he said, "if she has to mortgage the farm to make it."[1]

And so, in that simple and speedy way made possible by a town's smallness and intimacy, an enterprise was begun. The handshake partnership was formalized on September 28, 1886, when the two young men opened an account in the name of the Flint Road Cart Company. From the start it was agreed that Dort would supervise production, and Durant sales and financing. They were a good team. Durant had exuberance, curiosity, boldness, a nose for adventure. Dort was steady and attentive to detail, the perfect ballast when his associate soared high and fast.

Within another few days the contents of the Schmedlin and O'Brien shop were unloaded at Flint's Pere Marquette depot, to be transferred to a small building that Durant and Dort had rented. Durant then chose one of the two finished carts in the inventory, confided it to American Express, and ordered it crated and shipped to Madison, Wisconsin, where the Tri-State Agricultural Association's annual fair was about to open. Heavy sales in Illinois, Iowa, and Wisconsin were at stake, but the hour was late. The traditional selling occasions for carts, buggies, and wagons were these yearly expositions at which the farmers, the basic customers, gathered to appraise the past year's work and the new products that equipment makers were offering them. The season for such exhibitions was almost over at September's end.

Undismayed, Durant himself arrived in Madison on a Sunday, twenty-four hours before the fair's beginning. In bland disregard of the Sabbath, he called immediately on S. L. Sheldon, the president of the association conducting the show. Sheldon was a jobber of farm implements and vehicles. As was then customary, he carried several competing makes, exclusive dealerships not yet having become the practice. He told his young caller that he would consider adding a new cart to his line, provided he had exclusive rights to it in a reasonably good-sized territory, and Durant countered that that could certainly be arranged if the initial order was large enough and the territory not too extensive for Mr. Sheldon to give it the proper attention. And the dickering went on goodnaturedly enough so that, when Durant's demonstration model failed to arrive the next day, having got mislaid in Chicago, Sheldon obliged him by putting off the judging until Wednesday.

But when that day arrived, just as Durant had predicted, the Flint Road Cart sold itself. Put through its paces against some fifteen competitors under various loads and conditions, it was awarded the blue ribbon of first place, an event that Durant later memorialized by giving the name Blue Ribbon to a whole line of his vehicles. When he left Madison that afternoon, he had in his pocket a contract to deliver a hundred carts to Sheldon.

Then it was on to Milwaukee and an appointment with another jobber, George Cribbs. More talk, probably over cigars, with jokes, discreet bragging, the parry and retreat of negotiation. And Durant neat, serious-looking, listening respectfully and then leaning forward to talk softly and winningly in the special language of merchandising that was getting into his blood — percentages, discounts, margins, markups, premiums, cartage, allowances, shipments. Men, playing a game from which they excluded women, enjoying its familiarity and the spice of knowing that there was a danger of failure if one played badly too often. At the end of it, a somewhat qualified victory for Durant. For the first time he encountered the skepticism of bankers outside Flint. Cribbs said he would need the usual easy terms for payment, perhaps three or four months. Durant could not accept. His tiny company did not have the cash reserves to carry customers for that long. So Cribbs sent him over to his own bank, to see if it would "discount the line": that is, lend the jobber the cash to pay on receipt, taking the carts themselves as security. And, probably as Cribbs had expected, the bank said it would do no such thing; what kind of security was a new and unknown product? And Durant returned to Cribbs's office, and yielded to a "very flexible deal" in the matter of accounts due.

There was one more call on this first sales trip, on a man named J. H. Fenton, whose specialty was racing rigs, and who agreed to an order provided he could have some small, sporty-looking changes made, and market the cart under a house name, the "Fenton Favorite." That was agreed to, and leaving three friends behind, the first of a network of hundreds that would blanket the agricultural heartland, Durant climbed aboard a train bound home for Flint.

He was now a partner in a company less than two weeks old, with a factory capacity of two carts a day, and he had orders for the quick delivery of six hundred. He had duplicated his first cigar-selling triumph for Mr. Warren, except that it was much harder to expand production of carts than of cigars overnight.[2]

II Durant found the situation merely exhilarating. He would contract out his work to the biggest manufacturer in Flint, who was sure to have some excess capacity. On a Saturday morning, he found himself seated in conference with W. A. Paterson. He explained his predicament to the older man, and asked what he would charge to duplicate 1,200 Flint Road Carts. Paterson's hard environment had left him toughened and prone to cutting corners. He had no relish for helping a future competitor, but a dollar was a dollar. After a time, he agreed to turn out 3,200 road carts at $12 apiece. Durant, his problem solved, walked across the street to celebrate with Dort.

Within a short time he was on the road again, sprays of orders blossoming at each leap to a new city. All told, the company marketed about 4,000 of the practical but sprightly looking carts at about $22 each in its first year. But at some time around its anniversary, Paterson taught the youthful beginners in his business a hard lesson in misguided trust. After the first 1,500 carts had been delivered from his factory, the supply began to fall off. There were mysterious delays in deliveries, shortages that were explained evasively. It did not take Durant many questions among his jobbers to find the answer. Paterson was preparing to market a road cart of his own, suspiciously similar to the Flint Road Cart, and costing only $15.

Durant knew then and there that he needed his own facilities. By then there was a little money handy, and he and Dort were able to rent an abandoned cotton textile mill quickly and install new production facilities in it, which quickly made them independent of Paterson.

Under the best of conditions, he and Paterson could not have teamed together easily. Their entire approach to business was different. Paterson neither sold through dealers nor tried for volume production. During the spring and summer he would leisurely accumulate his annual stock of wagons and carriages, setting his production targets by hunch and long experience. When autumn came he would hire an auctioneer and conduct a combined sale and festival. From miles around the farmers came to enjoy the "entertainment and the simple spread that went with it, an annual field day at Mr. Paterson's expense." Mr. Paterson recouped the cost with sales that averaged $125 to $200 per vehicle. It was a rhythmic, seasonal business like farming itself: planting in the spring, garnering in the fall. God grew the crops, the farmers traded them for cash, and the merchants in turn reaped the cash. In general rejoicing at the conclusion of the cycle, Mr. Paterson's customers converged on him to gossip, to argue, to be amused, and to stuff themselves with relishes, pickles, biscuits, breads, pies, cakes, jellies, doughnuts, cookies, hardboiled eggs, pork, ham, chicken, salads, greens, preserves, dumplings, sausage, corn, cider, buttermilk, milk, tea, and coffee, grateful that they were not so intemperate as to drink intoxicating liquors. Then they would drive away in their new buggies and wagons for another round of subduing and replenishing the earth.[3]

Durant understood the human satisfactions of business at this pace and on this scale of closeness, but his progressive instincts forced him to update and enlarge it, and to reach for volume production, lower costs, wider markets. That could be achieved only by systematizing sales, stimulating buyers by advertising, and spreading the entire making and selling process more rationally over the year.

Yet he made one more trial of Paterson as a subcontractor. Once more Paterson spoiled it by sharp practice, and in so doing enlarged Durant's business philosophy. After a long period during which he was "swamped with orders" for road carts, Durant learned from his dealers that they saw good prospects for a four-wheeled family buggy carrying the by-now familiar Flint Road Cart Company label. Enthusiastic at the idea, Durant overcame his anger and bitterness and approached Paterson again. Time and success, he told himself, were great healers. Besides, he knew that Paterson, deep in his building projects, was in need of cash and ready to deal.

With two members of a growing staff, he developed a design for a buggy, then signed a contract with Paterson for two hundred of them. Once more he went posting off to display a sample and gather in orders. This time Paterson's competitive technique was even more direct and simple than before. He made follow-up calls to Durant's customers, whose names Durant had guilelessly let him know. To them, he explained that if they were impressed with the buggy that Mr. Durant had just shown them, they had good reason to be so. It was made in his own factory, and if they would order from him directly, he would give them a lower price.

When Durant learned of this treachery, the arrangement ended, and so did any possible closeness between the two men, though Flint was too small and their interests too linked for them to become open enemies. But Durant came to believe later that the episode was a turning point for him. In his own recollection, it was Paterson who had inadvertently shown him the virtues of vertical integration. Security lay in control of one's own production from beginning to end, from components to final assembly. After the second trial with farming out, objectives changed.

Our plan was to manufacture practically every important part of a buggy, and carrying out this idea, we did not stop until we had controlled or were interested in building a full line of bodies, wheels, axles, forgings, stampings, leather, paint, trimmings and various other items, even whip sockets; but not until our accessory plants were in operation . . . did we have a product that had no competition in value or price in the country. This gave us control of the business in that line as long as carriages were in demand.[4]

It is unlikely that Durant's business philosophy was born that simply, that quickly, or from that single incident. But by 1893, seven years after its founding, the lightheartedly launched venture of the insurance agent and the hardware store manager had grown almost miraculously. The two-thousand-dollar partnership of Durant and Dort was now incorporated and recapitalized at $150,000. It was one of the three major producers of the town, keeping pace with W. A. Paterson and Co., and the Flint Wagon Works. As for "Billy" Durant himself, everything was growing — his fortune, his warm contacts with dealers, his reputation as a winner, and his ambitions. His abilities were now concentrated, he was ready for higher flights, and he was collecting around him a nucleus of supportive and able associates who were eminently willing to help him.

III Durant was generally known to be the motive force of the company, but Dort was the president. Sometimes Durant accepted election as treasurer, and he was always a director after the incorporation. But he disliked and avoided the official headship. It tied him down to too many administrative functions when he needed to go out and see what was new among his customers and rivals and suppliers. In time he needed a sales organization behind him, and in the early 1890s it was managed by Charles H. Bonbright, who came to Flint after long experience in merchandising farm equipment in Des Moines, Muncie, and Chicago.

Dort, self-effacing and efficient, had kept the growing concern ticking smoothly, almost single-handedly at first. But in 1889, Fred Hohensee came on as production foreman and was soon showing a fine knack for keeping things in motion on the factory floor. In the same year, the firm acquired a youthful office manager, Fred Aldrich. Like Hohensee, he was a native of Flint. His father, Amon Aldrich, was publisher of the *Globe*, and was teaching him the printer's trade. But Fred had done some spare-time clerical work for one of Durant's outside undertakings, and this led to an offer of twelve dollars a week to join the Flint Road Cart Company's staff.

Fred presented this offer to his family for advice. Printing was a dignified and secure trade. It might even lead to journalistic heights. But Mrs. Aldrich spoke up with a fervency born of long experience as a country newspaperman's wife, struggling to keep the household going on the tardy provision made by delinquent subscribers.

"Do you get that in cash?" she asked. Fred nodded. "Then take it!"[5]

He took it. Before too long he was secretary of the corporation, and since he had a thrifty mind and invested his cash in its stock, he became one of its major owners as well.

Later in the company's life it got another executive of far more than ordinary competence. His name was Alexander Brownell Cullen Hardy, and he was the young superintendent of a carriage plant in nearby Davison, Michigan, when Durant reached out and gathered him in. Hardy's capacity for work was bottomless, and in two years he had learned so much so fast that when Dort was required to take a temporary leave of absence, he filled in for him flawlessly as president.[6]

In 1890, a twenty-six-year-old man named Charles Nash began work in the blacksmiths' department. His childhood had been the kind of horror that abounded in Victorian charity commissioners' reports. His parents were separated when he was six years old, and he was "bound out" to a farmer who was supposed to feed and lodge him, permit him three months of schooling a year, and deliver him to the world at twenty-one with a suit of clothes and $100. The man worked him mercilessly, kept him ragged and starving, answered his protests with beatings. At the age of twelve, Nash ran away. He found a carpenter to whom he apprenticed himself, and worked his way up to a wage of nine dollars a month. Out of this pittance, nonetheless, he managed to save some money. He was determined to break out of the trap of poverty. Eventually he had enough money put aside to buy ten sheep. "Unless you have had to debate between a warm pair of pants and a dollar in the bank," he said later, "you can't ever know how hard it was for me to buy those sheep."

Selling wool, part-time carpentry, farm odd jobs — all brought in some income, which was husbanded to the last coin. When he was a grown man, associates would tease him: "Charley, please show me the first nickel you ever earned. . . . You've got it hidden somewhere." But he could not help it; there were too many fears to allay, too many bad memories. By the age of twenty-two, he was managing a farm outside Flint for $20 a month plus a house and garden, and had a wife to support. So close to the bone did they live that they saved $150 in the first year, and put it out at interest. But the farm grind was too much for his wife's health; they moved into town and he took a job in a store. It was there that Durant and Dort both came to know him, were impressed, and hired him.

There would be legends afterward that he was "discovered" mowing Durant's lawn, or picking plums in Dort's backyard, or stuffing wagon cushions in the plant. But he was not a boy laborer who was found like a jewel in a trashcan. He was a mature man, looking for a ladder to climb. The Flint Road Cart Company gave him a bottom rung to step on, and never had cause to regret it.

His first job was pounding iron. Within a few days he walked into Durant's easily accessible office. "I'm wasting time," he said. "You can get a power hammer there. It would cost about thirty-five dollars and do more pounding in a day than I can do in a month." Durant took the suggestion, and Nash was moved over to working on a drill press that prepared cart braces for attachment.

The next time Durant came through the shop he stopped at Nash's machine. It looked like none of the others. Nash had rigged it with an overhead spring and a treadle that left both his hands free while working and doubled the output.

Durant weighed the implications of this. "Charley," he said, "we'll get another man here. See if you can't straighten out the trimming department for me." Promoted to the headship of that department, Nash wrestled with the problem of heavy expenditures on tacks. He found the answer in a short time. The carpenters held the tacks in their mouths while working. The cheap, roughly finished brand the company was using cut their lips and tongues, and they would spit them on the floor in exasperation and lose them. A better-grade tack proved to be the remedy.[7]

So Nash went on probing, correcting, climbing up to Hohensee's level and then beyond Hohensee to the highest supervisory ranks. "I craved responsibility," he explained.

They all craved it, all were inexhaustible workers, never tired of the constant round of ordering, taking inventory, figuring, checking, dictating. They could joke with each other, but it would never have occurred to them to regard what they were doing as anything less than gravely important. There are pictures of the officials taken in the 1890s. In one, a group of eight stares intently into the lens. Dort is at the center, very handsome, his wavy hair and luxuriant moustache in perfect trim. Durant, characteristically, is looking slightly up and away from the others. Hardy is already bald, his eyes set deep behind contemplative brows. Aldrich has pouches under his eyes. Six of them are wearing stiff wing collars. In the left-hand lapel of every one of the eight jackets is a flower.[8]

They knew each other as neighbors. Their homes were almost all within walking distance of each other and of the main office with its parlor-like atmosphere provided by a heavy table, wicker chairs, and—one touch of carefully controlled nature—pot of ferns, along with the rolltop desk. The boundaries between home and office, work hours and nonwork hours, were soft and permeable. Life was a unity, and the corporation was, in a sense that can never be recaptured, a family.

No one doubted that "Billy" Durant was the head of that family. Of his own, too, his pretty wife and curly-haired little girl and toddler son. Yet he did not fully belong to either family. He was too much absent in both mind and body. He was the planner, and the plans kept luxuriating almost faster than even the nimblest execution could keep up with them.

In 1892, as the pool of capital, customers, and managerial experience filled, serious expansion started. That year, Durant organized the Webster Vehicle Company and set it to making light spring wagons in an abandoned farm machinery plant. In 1894 he created the Victoria Vehicle Company to make a new line of rigs, and had a dual satisfaction as Rebecca's son in doing so. For its factory space he bought the old Crapo general store from Uncle James, into whose hands it had fallen, and then he gave the management of the operation to "the Doctor's" son George, the second Crapo cousin whom he had hired.

By 1895 the name of the Flint Road Cart Company was no longer adequately descriptive, and that November it was officially changed to the Durant-Dort Carriage Company. Webster and Victoria were subsidiaries, their factories sometimes known thereafter as Durant-Dort Plants Number Two and Number Three.

A few weeks later, during the Christmas holidays, Durant became pregnant with a new idea, a dramatically cheap buggy that would sell for cash only, the price cutback to be partly made up for by increased volume and by saving the cost of extending credit to the customer. For him, to have an impulse was to act, and he went immediately to the wall telephone in his home to call Dort. It took him two hours, standing, to convince his partner and left him, he said, paralyzed from head to foot. By New Year's Day he had decided to call the new item the Diamond Buggy and to hire A. B. C. Hardy as the works manager, and he immediately telephoned Hardy to come to Flint to discuss terms, summoning him from a turkey dinner which, Hardy ruefully recalled, he never had time to finish. Within half a year the Diamond Buggy, as well as an array of horse-drawn vehicles for every showy and utilitarian purpose, was in showrooms wearing the Durant-Dort label.

Now he moved in the direction of controlling components. The Flint Gear and Top Company began to make wagon subassemblies and accessories in 1897. The next year Durant bought the Imperial Wheel Company in

Jackson, to guarantee him the 50,000 sets of wheels that he needed each year. On learning that the organization's output was far in excess of this number, he promptly took to the road and sold 140,000 sets to other makers to justify the investment.

In 1900, alarmed by a rumor that a trust was about to seize control of the manufacture of steel axles and tires for wagons, Durant rushed to West Virginia to buy axle-making machinery, hired a superintendent from Wisconsin, and added the Flint Axle Works to Durant-Dort's other four establishments in the city. To do so he broke new ground, literally, in two ways. His other operations were clustered in the area just north of the Flint River where it crossed Saginaw Street, the historic magnet for industry since the sawmill days. But James Whiting pointed out to Durant that axle-making was a noisy process. If conducted on the edge of the downtown center, it would create a public-relations problem. Durant bought a farm two miles to the north of the river, a location so pastoral at that time that his new superintendent joked that he might still have a problem: the sheep and cows would not mind the din, but the hens' laying might be affected. The street that was cut to accommodate the factory traffic, Hamilton Avenue, later became the backbone of a second industrial district.

Finally, in 1901, stirred once more by whispers that a sinister combination was forming to kite the price of the linseed oil that went into paint and varnish, Durant created the Flint Varnish Works. With that acquisition, the company was almost totally independent of other suppliers. It had eight factories in Flint, since the Imperial Wheel operation was moved to town that year, and the three parts companies that it did not own or control were all in Flint, too. Durant-Dort bought some of its bodies from the firm of William F. Stewart, its springs from the J. B. Armstrong Company, and its whipsockets from the Flint Specialty Company, whose name was appropriate, since nothing could have been more specialized than the hollow cylinders it turned out at the rate of 3,300 a day to be affixed to dashboards and hold buggywhips.

In every year but three of a ten-year span beginning in 1892, Durant-Dort had added a new major division. Dort, worked nearly to exhaustion, had escaped for two years when he was forced to take his ailing wife to a dry climate. Hardy, who had replaced him, was so spent that he had to be furloughed on Dort's return in 1900 — in Europe, where the tireless Durant could not disturb him by telephone with fresh inspirations. Durant seemed to enjoy limitless work, although as the planner, the traveler, and the contact man he was spared the tedium of repetition, and not maddened by trivial and personal problems that consumed the energy of static executives.

In 1901, undisturbed by the presence of the automobile in the wings,

Flint's horse-drawn vehicle industry was having one of its best years. W. A. Paterson hit its production peak with 23,000. The Flint Wagon Works was somewhere in the vicinity of its all-time top of 35,000. Durant-Dort kept on growing, and actually reached its greatest single-year output with 56,000 units in 1906. By then the organization that grew out of Durant's chance encounter with John Alger in 1886 had nationwide, even worldwide, interests. It owned, or partially owned, subsidiaries that controlled thousands of acres of Louisiana forests. Its nameplates were found on heavy-duty wagons shipped as far away as Australia, and it also manufactured some vehicles marketed under the trade names of Montgomery Ward, the John Deere Company, and Rock Island Plow. Durant-Dort warehouses were found in Milwaukee and Waterloo, Des Moines and Columbus, Grand Rapids and New Orleans. As late as 1912, when the industry was dying and the survivors consolidated for final stands, the Durant-Dort directors bought shares in buggy, wheel, and body concerns in Ontario, Georgia, and Arkansas.[9]

At that late date, however, Durant had been long gone from the wagon and buggy business. He was no longer an active force in the company after 1901. Other men earned the credit for keeping the company viable and profitable so that it was later able to make the transition to the motor age, to accept it as a transformer rather than a shatterer. But they were men whom he had picked, nursing enterprises that were the projection of his instincts, his energies and persuasiveness. They were indebted to him for leadership that brought the inert machinery to life. Fred Aldrich summed it up.

Mr. Durant's vision, forecast and organizing ability and Mr. Dort's productive talents kept steadily onward and upward. . . . Mr. Durant went into the West and returned with contracts that required expansion of facilities and products . . . and Mr. Dort would meet the requirements fully. Expansion followed expansion and to be the largest producers of transportation vehicles was the natural result. Flint became recognized as the center for vehicles.[10]

At thirty-nine, Durant was rich. His stock in the company alone was worth several hundred thousand dollars, since it was now capitalized at a million and a half. Money had come easily, quickly. There was no outward sign of pride in his personal fortune. He seemed to take it for granted, and find his reward instead in watching the beanstalk grow, in climbing its leaves above the humdrum. To judge by his later behavior, what he savored most was the sight of his industrial creations, whose pedestrian looks made them no less beautiful in his eyes.

His success came out of a confluence of his enjoyment in putting corporate pieces together and the thrust of the national economy. From 1890 onward the advantages of large-scale combination in industry were so palpable that neither law nor exhortation could stay the avalanche of mergers. Durant-Dort had grown by generating, rather than absorbing, subsidiaries, but the end result was the same — an integrated firm powerful enough to dominate its field. Whether that enriching union of man and hour was a matter of vision or luck, it was a fact that had landed Durant on the top of the heap in Flint.

Flint had cause to be grateful to him and its other vehicle makers. Thanks to them, it had become a booming place once more. Its 1898 population was 13,000, and 1,500 of its men worked in the transportation industry. Three years later the city government had wrought-iron arches put up over Saginaw Street that carried a legend: *Flint. The Vehicle City.* By 1904 it was the tenth-ranked manufacturing city in Michigan, all of its products together valued at more than six millions, a pulsing fiber in the nation's industrial heart. It was ready for whatever mechanical tasks the future might ask of it. Of this readiness, Durant was among the proud architects.[11]

In turn, it had shaped him. At the new century's beginning, he had spent twenty-eight growing years there. The Flint that became fixed in his mind was a city that seemed able to match large-scale mechanical creation with neighborliness. Its human texture was still close-knit. There was no visible price tag on progress. Wagon making was, for all the impressive statistics of output, still a moderately easygoing process. Assembly lines and precision machining were not part of its scheme. Mechanical devices cut and smoothed and bored and bent pieces of wood and metal, but these were still put together mainly by hand. Buggies sat for days, waiting for as many as eighteen coats of brushed-on paint and varnish to dry. A picture of the Flint Wagon Works labor force taken around 1900 shows men dangling their legs from the loading dock, slouching in Whitmanesque poses, not yet hurried out of the certainty of their own personhood.

Everyone worked hard for small pay envelopes. The office staff's hours were from 7:30 A.M. to 5:30 P.M. six days a week, with an hour and a quarter for lunch. The average wage in the plants was between four and ten dollars a week. Even foremen got no more than fifteen or twenty at most. In the summer it was not unheard-of for schoolboys, including the sons of first citizens, to do small jobs in the factories for five cents an hour. But there was no need for a great deal of money to enjoy life. It was easy to get out into the country, hunt rabbits, picnic, ride a bicycle, take a sweetheart to the free summer serenades of Gardner's band, walk Saginaw Street on a Saturday night and watch the farmers' wives bartering eggs and butter for calico and shoes.[12]

There were understood social lines, but they were sympathetically veiled. Durant tried, in fact, to put a $1,200 modest salary ceiling on executive salaries. It was a well-meaning, unenforceable gesture when competition for talent became keen, and it was evaded by special bonuses. Charles Nash, for one, received $5,000 extra in deep secrecy when he became works manager.[13] Paternalism governed and softened employee relations, so that outside of cigar making, printing, railroading, and building, unionism made no headway. There were bonuses for old-timers, holiday parties for whole plants, gifts from management at weddings. In 1907 the Durant-Dort board of directors offered a free one-year subscription to any magazine of an office worker's choice. They also agreed to give forty dollars "no more than eight times a summer" to pay the admittance of plant workers to "League base ball games."[14] Baseball was a passion with the town, better patronized than Stone's Opera House or the town's first golf course, and by all classes. Mr. Cornwall, owner of the whipsocket factory, was an enthusiast, and when his favorites were at bat his rich baritone voice, which was the joy of the Episcopalian church choir, would rise above the shouts of the crowd and the players in a prayerful offering: "A dollar! A dollar for a home run!"[15]

Flint offered to Durant comforting reassurance of things that he wanted to believe about life in America. And at the same time, as he reached maturity, it became too confining for him. In middle age, when one's powers and limits are more clearly known, the basic structure of a personality is likely to appear clearly at last. It was demonstrably in Durant's character at this point to be bored without a challenge. There was no longer such a challenge in the horse-drawn vehicle game. It had obviously touched its high-water mark, although there was supposedly an inconclusive set of talks with James Whiting about melding a number of Flint and outside firms into a "wagon trust."[16] And there was no spice to simply enjoying wealth and its benefits in Flint, however well beloved the surroundings.

At forty, therefore, that age of transition and course-changing, William Crapo Durant left Flint for all practical purposes. He had always been traveling for long periods of time. Now he settled, except for occasional visits, in New York City. And he did so alone.

IV The fact that he went without Clara told its own story. The marriage had been going downhill. In time, the story would become part of a court record, the live emotions of pain and anger stiffened in the preservative of legal formulas. Clara complained that in the

1890s Durant began to neglect her for increasing periods of time. His trips from home grew longer, he wrote no letters of his own, and, she said, he did not answer hers. He was cold and withdrawn, refused to inform her of his whereabouts, and turned an unsympathetic face toward her distress, which led to tears, hysterics, and eventually to serious nervous prostration.[17]

Whatever the proportions of truth and exaggeration in these accusations, the reality was that from late in 1901 until at least the beginning of 1904, Durant was in New York. Letters passed between him and Rebecca, and their context made that clear. Hers were addressed to him at 52 Broadway, an office building in the financial district. "My dear boy," she wrote one day late in 1902:

This morning finds my thoughts more with you than any interest I might feel in the work at hand. If you were not so far away a telephone might satisfy, for I could hear your voice. As it is, we must have our chat on paper. How are you these days? Busy as ever—no time for rest?

Uncle William, she went on, had recently sent her a ten-thousand-dollar check, another plum plucked from the estate, bringing the total share of each heir to $189,000 as of that date. He had prudently added a warning to keep the matter confidential, lest it "prompt the assessors to higher taxes," and Rebecca lost no time in handing the unexpectedly large sum over to her absent "Willie" with a self-deprecating note that the money found her "as incompetent to look after and take care of as [she had] ever been to provide and produce."[18]

In summers, the letters came from "Barney's Joy," a cottage she maintained in Pentwater, on the Lake Michigan beachfront. "Here I am again, all settled, and would be so pleased could I hear you coming up the steps to visit with us for a while. . . . How are you and what doing? Is it hot in the city? And when are you coming. . . . Sorry you're working so hard where it's hot while we are comfortable . . . *many* things to talk over during some of our midnight vigils." Wherever she would write from, Rebecca included the kinds of detail that would have made sense only if the recipient was rarely at home. Clara was taking violin lessons "on Clifford's account," and both were enjoying their music. "One more accomplishment added to the family. I think it's nice, don't you?" Clifford was apparently having trouble settling his thirteen-year-old mind to the expectations of a boarding academy. "I do hope he has found the right school and will be contented." Flint was in year-end holiday flower.

Flint has been [very ?] gay—parties and clubs of every kind. From the rush one would think [illegible] was near at hand. Clara can tell you of her pretty harvest (corn husks and punkins) dance at the hall. . . . I have a quantity to help out with my Christmas decorations when you and all the family will be at home. I give you the [illegible] this early that you may make no other engagements. It's for breakfast through till bed time.[19]

The correspondence kept aglow an intense attachment between mother and son. Her pride and undemanding approval kindled grateful devotion in him. On her sixty-eighth birthday, in 1901, he told her of his "inexhaustible stock of love to draw from—the same yesterday, today and forever which I send with best wishes,"[20] and on his fortieth, in the same year, she poured out her heart with no sign of New England reserve.

My dear, dear boy—

How are you today? Wish I might take you by the hand—give you a kiss—and a mother's blessing. These two are eventful dates—and come but once in our lifetime—and to me mean so much. . . . You have been a good boy—thoughtful, kind and patient—doing always for my comfort. It is a joy to have a thankful son. I more than appreciate the blessing though the expressions are so few. But you do understand it all, I know—and feel the strong tie of affection that binds our love. May it continue to the end—more perfect as the years go on.

He responded in equally emotional terms.

My Dearest Mother:

How proud I am of you. How glad to be your son. You dear, good, kind generous soul.

May God bless you and spare you to us many many years, each Christmas brighter and happier, made so by *your own sweetness and charity*, of which I know and for which I love and honor you.

Your "birthday letter" I prize *beyond any gift* I ever received. It is among my treasures. It is a pleasure to write such a letter—a comfort and satisfaction to receive it. I trust my feeble effort will serve the same purpose. I think we understand each other and will grow closer and dearer to each other as the years roll on.

To be always worthy of your affection and esteem and to return "a little" for "the much" you have done for me is the hope and prayer of

Your affectionate Son,
Willie[21]

There was a subtheme running through the letters that carried the implications of a family crisis that would always remain shadowed. For in the first months of 1903, not only was William Durant living in New York apart from his spouse and children (though Margery was probably at that time in nearby Tarrytown at a girls' school called The Castle), but so was his sister. Hints gleam through the surviving, fragmentary Crapo and Durant papers. In January of 1901, Uncle William sent an estate check and an accounting to Rebecca, and then expressed regret that she had not had a chance to visit him in New Bedford while on a recent visit to "the East."

I understand, however, the unhappy circumstance which hurried you home. There are some things in this world it is difficult to comprehend and why the innocent are made to suffer so bitterly on account of the sins and transgressions of others is among the mysteries. However the pain is softened by the sympathy extended.[22]

Then there was Rebecca's own reference to the "two eventful dates" of her life in her letter on Durant's fortieth birthday. Presumably the other date was that of her first child's birth, and she had followed her remark with the observation that the years had passed quickly, "even with all the unhappy events and burdens so hard to carry." Then, on May 8, 1903, she wrote the one letter to her daughter that appears in the family exchanges that Durant inherited from her and kept. If one of Rosa's problems was that she stood too much in her brother's shade, then Rebecca delivered an unconsciously cruel stab.

Dear Rosie:

Have received a letter from your friend telling how you are situated. I am very sorrow [*sic*] to know you are so ill, and suffering as I am sure you must. Wish I might write some word to comfort you—a true mother's heart goes out to her child no matter what the conditions when sickness like this strikes. Your brother, *good boy*, telephones me that every thing is being done for your comfort, and for you to know that your children are cared for and protected by love must take away some anxiety. I would like to do something for you—to sooth[e] if possible the pains of heart and body—so long denied me. The kind and loving Father will not forsake his children. You have my sympathy and love with pity that you are away from a home. Wallace [Rosa's son] will leave for New York tonight and Willie will arrive in New York tomorrow night. Good-bye with love,

Mother[23]

Rebecca Durant Willett never read this letter. The day after it was written she died in what her death certificate described as a "furnished room house" on West Twenty-second Street, leaving a son and two daughters behind. The doctor who attended her lived only a few doors away and had been on the case for just a week—apparently someone summoned at the last minute. He recorded that she was a housewife, who had been resident in New York for two months, and had expired of a cerebral hemorrhage due to "exhaustion" at the age of forty-five years, six months, and fifteen days.[24]

In her not wholly coherent letters of bereavement, Rebecca spoke obliquely of her daughter's history, as if she could not bear to expose parts of it directly, even to private perception.

My dear, dear boy:

Could I take your hand in mine, feel your loving touch, your helpfulness and sympathy, it would express more than I can write. For even today my heart is full, my eyes overflowing with tears. . . . These last sad duties are always hard [even] with your brother love and deep pity for the unfortunate sister and the mother far away. . . .

But with all the sadness there is comfort in the thought that you could do it, and that she has never wanted for things she would accept. I try to feel no regrets, think only of the numerous blessings. Yet the mother love will grieve and the mother heart ache. . . . She is free from all harm, and the kind, loving Father, knowing . . . the good that was in her—for she had many lovable traits of character—will help her on to something better with him. . . .

I did feel anxious those few days of waiting . . . that something worse was to come—and that fear hanging over the mind, helpless to make it any different, has been taken away. . . .

. . . Glad to be away from the criticism of the natural[ly] curious. The report was generally known, and Anna [Rosa's daughter ?] was questioned as to the truth. To be away from it all is much better, although to be free from it, never. . . . I should not and will not let it blind me to the many things that are comforting. . . . Write soon, if only a little note, and tell me of your own dear self.[25]

What were the "sins and transgressions of others" that Uncle William lamented? The "unhappy events and burdens" that Rebecca mentioned in her birthday letter of 1901? Who was Rosa's "friend"? And why were there anticipations of "something worse," that were relieved by death? Was Durant's sister a drinker? A victim of mental illness? Or did she simply flee from her family alone, or with a lover? Whatever the answers, Rosa simply disappeared from further reference. Durant now had both a father and a sister who had died under obscure and disgraceful circumstances, as if there were some strain of weakness in Durant blood that it might be his good fortune to have escaped or his duty to resist. Whatever private thoughts he had on the matter remained private.

Yet at precisely that hour a streak of his father's character made itself manifest in him for the first recorded time. At least one of his New York activities, perhaps the only one, was available to scrutiny. A city directory listed the Durant-Dort Securities Company at 52 Broadway.[26] Once more, a William Durant was in the business of buying and selling stocks. Flint knew of it vaguely; rumors, which were inaccurate, gave him a seat on the New York Exchange. But even working through accredited brokers, he was watching and trying to outguess the rise and fall of the market, those tides of fortune and disaster under whose fathoms his father's hopes had been sunk in the mud.

The simple fact of being at the edge of Wall Street did not in itself argue that Durant had become a speculator. New York's stock market was at the nerve center of the country's financial life. Its tremors signaled every coming trend in banking and industry. The rail, the oil, the steel kings, and most of the manufacturing giants of the day eventually came to the great city in whose law and business offices the important deals were made. It was from there that they could best guide their empires.

But there was no telling what Durant intended to guide, or whether he planned at that time to settle for good in New York. He left no evidence that survived those years as to whether the market was for him a pastime or an apprenticeship, and if so to what. In this period of withdrawal and latency he was certain to be contemplating horizons ahead. He had decades' worth of energy still to spend. Something was bound to come at the end of this period that enclosed his separation from Clara, his sister's death, his satiation with the business he had founded. But what and where would it be? Did it ever occur to him that it might be back in Flint? That, like Jay Gatsby, what he was looking for was behind him where the dark fields of the republic rolled on under the night?

Whatever he was thinking was crystallized early in 1904, when Fred Aldrich came to speak to him with a proposition. A group of old associates in Flint wanted Durant to come home and help them in a losing struggle to break into the automobile business. For a second time, almost by chance, a local friend had suddenly shown him the goal toward which he had been moving without knowing that he did so. In looking over the new proposition as he had looked at Johnny Alger's cart, and then accepting it, Durant parted the curtains of a future that beggared any imagination except his own. He also stepped into the middle of a major stream of economic history that had been flowing in his home state, gaining tributaries and volume, for the preceding eight years.

3)

The Auto Comes

to Michigan

I Durant could not have failed to see how quickly the motor vehicle was
making inroads on the kingdom of the horse, nor the degree to which
Michigan was involved in the early development of American-made
automobiles. To judge by his later actions, he quickly grasped the pattern
that would govern the infant industry, and his ultimate success would be
incomprehensible and miraculous to those who did not also see the
elements of that pattern.

The automobile was not born in the United States. Both the machine and,
some say, the very name were European inventions. The first American
"horseless carriage" to be later duplicated for sale did not appear until
1893 in Springfield, Massachusetts, several years after German and
French models had successfully been driven. It was the work of two

machinist brothers, Frank and Charles Duryea, and was almost immediately followed by another handmade prototype, the work of Elwood P. Haynes in Kokomo, Indiana. Fittingly, these two acts of creation took place almost simultaneously in the two chief industrial workshops of the nation, New England and the upper Midwest.

There was little doubt that the machine would be quickly swept into national life on the forty-year tidal wave of technology sweeping the whole western world from 1875 to 1915. Or that Michigan stood an excellent chance of becoming an automotive center. During all of Durant's lifetime it had been shedding its youthful farming, lumbering, and copper mining skin. Its northern half was still a pleasant pastoral of lakes and forests, but to the southward a manufacturing belt rolled from Lakes Huron and St. Clair to Lake Michigan, studded with the cities of artificers—Detroit, Flint, Lansing, Kalamazoo, Battle Creek, Grand Rapids. The region was rich in mechanics, materials, transportation, and potential investors.

But in Michigan, as anywhere else, the task of making a *production* automobile would prove far more demanding than anyone at first realized. The simplest motor car was a costly collection of complex and temperamental systems—power plant, mechanical transmission, ignition, and cooling—whose large-scale duplication required new definitions of precision, planning on a massive scale, discouraging quantities of seed money. It was the very platonic model of a self-seller, but getting it from ideal to realization was a precarious odyssey. A whole new physical and economic landscape had to be prepared, an entirely fresh market and set of submarkets, brand new mechanisms of distribution and payment. The ultimate prize was certain and generous, but only a lucky, or rather, a well-financed and -led handful of companies, would reach the point of claiming it.

All of this was demonstrable in the drama of early automaking in Detroit, Lansing, and Flint.

The first horseless carriage to take to the streets of Detroit, or for that matter to run publicly anywhere in Michigan, did so just before the beginning of spring in 1896. It was the work of Charles B. King, the son of an army officer who had retired there. King was clever with his hands, liked machinery, and after beginning his working life as a draftsman, patented and began to manufacture one or two small inventions of his own that were useful in shop work.

In 1893, when he was about twenty-five, he visited the Chicago World's Fair and was taken with one of the displays, a small two-cycle gasoline engine, intended primarily for marine use, manufactured by another Michigan man, Clark Sintz of Grand Rapids. Like any machinist, King was probably fascinated by the inherent logic of the device — its light weight, the power it got from exploding a liquid petroleum derivative mixed with air in its cylinder, its intelligent application of general scientific principles to specific problems of motion. All mechanically minded young men in that nineteenth century of triumphant engineering felt in their bones what Robert Pirsig would articulate late in the twentieth, namely, that the machine was no more than the manifestation of a form of thought, of a logical system that posited that if *this* happens under certain conditions, then *that* must follow. The machine was "a miniature study in the art of rationality itself," and the world justly lay at the feet of the rational mind.[1]

King went home from Chicago with the idea of building a gasoline engine of his own, capable of running a land vehicle. It was far from an original concept. The United States, continent-sized, was powerfully transportation-conscious. The major work of its economy for three-quarters of a century previously had been the creation of its network of canals, turnpikes, steamboat routes, and railroad lines. The hope of a vehicle independent of fixed tracks, small and light enough to give everyone an individualized package of motion, was a natural progression. In the 1890s a bicycle craze had created what Marx might have called two "preconditions" for automobility, a demand for good, hard-surfaced roads, and a technology that produced lightweight frames, chain drives, and pneumatic tires.

Detroit was a highly suitable place for King's undertaking. It manufactured freight cars and Great Lakes vessels and stoves, and was full of men experienced in doing whatever could possibly be done mechanically. If capital were needed, it was available in the bank accounts of local magnates who had made money in cigars and garden seeds and general merchandising, and who lived on the margins of the city, sheltered from the noise and dirt of the processes that provided their wealth, for, as a local paper pointed out: "When a manufacturing business pokes its greasy nose among the fine houses . . . then good-bye to green lawns and quiet life."[2]

King rented a small machine shop from a mid-fiftyish Prussian immigrant named John Lauer, who became an assistant as well, and he hired as a second helper Oliver Barthel, a seventeen-year-old draftsman from an ironworks. For months they worked away slowly, with King getting ideas from magazines and from exchanges of correspondence with other "automobileers" who shared the enthusiasm of hobbyists everywhere. In November of 1895 he went up to Chicago and took part in a historic race sponsored by a newspaper publisher there. There were five entrants, competing over a 52-mile course to Evanston and back. King was an umpire in a German-made Benz, owned and driven by Oscar Mueller, a manufacturer of brassware. Thanksgiving Day dawned with a blizzard, but the open vehicles pushed ahead nonetheless, starting at 9 A.M. Mueller, King, and a passenger covered the first 26 miles in five hours and a half, and swung around for the return. In the late afternoon darkness the passenger, nearly frozen, fainted and had to be removed to medical attention by a passing sleigh. At 8 o'clock, Mueller likewise became unconscious. King pushed him away from the tiller and, clutching him to prevent his falling out, drove one-handed to an 8:53 P.M. finish, an hour and a half behind the winning car, a Duryea driven by the two brothers who had built it.

Finally, on the night of March 6, 1896, King had his engine mounted under the body of a wagon ordered from a firm that made circus vehicles. It sat crosswise, one end connected to the rear axle through a differential gearbox. He spun the crank, the cylinders gasped and gagged and trembled, and finally lapsed into noisy, measured explosions. King and Barthel climbed in and in seconds were clattering along, unbraked, on their landmark short trip. An alerted reporter for the *Free Press* was there to watch. Either too excited or too untalented to be precise in his use of words or original in his choice of similes, he wrote that the "most unique machine" was capable of running seven or eight miles an hour, and that "when in motion the connecting-rods fly like lightning."[3]

Thereafter King became one of the first auto pioneers to learn of economic realities that were far harder to master than mechanical problems. He wanted to build engines for other makers of cars, and managed to sell five, two of them to the Duryeas, who installed them in "motor wagons" that were exhibited at a horse show and a circus. Part of the motive was profit, but part was the sheer jazzlike fun of improvising and improving on known themes. "It wasn't money I wanted," King said; "it was to do things. I was bursting with ideas—bursting."[4]

But the working out of ideas in horsepower required too much more money than his business could provide. "The art is at present in a crude state," he reported to a national magazine, "and is mainly in the hands of the inventor, who has not as yet been encouraged by capital. The times are too hard at present for any development in the motor industry. I can see no other alternate except to wait until the clouds pass over and the people have money enough to enter this new field."

That did not happen soon enough for him. He had enjoyed a little backing from two wealthy friends, Henry B. Joy and Truman Newberry, brothers-in-law, but it dried up. He turned to making boat engines, for which there was some demand. But fundamentally he was no man of business. In 1900 he sold his engine works to the Olds Motor Company, later got out of his other ownerships, and went on to a long career of invention as an employee of Olds. At seventy-eight, he designed a small reflector device for his own car. Friends urged him to patent and produce it. No, was his answer. "I don't want to put anything into production. Just want to go on making things."[5]

II On that first Detroit run, the King automobile had been followed on a bicycle by a fellow automobile enthusiast, a plant engineer at the Detroit Edison Illuminating Company, Henry Ford. Ford looked on with open curiosity, since he was at that moment just three months short of testing a home-constructed road machine of his own. Literally millions of words would later come to be written about Ford's early youth, mechanical gifts, and struggles with unbelievers, but the part of his unfolding history that would most have interested Durant would be his seven-year struggle to go from building a single, experimental "quadricycle" to marketing an automobile successfully.

Ford built his car much as King built his, eclectically. He drew on his own job experience with steam and electric machinery; on the notions of auto-minded friends and fellow mechanics; on rare chances to inspect other cars; on "how-to-build-it" articles that appeared in 1895 and 1896 in *The American Machinist*. He was not a garage tinkerer, a romantic conception on a par with untutored genius. He understood what he was about. What he did not do was what no one had the will or the resources to do at the outset of motor manufacturing: namely, systematic research — defining a problem, accumulating data, testing materials and devices in the laboratory or on the bench, building and studying models. Trial-and-error, which is a costly long-run method of learning but requires almost no head-start capital, was what all the pioneers relied on. And by trial-and-error, Ford assembled the quadricycle in the wood and coal shed behind the two-family house that he occupied, buying parts piecemeal and on credit. He had his 500-pound vehicle, on its four bicycle wheels, ready to run some time after 2 A.M. on June 4, 1896, when he spun its two-cylinder motor into protesting life and drove his later-celebrated few blocks.

For a time Ford enjoyed showing the quadricycle to curious crowds in Detroit, sometimes chaining it to a tree or lamppost if he had to leave it, so that no enthusiastic showoff could jump in and try to drive it away. The attention he was looking for, however, was that of someone who would finance the construction of a second gasoline-powered "wagon," to become a prototype for quantity manufacture. Such a man appeared in the person of a friend of his father, William C. Maybury. Maybury was at the core of Detroit's civic leadership, twice a Congressman, once the city attorney, a future mayor, a Mason and an Episcopalian. He was willing to back Ford, and while he did not have much money of his own, he was an ideal man to round up other angels. He began with Ellery Garfield, an Indiana electrical-supply company official, whose interest was guarded, for he urged a thorough preinvestment examination of all other such machines under construction, noting: "It might save us a heap of money hereafter." Later, he went to Ford and asked if he could do something about "that horrible noise of the motor" and "also get rid of that smell of the Gasoline."[6]

Nevertheless, Garfield was won over to support by Maybury, and so eventually were ten others. The twelve of them formed the Detroit Automobile Company, capitalized at $150,000, though only $15,000 was at first paid in. The names would be forgotten eventually, but the business connections outlined a virtual economic profile of Detroit's upper class. Two were insurance executives, two had their money from the manufacture of railroad cars, two were officials of the Ferry Seed Company, one was a cofounder of the Diamond Crystal Salt Company, one had a brokerage firm, one a wholesale hardware company, and one was a lumber millionaire.

Ford had his backing at last, and was able to leave his job at Detroit Edison to give his full energies to the work at hand. But it was already August, 1899, and Henry Ford did nothing to accelerate a crawl toward the marketplace. In the familiar setting of a shop, equipped with a grinder, a lathe, a drill, and piles of nuts, ells, flanges, castings, pipes, collars, gears, and nipples, he gave free rein to his perfectionism and adamant unwillingness to respect any opinion other than his own. Each car was put together virtually bolt by bolt, with manual correction of poor fits, rearrangements of parts, the screech and sparks of reboring and regrinding, and Ford ultimately climbing into the seat, as someone once saw him do, and driving a partly finished car right in the shop, dodging posts, until it bucked and quit, and then saying: "Come on, boys, we'll have to try it over again." "You would be surprised at the amount of detail about an automobile," wrote the unhappy secretary of the company to a friend, while the production target of ten a month by early 1900 faded away, and the ultimate goal of two per day became sheer fantasy. The backers sighed, prodded, signed checks, and at the beginning of 1901, with $86,000 spent and twenty partly finished cars on hand, gave up. The corporation was dissolved.

Guiltless in his own mind, as he would always be, Ford managed, with the help of a few friends, to build a racer developing about 26 horsepower. On October 10, 1901, he took it out to a race at Grosse Pointe and before seven thousand spectators scorched it around a ten-mile dirt-track course in less than thirteen and one half minutes. As a result, the flame of faith was reborn in a few of his former supporters, and within a few weeks of the race they organized a new $60,000 corporation, the Henry Ford Company.

Less than four months later, Ford walked out, grumbling that he was "determined never again to put [himself] under orders." But the company he left behind did not die. Four of its stockholders were still convinced that there was a future in the automobile, though it seemed impossible to make it materialize through the medium of Ford. These four—William Murphy, Lemuel Bowen, Albert White, and Clarence Black—sought the advice of one of the best-known machinists in the city, a fifty-nine-year-old devout Baptist from Vermont named Henry M. Leland. With his son, Wilfred, Leland operated the tool-and-engine making firm of Leland and Faulconer. He hated tobacco, alcohol, and, above all things, the most microscopic imprecision in machinery. Under Leland's guidance, Murphy and his associates increased their capitalization to $300,000, hired workmen and space, and began to produce demonstration models of a car that they decided to name after the Sieur Antoine de la Mothe Cadillac, the governor of French Canada who had founded Detroit exactly two hundred years earlier. The city was ringing with bicentennial celebrations, and the name would be familiar and attractive. This new arrangement was floated about March of 1902. Ten months later the first four Cadillacs, powered with Leland and Faulconer engines, were on display at New York's annual automobile show, and in the spring of 1903 the directors' dream was fulfilled, and they were selling automobiles at $750 each. At the very end of 1904 they merged with their engine supplier, and Henry M. Leland became president of the Cadillac Motor Car Company.[7]

In the meanwhile, Ford moved onward, unswerving in his self-confidence despite six years of failure to emerge with a market-ready automobile and despite the foundering of two companies that had relied on him. For a third time he found financial helpers, this group, however, drawn from businessmen of lower social standing. His new principal supporter was Alexander Malcolmson, a successful thirty-six-year-old coal merchant with 110 wagons cruising Detroit's streets and bearing the slogan "Hotter Than Sunshine." Malcolmson was an optimist. He believed that he had the needed cash, and that he could get along with Ford.

Both ideas were illusory. Malcolmson badly lacked liquid funds (and would eventually break with Ford). His financial plight was well known to his youthful office manager, James Couzens, a stocky blond Canadian immigrant full of a fierce ambition to rise above modest origins. Couzens was justly regarded as a shrewd dealer, and Malcolmson wisely sought his advice on the new project. Together the two men worked out a series of maneuvers that managed to keep them at least one straining leap ahead of insolvency.

Ford was provided with a fresh assortment of machines, thriftily purchased by Couzens. He also acquired a Welsh-descended assistant named C. (for Childe) Harold Wills. Wills was impetuous, sporty, flashed jewelry, and loved hunting and fishing parties. But with a job on hand he could sweat indefinitely around the clock, as tireless as some two-legged pneumatic hammer or grinding wheel, knowing no gulf between work and passion.

A painting and carpentering contractor, Albert Strelow, who leased space in one of Malcolmson's coal yards, was persuaded to remodel an empty shop as a new, rent-free factory. And another important break-through was an ingenious contract with the Dodge brothers, machine-makers. These two were redheads from Niles, Michigan—picturesque throwbacks to the era of journeymen craftsmen who, like Ford, disliked being under orders. With success, they lost none of their shagginess, and could be found on a Saturday night liquoring up with workmen in some of Detroit's tough saloons. They were not stuffy about unusual business arrangements, and came to terms with Couzens on a huge order for 650 "running gears," each constituting engine, frame, and axles, at $250 each. Ford and Malcolmson, Ltd., would put up the $15,000 for the first 60 engines in three installments, provided that the Dodge brothers showed a matching investment, dollar for dollar, in tools and materials to fill the order. The next 40 engines would be cash-on-delivery. After that the balance of the $162,500 would be paid twice monthly. If there was a default, the Dodges got to keep all the unsold inventory.

Yet even with "gears" on credit, and wheels and bodies and tires on credit, there was still not enough money; there never seemed to be enough money. So there was a third reorganization. Ford and Malcolmson scrapped their partnership in favor of a new concern without the coal dealer's name, capitalized at $150,000 in 1,500 hundred-dollar shares. Five hundred shares to be held and not issued. Five hundred and ten to be divided equally between Malcolmson and Ford, giving them majority control. Four hundred and ninety to be hawked, pressed on buyers, thrown at creditors, proffered beseechingly to friends and kinsmen and associates, and somehow converted into a precious forty-nine thousand dollars.

Slowly they got ten other stockholders. Malcolmson's uncle, a Scot and a banker, by name John Gray, whose 105 shares earned him the right to be named first president of the concern. The Dodge boys put up $3,000 in cash and threw in $7,000 worth of materials for 100 shares. Others, none with more than 50 shares, included two of Malcolmson's lawyers, Horace Rackham and John Anderson, his cousin Vernon Fry, landlord Strelow, Couzens and his schoolteacher sister (who had one share), and the president of the Daisy Air Rifle Company.

So the ship was launched, the Ford Motor Company incorporated on June 16, 1903, seven years and twelve days after the quadricycle emerged from the coalshed. John Anderson, young and enthusiastic, wrote to his doctor father in Lacrosse, Wisconsin, that he was not throwing away his money. He had been to the "dandy" factory and seen the $1.50-a-day workmen putting together the piles of parts that came in from the suppliers. "That is all there is to the whole proposition," he said. "You will see that there is absolutely no money to speak of tied up in the automobile proposition." He went on to explain that the money would soon be sweeping in.

Now, the demand for automobiles is a perfect craze. Every factory here—there are 3, including the Olds—the largest in the country—and you know Detroit is the largest automobile center in the United States—has its entire output sold and cannot begin to fill their orders. Mr. Malcolmson has already begun to be deluged with orders, although not a machine has been put on the market and will not be until July 1st.[8]

Happily for the preservation of Anderson's innocence, he did not know that the mortality rate for new auto companies between 1900 and 1908 would turn out to be 60 percent. Nor did he examine the books of the Ford Motor Company for that summer. They were still cash-poor, for some of the stock had been paid for in promissory notes, some in materials, and some had gone to wipe out previous debts. One June 26 the corporation's bank balance was $14,500 and it owed the Dodges, Malcolmson, and a tire company $15,640. On July 2, after paying Ford a monthly installment on his $3,600-a-year salary and Couzens a month's worth of his $2,500 a year and a few other bills, they were down to $223.65 and owed the Dodge brothers $5,000, due within two weeks. They were saved in the nick when Strelow's $5,000 for his shares came in. A few deposits with orders came in to give them $3,831 on August 1, and after that they were on the way, but only after barely skimming the treetops on takeoff.

III There is no way of knowing how much Durant garnered from friends, letters, and the business press about the close details of Ford's early struggles. By the end of 1903, however, it was a safe bet that he had heard a good deal about the work of Ransom Eli Olds in Lansing. It was an encouraging story, and plump with suggestive possibilities for a mind nurtured in Flint, because Lansing was closer to Flint than Detroit, not only geographically but in its social and economic composition. And there in Lansing Olds had already managed to write the infant industry's first stunning scenario of success.

Olds was at home with both the business and the mechanical sides of the automobile proposition. His father was an Ohio blacksmith who scraped together enough capital to move to Lansing and open a shop that made and repaired the steam engines that powered farm machinery. That was in

1874, when "Ranse" was twelve. Pliny Fisk Olds prospered, and was soon servicing the machinery that ran such Lansing enterprises as a chair and furniture factory, a carriage manufacturer's, a foundry, two breweries, several gristmills, and an agricultural implement plant. His son learned the business willingly, intimately, even affectionately. Pliny had set up P. F. Olds and Company as a family-owned joint-stock venture. "Ranse" worked in the office and on the floor without pay at first, then for a salary that began at fifty cents a day, which he saved. When he had saved enough, he bought out his older brother and became his father's partner. He kept on buying until he was the major holder. At the end of the 1890s, Pliny, retiring, headed toward California and the sunset, and Ransom was in full command, a man of thirty, brought up to ripeness amid and by the grace of engines.

As early as 1892 he had designed a lightweight steam engine that used a gasoline-fueled burner to heat its boiler water. To the confusion of economic historians, he called this a "gasoline engine," and began to build such engines in his works. Olds mounted one of these "gasoline engines" in a road "carriage" as a first gesture toward making self-propelled vehicles. But by 1896 he, too, was working on a motor carriage powered by a genuine internal-combustion propulsion system.

He had it ready to test on August 11, 1896. Though cheered by its performance, he deplored its thousand pounds of weight; his goal was, as he stated in his patent application, "to produce a road-vehicle that will meet most of the requirements for the ordinary uses on the road without complicated gear or requiring engine of great power, and to avoid all unnecessary weight." But he thought that could be taken care of as he went into production. He may have expected at first that he could finance his "Motor Cycle" from the profits of the engine plant, but he quickly learned, as all the other would-be manufacturers did, that the dragon guarding the gate was capital shortage. To arm himself to overcome it, he had to look for help to the local masters of investment funds.

He turned first to Edward Sparrow, the Lansing embodiment of success and good citizenship, whose purchases of copper, iron, and timber lands had yielded the dollars that made him a cofounder and president of the City National Bank, and secretary-treasurer of the Lansing Improvement Association. Sparrow agreed to help line up purchasers of shares in the Olds Motor Vehicle Company, with a capitalization of $50,000, Olds getting half the stock for his know-how and ten thousand in cash.

Sparrow brought in other backers as promised, including a fellow officer in the Lansing Wheelbarrow Company, by name Eugene Cooley, whose father had been a distinguished jurist, and who was blessed with a candor rare among industry's founding fathers. Later, when things had gone well, other men who had taken stock in successful automobile companies would pat their vests, and clear their throats, and roll cigars between their fingers and modestly allow that if they said so themselves, they *had* enjoyed remarkable foresight. But Cooley admitted, "I am sure I did not see any great future for the invention and I do not think others did. . . . We felt that . . . a business could be developed which would show a profit. I am free to say that I had not the faintest vision of what has eventuated in the automobile business."[9]

The most important recruit was a severe, bearded man named Samuel L. Smith. Smith and Sparrow, by investing their mining and lumbering winnings first in railroads and then in Olds's enterprise, were living links between the two eras of Michigan's wealth — the first, based on a culling of the state's animal, mineral, and vegetable resources, and the second, reared on manufacturing. They were boosting the commonwealth into the new century, only three years away.

When Olds sat down at the new corporation's opening meeting, he was part of an alliance between inventor and capitalist that would be struck again and again in the industry's youth. Neither party was ever quite comprehensible to, or even comfortable with, the other. Olds was better off than some fellow inventors; he still owned the engine works, and he had half the stock and a director's seat in Olds Motor Vehicle. But he was a mechanic, and they were men of the countinghouse, and the difference in style was precipitated in the flask of an opening exchange between himself and Sparrow. The senior man turned a spectacled gaze toward Olds's end of the table, and announced: "Olds, we want you to make one perfect horseless carriage."

Olds shook his head. In the state of the art, perfection was not possible. "You shouldn't even expect it," was his warning.

Arthur Stebbins, Secretary, taking the minutes, neatly ran his pen through the word *perfect*, and made a small change. "Olds," the sentence now read, "we want you to make one nearly perfect horseless carriage."[10]

Making even nearly perfect cars, however, was harder than expected. In mid-1898, after a year of existence, the company had produced exactly four of them. It was not as disastrous a situation as appeared, since others were not faring much better. Nevertheless, the record had to be improved, more time and more money were imperative, so there was an 1898 reorganization that raised the capitalization to $100,000 and brought in more Lansing businessmen, including Samuel L. Smith's son Frederic, who, like Eugene Cooley, seemed free of self-importance and was blessed with a sense of humor. It was his view that some of the city's "cold-nosed wealthy" bought into Olds's auto company with no great hopes for it but thinking that it might give them a chance to move in on the engine works, which were paying well.

And there was still not enough, so that a third reorganization was undertaken at the end of 1899, and a full $500,000 worth of stock was authorized, though only $350,000 of it was distributed. Among the new takers were in-laws of Samuel Smith, and he in turn talked several Detroiters, including the president of the Michigan Central Railroad and a former president of the American Banking Association, into investing. As new directors, these men urged a move of the Olds auto operation to their city, which had better assembly and sales facilities. On New Year's eve of 1900, Ransom Olds walked into the bedroom of his two small daughters in their new home in Detroit just as midnight was striking, and shook them awake, explaining that "they would never again have the chance to see a new century born, and he didn't want them to miss it."[11]

And with a new century and a new location, there was a new name for the cars that were going to be manufactured—Oldsmobile. All of these beginnings were encouraging to those involved, with the possible exception of some Lansing leaders who were sorry over the escape of even an infant business enterprise from the community.

During 1900, Olds worked on the design of that uncomplicated and lightweight road vehicle that he had envisioned in his patent application. Some time during the year he readied his prototype, a 700-pound creation on bicycle wheels, with a single-cylinder under-the-body engine, simple enough so that "anyone could run it, and the construction such that it could be repaired at any local shop." It came to be known as the "curved-dash Oldsmobile," and it was to become the first American best-selling automobile.

Like Durant's road cart, it was somehow individual and intimate, so small that it looked as if it were meant for only one person. Its tufted leather seat perched on top of what seemed to be nothing more nor less than a rectangular box. The floor under the rider's feet swept up and curved back on itself like a wave in motion. On either side, two brass lamps made a bright show that encouraged forgetfulness of how unequal to the darkness they really were. The bulb horn at the driver's left hand was pleasingly impudent; the gearshift lever on his right a magic wand to summon the spirit of motion. The whole body was set high on its wire wheels, riding its springs like a pleasure craft on the tide. It was not a workhorse but a companion; drivers leaned forward going uphill to give it friendly (and needed) encouragement. Its very market name, a "runabout," expressed the freedom that the ownership of an automobile could convey.

Olds planned to assemble a great many of these cars in 1901, and *assembly* was the most truly descriptive word for what the few auto manufacturers of that day were doing. None of them had resources for making parts, and contracting-out was the course that a trade journal pointed out as safest. It "involves the least risk," said *Motor Age* at the time, "gives the most rapid turn-over of what money is invested, and finally, leads to success by the straightest and easiest road."[12] Olds ordered roller bearings from a New Jersey firm founded by John Hyatt but recently taken over by a young graduate engineer, Alfred P. Sloan. He bespoke wheels and axles from a Utica, New York, corporation called Weston-Mott. Its head was likewise youthful and college-trained. His name was Charles S. Mott.

For engines he went both to Leland and Faulconer and to the Dodge brothers, since his own company in Lansing was busy fulfilling contracts of its own. And for radiators he turned to a sheet-metalworking company owned by two brothers, Benjamin and Frank Briscoe. Ben, thirty-three, was the older and the leader. When Olds first showed him the drawings of what he called a "cooler," Ben scratched his head. He had seen nothing like it before. He said it resembled "an antiquated band instrument."[13] But they were both glad of the contract, and after a time they were not only doing Olds's radiators, but making fenders, gas tanks, and other auto parts for several manufacturers.

On March 9, 1901, what seemed to be a disaster occurred. A fire swept through the plant and wiped out everything in it. But Olds was able, all the same, to put together 400 of his runabouts in various rented spaces before the end of the year, and Detroit's misfortune was Lansing's second chance. The Business Men's Association there put up $5,200 to buy a 52-acre plant site, which had once been used for agricultural fairs, and the Grand Trunk Rail Road agreed to build appropriate sidings and make special rate concessions. With such boons in prospect, the Detroit influence on the board was overridden, and the new factory for Oldsmobiles was raised in the owner's hometown, though the Detroit works were rebuilt and used for three years to provide overflow capacity.

Then the glory years began for the "merry Oldsmobile," although the song that celebrated it was not composed until 1905. In 1902, the Olds Motor Vehicle Company sold 2,500 runabouts. The sales were fed, as all early auto merchandising had to be fed, by a series of promotional races and cross-country runs including a "dash" by Roy Chapin, a young mechanic and test driver for Olds, from Detroit to New York. The 800-mile trip took 7½ days, 30 gallons of gasoline, 80 of water, and many repair stops. But it proved that the curved-dash Oldsmobile could survive over distance. It struggled, it protested, its underpowered engine swooned on hills and sickened from any protracted exertion, but eventually it got there, and was a bargain at $650 in 1902.

The next year, some 4,000 units were sold for a total of $2,325,580. The net profits of around $900,000 were enough, after various reserves and reinvestments were set aside, to pay $327,000 in dividends to the delighted stockholders. Oldsmobile agencies proliferated in New York,

Washington, Pittsburgh, Chicago, Minneapolis, Omaha, San Francisco, Houston, Denver, Cleveland.

In 1904 5,500 runabouts rolled from the factories; in 1905 the total was 6,500, which did not include other models in production. By then Olds had left the company, the quarrels between him and the other directors intensifying and deepening until the point of fissure was reached. He went into a second automobile enterprise, and Frederic L. Smith became vice-president, general manager, and effective head of the corporation.

The trick had been turned. What Durant could see in May of 1904 was a thriving automobile concern in Lansing. And he or anyone who might be looking could catch the vibrations from Detroit of at least four successful motor companies, with others tuning up for a start. There was the Detroit subsidiary of Oldsmobile, and Cadillac, and Ford. In addition, late in 1903, James W. Packard, who was producing in Warren, Ohio, a salable car bearing his name, was induced to move to Detroit by a syndicate whose members included Henry B. Joy and Truman Newberry, Charles King's old friends, and some veterans of Ford's defunct Detroit Automobile Company, ready to hazard anew. Eight hundred autos were owned and operated in the city, and the factories that made them were already an exciting display of industrial power, as a reporter observed.

Rows upon rows of special machinery are humming and buzzing away, bewildering the onlooker with their number . . . each with its own peculiar work to do. . . . In the assembling room the same orderly process is to be observed. The engines move along from one group of men to another until they are ready for the car, thoroughly tested and proved worthy of use. . . . One little imagines . . . the immense amount of detail and careful manipulation that have been necessary on the hundreds of parts before they have all been brought together and adjusted to form this engine of commerce and pleasure.[14]

Michigan was in full procession into the automotive future. And Flint, the Vehicle City, was behind the parade.

IV That was precisely the opinion of the Flint *Journal* at the time. It proclaimed:

Flint is the most natural center for the manufacture of autos in the whole country. It is the vehicle city of the United States and in order to maintain this name by which it is known from ocean to ocean there must be developed factories here for the manufacture of the automobile.[15]

By then, the automobile had made its appearance in the city, and one attempt at commercial manufacture had been launched and lost in the city that Durant had left behind him.

The first car built in Flint was handmade by a local Leonardo, Judge Charles H. Wisner, the son of a former Michigan governor. He was not only an attorney but an amateur photographer, architect, landscape painter, woodsman, and machinist. In a carriage house behind his home, he had a completely equipped workshop in which he built a fishing reel of his own invention, and X-ray machine for his friend Dr. Edwin Campbell, and finally an auto, making all the parts of his creations himself down to the very nails and screws.

Wisner took his car onto the streets late in 1900, according to cobwebbed local memories. It was apparently very noisy and willing but weak, for while it could negotiate the streets well enough, when it came to the raised wooden crosswalks at main intersections it thrust itself against them, grunted, and died. It was even said later that one Sunday morning Wisner took his friend Mr. Durant out for a trial spin, and that the two of them had to restart the machine frequently, to the amusement of the churchgoing passersby who looked on.

In the following year, Wisner undertook to make two more autos, enlisting the help of James Parkhill, a mechanic at the Armstrong Spring Company. Meanwhile, a second gasoline-powered auto made its appearance, assembled by (or commissioned by) Dr. H. H. Bardwell. The doctor had his picture taken in the boxy little vehicle. He sat bolt upright, uniformed according to his class, not in a duster, but in a business suit and fedora. Even his beard was in perfect plumb as he extended one firm hand to grasp the tiller and ride to the relief of his patients.

By early in 1902, Flint's population of automobiles would include at least Dr. Bardwell's and Judge Wisner's cars, a "steam mobile" belonging to another physician, perhaps an electric vehicle—there was certainly one there in 1903—and possibly a French-made import. It was at that time that the first flyer into quantity manufacture was taken, and the entrepreneur was A. B. C. Hardy, the former interim president and key executive of the Durant-Dort Carriage Company.[16]

At the carriage-works Hardy had proven a tireless doer, a formidable straightener-out, a thick-and-thin loyalist. His capacity for hard work was profound, but not infinite. After four years of fighting production bottlenecks, supply trusts, competitors, and the knots and resistances of sales and transportation organizations, he was weary. It was hard for him to get any rest on vacations because of Durant. "The Boss" was a kindly man who liked and was liked in turn by subordinates, but who was inexhaustible and simply unaware of fatigue in others. Whenever Hardy tried to get away,

Durant pursued him by telephone down whatever labyrinthine ways he had fled.

In January of 1900, Hardy escaped briefly for a few days to New York, where the first National Automobile Show was in progress. Carriage makers milled around curiously, trying to read omens of the future on the floor. Hardy fell in with his fellow townsman, James Whiting, of the Flint Wagon Works. Together they accepted from a French exhibitor an invitation to free rides, available to anyone who applied at a lower Fifth Avenue address.[17] Whether or not this was a transforming experience for Hardy he never said. But the following summer, he took his vacation in Paris, which was beyond telephone reach then, and which was also the scene of a great industrial exposition, where there were more French and other European automobiles to look at.

The foreign makers had got beyond the horseless-carriage stage. Their creations already had the look of the modern car. The engines, often multicylindered, were in front of the dashboard, under hoods. Power was transmitted to the rear wheels through a driveshaft that ran under the chassis. Steering was by wheel. Some already had partly or wholly enclosed bodies. Not all the autos at Paris were so advanced, but enough of them were so that Hardy knew that he was looking at the next generation of automotive history. He returned to Flint for a short time, then announced to his Durant-Dort associates that he was resigning, turned around, booked passage, and was on his way back across the Atlantic for another eleven months.

He would afterward admit to having spent that time "crawling under every car he could." A legend arose that he returned to tell the carriage manufacturers in prophetic tones that the days of their kingdom were numbered, their shafts and whips and varnish pots doomed, and that they must "get out of the carriage business before the automobile [ruined them]."[18] The story might have been true, or it might have been merely a convenient imaginary peg on which to hang many such warnings that would have echoed in the air in those years. But, true or false, Hardy himself was ready for a new era. He scraped up a small amount of capital, a mere $5,000, rented shop space in a location in which Abner Randall and his brother Frank had once made their wagons, and began to turn out cars. He was the junction point for Flint's vehicle-making past and future.

His gifts were impressive. While other, better financed operations sometimes took years to produce a first tentative handful of autos, Hardy, in cramped quarters and on almost no money, turned out fifty-two in eighteen months. He called them Flint Roadsters. They did not incorporate the costly European influences, except for a steering wheel. Each had a one-cylinder engine under the chassis that developed a mere 8.5 horsepower. But each was an attractive little runabout, with leather seats and polished lamps, wide fenders, artillery wheels — that is, with wooden instead of wire spokes — and, as a buggymaker's touch, many glistening coats of red paint, altogether a bargain at $850.

Then the weight of the law suddenly descended on Hardy. Among his customers had been a skeptical-appearing man who asked for a list of all "satisfied users," and received from the confident manufacturer a list of fifty-one names. Shortly thereafter, Hardy was served with fifty-two injunctions, one for each car he had made, commanding him to desist from further manufacturing until he had paid royalties to, and made satisfactory future arrangements with, the holder of the basic patent on the gasoline-powered motor vehicle. The said holder was a recently formed organization known as the Association of Licensed Automobile Manufacturers, and the curious "customer" had been acting as their agent.

Behind and ahead of that moment stretched a story full of critical, but slow-moving, legal and financial evolutions. In 1879 a Rochester, New York, attorney, George B. Selden, had applied for a patent on a road vehicle utilizing a liquid hydrocarbon internal combustion engine. As Hardy learned, Selden delayed formal registration of the patent for fourteen years, but when it finally became effective it gave him a powerful priority of claim.

Selden's next step was to find a manufacturer with whom to share the benefits of the patent. This turned out to be the Electric Vehicle Company of New Jersey, which was not intending to produce liquid-hydrocarbon-using cars, but thought that it might use the patent to prevent any other firm from doing so, leaving a clear field for electrics. Selden and Electric Vehicle concluded an arrangement in 1899, and immediately sued Alexander Winton of Cleveland for infringement.

The case moved with the law's majestic deliberation, and was finally decided in March of 1903, in Selden's favor. By then, various new elements had entered the picture. Winton was willing to settle out of court. Several other manufacturers, including the makers of the Packard and the Oldsmobile, were ready to come to terms with Selden. The Electric Vehicle Company no longer had realistic hopes of keeping the gasoline engine off the highways. These circumstances had readied the soil for the planting of confederation. Soon after the patent was affirmed, the principals formed the association. Each of the founding gasoline-car companies would pay an initial fee and a future royalty on every car manufactured. Of the fund accumulated, Selden would receive 20 percent, the Electric Vehicle Company 40 percent, and the remaining 40 percent would be held by the A.L.A.M. for good works, including future defenses of the patent. At its discretion, the A.L.A.M. would license new manufacturers.

The A.L.A.M. harbored what it thought to be worthy purposes. It spoke of using its licensing power to establish standards of quality and prevent investors from being taken in by unscrupulous promoters of shadowy companies. "It will," said the magazine *Motor Age* when the association was formed, "prevent the incursion of piratical hordes who desire to take advantage of the good work done by the pioneers to flood the market with trashy machines, made only to sell and not intended to go—at least for any great length of time."[19] But it was clearly an auto trust, and while many new producers joined, and paid, a few independents continued to battle in the courts and eventually, in 1911, broke the monopoly.

The year 1911 was far in the future when Hardy was presented with the A.L.A.M.'s bill, however, and he lacked both the money and the temperament either to fight or to join. The back payment could have been managed if he had chosen, but he was already rich in wisdom about auto production, and it is very likely that he realized that small-scale operations would not long survive, and that for him there were impassable obstacles to enlargement. He quit the field and left Flint, and disappeared for a time in Iowa, where he superintended yet another carriage company. In this retreat he awaited events and enjoyed a more tranquil existence than the preceding five years had allowed him.

Almost simultaneously with his departure, Flint's second essay to join the ranks of auto-making cities began under unpretentious and inauspicious conditions. Its beginnings were sunk in a failure elsewhere—the unavailing four-year struggle of David Dunbar Buick to produce a car in Detroit.

Some time around his forty-fifth year, Buick posed for a portrait. He wore a jacket, a high collar, a properly knotted tie. His hair stood up in a stiff and correct pompadour, his mouth was set in a serious, straight line below a heavy moustache. But the camera caught what seemed to be a look of discomfort in his eyes, something oddly poignant, a manifestation of some perceived imbalance. It might have been a simple uneasiness in clothes appropriate to a banker or a school principal when in fact he was happiest as a mechanic. Or it might have reflected that Buick was feeling the first inward tremors of shocks that would shake apart his life and send a career that had taken him from shophand to businessman into sudden eccentric and self-destroying patterns. "Fame beckoned to David Buick," said one of his contemporaries. "He sipped from the cup of greatness and then spilled what it held."[20]

He was a Scottish machinist, the storybook embodiment, therefore, of thrift and exactitude. He was brought to Detroit by his immigrant family when he was two years old, in 1856. At an early age he was apprenticed to James Flower, one of three English-born brothers who ran a factory that turned out brass and iron castings, valves, fire hydrants, and other metal devices and fittings. Like the Lelands, the Flowers were known as perfectionists, and their thorough training of their students, one of whom, after Buick, was Henry Ford, included the requirement that a youngster "draw his blueprints for a job, and, if necessary, make his patterns, mould his piece, finish and install it."

Buick completed his training and began to work for a plumbing supply company. In his spare time he devised and patented a process for bonding porcelain to cast iron. The result was the enameled bathtub that became standard in the industry. With a partner, William Sherwood, Buick began to manufacture this popular item in quantity. By the late 1890s he was another successful Detroit businessman modestly enjoying the fruits of his innovation.

Then the automobile fever that was in the air of Detroit infected him. In 1899 he organized, on his own, a second company to make nothing but gasoline engines, with the catchy name of Auto-Vim and Power. The engine-fabricating purpose, however, barely masked the real quest to make a production car. Buick worked at that with increasing absorption, assisted by the designer he had hired, Walter Marr.

Marr was no ordinary employee; he was one of those men who never truly work "for" anyone. Like a cat, which merely consents to live with a provider, Marr would accept wages for doing what it was in his nature to do, provided conditions suited him. He came from Lexington, Michigan, and had learned machinecraft in Saginaw, at the mouth of the Flint River, making power for sawmills and steamboats, the power that was coming to be as much a Michigan resource as wood and water were.

In 1888 he built his first gasoline engine. In 1898, striking out on his own, he opened a bicycle factory in Detroit. Joining the engine and the bicycle was merely the working out of a natural curve of inclination; by 1899 he had put together a "motor tricycle" as well as a "motor wagon." He and Buick met, and Buick convinced him to leave the bicycle business behind and plunge headlong into the development of a superior car. Buick himself could be nothing less than in earnest, for he burned his bridges through the sale of his plumbing business for $100,000, which it took him little time to lose.

He and Marr seemed born to stimulate and to trouble each other. Marr belied the cliché that engineers are steadygoing whereas artists have "temperament." He was a gifted designer of parts and improviser of tools, wholly possessive and demanding of and on behalf of his creations, clinging to them for yet a little more improvement until colleagues managed to seize the model or blueprint from his resisting hands and get it into production. He wore a derby hat in the shop; his spade beard bobbed up and down in frequent argument. Buick himself was likewise full of confidence in his own judgments, "a crank and a hard man to do business with."[21]

They lurched through a collaboration of continued crisis. Buick's crankiness was sharpened by an ineptitude in handling money that was astonishing for a middle-aged man who had been a business success. The automobile seemed to have deranged his compass. His debts compounded; he offered to sell out to Marr, but was refused. And finally, Marr walked out on him and tried an unproductive track for a while, designing something that he called the Marr Autocar, which failed to win backing.

His place was taken by a French-born engineer from Philadelphia, Eugene Richard, who had worked for the Olds plant in Detroit. Richard and Buick continued to tinker and test and combine their ideas with those that Marr had already set in motion, with the result that none of them was the exclusive author of the finished product. It took them until the middle of 1902 to bring forth a single automobile, later to be known as Buick Model A. Whatever had been the difficulties of its birth, it was the nucleus of a superior piece of automotive engineering. Its major asset was a new kind of engine that Richard, Buick, and Marr were responsible for, known as a "valve-in-head" type. In it, the valves that admitted vaporized fuel to the engine and exhausted the gases left by its explosions were set directly in the tops of the cylinders, an improvement on earlier practices that resulted in better combustion and more power. In time, cars equipped with it could outstreak rivals on the road.

By the time this prototype was shown, Buick had not a cent left for development. He turned to various sources, and finally came to the Briscoe brothers, to whom he already owed money for various parts they had supplied him. He was apparently desperate, since he proposed that if they would write off his existing debt, and advance him a mere $650 additional, he would turn over to them the full rights of production and sale of the car that his company, which he had now renamed for himself, was putting together. The brothers could scarcely say no to such a modest gamble, and agreed to advance Buick money as he needed it. He needed a first installment within twenty-four hours, then another, and another, modest and birdlike dips into the well of capital by industry standards, but enough to make the Briscoes pause. In March of 1903, Buick owed them a fresh sum of approximately $2,000 and asked for another $1,500. They agreed, but at the price of a curious reorganization.

The newly styled Buick Motor Company was to be capitalized at $100,000. Of its stock Buick himself, the inventor and founder, would hold exactly $300. The other $99,700 would belong to the brothers. If, however, within six months Buick repaid the $3,500, they would yield their entire interest to him. In effect, they were asking him to put up the entire business as security for their $3,500, and they evidently preferred to collect the debt rather than claim the security, for by then they had lost all confidence in Buick's capacity to get on with the actual quantity production of his machine. Nor was their judgment wrong. In September their debtor was still insolvent, and too beaten or too preoccupied to argue that he ought at the very least to have some more generous share of the stock for his nonmonetary contributions. The company passed to its now-unwilling owners, the Briscoes. As it happened, it stayed with them only for the blink of an eye, for by then they had managed to unload it.

The sale came about through an accident of consanguinity. Ben Briscoe, who was the actual head of the partnership, was married to a woman whose cousin was Dwight Stone, a Flint real estate dealer. Stone's father had put up the town's successful woolen mill back in 1867, and later built the auditorium downtown that was a cultural replenishment station still known as Stone's Opera House when Mr. and Mrs. Briscoe came for a kinsmen's visit in 1903. Dwight Stone learned of Briscoe's urge to sell his new acquisition, and was at once interested, for he knew that James Whiting, on behalf of the directorship of the Flint Wagon Works, was looking for an automobile property. It would be something to operate in addition to the wagon factory, a hedge against the inevitable future that was visible to the intelligent men of Flint even while their existing vehicle business still flowered.

Stone made the appropriate introductions, and after some negotiation, a bargain was struck. Whiting paid ten thousand dollars to acquire the Buick Motor Company. In consideration of that sum, its inventory and physical assets were moved to Flint and into a new building that was put up adjacent to the Flint Wagon Works. Buick came along with the deal, and so did Marr, who had decided to rejoin him after another of his flings at self-employment. Richard did not come along; he had left Buick by then.[22]

The brick walls of the new home of the Buick Motor Company rose, and so did the hopes of its latest owners. But weeks went by and turned into months, winter fastened Flint in its frigid grip, gave way to muddy spring, yielded to the dusty warmth of summer. And David Buick asked for more money, and, with Marr, tinkered and tested and kept putting together and picking apart what was to be the Buick Model B. Though Whiting's initial, cautious design was to start with engine manufacture only, he was coaxed by the two builders into authorizing production of their second essay at a roadworthy vehicle. Its first test drive on July 9, 1904, was a landmark in Flint's history. Marr and Tom Buick, David's son, climbed into what was virtually a stripped-down chassis and headed it for Detroit. They arrived there without noticeable difficulty, and three days later returned over a course lengthened by an unplanned detour to 100 miles. They took just

over three and a half hours to wind through the gaping little towns of
Pontiac, Orion, Oxford, Lapeer, and Davison, and pulled up mud-spattered
but triumphant in front of their departure point, vindicated conquerors of
distance.[23]

But exhilaration alone was not the stuff of dividends. In all of 1904, fewer
than forty cars were produced, a tiny fraction of what was needed even to
return costs. The leadership of the Flint Wagon Works had borrowed the
considerable sum, for the city, of $75,000 in working capital, spreading it
among three banks, and seemed to stand a good chance of losing it all, a
blow that would be felt throughout the city's financial community. The
Flint of midyear was beginning to know the auto as a presence. Nearly
thirty of them were on its tax rolls. But its record as a nursery of
auto-making companies stood at one thwarted and one foundering.

It was at that point that Fred Aldrich came as an emissary to Durant and
asked if he would be interested in reorganizing and leading the Buick
Motor Company.

4)

The Buick Years

I Whatever was in his mind when he agreed to consider the idea of coming to the Buick's rescue he never said, to anyone's recollection. It could have been loyalty to Flint friends and associates, or an urge to touch known reference points again, mingle with familiars, perhaps even accommodate his neglected wife. It might have been that whatever he was pursuing in New York was hidden behind doors that still were not far enough ajar for a small-town Michigan carriage maker to slip through.

Those who knew Durant best, then and later, believed that the real bait was the chance to start something new and promising. The initial difficulties only sharpened the interest of a man who had the winner's confidence that came with early, easy success. "He loved to create," one of his longtime associates of his riper years said. "He was constantly looking for

(83)

11.
David Buick. Taking over his struggling infant made Durant famous.

12.
Albert Champion ("Shom-PYON"), whose name became synonymous with spark-plugs

13.
Vignette of 1910. A Buick waits for the right-of-way.

14.
The quintessential Buick: the throbbing "Bug" racer

15.
A Buick "White Streak," around 1908, driven by H. M. Bassett, superintendent of
the Weston-Mott axle plant behind him

16.
Durant, dressed for the road around 1909, with the
smile of the yet unbeaten

17.
Flint when Buick boomed: quitting time at the plant

new industrial worlds to conquer.'"[1] Even if his 1904 aspirations had not yet ballooned to take in whole worlds, the prospect of mastering another game and making it yield fortunes hidden within it would be enough to stir him. By 1904 it was clear enough that the motor industry was just such a high-risk adventure, whose end product was not merely profit for its backers, but a machine that was the metallic embodiment of progress itself. It is hard to conceive that at that late date he needed to be sold on the auto.

But he did need to be persuaded of the viability and promise of the Buick. Enough was said in whatever initial conversations he held with Whiting and others to interest him in a trial, and he began it on September 4, 1904, when he climbed into the seat of a Buick owned by Dr. Herbert C. Hills. The doctor had placed his order as soon as the company moved to Flint, and had been assigned the second car produced there, but on condition that he allow its use as a demonstrator until more Model B's were completed. After that first ride, Durant had another Buick made available to him, learned to drive it, and began his own test program.

William Paterson's son-in-law later became an automotive historian, and found the memories of Flint people still impressed with Durant's thoroughness.

[He] drove that two-cylinder Buick back and forth over a wide range of territory devoid of good roads save for a few gravel turnpikes built by toll companies. He put it through swamps, mud and sand, and pitch-holes for almost two months, bringing it in again for repairs and consultations and then taking it out again for another strenuous cross-country run. He had every sort of mischance chronic in the motoring of the period, often, of course, being stalled in out-of-the-way hamlets for lack of repair parts or fuel and oil. During these enforced waits, perhaps in a country blacksmith shop which would some day be a garage, this impetuous and eager mind wrestled with the future of transportation.[2]

He did in fact have long-range purposes in his wheeled excursions on the back roads. The auto's promise would never be fulfilled until it could negotiate long intercity trips. Americans were a nation of travelers, spread over a wide domain. And a big share of the auto market would have to be found in that large part of the population which, even a few years after 1900, was still rural. The farmers who had been his wagon and buggy customers would have to be converted to the motor age by a demonstration that the auto was applicable outside the towns. In his first few years as a manufacturer, Durant enjoyed spreading the gospel in person. He took long cross-country drives, two of them especially well remembered by Margery, who was with him. They bounced and roared over the dusty, pitted dirt roads, and she saw that he gratefully accepted the small disaster of a broken spring or axle as a chance for salesmanship.

They would find their way to the nearest farmhouse, and Durant would ask directions to the next town where there was a garage, telephone ahead if it were possible, or arrange for the farmer to tow him. And if it were late, he would offer to pay for a meal. At the table, he would talk on about the motor car and how its small mechanical problems would soon be cured; how it would enable farmers to go more swiftly and profitably about their business, bring them and their families closer to the amenities and essential services of the city, break the grip of isolation that held their children back in competition with townsfolk. He would invite a close inspection of his own car, even a demonstration ride if the damage permitted. It was not necessary to convince his hosts that the auto was a wonderful, modern machine; they knew that. The important thing was to show them that it was not some distant presence like the dynamo, but rather affordable and usable by ordinary people such as they were, in their own setting.[3]

After these first two months of autumn rural rides in 1904, Durant himself was persuaded, and he had also taught himself enough of the details and costs of making, operating, and maintaining a Buick to feel safe in a decision. One late October day, he and Whiting drove around Flint for a long time in earnest conversation. At the end of it the severe-looking Whiting, who was rarely quoted at any length, walked in and addressed his expectant family.

"Billy's sold," he said.[4]

II The new Durant style became manifest within the first sixty-five days of his assumption of leadership. The Flint men who had bought the Buick Motor Company from Briscoe had cut its capitalization from his $100,000 to what they thought of as a more reasonable figure of $75,000. On the day of his takeover, Durant raised it to $300,000. Two and one half weeks later, he made it $500,000. Six weeks after that, he went to the Automobile Show in New York and returned with orders for 1,108 Buicks, or 1,071 more than the entire preceding year's output — for that matter, many more than the eventual 1905 output of slightly over 700 machines.

Ten months after his November 1, 1904, agreement with Whiting and the other original Flint owners, he raised the amount of the company's stock to a million and a half dollars, a twentyfold step-up. The full pyrotechnic impact could best be appreciated at the end of a complete year of his reign.

The details of his plan emerged in a step-by-step unfolding. Both the grand design and the parts reflected what Durant had learned in New York, and in his third of a century in Flint, about the management of men and money. They also demonstrated the emergence of either a new or previously unrecorded will to power and financial adventure. Durant lunged into the battle to save Buick as if, at midlife, something had released in him even more vital energy than his townsmen had suspected.

From the start, he made it clear that he required absolute control. That was part of the arrangement. His title was simply (at first) treasurer and chairman of the board of directors of the company, but he did not expect to be, and was not, outvoted on any question. Charles Begole held the presidency, the very model of the kind of first citizen who could adorn the role and inspire confidence.

Durant had a threefold job facing him. The first was to raise money. He grasped the central principle that the early auto makers' experience taught — that largeness of scale was all. Only money begot money, and small plans would be automatically weighed in the balance and found wanting. With adequate backing in hand, the second assignment could be faced, which was to build a car that would lure buyers. Finally, the manufacture, sale, and servicing of that car would have to be systematized and given a structure that could accommodate growth. Durant would be at the center of the grid, the personal coordinator of all three operations, and almost alone in the financial one.

The key to funding lay in having shares of stock to deal with, and the secret of Durant's power rested in his ability to capitalize on the difference between the theoretical meaning of incorporation and what actually took place when security issues were authorized by law and thrown onto the market. Supposedly, the shares of stock in a corporation stood for its assets, which included such tangible objects as machinery, real estate, and inventory, but also embraced more nebulous entities of purely potential value — the concern's "goodwill," the patents it held, the skill of its management and technicians, and the extent of its sales network.

The original incorporators divided the total value of these items into portions represented by shares of stock, which they then bought themselves and sometimes sold to others, who thereby became co-owners. This process provided working funds and offered an alternative or a supplement to borrowing. The problem with borrowing was that the money had to be repaid, principal and interest, in a fixed time period regardless of the company's fortunes. Stockholders, on the other hand, were expected to be patient and wait out economic storms before collecting their cut of the profits, in the form of dividends.

If things went well and the undertaking prospered, its assets multiplied, and a new, enlarged capitalization was sought, as had happened several

times with the Durant-Dort firm. New shares were issued covering the
increased values, and their sale enlarged the family of owners, as well as
the available resources. As laid out in textbooks of business practice, the
system was pleasantly logical. Profits made a degree of expansion possible,
and expansion justified the sale of more stock, which in turn stimulated
new growth and profits, and so it went on in a pleasant succession of
growing seasons.

In practice, however, the entire operation was more flexible and
metaphysical. The assets of a company could be inflated by friendly
assessment and eloquence to a point where buying a share in them was
really an act of faith in things unseen but hoped for. (Genuinely unscrupulous promoters, in fact, had been known to issue "watered" stock against
wholly imaginary properties.) But neither did the incorporators always see
actual cash for each share bestowed on a new owner. If an issue were
marketed through a bank or brokerage house, the house might take some of
the shares free as its commission. Shares could likewise be given in return
for property or for services, or merely to win friends among influential
citizens. They might be held in the company treasury as a reserve against
future needs, or pledged as collateral for loans. And they could be sold for
only a fraction of their face value, with the balance to be paid up out of
dividends. They could, in practiced hands, substitute for cash.

The textbook model of the corporate marketplace depicted companies as
offering shares of hard assets in exchange for tangible dollars. The actual
situation early in the century—when securities markets were largely
unregulated—was one in which pieces of paper suffused with expectation
were often traded for promises, services, and supportive gestures that were
themselves a highly impalpable kind of capital. Yet a creative entrepreneur
could go far on this process if he dealt in a product that had a genuine
future. And few men were as adept as Durant in working in this bazaar of
illusions. In his hands, shares became instruments for getting things done,
and he employed them with a virtuosity that dazzled beholders.

The first boost in capitalization was achieved by floating 3,000 shares
with a par value of $100 each. The original incorporators in Flint could
trade their old stock in for the new issue, each share so given up bringing a
share of 7 percent preferred stock and a quarter-share of common.
Preferred stock was the safe and premium investment. It had first call on
the division of profits, but could earn no more than the rate stated on the
share's face. Common was the risk-taker's stock. It might yield nothing, or
it might yield dividends to which there were no theoretical limit. Its price
fluctuated most widely with the supposed fortunes of the corporation. Even
after the exchanges were made, the initial issue of new stock left Durant
extra securities for marketing and dealing.

The second increase, to $500,000, better illuminated what was about to happen. Durant had $325,000 worth set aside for himself, held in trust. The remaining amount was for the former owners, which allowed for a fresh exchange and left a surplus for the treasury or other potential uses. Durant now once more set aside from his block $22,000 in stock for Begole, and $101,000 for Whiting in return for their management services in the plants he was contemplating. Of the remainder, he conferred a substantial amount on the Durant-Dort Company, in return for which they leased to him the factory of their subsidiary, the Imperial Wheel Company, in Jackson. It had stood empty since they moved wheel-making to Flint in 1901. They may, in addition, have paid for some of the stock in cash.

With an empty plant at his disposal, Durant planned to speed up production by contracting his body work to the W. F. Stewart Company, having the engines alone built in the three-story building that Whiting had put up to house his purchase of the year before, and assembling the finished cars in Jackson. Despite the extra shipping involved, the arrangement would offer immediate expansion of capacity. But there was a shrewder motive, which was nothing less than to hold over Flint businessmen's heads the threat of taking Buick away from them altogether. Loyalty was a virtue, Durant knew, but his hometown friends might need a prod to remind them that they were expected to make some initial sacrifices of their own if they expected long-run blessings from a healthy Buick enterprise. He did nothing to diminish the attractions of Jackson's own potential as a final home for Buick, and they were in fact impressive. They included several wheel, spring, and axle works, machine shops, repair depots for interurban electric-railway lines running to Detroit and Lansing, a location at the junction of three major railroads—even an existing auto factory, which produced an auto known as the Jackson (or Jaxon), whose sales slogan was: "No Sand Too Deep, No Hill Too Steep."

He played a slightly teasing game, possibly hinting that Jackson had capitalists who would be able to show their appreciation for an immigrant industry; going up to Bay City, another old sawmill center on Lake Huron, and passing the word that he would match a farsighted donation of $100,000 with a like amount of his own plus the Buick plant; playing the executive who is still open-minded on the matter of where to settle. Flint understood. On April 24, 1905, the directors of three of the town's banks agreed to subscribe for $100,000 in Buick stock, on the written understanding that the Buick corporation would "discontinue its Jackson plant and locate its entire business at Flint, commencing construction work upon its new buildings as soon as plans [could] be prepared and the weather . . . permit."[5]

Harmony reigned in Flint; for the banks it was a happy choice, even if one clouded by a slight compulsion. Not only was Jackson totally eliminated, but for the $100,000 worth of stock they paid $80,000, earning a commission of 20 percent, a profound easement to a sense of being used. Durant, fresh cash in hand, rushed back and forth between downtown Flint, other points, and the Hamilton farm, which he had bought at a thrifty price in 1898 to locate the Flint Axle Works, and which was to become Buick's production center, where he watched things progress.

The first two expansions of capitalization had required some assistance from Durant's friend and lawyer, John Carton. Carton was a steady figure of phlegmatic evenness, willing to take advantage of the winds of change but not uprooted by them. Though he was described as deadpan, there was actually a cast to his mouth and eyes in photographs that suggested a constant and rarely disappointed expectation of outlandish requests from his clients, most especially Durant. It was his conviction that Durant possessed a gift for high flights that could easily end in spectacular crackups, and that without the restraining hands of practical men like Dort, Nash, and Aldrich, "Billy . . . just soared high, wide and handsome" into air too thin.[6]

Nonetheless, Carton took charge of registering the first, $300,000 issue of new stock with the state's Bureau of Securities and Corporations. The law demanded that the shares represent genuine properties and not mere expectations. Carton had no trouble with $300,000 or even $500,000. The Jackson assembly facility alone was highly valuable, there were inventories and orders on hand, and the rules did not exclude such things as patents and good will, so that it was no great matter to pass inspection.

But when, in September of 1905, Durant proposed to organize anew, this time with $900,000 in common stock and $600,000 in preferred, Carton's ingenuity was taxed to the utmost. The corporation's holdings were growing nowhere nearly as quickly as its treasurer was valuing them for stock-emitting purposes. Carton managed to make the total come out right by resorting to such expedients as a $60,000 item labeled "the value of an engine improvement invented by Walter L. Marr, but on account of business reasons not patented." He was, however, aware that he slipped this by the Republican Secretary of State only on the strength of his own party credentials. He himself had served as Speaker of the Assembly only recently, and would soon do so again. As it was, the legislature at its next session banned the future use of such intangibles in applications for incorporation.[7]

There was now an abundance of stock to sell, and Durant had no trouble in finding takers. He claimed to have disposed of shares to the value of $500,000 the very day that the new issue was approved, and it was probably not an exaggeration, for he had institutional customers whose large orders made short work of the sales process. Foremost among them was Durant-Dort. He no longer played any role in its operations, and had asked to be removed from the salary roll of officers in 1901. The request was denied, one of the few things that the directors would deny him. The bonds of gratitude were strong, and if they were not enough, there was a practical motive for the company to buy as much as it did. Dort was quick to perceive that by investing profits in automobile stock, the carriage makers were building a new successful business within the shell of the old. It was a thought that was also entertained by the other leaders of the industry whose day was ending. The Flint Wagon Works owners, both corporately and in their own names, increased their Buick holdings, and even W. A. Paterson bought enough to become a Buick director. Durant did not let ghosts of injuries past stand in the way of selling stock to the old man. Durant-Dort was at the head of the list, however; by the end of 1905 it owned between one-quarter and one-third of all Buick common stock outstanding. The following spring it took another $100,000 worth from its persuasive founder. "Within reason," said Fred Aldrich, "our resources were always at his disposal."[8]

Besides the many shares in the possession of the Durant-Dort Company, and Flint Wagon Works' corporate 500, and the just-under 1,600 in the portfolios of Whiting and other Flint Wagon associates as individuals, there were some large institutional purchases. By coincidence, the very day that Durant took over Buick was also historic for the Flint Gas and Light Company, for which he had worked as a youth. It sold out, for $325,000, to a larger concern, and a part of that price soon found its way into the Buick treasury.

The banks were called on often, and Durant no longer had any hesitation about invoking the ties of blood, money, and old history that bound him to their officers. Willingly, he took the cash of the Citizens Commercial and Savings Bank, whose head, Robert J. Whaley, had lent him his first stake when he was a young man fearful of the mockery of his relatives and friends if he lost money for them. He had other links to Citizens Commercial, too. George L. Walker, a Flint Wagon Works founder, and John Carton were both directors. As for the Genesee Savings Bank, it was still practically a family institution with two uncles and two cousins in its directorship, and with a president, Arthur Bishop, who had become a firm friend. Bishop was one of Durant's most faithful well-wishers, once proudly showing a visitor a spindle on which a thick sheaf of papers was skewered. "Those are Billy Durant's notes," he said, "the ones that I thought it best not to put through the bank, so I let him have the money myself and just carry these along until it is easy for him to meet them. Billy always gets what he wants here."[9]

Durant had driven the roots of Buick deep into Flint. It was almost a family firm, if the elite of the town, with a total 1900 population of about

13,000, was considered as a form of extended clan, comprising thirty or forty families laced together by shared interests, ancestry, trust, and marriage. He ran down the list of directors for the prospectus of a new subsidiary he thought of launching in 1906, and his pen noted that seven of the nine, himself included, were Flint men. The other two were Buick and H. G. Field, president of an architectural and engineering firm in Detroit, though his address was given as Jackson. Durant offered their reputations as inducements to investors as if they were dainties on a platter. Whiting was "a man of some means and stands high in the community"; Paterson, "one of the largest manufacturers of vehicles in the country," had "considerable means," and so did W. F. Stewart, whose factory made 220,000 carriage bodies in a year. Nothing was said about George Walker's means, but he was described as "a man of considerable executive ability." Of William S. Ballenger, the treasurer of the Flint Wagon Works, Durant said directly that he was "not a man of large means but stands very high in the community," which was wholly accurate. Ballenger was then a recent Flint arrival, a thirty-nine-year-old native of Cambridge City, Indiana, who had gone to business college in New York State to learn bookkeeping, and been hired from there by Whiting. He was already known as a diligent, loyal, self-effacing team man.

Begole was listed with only one of his many credentials, the presidency of Flint's water and utilities companies. Durant described Buick, listed as living in Flint, as "a gas expert . . . very largely responsible for the creation of the marvelous motor which bears his name," and then threw in for support the notation that Buick was contracted to the company for a term of years, "as is also his associate, Mr. W. L. Marr, equally well known and talented."

And for himself the entry read simply: "Mr. W. C. Durant, Treasurer of the Durant-Dort Carriage Company of Flint, Michigan, builders of Vehicles; also Treasurer of the Imperial Wheel Company, Flint, Michigan, builders of carriage and automobile wheels."[10]

He used Flint's strength, its cohesiveness, as his own asset. In less than a year he had gotten a plant and plant managers for no cash outlay, and raised at least $100,000 in working funds without once stepping outside the local boundaries that he knew by heart.

It might have occurred to doubters that something was slightly amiss. Durant had been summoned because some men worried that Flint was tied too tightly to the fortunes of the then-staggering Buick company. He had made the knots tighter than ever. They were all roped together on the slope now; if he slipped, they would go flailing into the abyss together.

But he had no intention of slipping. He was climbing steadily toward the sun.

III At the plant they were creating magic for him to sell. Marr and Buick were working on new engines, along with fresh recruits, Enos De Waters and an expert hired from Cadillac by the pre-Durant management of Buick, Arthur Mason. Mason had a passion for his work that inflamed many of the early inventors, and that was not yet diffused through the sluice gates and budgetary channels of a large research organization. He knew nothing of clocks; none of them did. "We worked until we had the day's job done," said Buick, "and were ready for tomorrow, and then we went home—and not until then."[11] Mason struggled, as 1904 ended, to develop an engine that operated at 4,000 revolutions per minute instead of the then-customary 1,800. For weeks he was cutting, trying, prodding his creation toward life. Then Durant heard about it, and was warned by a friend in conversation that he had better have outside advice on such a new departure.

Durant brought in a consultant who poked at the engine like an examining surgeon as it lay on the bench. The prognosis was unfavorable; the concept violated unimpeachable engineering laws. "I would suggest," the visitor said, "to whomever buys one of these cars to purchase a bushel basket with it in order to be able to collect the pieces." The pleasantry was repeated and laughed at. Mason was not among those who appreciated it. He called Durant over to the bench sometime thereafter, urged him passionately not to reject the new idea, then suddenly bent down and seized the engine in a lover's embrace, his head resting on the greasy cylinder block. "Start it up," he pleaded. "If it goes, I may as well go with it."[12]

Durant was delighted with that spirit, allowed Mason free rein, and was rewarded when the engine did, in fact, perform beautifully, and gave him the keynote of a campaign.

Power, the achievement of Mason's long experience and hard work became the synonymous [sic] of Buick. We played on that one item: Power! Power to outclimb, power to outspeed anything on wheels in our class. With Buick we sold the assurance that the power to perform was there.[13]

For the Model C, a two-cylinder, 22-horsepower Buick, the slogan was: "We do with two cylinders what others try with four." Durant was happy devising such sentences. "Buick customers are our best salesmen" was another peppy 1905 invention, and sometime later Durant wrote and used an advertising claim whose last nine words were the company's public boast through generations of models: "We build nothing but high grade automobiles, and when better automobiles are made, Buick will build them."[14]

In 1906, Durant put $5,000 worth of stock in trust for Mason, who would be a lifelong associate. At the same time that Mason entered the ranks of Buick stockholders, the man for whom the company was named was drifting out of them. David Buick was never at home in the new order of things, and as unable as ever to cling to money. For months he left a legal bill of Carton's unpaid. The sum was only $92.58, but when Durant finally paid it for him, he sent a covering note to the lawyer explaining: "Mr. Buick wishes me to say that until a few moments ago this was more money than he had in the world. He disliked very much to make this admission and possibly this is the reason why you have not heard from him before."[15] In 1906, finally, the strange inventor who seemed unable to handle either success or failure resigned, was paid an undisclosed sum by Durant, and headed out from Flint on a wandering, impoverished course that led to an obscure death some fifteen years later.

Ironically, as he sank out of sight, his name was stamped on the consciousness of increasing numbers of Americans each year as Durant sold more and more cars, welcoming the tests of ingenuity that came with having virtually to invent a national sales organization. Some Buicks were displayed in Durant-Dort showrooms, a useful way of showing off the car to the rural trade and still another use of the carriage company's available resources. And Durant roved incessantly, seeking out dealers whose energies and powers matched his own, men like Harry Pence of Minneapolis, who would head westward into the wheatlands with a procession of Buicks behind him, showing them off, taking partial payment in produce, dropping sold cars off his train and sending their drivers home. Or like Harry Noyes, a New England dealer who operated in much the same way, stopping at hamlets in the Berkshires to gather a crowd, haranguing, selling the demonstrator to a live prospect then and there, and making his way back by "oxcart" and rail, contentedly counting receipts.[16]

Durant himself was their guide and model. Legends of his prowess grew like campfire stories, getting taller with each new telling. Once, the tale would begin, he had a layover of an hour or so in Detroit, waiting for a New York train. He went over to his dealer on Jefferson Avenue, and got a list of hard prospects. And wouldn't you know, in half an hour he was back, slapped a couple of order forms and deposits on the desk, and grabbed a cab for the depot? Laughter, head-wagging, tongue-clicking. A parable of the master, true at the core even if embroidered, and inspiring.[17]

Another link in the organization was forged by an unusual Massachusetts dealer, Harry Shiland. He was a skilled mechanic who, out of pride and a desire to keep customers contented, personally overhauled every machine he delivered. It was an absolute necessity. Nothing was yet standardized, breakdowns were frequent and expected, and one ventured forth on the road armed with tire patches, pumps and rim tools, spare parts, extra grease and oil, hammers, wrenches and pliers, twine and wire, and hoped for exemption from the inevitable.

Shiland was not impressed with early Buicks. He found too many poorly machined parts, loose connections, missing elements, and other "normal" deficiencies. He protested by letter, and Durant responded by asking him to drop in if he were ever visiting Jackson. A blunt, direct man of action, he took up the invitation, and launched a fresh stream of criticism so accurately targeted that Durant took him on an inspection tour of the plant and decided at its conclusion that Shiland was wasting valuable talents in New England. He urged Shiland to join the Buick staff as service director, and Shiland did so, building a parts and "complaint" department on the principle he had imparted to Durant: "You aren't selling cars to mechanics. Cars have to be foolproof for the average doctor or lawyer or business man to want them."[18]

In the summer of 1905, still only a few months into his new career as an auto executive, Durant learned that behind the sales and service networks must stand a production effort far more highly disciplined than in the carriage business. At the helm of Durant-Dort he had comprehended the need for guaranteeing supplies of parts. The Flint Axle Works, Flint Varnish Works, and Imperial Wheel Company were proof that he had mastered that lesson. But the automobile, with its many more intricately-arranged components, demanded even tighter and therefore more vulnerable scheduling. "Every piece of the motor car is essential," one maker wrote later, "in the sense that the automobile is not complete unless every part is available. Delay in delivery of any part stops the work."[19]

The bottleneck that first summer of Durant control was axles. He was buying them from the Weston-Mott Company in Utica, but suffered at the mercy of railroad freight dispatchers who did not share his conception of what a priority shipment meant. Some parts makers, like Alfred Sloan of Hyatt Roller Bearing, even kept on the payroll agents whose job was to ride the caboose and "cajole, bribe, or fight, as the occasion demanded," to keep the bearings moving. Durant tried ordering axles by express, but this device rocketed costs out of sight. He was desperately eager to lose no time. The option of building an axle plant, as he had done for wagons and carriages, was too slow. But there remained another. On June 5, 1905, he wrote a letter to Charles Stewart Mott.

Would you entertain a proposition of removing or establishing a branch factory at Flint, Michigan, provided the business of three or four large concerns was assured for a term of years? Flint is in the center of the automobile industry, a progressive city, good people, with conditions for manufacturing ideal.[20]

Mott was a man who liked a challenge, too, and had already faced several in a short business life. Weston-Mott was a family firm. Mott's father and uncle had bought it from in-laws in 1896 when "Charley" was twenty-one, a young man with a mechanical bent polished by a technical education at Stevens Institute in Hoboken, New Jersey. The company made bicycle wheels, and he willingly joined it.

In 1898 he came back from navy duty in the Spanish-American War — moustached, handsome, energetic, ready to climb the ladder — and found that the bicycle craze was over, the bottom out of things. But he, his father, and Uncle Fred scrambled. They relocated and renamed the company and dug for new markets. They made wheels for pushcarts, rickshas, invalids' chairs, and for some early horseless carriages, which rode on wire wheels like those that equipped bicycles, only stronger.

John Mott died; Uncle Fred retired. Prosperity came to Charles Mott's concern when Ransom Olds used him as a supplier for the curved-dash runabout in its first year. Then a second collapse. At the end of 1902 Olds announced that he would switch to artillery wheels. Mott, his chief customer untimely ripped from him, and left "with the responsibility of a factory and payroll and very little business or income" at twenty-seven, took to the road, knocking at automakers' doors. He found that they no longer wanted simply wheels, but that they also wanted the axles that joined them: heavy axles for the newer cars, capable of taking the strain of chain drives or incorporating differential gears to be coupled to a drive-shaft.

Mott had never made an axle. Nevertheless, he took orders for a quarter of a million dollars' worth, including five hundred for Cadillac. Then he rushed back to Utica and marathon days of studying, hunching over drafting tables, rushing up and down factory aisles, thumbing machinery catalogues, figuring specifications. In a time astonishingly compressed by urgency, he made Weston-Mott an axle producer. In the process he struck up a friendship with Alfred Sloan, almost exactly his own age, an alumnus of the Massachusetts Institute of Technology. Sloan's roller bearings would go into Mott's axles. The two men came to trust and respect each other. What Sloan said about himself and his business partner, Peter Steenstrup, might have applied equally well to his relationship with Mott. "Neither one of us ever took any pride in hunches. We left all the glory of that kind of thinking to such men as like to be labeled 'genius.'"[21]

Mott was ripe for bold moves, and Durant's invitation was bound to appeal, with its offer of proximity to the "center of the automobile industry." During the summer Durant worked on Mott through various exchanges and mutual visits. Seriousness set in when wives were brought along, however. On the Friday before Labor Day, Durant and Dort traveled to Utica, and when they returned Mr. and Mrs. Mott were with them and a trained nurse was behind, taking care of the Mott children.

Ambassadorial rituals followed. Bishop, Whiting, Ballenger, Carton, and Clarence Hayes (of Imperial Wheel) met them at trainside. There was dinner at the Bishops', followed by other dinners, rides about Flint. The Motts were shown pretty homes on tree-lined lanes, and Saginaw's lively avenue of commerce still decked with souvenirs of the fiftieth-anniversary-of-incorporation celebration that had taken place in June. The Vice-President of the United States himself had been there to speak.

Mott was taken out to see the work at the Hamilton farm. Shovels tore at the earth, cranes whirled and bowed, wagons shuttled under burdens of iron between sidings and unfinished structures, whistles shrieked and hooted warnings. Bare ground and construction shanties were giving way to the Buick factory, and there would be room for more to come, for workers' housing, for water and power lines, for the necessary streetcar tracks. Mott looked and listened as Durant and the others promised to subscribe for $100,000 of stock in a new, half-million-dollar corporation, Weston-Mott of Michigan, donate the site for its factory, and award it all of Buick's axle business.

When Mott stepped aboard the train Monday afternoon, the contract was signed. The plant was completed and began operations, with the machinery moved from Utica, on February 1, 1907. Mott became, in time, a leading citizen of Flint, a human acquisition of even more value than the assets which he imported. Sloan called it "the first step in the integration of the automobile industry. Thereafter, bit by bit, we were to see a constant evolution bringing the manufacture of the motor car itself and the manufacture of its component parts into a closer corporate relationship. All were to cohere as if drawn together by some magnetic force."[22]

The full pulling power of Flint's magnetic force, William Durant, was not felt until the beginning of his second year of active Buick leadership, the winter of 1906–1907. At that time the Jackson operations were brought to their new home on the site of the vanished farm, next to Weston-Mott's plant, so that Buicks were now Flint-made from beginning to end. The consolidation added two more strongly effective production men to the team: Harry Bassett, who came with Mott and whose joviality did not detract in any way from his insistence on copious, high-quality output; and William Little, a onetime maker of buckboards in Massachusetts, whose efficiency at Jackson had marked him out for an important future.

Working intensively, the men and the capital gathered within the Buick fold began to run up the production totals. In 1906 1,400 cars had come off the line, and in 1907 the output was 4,641, which alone was nearly half the entire number registered in the United States two years earlier. They were vehicles of steadily improving quality and performance, bringing new credit to the engineers every time they took the road in one of the racing and touring competitions that were still necessary to demonstrate the automobile's potentialities to the unconvinced. The 1906 Model F, a two-cylinder touring car that sold for about $1,200, won wide acceptance when one example of it ran from New York to San Francisco in 24 days, 8 hours, and 45 minutes. A Model G, lighter-bodied in runabout style, but with the same 22-horsepower engine, swept to the finish ahead of a Cadillac, a Ford, two Maxwells, and other now-forgotten makes in a well-publicized race in Illinois. Glowing with accomplishment, Durant discovered that no matter how swiftly the supply of new Buicks multiplied, demand continued to outpace it. An investors' prospectus crowed exuberantly as it outlined progress on new additions to the factories which would "very nearly double the capacity of the present plant."

Notwithstanding the buildings, additions and improvements above referred to, the demand for our product is so great that we are totally unable to handle the business offered us, and we find it desirable, for many reasons, to still further increase our output.
The enormous business which has been built up by this Company (established less than eighteen months ago) is due to the fact that we are manufacturing a machine of rare merit at a very reasonable price. . . .
You fully appreciate our position in the trade and the rapid strides which this Company has made during the past year, but it is possible that you are not aware that we have today in excess of *one hundred direct agents*, including many of the largest and strongest dealers in the country, *seven of whom* are in position to take the entire product of this factory which is now producing from fifteen to seventeen finished automobiles per day.[23]

Durant's excitement reflected the feelings of other successful auto makers as the young industry began to thrum with a sudden acceleration. The first, halting decade of experimentation was over. Cars were larger, stronger, more standard in design, and more desirable. Within a very short time there would emerge a near-frenzy of anticipation of large markets, rarely checked by slumps and then only briefly, and catching up everyone contributing to the finished auto in its grip. Sloan perceived that the watchword was *tempo*.

Speed! Do what you have been doing, but do it faster. Double your capacity. Quadruple it. Double it again. At times it seemed like mad-

ness. Yet people clamored for the cars. There were never enough automobiles to meet the demand. The pressure on production men was
desperate.[24]

IV Amid this hurly-burly, Durant flourished as if he and the moment
were made for each other. Friends and family noticed, or at least
for the first time began to record, a behavior profile in which
outward calm and conformity were thinly stretched over kinetic impulses
to unpredictable action. He was always neatly dressed and barbered, "a
very clean man, an immaculate man," Margery said. His face was pink and
smooth, his eyes dark and shining, and constantly darting from face to face,
lighting first on one object and then another. But he did not give the
impression of inattention. Instead he kept his head tilted slightly toward
anyone who was speaking, and in a group he gave others priority in
expressing their views, even prodding them on with questions. When he
himself spoke it was often as the last, and in a voice so modulated that a
reporter said of him: "If he had to turn in a fire alarm, chances are he would
whisper it."[25] Yet he dominated the conversation simply by the intensity of
what he said, by some enormous power of projecting what was in his mind
into his listeners' consciousness to the exclusion of all else. Despite his
short stature and light weight — less than 120 pounds at this time — he was
the largest figure in the room.

The all-embracing interest of existence was business. He swept hurried-
ly through meals, eating what was set before him with neither praise nor
complaint, and taking little notice of his children when they were small
unless they distracted him with an excess of high spirits. Clifford was prone
to do that, his sister recalled, and Clara sometimes bought peace with a
payment of five cents for every well-behaved mealtime. After meals, or
sometimes during them, a procession of men swept into the house, and far
into the night they would sit with Durant, "emitting an unending stream of
facts, figures, suggestions, protests," filling the air with smoke, the parlor
with their boisterousness.[26]

Even a housewife of strong nerves and total dedication to her husband's career would have struggled to cope with this invasion of her
domain's curtained and upholstered tidiness, and for Clara Durant,
during the earliest years, it must have been an additional burden. After
the spring of 1906, however, it no longer mattered. Margery married,
and thereafter Durant lived with her and his new son-in-law while
in Flint.

The wedding was a Flint social highlight. Margery came almost directly from her last formal schooling, a brief period in a "seminary" in Washington, to the bridal bower. Her groom, Dr. Edwin Campbell (he for whom Judge Wisner had constructed his X-ray machine), was far closer in age to Durant than to Margery's eighteen, but he was an undoubted catch. His patients were drawn from the town's best families, and it was a local understanding that to be considered well-born one must have been delivered by him. So much cachet went with the match that it overwhelmed any question of why a girl so young would choose a contemporary of her father rather than a more youthful suitor. The ceremony took place in St. Paul's Episcopal Church on the evening of April 18, 1906. As Durant led his daughter up the aisle with short, hurried steps, she whispered a rarely heeded piece of counsel to him: "Don't go so fast, dear."[27]

After the honeymoon trip, the couple settled into their new home, in which a bedroom on the first floor was set aside for the use of Durant. The bonds linking him to both wife and husband were unusually strong. Margery had always given "Pops" undemanding adoration. Granted that much acceptance of his fundamental self-absorption, he was able to respond with generosity and a universally noticed attractiveness. The doctor continued his appointed rounds of dosing and splinting and easing humans into and out of the world for a time, but to an increasing degree took to helping his father-in-law with business affairs. Margery helped to clear the way for this by keeping Campbell's own books and mailing out the bills, so that they were both willingly in Durant's gravitational field. At the end of some two and one half years, about the time of the birth of their first child, Campbell gave up his practice entirely to devote himself to financial matters.

Durant's room was a simple one, equipped with a plain brass bed, a chiffonier for his clothing, and a table with two or three straight-backed chairs. It was kept clean by Margery herself with the help of a single maid—at least so Margery said. Her status was apparently not compromised by this simple establishment any more than by her secretarial work for her husband. Wealth was worn quietly in Flint, and thrift marked as a virtue in any young bride. In any case, her father's quarters required little attention, since he was so rarely in them. He was constantly in transit between Flint and Jackson, Detroit and Utica, and the many cities, major and minor, where his showrooms and suppliers demanded his shepherding. He always kept a suitcase in his room packed with clean linen, a couple of suits, and a conservative tie or two; the suits were ordered sent up on approval, and hung on the rack until he had time to look them over and make his selections.

Before he took to a chauffeured car, he relied on a public hack driver named Harry Jewel to get him to the depot on time. He would inform Jewel of his scheduled departure, usually on short notice because he hated to make travel arrangements long in advance. He found that when he did that, he was handcuffed by scheduling; either he had to cut short some piece of work or was left with time on his hands if he finished too early. But when Jewel knew the right hour, he would station himself outside office or home, and just as he heard the whistle bay at a familiar crossing, he would knock, fling open the door and shout: "Come along, Mr. Durant! You've got to leave! Train time!" And Durant, while Jewel seized his bag, would hustle into a topcoat if the season demanded one, clap on his head the plain black derby that he wore in those years, and be whirled away and deposited in his coach, still meditating on some problem, just as the cry of "All aboard!" echoed under the shed.[28]

Where others would have been pained by the broken life-rhythms that travel imposed, Durant felt none. He slept for only a few hours a night, and sometimes not at all. On more than one occasion he had himself driven to evening meetings, left instructions to wait, and appeared the next morning in wordless unawareness of anything unusual. When he did sleep he testified that he did it soundly. Anxiety never seemed to be visible in him, perhaps because he dwelt in regions beyond its reach. "To him," said a contemporary, "the immediate future was remote; the remote future near and vivid," and it was the dread of tomorrow morning's crisis that made most men toss and perspire.[29]

It was while going at this breakneck pace that he encountered his first real obstacle in his period of captaincy of Buick, and powered his way through it. Early in 1907 there was a sharp break in the stock market. It was followed by a period of loan reductions and call-ins by banks, and a general business contraction that tightened and squeezed the country until, in autumn, it was in the grip of recognizable panic. Credit evaporated, and weak firms staggered toward collapse. Buick was especially vulnerable to any difficulties in the money markets. Its growth required an unfaltering cash flow to meet payroll and other expenses that could not be handled with promissory notes and stock. And cash was an unobtainable item. Mott, whose customers were paying him with I.O.U. certificates, which he endorsed and passed on to his own creditors, was reduced to asking Carton to wait for an annual legal fee of a mere $250 until the pinch relaxed.

Prudence dictated cutbacks in operations, and the conservation of funds through layoffs and reductions in orders to restock inventory. But Durant chose not to live off fat. He operated on the instincts of a flier at the point of a stall; safety lay in a plunge to gain more speed. Somehow managing to keep collectors at bay, he kept his factories working at full blast. When demand slackened and finished Buicks clogged the factory yards, he stored them in barns and empty warehouses, confident that the country's seizure was temporary, and not the first sign of an oncoming major depression. His judgment was entirely correct. When the clouds blew away at the year's end, Buick dealers had cars to offer while customers of other makers were asked to wait for months of working off backlogged orders. The natural result was a fresh surge of Buick sales, and the power at last to pay up and pay off. "He was one hell of a gambler," Mott mused when it was all long-past history. "To this day, I don't know how he was able to handle it financially, but he did it."[30]

The climb was resumed. Durant wanted to enter 1908 with a light and inexpensive, but fast, car, and he found time to goad on his production men, poking into every detail of the composition of their creations, undiscouraged by his lack of technical knowledge or by occasional misadventures. One day he came into the plant and demanded almost overnight improvement in the brakes of one of the Buick models. There had been complaints. William Little and assistants worked feverishly, rigged a test car with the results of their efforts, and invited Durant for a demonstration ride with Little at the wheel.

Willingly, Durant climbed into the back seat to play the role of demanding consumer. Little gunned the engine, then slammed down his foot. Behind him, William Durant rose, arms outthrust vainly against the unresisting air, like some strange flying fish. He plunged downward to smack wetly against the leather of the front seat, slid through the doorless opening on the passenger side, and landed splayed out on the dirt of the factory yard. Horrified, Little leaped down from the height of the driver's seat and rushed around to the fallen form of his employer. Durant was already brushing himself off. He gave Little a long look before speaking.

"You certainly got some brakes, Bill," he said.

Exhaling what must have been the largest sigh of relief of his life, Little helped finish the cleaning up, then bade Durant to get back in for the return trip.

"No thanks," was the response. "I'll walk."[31]

The goal of the engineers' striving turned out to be a Buick that had a relatively brief life span but became a classic. Its official name was Model 10. It was a four-cylinder runabout of 18 horsepower and 166 cubic inches in engine volume, with a simple, two-speed planetary transmission operated by foot pedals. The technical data had little meaning for the public, which, then and later, wanted simply the assurance of that speed which was already its automotive drug. The Model 10 had it. It was advertised as a car for "men with real red blood who don't like to eat dust." An even more effective sales device arose from the fact that the Model 10 emerged from the factory painted in a bone-colored shade that allowed it to be nicknamed the White Streak. Behind the driver and passenger was a flat rear deck on which a third seat was mounted, sometimes referred to as "mother-in-law's." Even so adorned, however, the Model 10 looked unencumbered and eager for adventure, a companion of the road. Though it stood high off the ground, as all cars were obliged to do to clear obstacles in country trails and allow room for the crank to turn, its rakish fenders and convex cowl softened any boxy appearance. It was easier to drive and maintain than comparable cars, and most important, it could be marketed for a thousand dollars or slightly less.[32]

The price consideration was weighty. Durant read a trend in sales reports. The hard year of 1907 was being succeeded by an upward surge of auto buying that was more than merely temporary. Roughly 62,000 cars would be made in 1908, twice that number in 1909, and three times as many in 1910. And they were no longer bought merely by the fortune-favored. Sales of cars priced under $1,375 began to grow from about one-third of the market in 1907 toward a high of 90 percent in 1916, which would be a record-setting production year. A car for the average-income buyer would reap millions in profits that were out there waiting for the sickle.

Model 10 was Buick's entering wedge into that beckoning low-priced field. Henry Ford had identical premonitions of the future in 1908, and began to develop the Model T. It became a more utilitarian car than the Model 10, and Ford took the extra step of making it his factory's only model, freezing the design and thereby opening the way for continued, relentless cost- and price-cutting. It was a gamble that paid off for Ford almost beyond the limits of fantasy in the long run.

Durant had no desire, risk-taker though he was, to follow that path of concentration on a single card. His instinct was, in fact, quite the reverse—to invest heavily in diversification. From 1908 to 1910 Buick not only made the Model 10, but it continued an earlier luxury offering, the Model D, a 5-passenger, 25-horsepower vehicle that sold for $2,500 at its 1907 introduction. It also offered two additional models that were costlier than the White Streak. But all together, they justified the most buoyant hopes. Durant's corporation produced 8,487 cars in 1908, to lead the industry. Ford was second with 6,181 and Cadillac third with 2,380. The following year was even better, for Buick sales were 14,606 out of a total national production of about 130,000, and in 1910 the comparable figures were 30,525 and 187,000. Almost every sixth new car bought that year was a Flint-made Buick.[33]

V Flint was in another economic renaissance, its third since sawmill days. Curiously conservative in one way, it was slow to adopt the machine on which its new wealth was footed. By 1910 it had a mere two hundred autos licensed, and it was only in that year that the police department bought a motorized paddy wagon, the firemen a pump truck, and rural mail carriers horseless delivery vehicles. Only then, too, did Saginaw Street begin to be prepared for the new era, when two nine-foot-wide lengths of macadam paving were laid along its busiest stretch.

But there was nothing slow about the pace of factory construction. On the 220 acres of the Hamilton Avenue complex, six separate buildings went up one after another, not counting a drop forge and foundry and the Weston-Mott plant. In 1908 one of those new buildings, Buick Plant Number Two, temporarily worked around the clock to keep up with orders, while the others operated until midnight. The city's work force, a good share of which was employed in those factories (and in the still-active horsedrawn vehicle plants), was judged to be near 15,000 in 1910. The total Flint population was 38,550, a threefold jump in the preceding ten years, and it would reach 45,000 by 1914.

On Saturday nights an approximate $125,000 in pay was dispensed, and a tide of liberated workers swirled noisily into downtown streets, each man clutching an average of fifteen to eighteen dollars for the six nine-hour days he had put in. Banks stayed open late to cash checks and break bills, and under the lights the successors to the lumberjacks strolled, shopped, ate, drank in one of the many saloons — one for every thousand residents — roistered and brawled, with little incentive to go home. Housing was critically short, and hundreds of families were quartered in tents and tarpaper shacks. Foremen, eager to keep desirable employees, begged for speedier residential construction and moved among their workmen, moderating squabbles in several immigrant tongues, bailing out those who had got in too deep at the moneylenders', engineering reunions and relocations and school enrollments and hospitalizations on occasion. It was a last effort to cling to the old paternalism, protect it against dissolution in a new, more frenetic order of things that saw men eddying in faceless swarms through the gates in the morning, brought by streetcar from distant points to spend many hours as anonymous pairs of arms turning thousands of tons of wood and metal and fabric into hundreds of cars every week.[34]

Yet for all the change that the automobile was imposing on it, Flint was still not Detroit. It kept a savor of intimacy among its top families and especially among the leaders of Buick. They were still a small group, whose pranks and idiosyncrasies resounded through a closed arena. The members of the Buick racing team—Lewis Strang, Bob Burman, the Chevrolet brothers, Louis and Arthur—were universally recognized and admired, and no one complained when they practiced by roaring up and down the streets in their souped-up machines during traffic-free holiday morning hours. The arrival of the factory executive group in the dining room of the Dresden Hotel was the starting signal for boisterous joshing, especially between Harry Bassett and William Little, both hearty and outgoing men. Little loved to arrive downtown in his car, commanding attention by his parking technique, which consisted of skidding to the curb in a U-turn. When Bassett once ordered a Model 10, Little made the delivery unforgettable. Precisely as every factory whistle in the complex screamed that it was lunchtime, Bassett emerged from the Weston-Mott office door to see his car being driven up, "gaily decorated," the mother-in-law seat removed from the deck and replaced with a barrel of beer.

Even in off-hours, if there were in fact any off-hours for them, the clubby atmosphere of the shop prevailed. Bassett and the factory manager, shipping superintendent, and treasurer of Weston-Mott lived in the same group of apartments; Little was only next door. When one member of the group, on a rare holiday, caught a fine fish or bagged a pair of birds, all sat down as one to enjoy the feast. Doors were unlocked and almost unnoticed. On one occasion Mott arrived the evening before a payday carrying two valises that contained $60,000 in cash and calmly left them in one of the apartments overnight.[35]

Durant was not in the center of these bouts of conviviality. He was too much his own man, too frequently away, too distant in several senses. It was not entirely a matter of informal corporate ranking, for old friends of the carriage-making days called on him with comfortable familiarity, and treated him with something far short of deference. On an evening in 1906 Dort and Nash came to the Garland Street house for dinner and the talk of business that none of them could or wished to escape, and the subject turned to the future of the motor car. Durant sat for a time fingering the keyboard of what later memories recalled either as an organ or a player piano, and fell into a verbal rhapsody of future growth. The day would come when one company alone might sell ten, twenty, fifty—yes, a hundred thousand and more automobiles a year. When he had concluded, the other two looked at each other.

"Dallas," said Charles Nash, "Billy's crazy."[36]

But they were especially close and longstanding associates. Few recent arrivals to Flint could speak to him in that way. And they knew, too, that if he was "crazy" it was the mark of wizardry, not moonsickness, that sat on him. Even more than in the wagon era, when two other firms had shared the credit for prosperity, Durant was deservedly the city's hero. He had taken

Buick to the heights in four short years. Its early capitalization had been based on patents and good will and whatever hardware had been accumulated by the small amount of cash paid in from the cautious purses of the first investors. At the end of 1908 its net worth was $3,417,142, with all intangibles written off the books, and almost all the growth attributable to reinvested earnings. Durant had reason to trust his own credentials as a miracle worker, to run toward the future with eagerness to clasp it. If there had been youthful uncertainties, questions about his rank in the hierarchy of Crapos, or unvoiced fears of a tainted inheritance, they were behind him now with the expiring lights of the wagon and buggy business. In a mood of farewell and renewal, he took at last the decisive symbolic steps of divorce and remarriage.

Officially it was Clara who divorced him. In the legal formulation mandated by custom, her petition filed in the Circuit Court for the County of Genesee in Chancery on the twenty-sixth of March, 1908, begged relief from her union to a husband who had "been guilty of the usual [sic] wanton and extreme cruelty" toward her. But the statutes of Michigan permitted a marriage to be ended only by reason of one party's insanity, desertion, or, precisely as worded in the complaint, "extreme cruelty," and the marks of collusion were evident everywhere in the proceedings as the prescribed drama was played out. Clara, the "oratrix," prayed for the bill of divorce. Durant made no response, thereby "confessing" to misconduct, and allowing a commissioner of the court to take "proofs" for presentation. These turned out to be the affidavits of three witnesses — De Witt Blue, the Durants' sixty-three-year-old handyman, Anna Callahan, their maid, and Dr. Campbell, their son-in-law, who had helped to negotiate the proceedings and the settlement which followed them. All three of the statements were virtually identical in language.

Together they fleshed out the story that must have been suspected in the small town for a long while. Durant's lengthy absences would have been noticed, and the testimony simply added that during them he had "refused and neglected to answer her letters or give her any attention whatever," and that even when at home he had continued his indifference, "frequently paying her no more attention than a stranger." Clara submitted, whether truthfully or in fulfillment of legal requirements, that she had

tried to induce said defendant to change his conduct and to treat her as a husband should; yet he [had] coldly and with a cruel indifference repulsed any and all advances made by your oratrix and [had] used profane language to her, and informed her that he would do and act as he pleased.

That Durant would "do and act as he pleased" would have surprised no one who had long dealt with him. The image of him as icy, however, was in sharp conflict with the public "Billy" Durant, whose persuasive tongue successfully wooed the consent of bank presidents and mechanics alike. Yet there was a capacity for anger both hot and chilly. One associate, at least, stated that "it was not difficult for him to give an impression of coldness if he felt that way,"[37] and behind the veil drawn over his home life with Clara he felt that way for extended periods of time.

Notwithstanding the widening rift, Clara swore, they had "cohabited together" until September of 1906, after which time they occupied different rooms in the house. Reduced to a "nervous wreck," Clara had spent part of the following winter at a rest home in Pinehurst, North Carolina, accompanied by a nurse under Dr. Campbell's orders. There had been no word of concern from her husband. On at least one other undated occasion Campbell had recommended her hospitalization, in Philadelphia, for six weeks. So the sad dance of mutual infliction of pain had gone on, Clara trying to hold Durant to Flint-scale husbandliness, and he building higher and higher the walls of a private fastness from which she was forever barred.

Making whatever private allowances for exaggeration he chose, Circuit Judge William Gage was satisfied with the offered demonstrations. He granted the decree of divorce on May 27. Judge Wisner would ordinarily have been sitting at that time, but was away on a fishing vacation, possibly a tactful intentional absence. Gage ordered that the record be "suppressed," meaning that it did not reach the newspapers. Flint would find out gradually, and as gracefully as the parties concerned could manage it. Clara received $150,000 in cash and "approved securities," and turned back to her former husband some Durant-Dort stock that he had registered in her name.[38]

On the next day, in New York City, far from the eyes of Flint journalism, Durant married Catherine Lederer, of Jackson. She was nineteen years of age.

Nothing was ever said to anyone's public recall, nor any scrap of paper preserved, to indicate that Catherine was the precipitating factor in the final breach with Clara, or that her relations with Durant were anything but proper—or at least as proper as the circumstances of the courtship allowed. That issue had been raised at the very outset by her mother, when Durant appeared to ask if he might "call on" her high-school-aged daughter. The answer was naturally negative. Mr. Durant was still married. "Of course," Catherine smiled at an interviewer late in her life, "that made no difference."[39]

They met during one of Durant's extended business visits to Jackson.

Cliff and Margery sometimes visited him there in his quarters at the Hotel Otsego, and Margery met Catherine through a circle of young friends, and that led to an introduction. Some time afterward, Durant gave Catherine two tickets to the theater, one for herself, and one for a friend. At the end of the performance, he picked up the two girls and drove them home—Catherine last, giving him some private moments with her. It was then that he made his formal request to become a suitor. Catherine's willingness to ignore her mother's disapproval was not surprising, since Margery would almost surely have told her that Durant's marriage was in fact moribund, and Mrs. Lederer herself may have changed her mind when the facts were explained to her. She developed, in time, a warm relationship with Durant, once she accustomed herself to the idea of a son-in-law of her own age. Durant himself had just such a son-in-law, and after that May of 1908 he and Margery each had, in their spouses, a counterpart of the other.

That the marriage was exciting for Catherine was beyond doubting. Durant was at the peak of his powers and energies, still attractive, still youthful-looking, eager to love in his fashion. Catherine was, in her turn, a perfect match for his needs. She was beautiful, innocent, uncritical, and shy, the perfect princess to install in the castles he was building in his mind. There she could be adored and bedecked with gifts and left to herself for long periods while he sallied out on his quests. She asked no more of life or of her mature gallant. Her great strength was loyalty, and in a far future time it would be tested and found good.

Among the insiders who know of the impending change was Rebecca. She was told as soon as the divorce petition was filed, and had to contend with the realization that her "boy," even as she, had shipwrecked in marriage. She treated it as a misfortune for which she would not assign responsibility, one more of God's mysterious burdens to prove the soundness of heart of the faithful. Either excess of emotion or her seventy-five years made her pen skip words and phrases as she poured out consolation.

I understand in a certain way what it means to you, this hard work and struggle both in body and mind—it is wonderful [that under ?] the strain [you have ?] not given away. Do not let me add in any way one more burden or give you an anxious thought. I want to be brave for you, a help in every way. My heart aches with sorrow for you. I would have made any sacrifice to have spared you from this disappointment—a broken home. We will meet it as best we can—not [let it ?] blind us to many good things that are about us and which we may enjoy if we will. It's hard to see what good can come from so much trouble, but one sure thing—we have to meet it and accept it with good grace—do the best we can, keeping a courage that will take us to the end. So, my dear boy, keep up a good heart. It might have been something worse. Take good care of your health. When one is good and strong they can endure trouble and hard work better. . . . Good bye — we shall be glad to see you back again. It is so different when you are here.

With a great deal of love,
Mother [40]

So it was over, finally, in that 1908 springtime, and there would be a home again, but not for any length of time in Flint. Flint, where he was known by many under the most simple and respectful of titles, simply "the Man," was at his feet, but he would not stay to take up what it offered. That was not enough. To rest in safety and enjoy yesterday's gains would never be enough. His mind was already brimming with new plans that had been in motion for several months — plans that went back to an afternoon when the telephone had rung and the voice of Ben Briscoe, speaking from Chicago, had crackled through.

"Hello, Billy," said the voice. "I have a most important matter to discuss with you."

"What's the big idea, Ben?"

"Don't ask me to explain. There's millions in it. Can you come?"[41]

5)

General Motors:

Creation and Crisis

I On the date that Briscoe's call arrived, Durant was not free to drop what he was doing and leave. He proposed instead that Briscoe take an overnight train and meet him in Flint for breakfast. Since it was he who had an idea to sell, Briscoe agreed. Early on the following morning, the two men sat facing each other over a tablecloth at the Dresden Hotel. There, amid the stir of a fresh day getting under way, Briscoe dropped into the furrows of Durant's imagination the seed he was carrying with him, the idea of a great combination in the motor industry.

It could easily have occurred to Benjamin Briscoe as he sat there that, given a slightly different fall of the cards, he might have been occupying Durant's seat as the head of Buick. If he had been able to handle the erratic inventor better, or to find significant backing in 1903, another outcome to the story would have been conceivable. For, ironically, in the five years since selling the firm, he had forged excellent links to the national banking community. His problem was that these connections never produced for him on the grand scale of his expectations. He lacked the touch, or simply the luck, that allowed Durant to spin straw into gold.

Still, Briscoe had grounds for a generous measure of self-esteem. What he possessed in life he had justly earned. Born in Detroit in 1868, he had entered the sheet metal business at the age of twenty with only $452, an inheritance, in initial capital. He and his younger brother and later partner, Frank, were an unusual pair among the city's businessmen, who seemed, in many cases, to be human counterparts of the machines by which they lived. By contrast, Frank Briscoe was musically talented, spent long periods of residence in France, and regarded business as simply a livelihood, or at best merely one of a number of absorbing interests. Ben, though more deeply engrossed in his work, was something of a sport and high roller, a man for whom life was not measured in microscopic tolerances nor enclosed by balance sheets.

Ben's failure to achieve anything with Buick had not blunted his desire to enter the automotive field as a maker in addition to being a supplier. He found another engineer, Jonathan D. Maxwell, whose experience appeared impressive. He had worked on three early cars, the Haynes-Apperson, the Oldsmobile, and a Detroit creation called the Northern. Briscoe bestowed $3,000 on him to produce a prototype, and he set to work in the machine shop of John Lauer, which had also been the hatchery of Charles King's path-breaking auto. By the end of 1903, it was ready.

To Briscoe's disappointment, the Detroit investment community looked upon his handiwork and found it resistible. The time was out of joint for him, since the city's auto venture capital had been heavily absorbed in the preceding two years by the producers of the Oldsmobile, the Cadillac, the Ford, the Northern, and two other short-lived makes called the Reliance and the Queen. He was forced, as he saw it, to go hunting in the unfriendly surroundings of Wall Street, but once there he bagged a spectacular quarry. J. P. Morgan and Company helped him to raise $250,000 through the sale of bonds. Either as a condition of the arrangement or as a prudent afterthought, he decided to locate his operation within virtual eyeshot of "the Street." The plant of the newly formed Maxwell-Briscoe Company went up on a flat stretch of ground between the New York Central tracks and the Hudson River at Tarrytown, a suburban village forty minutes north of the heart of Manhattan. There, amid hills that Washington Irving's stories had peopled with bucolic Dutchmen and ghostly elves, the first Maxwell-Briscoe production cars were completed in 1905. By a year later they had caught on, and were soon selling very respectably.[1]

In spite of that, Briscoe's mind was not at ease as the 1908 season got under way. He saw the industry as a theater of combat where wariness was a necessity for survival. He had refused to join the A.L.A.M. and had linked himself instead with a loose rival organization of independents, the American Motor Car Manufacturers' Association. Through that group he was receiving unsettling information about the condition of things.

In 1902, there had been only twelve significant producers of autos. In the ensuing five years, thirty-seven new manufacturers — counting only those who actually got into the marketplace for any length of time — had joined the game, while five had gone under. The forty-four survivors of 1907 may not have realized just how precarious a calling they had chosen. Nineteen years later the number of makers would still be forty-four (not all the same ones), but in the meantime over 125 companies would have come and gone, half of them enduring for fewer than six years, and the median life span for all being only seven. Yet even without prophetic foresight, 1907's auto executives could see a difficult pattern in nearly four dozen of them competing for a still undefined and tiny market: 43,300 cars in all being sold that year. Nor were they contending for equal shares. Already the top 25 percent of all producers accounted for three-quarters of the total output. Below them the others struggled for a remnant that could not possibly support them all. What kept marginal producers alive temporarily was a curious credit pattern by which all the makers profited but which was indispensable to the weak. Auto buyers, whether dealers or individuals, paid in cash — usually 20 percent as a deposit with the order, and the remainder when the merchandise arrived. Each auto came with a sight draft — in effect a check drawn on the buyer's account — for the balance of the price attached to the bill of lading. It had to be signed before delivery was completed. On the other hand, the makers of automobile components were willing to extend credit to the assemblers (which car makers basically were), who could therefore ship out and collect on cars for whose materials they still owed. Roy Chapin, a manufacturer, explained it in recollection: "Dealers' deposits often paid half the sum necessary to bring out a full year's production, and if the assembling were efficiently directed, drafts against the finished cars could be cashed as rapidly as bills from the parts-makers came in."[2] It was a system that worked well provided there were plenty of orders and deliveries to keep cash flowing to the parts makers, who, as a practical matter, were financing production. But it allowed little room for even the most temporary hard times.

In theory, successful makers should have welcomed a pruning of the field by an occasional slump. But the reality of economic life was that the strong were vulnerable to the shock waves set up by the collapse of the weak. The industry was still experimental enough so that the crash of a few firms shook buyers'—and, more importantly, bankers'—confidence, and shrank the supply of customers and credit. In addition, no company or group of companies was yet secure enough to set standards of quality and price that could resist desperate competitive tactics by an organization in its death-throes taking a last, despairing chance. Or by a newcomer promising miracles of inexpensive quality that he could not deliver. Briscoe summed it up in this way: "Not a few of the concerns of the day were run by what might have been called 'manufacturing gamblers.' In many cases the management had adopted methods that were described as 'plunging.' In fact we all plunged, and conditions came about which were thought by some of us to predicate disaster."

For these perils, as well as those posed by what he called "skimmers," or concerns that stung stock buyers with a trashy car but an eloquent prospectus, Briscoe thought he saw an answer written in the financial history of the preceding years.

In this year of 1908 many of us thought that the industry was beset with difficulties and so came the desire to some of us to form a combination of the principal concerns in the industry, not with the desire to sell all of the automobiles that were to be sold, but rather for the purpose of having one big concern of such dominating influence in the automobile industry, as, for instance, the United States Steel Corporation exercises in the steel industry, so that its very influence would prevent many of the abuses that we believed existed.[3]

That Briscoe should have chosen United States Steel as his model for a stabilizing auto trust was not accidental. It was the ultimate in mergers, the first corporation with an authorized capital of over a billion dollars, controlling 10 companies, which owned 149 steel plants, 84 blast furnaces, 112 Great Lakes vessels, 1,000 miles of railroad, and thousands of acres of coal, ore, and limestone lands. Most importantly, it was under the controlling guidance of the country's money master, the one man who could have arranged the extraordinary financing involved, J. Pierpont Morgan, to whom Briscoe had access.

That was Briscoe's message with "millions in it." He believed that he could arouse Morgan interest in underwriting a consolidation of major auto makers, and the first step was to get the potential members together with a proposal to take to the bank.

The proposition immediately kindled Durant's interest. Whether or not he fully shared Briscoe's concern for stability, he had a distinct interest in uniting companies whose cars appealed to several markets, just as he had done in his Durant-Dort days with his Diamond buggies and Victoria vehicles, so that the purposes of the two men easily coalesced. They talked on through the morning at the hotel and at the Buick offices, long enough to outline differences between them.

Briscoe wanted to bring together a conclave of some dozen makers, large and small. Durant was suspicious of that. There would be too many discordant voices. He had a countersuggestion. Since the bulk of production was already concentrated in a few firms, why not link a handful at the top? They would be strong enough to set the pace and tone for the others.

Durant had candidates to name, too, who must already have been on Briscoe's list. Buick and Maxwell-Briscoe, naturally. And Ford, who was the major producer in the industry along with Buick. For a fourth, Durant's choice was Ransom E. Olds's new firm, whose car, the Reo, bore his initials. Olds had quarreled and broken at last with his former associates in 1904. Leaving them behind, as well as the Oldsmobile name, to which they were legally entitled, he had found new backers and begun afresh with a touring car and a runabout. His advertising men capitalized on his successful experience. "The world moves. You need no longer pay fabulous prices for intricate mistakes and doubtful experiments — Mr. R. E. Olds has built the Reo Car." In two years from the introduction of the curved-dash winner, he had become an elder statesman. The approach and the new car both worked, and Reo sales for the year that ended on August 31, 1907, were a gratifying 3,967.[4]

Durant argued that a merger of these four would control the production, even at 1907 levels, of 22,000 cars a year. He convinced Briscoe that this alliance would be both manageable and strong in impact, and when they said good-bye it was with the understanding that Briscoe would arrange a meeting of the two of them with Ford and Olds in Detroit as soon as possible. In the interim it is likely that he reviewed what he knew about earlier essays in combination in the industry as it groped its way toward some ultimate form.

The Association of Licensed Auto Manufacturers itself, though a coalition rather than a consolidation, represented an effort to regulate the individualistic impulses of the licensees in the interests of auto-making society as a whole. That was what *Motor Age* discerned in praising the A.L.A.M. for resisting the "incursion of piratical hordes." Whether or not Durant saw it that way, he had pragmatically joined the A.L.A.M. without any noticeable qualms.

There had been a one-man effort to create a motor empire as well. Its mastermind was Colonel Albert Pope, whose long life stretched back to Civil War service, and who had been a successful bicycle manufacturer in Hartford, Connecticut, when the light of the auto age broke in on him. The colonel was ready to move with the times. He created a "motor carriage department," specializing in electrics, since he was convinced that no one would want "to sit over an explosion." This became the nucleus, with some outside capitalization from the financier William C. Whitney, of the Electric Vehicle Company, which bought the Selden patent. In 1903, yielding to the inevitability of the gasoline engine, Pope launched the Pope Manufacturing Company, which put out a varied line of autos known by hyphenated names such as the Pope-Tribune, the Pope-Toledo, and so on. In 1907 it was a 22.5-million-dollar enterprise, with factories in Hartford, Hagerstown, Toledo, and Indianapolis, but the colonel could not make it pay, and it collapsed into receivership.

In 1906 Herman Cuntz, the secretary of the A.L.A.M. at the time, undertook an exploration of the possibilities for a large-scale merger among some of the members. The course of his investigations led him to sit down eventually with one of the era's most powerful and interesting financial forces, Anthony N. Brady. Brady lived a long and affluent life that began with birth in Lille, France, and brought him to the United States as a youthful immigrant. He opened a tea store in Albany, New York, in 1864, when he was barely twenty-one. He turned it into a monopoly, sold it, and put the profits into granite quarrying, prospered at that, too, and then plunged into two industries bound to succeed, with any kind of good management, in an urbanizing nation: street railways and utilities. His specialty was consolidations. In 1900 he had major holdings in gas and electric companies and trolley lines in New York, Washington, Philadelphia, Utica, and Albany. Brady listened to Cuntz's argument that the hour was ripe for sagacious investment in a motor car trust, and agreed, but only in part. The idea was good but the timing off. Brady could smell the coming panic in the air; the bubble of prosperity was swelling, stretching too thin. Let it burst, and auto properties could then be picked up cheaply by consolidators. The prudent thing was to wait.[5]

A by-product of Pope's failure and Brady's caution was that New England and the Northeast lost finally and forever the opportunity to seize the leadership of the motor world. When consolidation came, its operating (though not its financial) headquarters were to be in Michigan. But it was bound to come from some quarter. Neither Briscoe nor Durant could claim the paternity of the naked idea of consolidation, shorn of any particular corporate form. It was in the very air. In 1900 there had been 185 large industrial combinations, with a capitalization of three billions, producing 14 percent of the national industrial output. In 1904 their number had jumped to 318, the value of their stock to over seven billion. They dominated the production of steel, petroleum products, farm machinery, copper, electrical apparatus, packaged meats, refined sugar, tobacco products, and all the foundation stones of the economy.

The trend to combination was swiftly, unceasingly, and irrevocably transforming the old America of farm and hamlet. The automobile was on the verge of doing so as well. It was fated that these two powerful forces should flow together. And it was appropriate historical dramaturgy that brought the house of Morgan, the royal matchmaker of American enterprise, into the initial maneuverings of 1908. Durant was getting into majestic company, but he was not awed.

II The four of them gathered for the first conference in a public room of Detroit's Penobscot Building a short time after Briscoe's visit to Flint. Looking around, Durant worried about the location. If it were known that four major auto company heads were in a meeting, rumors would begin to fly that might send shudders through the market for automobile securities. Durant himself now had two millions' worth of Buick common stock and $600,000 in preferred to worry about. That was the total amount outstanding under a new capitalization of June, 1907. He suggested that the men leave separately and arrive, one by one, a little later at his suite in the nearby Pontchartrain Hotel, where he would provide lunch for them.

Over the cups and dishes there, they talked in the figures that were for them a second language in which the essential discourses of life were comfortably conducted. The first question was one of allocation. Each company would trade in its own stock for that of the new combination, but in what proportions? They decided that a firm answer would have to await audits. James Couzens, who had come with Ford, scribbled a few notes. They were thinking of a capitalization of $35 million. Of that, $27.5 million was to be divided among the firms in payment for their assets, and another $7.5 million was for extras such as commissions to the bankers who would float the issue and bonuses to the promoters themselves.

They left that subject in the air and turned to the form of a consolidation. Would it be an operating merger, with central departments for purchasing, engineering, advertising, and sales? That was Briscoe's idea, a strangely canny prefiguring of what the corporation that grew out of the talks would finally look like, long years in the future. But Durant preferred a simple holding-company arrangement — the combination simply to own the stock of the constituent concerns, whose executives would remain free to function as they thought best in all areas. He believed that things were still too fluid in the industry for a standardization that might shut off experiments, and he clearly had no intention of yielding his own liberty of maneuver. Briscoe put the difference between them succinctly: "Durant is for states' rights. I am for a union."[6] But he said it with a laugh, and the discussion was harmonious enough so that all agreed to meet again in approximately a week, in the location that would really matter — the downtown New York offices of Ward, Hayden and Satterlee, the ultraprestigious law firm whose head, Herbert L. Satterlee, was the son-in-law of Morgan himself.

They kept no minutes of the sessions held in those offices, so that there was no certainty afterward of exactly who participated. Almost surely Morgan himself was not there; he left preliminaries to lieutenants, especially when they involved only $35 million. But his presence radiated from the very walls; the implication that his consent was necessary overhung every uttered proposal. He did not have to be seen to be believed in.

But Satterlee as his surrogate was impressive enough, and carried in his own person enough contrast with the four auto makers to make the conferences into what the nineteenth century would have called "tableaux." Facing him across the table, figuratively, they sat — all self-made midwesterners in their forties. Briscoe, the most junior in years and most probably in fortune, was unknown outside the auto industry. Durant himself was far from famous, since he alone of them did not have his name on the automobile that made him rich. He was the aristocrat of the four, grandson of a governor that he was, even though he had chosen to earn his way up from the bottom. But he was not even a high-school graduate. Olds and Ford were fundamentally educated in machine shops. Olds was best known, his name boosted into notoriety on the upsweeping sales curve, five years earlier, of his runabout. Ford's fame would eventually outshine all of the others', but it was still ahead of him that spring as Model T took form in preliminary sketches and specifications.

And Satterlee, who was just Ford's age and two years younger than Durant? His name belonged to an old New York family, he held bachelor's degrees in arts and law (and a doctorate) from Columbia, and his first job on completing his legal studies was as private secretary to Senator William M. Evarts, formerly counsel to President Andrew Johnson in his impeachment trial, formerly Attorney General, formerly Secretary of State, withal one of the country's most distinguished attorneys and a perfect conduit into the corporate practice that Satterlee soon undertook. Satterlee had been married to Louisa Pierpont Morgan since the autumn of 1900, and a year after these auto talks would become Secretary of the Navy.

His function was to see if the proposition of the provincial businessmen was worthy of the financial establishment's midwifery. The house of Morgan was in no hurry to step in and supervise the growth of the automobile industry. It was early yet; time was needed for new auto-related inventions to prove themselves, for weak managements to betray their failings as they always helplessly did in the long run, for public taste to settle on the models of its desire. Morgan was in on these explorations, through Satterlee, to keep informed and also because the return on the money raised for Briscoe was a comfortable 20 percent annually. Yet essentially the Morgan view was that expressed a few years later by another banker, Eugene Meyer. "The business was lively, adventurous, had a great future."[7] *Adventurous*. Not a word that sat well with the house.

How far Satterlee would commit his principals to the support of the four-firm consolidation suddenly became a moot question after an unrecorded number of meetings and on a date lost to history, but probably in May. For Henry Ford, with the blunt impulsiveness that made others think of him both as a genius and a terror, suddenly announced a position and snapped his jaws shut in a way that recognizably meant "no budging." He did not want stock in the new concern over and above the value of his business. He did not, in fact, want stock for the Ford Motor Company. He wanted cash. At least three millions in cash. And thereupon, Ransom Olds spoke up and said that in that case he, too, would want his share in cash — the same amount.

These announcements came as a total and unpleasant surprise to Satterlee. Asking for a halt in the meeting, he requested that Briscoe and Durant step into an adjoining room with him, and there demanded to know what was going on. Durant confessed total ignorance. Briscoe, with embarrassment, admitted that in his first approach to Ford he had been told something like this. But as the talks had developed, Ford seemed increasingly interested in a role in the merger, and Briscoe had assumed that in time he would come around.

The new demand actually forced to the surface a division between Briscoe and Durant, on the one hand, and Ford and Olds, on the other, that went beyond money. They had fundamentally different ideas of what they were talking about. For Briscoe and Durant the merger was to be a beginning. They were going to scale new peaks of auto-making achievement through its agency, if their visions materialized. But Ford and Olds, apparently, simply wanted to sell out and quit the game.

Olds had little patience with administrative details and with the necessary compromises of dealing with backers. His creative urges in the field had twice been satisfied within ten years by the development of successful cars. From 1906 onward his involvement in Reo's affairs had been "minimal." He spent increasing periods of rest in Florida's winter sunshine and northern Michigan's summer outdoor pleasures. Even in Lansing, less of his energy was expended in the office, and more in various civic projects as he cultivated the garden of benefactorship.

Ford, always mysteriously moody, was also in a frame of mind described by those around him as dejected and listless. The captaincy of his own concern bored him. "He would come in maybe once or twice a week, and then just roam around," an associate reported.[8] Stockholders were parasites, the apparatus of executive decisionmaking a mere waste. Combinations tended only to raise prices anyway, whereas what he wanted to do was to put every American in the lowest-priced car possible. In 1908 he did not seem to see his way clear to do that yet. Selling out and getting out were perhaps the only choices.

The inner compulsions of Olds and Ford were not part of Satterlee's concern, but their new stance called for a complete recalculation of the odds. If the potential combination had four proven achievers in its directorate, and if they were willing to take its stock as an evidence of their own good faith, then the proposition was something that the Morgan interests might profitably encourage. As a second choice, if Ford and Olds retired, taking stock in the combination for their properties, with an additional bonus to stay out of competition thereafter, that would still leave an entity possibly worth nurturing.

But for the house to put up six million — or it may have been eight million — in cash in order to pasture Ford and Olds and create a new enterprise for Durant and Briscoe — no, indeed. Satterlee reconvened the meeting and made a crisp statement. The initiative had changed hands. The conference would now break up. The bankers would thenceforth reserve the handling of financial arrangements exclusively to themselves. When they had a plan ready, they would let the others know.

There was no ambiguity in the message. Ford and Olds dropped out, their demand denied. Belated rumors of a four-way linkage seeped into the trade press in June, but by then they were void.

Durant, however, had come too far and was too much on fire to let it end there. Either as the meeting was breaking up or later he addressed a six-word message to Briscoe: "Let's go it alone. We two."

III Briscoe willingly accepted Durant's bid to pursue matters. There was no reason to doubt that a smaller combination was feasible, and might even be more attractive to the bankers as a trial model. Between them the Buick and Maxwell-Briscoe factories could produce 13,000 cars a year, 20 percent of the total projected 1908 output, and a most comfortable beginning base. The lead in the negotiations now passed imperceptibly to Durant, who was first referred to Curtis R. Hatheway, a junior member of Hayden, Ward and Satterlee, and by him to a Morgan partner at the very center of things, George W. Perkins.

The two met in a special setting of speed and power perfectly suited to the final flourishing of the age of steam. Perkins was a busy man and a constant traveler. So was Durant. They found it most convenient to meet in Perkins's private drawing room on a crack express bound for Chicago from New York. It was like holding a parley on a landborne yacht. Both men got on, and three hours later Durant descended at Albany for an easy return trip on one of the plentiful trains, warmed by the attentions of white-jacketed stewards and by Perkins's encouragement.

They were the kind of men who would have liked each other. Perkins was also a former salesman, who had won admittance to the Morgan "family" on sheer merit. He came from Illinois, where his father had been superintendent of a reform school. As a young man he got into selling insurance, and rapidly rose through the ranks. He was third vice-president of New York Life at thirty, and chairman of its finance committee eight years later. His specialty was in selecting the best foreign investments for the accumulated premiums and then negotiating them on favorable terms for the company.

These achievements came to the attention of Morgan, who hired him in a characteristically terse way. Perkins walked into the main Morgan offices one day to solicit a contribution from him to help save the Hudson River Palisades from destruction by quarrying. Morgan sat behind a glass partition in a room full of other associates, protected from disturbance by an awesome power of concentration and a reserve that needed no physical walls. Morgan heard Perkins out, then announced that he would raise the entire fund necessary himself, if Perkins would do something for him in return.

"What?" asked Perkins.

Morgan swept out an imperious arm. "Take that desk over there."

Perkins did so at the start of 1901. The next year he organized the International Harvester Corporation for Morgan from five separate, quarrelsome companies. He was soon known as Morgan's right-hand man, and enjoyed the role and the power openly. On a trip to Europe in 1905 he sent back a playful wire: "Have changed government of Russia, separated Norway from Sweden, and welcomed the King of Spain to Germany. Am leaving for France tonight. If there is anything you think needs attention there, cable me at Paris."[9]

Perkins told Durant to keep going, and went so far as to suggest a name for the emerging company. Briscoe and Durant had apparently let drop a tentative title of "United Motors." Perkins suggested "International Motors" instead, perhaps because it reminded him of International Harvester or of a Morgan-created consortium of shipping lines called International Mercantile Marine.

Gratifying as Perkins's encouragement was, it might have spared Durant some wasted moments of optimism if he had gotten an exact explanation of what was involved when Morgan underwrote a consolidation. Perkins had himself described it to Cyrus McCormick a few years earlier when arranging the merger that became International Harvester.

Morgan and Company would investigate, consulting and questioning the various producers in the field as to their interests and opinions. Then the firm would prepare a plan and submit it to the chief corporations in the industry. If approved, the House of Morgan would estimate the working capital necessary to organize the new concern, and form a syndicate to raise this money. If $10,000,000 were needed, the syndicate would issue $15,000,000 in stock, the extra millions representing the syndicate's "bonus." . . . Morgan would also insist upon choosing all the officers and directors of the new company. "This point . . . Morgan & Co. have found indispensable in making their combinations."

Unaware of what was going to be expected of him in the way of yielding control, Durant sailed along, taking his own preliminary steps. Possibly even before the late June or early July session with Perkins, he had gotten Buick's stockholders to deposit their endorsed certificates in John Carton's hands, with the understanding that they were thereby giving consent to William Durant to "sell" them in exchange for preferred and common stock in a new combination on whatever terms he chose. There was no problem in getting so sweeping a delegation of power. At that moment, Flint's faith in Durant was whole and perfect.

Disillusionment came, however, with the discovery that Perkins was not the final authority. Doing business with the Morgan firm was like dealing with a foreign nation. Men referred to its head offices at 23 Wall Street, the corner of Broad and Wall, simply as "the Corner," in exactly the way they might have said "Number 10 Downing Street," or "the Quai d'Orsay." An outsider got to the central circles of decision only by slowly threading a maze of offices. So Durant, who was accustomed to concluding deals by walking two blocks and sitting down with a friend or cousin in the bank, was informed by Hatheway that the parley on the New York Central had merely opened the way for another meeting, this one with still another Morgan attorney, Francis Lynde Stetson.

Stetson's towering altitude dwarfed even Satterlee's. He was sixty-two years old and the dean of the New York bar. At the age of thirty he worked in the law firm of Samuel Tilden, and presented to Congress the case for awarding Tilden the disputed presidential election of 1876. Counsel for the opposing side was William Evarts, for whom Satterlee later worked. That Stetson lost was no drawback to a brilliant career, nor was the fact that he was a Democrat, albeit a rich one, in a generally Republican world of corporation attorneys. It was, in fact, an asset. By 1894 Morgan had met Stetson and made him his favorite personal counsel. That year, the Democratic President, Grover Cleveland, was sorely beset by the problem of a severe national gold shortage. Stetson was not only his friend but his former law partner, and Stetson arranged for meetings among himself, Cleveland, and Morgan, which ended with Morgan heading a syndicate that lent the United States of America enough gold certificates to ease its way through the crisis. It was not surprising that Stetson was called "Morgan's Attorney-General," which was exactly the way that Morgan thought of him. Threatened with an antitrust prosecution by Theodore Roosevelt, Morgan wrote to the White House: "If we have done anything wrong I can send my man to see your man and they can straighten it out."

By appointment Durant called on Stetson, who measured the small, smiling man from Flint with a skeptical mental survey. For Stetson was a man of deep fiscal conservatism, and it was known that Durant, despite Buick's excellent record, had begun its expansion by issuing stock that was overvalued well beyond the assets it stood for. In addition, the Morgan entourage kept an eye on every sparrow who fluttered into the Exchange, so Durant was probably marked as a player of the market. That being so, was it possible that Durant's merger talk was simply a device to boost the price of his own company's stock? On the informal Detroit market for auto shares (which were not yet listed by the New York Exchange), Buick had recently jumped from 90 to 125.

Stetson, a man of "exquisite courtesy," did not raise these points in conference, but he did bore in with doubts and reservations. How good was Durant's title to the Buick shares he was planning to exchange? Did the stockholders who had endorsed their certificates to him know the actual details of the proposed merger — how much common they would receive, how much preferred, what Buick's proportion of the whole would be? If some of them later were dissatisfied they could create legal complications. It would be much safer to announce the complete plan first, and then secure their consent. And it might be well, too, during the negotiations, to freeze dealings in Buick stock.

All these suggestions fell like blows on Durant, now poised for action. He explained to Stetson that his attorney in Flint, Mr. John Carton, believed that the existing form of transfer was entirely satisfactory. Stetson's courtesy must have been stretched to its limits. What Durant had done was tantamount to a layman's telling a Cardinal not to let a point of canon law stand in the way of a dispensation, because his parish priest was sure there was no problem. The talk ended on an inconclusive note, with Durant neither convinced, nor on the other hand absolutely rejecting Stetson's demands, but overall filled with distrust. He wrote to Carton:

[After] a long hot session with our friends in New York . . . was pretty nearly used up at the finish. If you think it is an easy matter to get money from New York capitalists to finance a Motor Car proposition in

Michigan you have another guess coming. Notwithstanding the fact that quoted rates are very low, money is hard to get owing to a somewhat unaccountable feeling of uneasiness and general distrust of the automobile proposition.[10]

He passed on Stetson's objections, and Carton's answer affirmed what they both believed — that any dissidents among the stockholders could be dealt with Flint-fashion, one at a time and face-to-face. "If any of them should refuse to sell their stock without the knowledge of these details, then it would be a matter to be taken up with the individual," Carton wrote. "I do not think that will be required."[11]

It was now mid-July. Durant returned to Flint and began to move at his own pace. First he took an important trip to Lansing, which he kept secret for a time. Then, in apparent capitulation, he wired Curtis Hatheway, "Prepare and mail any kind paper satisfactory to Morgan attorneys for signature our stockholders. List large and widely scattered and it will probably take several weeks to complete signatures." But rather than a surrender it was a final concession to get things moving. The "Morgan attorneys" were making other maddening requests as they revealed the full implications of what it meant to petition New York bankers. They wanted the stock of both companies sold in a single transaction, themselves to name the vendor. They wanted a separate resignation from each Buick director. They wanted Carton and Durant in New York, though Carton was about to go on vacation and Durant was immersed in Buick matters. Durant would agree, with reservations, or at least discuss each point further, but matters must march. "You must admit that I have been patient and long suffering. I now think it is up to us to get busy." Behind the new, almost peremptory, tone was something that Durant hinted to Hatheway on the last day of July. "We are not interested in the Maxwell-Briscoe proposition."[12]

The tie to Briscoe was about to break. The rupture was hurried along when *The New York Times* suddenly blazoned a full account of the exact stage that had been reached. The merger would soon take place. It would be called International Motors, issue $11 million in common stock and $14 million in preferred, have four Morgan nominees in its management and a target goal of 15,000 cars in 1909.

If anything outraged the Morgan partners it was a news leak. Secrecy was a necessity to avoid speculation in shares, price changes, new demands, anything that would upset a deal in the making. It was as much their need and their prerogative, they believed, as it was for foreign ministers. They let Briscoe know of their displeasure in emphatic terms, and Briscoe passed it on to Durant. "It seems that on account of the publication of the details in Friday's 'Times' that the people on 'the corner' are very much upset." Hatheway was even more explicit. It was all off. He wired to Flint that "they" would no longer cooperate due to the exposure of "[their] plans."

Briscoe, at the end of a downward trail from being the initiator of the whole procedure, apologized to Durant for the Morgan withdrawal, just as he had been obliged to apologize earlier for the defection of Ford and Olds. It was his misfortune to be unable to deliver on promises. "I recognize that the procrastination in pushing the matter through has been very disappointing and disconcerting to you, as it has been to myself," he said. Then he added a last token of earnestness. He would even come in without Morgan. "We have both concluded that a million dollars in cash would be enough to finance the proposition, and I will eat my shoes if we can't raise a million dollars between us."[13]

But Durant no longer needed or wanted his Detroit friend now. Late in August he went back to Satterlee, whose firm he had decided to use in carrying out what he had in mind. He was the last of the four manufacturers whom Satterlee had confronted early in the year. He explained that he had lost months in waiting, and wanted to use the Buick stock placed in his hands before the owners gave up on him. "I must have a consolidation," he said.

Satterlee regarded him for a moment, and asked the obvious question. He was the only one left. How was he going to create a consolidation with only one company?[14]

Then Durant, with the successful poker player's joy, pulled out the card that he had been quietly holding for over a month. He had two companies. He was holding an option to buy 75 percent, at least, of the outstanding stock of Oldsmobile.

It had happened in those July days following the talks with Perkins and Stetson. Durant had learned that the Olds Motor Company, now controlled by Samuel Smith and his sons, was in trouble. Production had dropped to 1,000 a year, one major stockholder was trying to sell out at $5.00 per share and finding no takers, and Samuel Smith had advanced the firm a million dollars out of his own pocket, which he despaired of recovering. Durant made telephone calls, probably to Fred Smith, who was a warm, close friend, and announced that he wanted to visit Lansing with a proposition. Deliciously free of the galling need to wait upon the glacial tempo of business as practiced by "the Corner," he chose an hour that was characteristically and exclusively his own. Taking a late train after a full day and evening of work in Flint, he arrived at the Olds offices at 3 A.M.

It took little time for him to explain that he hoped to merge Oldsmobile and Buick, and, considering their situation, probably little more for the

Smiths to accept. Then Fred Smith, always amused at Durant's style, asked if perhaps "Billy" did not want to inspect the property he was buying before papers were signed. Of course, of course, agreed Durant, who rarely needed to look at the things of brick and iron and steel that he owned because he could see them all beautifully in his mind's eye simply from reading a balance sheet, in the way that a doctor could reconstruct the entire course of a disease and cure by a glance at the marks on a patient's chart. But for form's sake he undertook what Smith called a "gallop" up and down the factory aisles, nodding at the lathes and stamping presses and assembly racks and test beds and bins of rods and wires and nuts and bolts and cushions and batteries and piles of doors and tires and cranks, and after fifteen minutes went back to the office and got everything settled in time for breakfast.[15]

That was why he had walked so confidently into Satterlee's office on the heels of the Morgan break-off, and now all that remained to do was to incorporate the new entity in New Jersey, whose laws smiled on holding companies, and to give it a name. Durant was still perfectly satisfied with International Motors, but when Satterlee went back to Perkins he found that Perkins wanted to hold onto the name for a possible future motor merger, and if Durant desired quick action it would be best not to fight the matter. Hatheway's researches unearthed a United Motor Car Company in New Jersey, which seemed to rule out United Motors, the original working title. "We suggest," Hatheway wrote, the name 'General Motors Company,' which we have ascertained can be used."[16]

On September 16, 1908, the General Motors Company was incorporated by three directors, George E. Daniels, Benjamin Marcuse, and Curtis R. Hatheway, with an initial capitalization of $2,000, to give it legal existence. Less than two weeks later a legal ritual was enacted when Durant appeared before the trio in his capacity as Buick treasurer and tendered to them 18,870 shares of his company's common stock, worth approximately $3.4 million. They in turn voted to raise General Motors' capitalization to $12.5 million, and paid Buick with $2.5 millions' worth of GM preferred, $1.25 millions in GM common, and $1,500 in cash.

Six weeks later a similar transaction was completed with the Olds corporation, with General Motors giving $3 million in its own stock for Olds shares worth about $2 million, and likewise agreeing to pick up a million dollars' worth of debts owed by the company to Samuel L. Smith. Once more, a relative pittance in cash — $17,279 — was part of the price. So at last the consolidation had come about, the long labor proven finally productive. The broad concept might belong to no one person in particular, and the triggering impulse might have come from Benjamin Briscoe, but it was Durant who had persisted through the quarrels and walkouts and slowdowns, and completed the work. General Motors was what he proudly called it throughout his life: his "baby."[17]

VI The curious circumstances of General Motors' creation meant that it started its existence as a one-man operation. The net effect of Briscoe's misjudgments, the haughtiness of the Morgan firm, the stubbornness of Ford and Olds, was to leave Durant the untrammeled master of the new enterprise. That might well have been the only outcome that spared the corporation early and disastrous bloodshed in the board-room. It was inconceivable that such arrant individualists as the original conferees could have worked together for long without quarreling furiously among themselves or with Morgan or any other financial regulator. As it was, the chances of the game gave Durant total power without a struggle. Authority, like money, had come to him easily, unquestionably reinforcing his unarticulated sense that he was fortune's darling. That conviction spurred him to fresh bursts of creativity.

He was emboldened as well by the power placed in his hands through the control of millions of dollars in stock. Those certificates, handsomely engraved and printed, became an enchanted currency under the spell of his promises, always growing in value, always able to set machines and men in fruitful motion. It had taken sixteen years for his carriage-making proper-ties to justify $1.5 million in stock. It had taken three for Buick to reach the point of issuing $2.6 million. Now, at the very beginning, Durant had $12.5 millions to manipulate, with more at command from the directors if he liked. With such resources, his ambitions soared as if freed from some long-irksome encumbering ballast.

There was no overall design at first, simply a determination to be ready to rush into production with whatever caught the public fancy. "He wanted a lot of 'makes,'" a friend explained later, "so that he could always be sure to have some popular cars."[18] In pursuing "makes," he was by turns shrewd and calculating, or impulsive and foolhardy, a commander whose moves occasionally baffled his own staff as much as they did the enemy's. The gifted and the incomprehensible choices often were made simultaneously. Experience could have shown him the risks as well as the gorgeous opportunities inherent in his style, but he rarely gave it any time to sink in.

The Olds purchase was an example. In spite of its excellent early record, it was a floundering organization when he acquired it, and overvalued at three millions. Durant knew as much himself. Aware that the Olds management had tried to recoup its position with a heavy advertising campaign on billboards, he remarked that the sum involved was "a hell of a price to pay for a bunch of road signs."[19] But he needed to make a beginning somewhere, and with Olds in hand, he reached out for a third company, this one located in Pontiac, just north of Detroit, manufacturing an auto named for the county in which the plant sat — the Oakland.

Oakland's father was Edward Murphy, who had been the head of the Pontiac Buggy Company, and a friend of Durant's since the 1890s. In 1907 Murphy belatedly felt the chill of approaching death for the horse-drawn conveyance, but managed to find a retired lumberman who helped him raise $200,000 to convert to car-making. In mid-1908 another $100,000 was raised, and a four-cylinder machine called the Model K had been designed, but at that year's end total output was a forlorn 278. All the same, Durant decided that there was a place for this struggling infant in General Motors, and made a bid to its stockholders. As he recalled it, Murphy himself was the last to be convinced, and then only after he was outvoted, but the others must have been at least moderately hard prospects, too, since the General Motors treasury had to part with approximately $201,000 in cash for the 19,000 Oakland shares that gave it control. The remainder of the outstanding Oakland stock was secured with notes and with shares of GM.[20] The outlay was modest enough for a car that was to become the Pontiac, but the directors of General Motors may have found it curious that more than ten times as much cash was laid out for the unproven Oakland than was spent on buying Buick and Oldsmobile. They did not argue, however. Durant had carefully chosen a board of little-known men who would raise no issues with him, and he was rarely disappointed by his selections.

By the time Oakland was formally acquired, Durant had already bagged another and truly impressive quarry. With Oakland, General Motors would be established in Lansing, Flint, and Pontiac, but he urgently wanted it to have a facility in Detroit, which was clearly emergent as the industry's center. To achieve this, he reached for nothing less than the Cadillac Motor Company, which was successfully marketing the best-reputed high-priced car in the country. As well as it was doing, its owners were accessible to an offer early in 1909, for Durant learned that Ben Briscoe, who still had expansionist urges of his own, had been offered an option on 60 percent of the outstanding stock at $150 a share, but had been unable to come up with the money. Cadillac was going to be expensive, but worth it.

The car's good name owed everything to the fanatical perfectionism of Henry M. Leland. Alfred Sloan was one of many parts makers who could testify to that. Early in his career his factory received a large order for bearings from C. S. Mott, who used them in a shipment of axles to Cadillac. Sometime after the delivery, Sloan got a frantic call from his partner Peter

Steenstrup, who was on a sales trip. "Old Leland's on the warpath," Steenstrup reported, and begged for Sloan's help. "I'm no mechanic. I'm a salesman. We're not speaking the same language."

Arrived in Detroit, Sloan sat humbly opposite Leland while the white-bearded autocrat set a pile of Hyatt bearings on his desk, and picked up a micrometer in his broad brown fingers. One after another, he measured the bearings and noted a series of variations in their diameter. In the intonations of a preacher scourging some particularly flagrant sin, he thundered: "Your Mr. Steenstrup told me these bearings would be accurate, one like another, to within one thousandth of an inch." Then he rose dramatically and led Sloan to a window overlooking the factory yard. There lay piles of discarded axles like stiffened corpses. "Unless you can give me what I want," Leland threatened, "I'm going to put five hundred Weston-Mott axles out there beside those other rejects." Sloan rode home to order changes in his production line, his ears ringing with Leland's advice that he must grind his bearings so precisely that, no matter how many thousands he made, the last should be the exact counterpart of the first. He professed to be improved by the experience. The old man, he said, had given him "a genuine conception of what mass production should mean."[21]

The payoff for such demands, however, was impressive. In 1906, Leland had won the Dewar Prize of London's Royal Automobile Club, awarded annually for the greatest improvement in an auto during the year. Three Cadillacs were shipped to the club's test track at Brooklands, outside London. They were there broken down and their parts thoroughly scrambled, after which a different set of mechanics proceeded to reassemble them, using only hammers, wrenches, pliers, and screwdrivers. The three cars were then driven for 500 miles without a breakdown, an extraordinary feat in the crude state of the art. Precision manufacturing was well established in many industries, especially arms-making, in which Leland had been trained, but the sheer number of parts in a car, and the hard and unforgiving use to which they were put, posed a special kind of manufacturing challenge.

Nineteen-seven had been a hard year for Cadillac as for most companies, one nervous stockholder greeting Wilfred Leland, on his return from a wedding trip, with "We are bankrupt! All our money is lost."[22] But the moment of despair had passed, 1908 had been better, and in 1909, with a four-cylinder Model 30 selling briskly, Cadillac was on the way to a 6,000-car year. Both Lelands, father and son, and their backers were therefore disposed to drive a hard bargain when invited to join a new consolidation. Their answer to Durant's first approach was rendered in firm New England tones. The price was $3.5 million in cash, not stock, and it would hold good for ten days. After that, it might rise.

When Durant was anxious to have something, he was neither inclined to dicker nor to raise any outcry if he lacked the purchase price. He thanked the Lelands and departed, and did not reappear for several months. Later, Wilfred Leland claimed that an agent of Durant had offered him a personal bribe if he could bring his father and his partners down by half a million, which was refused. The story rested only on Leland's word. Whether it was true or not, Durant finally made a second formal approach about midway through the year, saying that he now thought he could raise the money. He was informed that the price was now $4.125 million, again for ten days only. Once more he went into the money markets, and came up empty-handed. Once more he came back after the expiration of the time limit. And once more the figure rose, to $4.5 million.

This time the head of the General Motors Company (still without any official title save director) had an acceptable formula, of the kind his nimble financial intellect delighted to produce. General Motors itself had nowhere near that much cash. Its entire growth rested on the willingness of stockholders in the constituent companies to trade their existing shares for GM shares that were supposed to become more valuable in the long run through the enhanced power of the holding company—to place a bet, in effect, on the future of combination. If the owners of Cadillac were unwilling to be that venturesome, however, there was an answer. The Buick Motor Company, General Motors' backbone, had plenty of cash. Buick would buy out Cadillac, putting up $2.5 million immediately, and giving eighty promissory notes of $25,000 each for the balance, one-third of them due in six months, one-third in eight, and one-third in ten. Then General Motors would repurchase the Cadillac stock from its own subsidiary later, paying $500,000 in cash and approximately $5 million in GM preferred stock, the extra amount apparently a bonus for Buick's cooperation.

Whether the Lelands were struck by the cleverness of the device, or indifferent as to how Durant handled the internal cash transfers of General Motors, the important thing was that the money was there. On a hot July day in Detroit, the ten stockholders who had created the Cadillac concern in 1902 met in a bank to be paid off at $300 a share. Afterward, Durant asked Wilfred and Henry Leland to meet him at his hotel and there asked them to continue in their executive posts. Their recollection was that they demanded absolute freedom, and that Durant slapped his knee and declared: "That is exactly what I want. I want you to continue to run the Cadillac exactly as though it were still your own. You will receive no directions from anyone."[23]

In stripping the Buick company of so much of its cash, Durant was taking a major business risk, akin to a general's depriving a successful army of all its reserves in order to throw them against an objective on another front. But his own mind invested gestures that a banker would have found demented with logic. Winnings were to be used, not hoarded, and if the aim was to blanket the market in the long run, so that somewhere some General Motors–owned company was always sure to be prospering, then there was nothing wrong with the successful members of the combination temporarily carrying a few stragglers. Not that Cadillac was in any sense a cripple. On August 31, 1909, it showed a net profit for the preceding year of $1,969,382, almost half the acquisition cost earned back, as Durant happily pointed out in General Motors' first annual report a few weeks later.

Stimulated, energized, almost intoxicated with the sense of how easy it was to buy motor companies, Durant rushed ahead, sweeping up new firms as if they would rot left unpicked. He bought the Marquette Motor Car Company of Saginaw and the Reliance Motor Truck Company of Owosso and the Welch Motor Car Company of Pontiac, the maker of what one Durant associate called "the super passenger car of its day, as big as a freight car." Its incidental virtue to General Motors was that A. B. C. Hardy was recalled from his Iowa sanctuary to take charge of the operation. Durant went on, buying the companies that made the Elmore, in Clyde, Ohio—"a two-cycle monstrosity junked in infancy,"[24] in one skeptic's evaluation—and the Randolph, in Illinois, and the Cartercar in Pontiac, that one equipped with a friction drive that was supposed to eliminate difficulties of gearshifting. In 1910, reviewing his whirlwind progress through the bazaar, the magazine *Motor World* commented:

At all times Durant's faith in himself was admirable. When his wisdom in acquiring a lot of "lame ducks" was questioned, he declared that lameness was the fault of mismanagement and that under proper direction—his own—the lame could be made first to walk upright and then to gallop to the goal of prosperity. Some of the General Motors purchases, however, proved very lame, indeed. . . .[25]

Their lameness was not apparent at the conclusion of General Motors' first year of existence in September of 1909, however. The records showed sales of slightly over $29 million, with $9,114,498 available for dividends. Having already paid $3.50 on the preferred stock in April, Durant and his fellow directors, who now included Curtis Hatheway and Fred Smith, increased the capitalization of the company to $60 million, and declared a 150 percent dividend, payable in stock, on the common. While a stock dividend, like a stock split, put no immediate dollars in shareholders' accounts, it hugely increased their potential gains as the corporation prospered.

His appetite growing by what it fed on, Durant's heart leaped when a rumor was brought to him that autumn that once more a restless Henry Ford was considering the sale of his company. The price would be high, since the Model T was beginning its phenomenal sales career, and even in 1908 a profit of $2.5 million had been turned on some $9 million in sales. But that was never a barrier to exploration, and so on a late October evening, Durant found himself once more talking to James Couzens, in the lobby of New York's Belmont Hotel, just across the street from General Motors' first New York offices in the Terminal Building, at Park Avenue and Forty-first Street. Ford was in town, too, but upstairs in his hotel room, suffering from an attack of lumbago.

Couzens was eager to see the sale made. At thirty-seven, he had three children, a great deal of money, graying hair, migraine headaches, and an ambition to move onward from the tempests of five years as Ford's chief executive and partial partner. After he and Durant had talked, he went upstairs and announced to Ford that General Motors would pay $8 million. "All right," was Ford's response from the floor, where he was lying to ease the pain in his back. "Tell him he can have it if the money's all cash. Tell him also, I'll throw in my lumbago."[26]

They went from there to the very brink of consummation before the banks parted them. On Sunday the twenty-fourth of October, the three of them checked inventories at the Ford plant, and two days later, the General Motors directors gave the expected authorization to Durant to proceed. Couzens made life easier by saying that he would buy enough additional Ford shares to raise his holdings to 25 percent of the company, and he would be willing to take GM stock for his part. The other six million could be paid with two million down and the remainder in three-year, 5 percent notes. Yet Durant could find no bank whose loan committee would tender the money. If they had any inkling of the gigantic profit potential in Ford, it was counterbalanced by concern that Durant might dissipate any amount of profit in his quest for "lame ducks"; that even the combined resources of Buick, Ford, and Cadillac could not meet the huge fixed expenses that were accumulating as Durant's automotive empire grew.

Checked but not halted, the slightly built man from Flint continued to seek diversity with the same manic insistence that Ford showed in his later unending drive to cut costs, once he resigned himself to remaining an auto maker. Durant won board authorization that same October of 1909 to go after the E. R. Thomas Company of Buffalo, makers of the Thomas Flyer, which had just won a race from New York to Paris via Siberia. That fell through, as no satisfactory agreement could be reached. Then Benjamin Briscoe appeared on the scene again. This time he was a potential seller of the triad of companies that he and his brother owned, the parts-making

Briscoe Manufacturing Company, the Maxwell-Briscoe plant, and another that made an auto known as the Brush Runabout. Though these themselves could have been the nucleus of the combination that the lively Briscoe still yearned in vain to start, he was willing to let them go for money to make a fresh start, specifically five millions, two of them in cash, the last demand possibly being an addition from his backers on "the Corner." Again, his friend "Billy" could not find bank support, and had to forego the opportunity. There was no second Buick company in the background whose treasury he could use to circumvent the credit markets.[27]

There was a creator's egocentricity in Durant's insistent reliance on his own erratic hunches to unfold the next direction he should take. He answered reproaches to his judgment by telling Hardy one day:

They say I shouldn't have bought Cartercar. . . . Well, how was anyone to know that Cartercar wasn't going to be the thing? It had the friction drive and no other car had it. Maybe friction drive would be the thing. And then there's Elmore, with its two-cycle engine. That's the kind they were using on motorboats; maybe two-cycles was going to be the thing for automobiles. I was for getting every car in sight, playing safe all along the line.[28]

Any systematic survey, however, would have shown that in 1909 there was not very much uncertainty about what was going to be "the thing." The four-cylinder auto, using a front-mounted four-cycle engine, delivering its power to the rear wheels through a driveshaft, and equipped with an H-slot sliding gear transmission, was becoming "well-nigh universal."[29] But offsetting this misplaced bet was the pattern of drawing components factories into the General Motors network, as had been done on a smaller scale with Durant-Dort and Buick. Even if the motive was less a rational calculation than an instinctive yearning by Durant to have a ready supply of parts at command, he put himself near the head of the procession marching toward the vertical integration that was the industry's unfolding model of success.

He began the process almost simultaneously with the creation of General Motors. One day, when he was in Boston on Buick business, he was called on by a bald, moustached man who explained that he liked to have his name, Albert Champion, pronounced in the fashion of his native Paris— "shom-pee-YOHN." Champion, whose surname was so perfect a trademark, had in fact a product which carried it, a spark plug of his own design. He had developed it out of an interest in good engine performance that dated back to a brief American career as an auto racer, which he had given up as too hazardous. Before that he had been a prize-winning bicycle racer in France. Detroit's auto-minded community remembered Champion from the early days of the century. He would appear in the barroom of the Pontchartrain, an unofficial headquarters for the trade, bringing with him an "elaborate electrical set" which he would assemble to demonstrate to buyers his "supérieur" porcelain plugs. Eventually, he had found backers who set him up in Boston as the director of the Albert Champion Company.[30]

Durant was impressed with Champion's demonstration. He was paying thirty-five cents each for plugs for Buicks that were not as good. If Champion were set up in Flint, he asked, with a guarantee of a market for every plug he could make, could he improve on that price? Champion could. Leaving his dismayed Boston angels behind, he moved to Buick's home base, where he began to make plugs in a corner of the auto plant, not achieving a factory of his own until 1912. His new firm was called the Champion Ignition Company of Flint, the lengthy corporate title being chosen to avoid confusion with the original Albert Champion Company, whose owners refused to give up Champion's name along with Champion. Durant sold his interest in the concern to the growing motor combine in 1909. Much later, General Motors retitled its partially owned subsidiary (which it would absorb completely in the long run) the A.C. Spark Plug Company. The French millionaire-to-be thus came to share with Ransom Olds the odd distinction of having two companies making his product, one under his name and the other under his initials.

A.C. Spark Plug was only one of the earliest makers of ignition and electrical gear, transmissions, wheels, brakes, engine castings, springs, body panels, and other elements of finished autos that were gathered into the General Motors fold in its first year and a half. There was an array of them, some wholly owned, and some in which General Motors had only a partial interest. Weston-Mott, of course, and Michigan Motor Castings of Flint; Jackson-Church-Wilcox in Jackson; Seager Engine Works in Lansing; Lansden Electric in Ontario; Michigan Auto Parts and Northway Motor and Manufacturing Company in Detroit; Brown-Lipe-Chapin in Syracuse; Dow Rim in New York City. Less subject to vagaries of taste than the auto concerns themselves, most of them were destined to have long and successful lives within General Motors. One, however, was a disaster in which Durant searingly illuminated the weaknesses that lay at the heart of his method and his personality, which were fused into one. That acquisition was a cluster of small corporations linked together as the Heany Lamp Companies.

Practical auto headlights were not yet in existence when General Motors got under way. Motorists descended as darkness fell and struggled to light acetylene or other gas lamps, prodigally expending matches and curses in an ordeal that was sharpened if there were wind and rain. In January of 1910, Durant became convinced that John A. Heany could provide relief with an electric lamp of his own making, sturdy enough to withstand road shocks and to operate on the current furnished by an automobile generator and storage battery. He bought out Heany's operation for 8,290 shares of GM preferred and 74,775 shares of GM common with an astonishing total face value of some $7 million, plus $112,759 in cash. Yet the slightest investigation would quickly have shown what immediately became clear. The property was worthless.

Heany was one of those characters who sometimes emerge from the shadowlands of American technology, claiming to have invented something basic and then to have been robbed of credit by better-financed aspirants. In 1907 he applied for patents on various "improvements" in the electric light bulb. The General Electric Company, which controlled the basic inventions in incandescent lighting, brought suit to void them even while Heany was setting up his manufacturing facilities. While the case was struggling through the barbed wire of motions and filings, Heany, his attorney, and a clerk in the Patent Office were indicted on the charge of tampering with the applications so as to give Heany a false priority of date on certain ideas. The lawyer and the clerk were tried and convicted. Heany, either very lucky or very able, walked out free, and into his profitable encounter with Durant. Soon thereafter, the Commissioner of Patents threw out the Heany applications. General Motors had to write the Heany investment off the books. The stock that it had turned over went on appreciating in value and accumulating dividends until, according to one estimate of 1927, the compounded value of Durant's mistake at that point was over $370 million.[31]

What was behind the blunder? John Carton had a hard suspicion, shared by others. It was that Durant knew that he was buying a false front and did not care. The purchase furnished an excuse for issuing extra GM shares that would find their way to market disguised as representatives of objects of value. The practice of authorizing issues with nothing behind them, known as stock-watering, had a long and dishonorable entry in the annals of deceiving investors. It was Carton's expressed view, after a time, that "Billy" had "never thought that General Motors would become the big manufacturer that it did; what [he] desired, most of all, were large stock issues in which he, from an inside position, could dicker and trade."[32]

It was a judgment that overlooked two facets of the Durant nature. One was his pure joy in selling good products, a delight too rich for him to regard the output of his factories as merely incidental to the stock trading, which, no one could doubt, he also savored. The other was his honest American businessman's conviction that almost any well-managed company would prosper in the piping times that were the natural and expected state of things, so that even a little excess valuation would prove, in time, to be understated as performance unfalteringly overtook and passed promise. This credo alone might have explained a transaction whose ultimate truth would be buried with Durant, if he ever confronted it himself.

By the second summer of its life, General Motors was a collection of some twenty-five firms, some partly and most wholly owned, making automobiles, taxicabs, trucks, parts, and accessories. They were straddled over three states and Canada. One of the best moves Durant had made was the purchase of a 40 percent interest in the McLaughlin Motor Car Company of Oshawa, Ontario, which began to manufacture Buicks under license and to lay the foundations for General Motors of Canada. As of September, 1910, Durant's youthful empire employed some 14,000 people, and was responsible for about one-fifth of the total national auto production — 21 percent by volume, 22 percent by value. The value of the fixed plant investment was some $14 million, and of the inventories on hand approximately $40 million.

The creation of this infant prodigy was an exercise in fiscal gymnastics that outshone the performance at Buick. Durant and his directors had brought it into existence by laying out approximately $6.2 millions in cash, and $26 millions in stock. Of that stock, around $6.25 million had been issued as a dividend at the end of the first year, and another $14 million had been issued in exchange for the stock of the constituent companies. Only $5.75 millions' worth had been marketed to raise cash, and had yielded a net of only $4.5 million.

The difference between that and the $6.2 millions of cash spent came out of earnings, predominantly Buick's. Almost three-quarters of the cash outlay was in the payment for Cadillac, while the remainder was spread in morsels among the other almost two dozen acquisitions. Durant, in summation, had bought properties worth $54 million inside two years; they were earning annual profits in the range of $10 million; they had cost him under $33 million, and less than a fifth of that had been in cash.[33]

He had good reason to swell with ingrained optimism as he looked down from the height he had reached in fewer than six years in the business. Suffused with pride, he was blind to two weaknesses in General Motors' structure. One was that it badly needed to be better administered and also pruned, freed of the weight of some of his wrong guesses. The other was its frightening vulnerability to interruptions in cash flow; he had multiplied its obligations and thinned its reserves in the same process of steady buying. Before 1910 was over he was to have a brutal lesson in just how precarious was the ground on which he stood.

V He was the center of the empire. Its headquarters was located wherever he sat. He was incapable of sharing responsibility, as *Motor World,* summing up the first two years, perceived.

It was quickly made plain that General Motors was a "one-man institution." Durant was its general and he was his own colonel, his own major and his own lieutenant. He dominated it from top and bottom and brooked no interference. He is a prodigious worker and the wonder is how he attended to so many details, great and small, and lived through it all. He kept one eye on his factories and another on the stock ticker, and the while he dreamed of world conquests.[34]

Writers fell helplessly into trite military analogies in describing him, especially since his short stature made the comparison with Napoleon almost irresistible. Even his chauffeur in Flint had that thought in mind when he watched Durant pacing the train platform one morning, awaiting an express. His head was sunk in the fur collar of the long overcoat he wore against the cold, which he said made him shrivel up; his arms were folded in front of him, his whole being drawn inward into some central reservoir of thought. But if he was Napoleon, it was not the time of Austerlitz, but of the Russian campaign—forces widely dissipated, flanks open, communications lines wavering.[35]

The two sides of his nature were in conflict. Like Henry Howland Crapo putting together logging camps, sawmills, lumber yards, and railroads in an intelligent sequence from forest to furniture, he could appreciate how many disparate parts he needed to round out his operations. But—perhaps like his father—he was impatient of routine and dull necessities. Sometimes he was not merely ahead of other men's reality, but in flight from it. Every new addition to General Motors made administrative and financial demands, created problems of coordination that had to be solved if the enterprise were to develop its fullest efficiency. These were not the kinds of challenge to arouse him. He almost seemed to enjoy operating in the midst of the frequent crises that lack of planning bred. "You know," a friend once remarked to one of Durant's advertising executives, "W. C. is never happy unless he is hanging to a window sill by his finger tips."[36]

He was in constant motion among his companies, rushing from outpost to outpost, though the main axis of his travel was between New York and Flint. In the middle of 1909 a young friend and assistant entered his life and got a vivid introduction to what it meant to keep up with "the Man." Winfred Murphy, in his mid-twenties, was a shorthand expert who had done secretarial service for Michigan's Republican State Committee, its governor, and its upper house, and then, deciding that "there wasn't much in politics," gone to work for the general manager of Oldsmobile. Durant, on a trip to Lansing, needed a stenographer quickly, borrowed Murphy, and was impressed. Shortly before Christmas that year he came to Lansing again, offered a job, but warned that there would be "some travelling," and that Murphy might better pass it up if he were married. Murphy was a bachelor, as it happened, and gladly came down to be set up in an office next to Durant's in the Buick administration building. Within a week, Durant burst in on him with a crisp announcement: "Well, we're going to New York," meaning in a matter of hours. That night Murphy slept on the Wolverine, and the next morning was led into a room piled ceiling-high with unfiled correspondence dating back several months. Working day and night, he had barely conquered it, when a summons came for immediate departure. From then on his life consisted of more or less alternate weeks of catching what sleep he could in the Murray Hill Hotel in New York or the Dresden in Flint, his employer's definition of "some travelling."[37]

Durant was a bridegroom rarely seen by Catherine, who did not yet have a permanent home to share with him. He scheduled his work with no regard for clocks. "I'll meet you at one-thirty A.M.," he told one importunate visitor seeking a few moments of his time. "You mean one-thirty P.M., don't you, Mr. Durant?" "No, we'll get to this yet today. I mean one-thirty A.M." But he was "always among the first to be at the office the next morning, fresh and smiling."[38] He needed to maintain a desperate pace simply to keep up with his own inspirations. The acquisition of a single industrial property normally requires many months of proposals, conferences, audits, draft contracts, paperwork by banks and lawyers and stockholders. Durant was buying companies at an approximate rate of one every thirty days. "Only the most phenomenal memory could keep his deals straight," said Lee Dunlap, Oakland's general manager. "He worked so fast that the records were always behind him."

When Mr. Durant visited one of his plants it was like the visitation of a cyclone. He would lead his staff in, take off his coat, begin issuing orders, dictating letters, and calling the ends of the continent on the telephone, talking in his rapid, easy way to New York, Chicago, San Francisco. That sort of thing was less common than it is now; it put most of us in awe of him. . . .

On this visit of which I am thinking, early in 1910, I expected he would stay several days as we were to discuss the whole matter of plant expansion. But after a few hours, Mr. Durant said, "Well, we're off to Flint." In despair I led him on a quick inspection of the plant. Instantly he agreed that we would have to build, and asked me to bring the expansion plan with me to Flint the next day. There wasn't any plan, and none could be drawn on such short notice, but his will being law, and our need great, something had to be done.

So I called in a couple of our draftsmen to help me and that night we made a toy factory layout—existing buildings in one color, desired buildings in another. We drew a map of the whole property, showing streets and railroad sidings, and then glued the existing buildings to it in their exact locations. Feeling like a small boy with a new toy, I took this lay-out to Flint and rather fearfully placed it before the chief. I needn't have been alarmed at our amateur lay-out. He was pleased pink. We had a grand time fitting our new buildings into the picture as it was spread on his desk. We placed those new buildings first here, then there, debating the situation. When we agreed as to where they should go, he said, "Glue them down and call W. E. Wood."

Mr. Wood came in after a few minutes and received an order for their construction. In the whole history of America, up to that time, buildings had never risen as swiftly as those did. Contractor Wood had men, materials, and machines moving toward Pontiac within twenty-four hours, and we were installing machinery in part of the structures within three weeks. But, of course, we could not be equally swift in paying for them. That was something else. But for the time being none of us worried too much over that; we figured the "Little Fellow" would find the money somewhere. Which he did, in the end, though we know there was plenty of trouble before the bills were receipted.[39]

Though in theory the separate plant managers were independent, Durant enjoyed his incursions into their domains. He was proud of how he had personally designed Oldsmobile's basic 1910 model, just after his take-over. He did it by having a White Streak driven to Lansing, its wooden body sawed in quarters, and the quarters separated to give a longer and wider profile, which the engineers were commanded to duplicate.[40] He loved the road testing of the cars themselves, though after a time he became so absorbed in work that driving was a pleasure which, like cigars, he abandoned. Nonetheless, in 1909 and 1910 he was at the wheel of a Buick in the annual Glidden Tours. These were cross-country races of stock models, over New England back-road courses, designed to prove the sturdiness of each manufacturer's entries at a time when, despite the achievement of Leland with Cadillac, most motorists found that "to start out for a ride was an adventure; to return with no parts missing, and all parts functioning, was a miracle."[41] In both cases, Durant lost, once because he stopped to help a fellow driver in trouble and was disqualified.

Murphy never forgot one particular moment that distilled the essence of the Durant encounter with the road. They were on the way from Flint to Detroit to catch a train, with a brief scheduled stop at Pontiac, and Durant was pushing hard on the accelerator when they were blocked by a slow-moving farm wagon. Hardly hesitating, he swung sharply left into a deep roadside ditch, roared past the obstacle, and wrestled the car back onto its course. As he did so there was a gunshot-like sound, and the car swayed and emitted a metallic screech from its bowels, like a stricken creature. Startled and horrified, Murphy started to rise in his seat, expecting to get down and look for the damage as they braked to a halt. But Durant fed the engine more gas and pushed him back. "Never mind," he shouted. "We're still moving." And they came squealing into the Oakland factory, the car canted over and jerking, and only then did they hit the bump that jolted loose two pieces of a spring that had snapped in half.[42]

Yet while riding these whirlwinds he kept a human side alive. A young Flint reporter, Arthur Sarvis, discovered that he could catch Durant in the small hours at an all-night restaurant, where the master of General Motors unassumingly slipped for a cup of coffee during marathon work sessions. He was always "kind, courteous, approachable," and good for a story.[43] Another writer for the press who interviewed him was entirely won over. He found, in Durant's "trim, lithe body" a hint of "illimitable static force." His manners were "refined and cordial," he expressed himself with "zestful conciseness."

There are no harsh lines in his face, no note of autocrat in his speech or act. In fact he is a man of extreme reticence. . . . Yet there is something about him that makes you feel that here is an extraordinarily virile personality. . . .
It is often remarked that he is calmest in the time of stress and cheeriest under the heaviest burdens. It is at such times that he invariably smiles — and his smile . . . is as innocent as a child's and as philosophic as a sage's. . . . Mr. Durant is a man of heart and very attractive human failings.[44]

And a man who could laugh at himself. Theodore McManus, a Detroit newspaperman and public relations counsel, once doubled him up by thrusting at him a poem scribbled during a long wait in his outer office.

> *I'm glad I'm not a vacuum*
> *I'm glad I'm not a myth*
> *I'm glad I'm not the sort of stuff*
> *They fill pin cushions with*
> *But most of all I'm glad, O Lord*
> *You did not make me Henry Ford.*[45]

"Oh, you villain!" gasped Durant. "Did you write this? Can I have it?" and he dashed off with the paper in a firm clutch. In the midst of "tremendous operations," McManus said, he would burst into "the pranks of a boy." Murphy knew what that meant, too. Durant took him along once on one of his summer dashes to Pentwater to visit Rebecca; he needed a secretary at his side almost constantly. After some time spent in the cottage, Durant beckoned Murphy to follow him, saying there was something he wanted to do that his young employee might enjoy. They climbed to the top of a high sand dune, where Durant gazed at Lake Michigan for a moment, settled himself down on the seat of his pants, and delightedly slid down several hundred feet to the beach.[46]

It was a smile of victory that lit his face from deep inside, that golden year, for him, of 1909. Ahead of even his most optimistic competitors, he had picked up the vibrations of the coming auto revolution. The car was already, in one magazine writer's prophetic formulation, "the idol of the modern age." Another wrote: "There is no question but that the business is going to get steadily better. . . . The automobile is essential to comfort and happiness." From everywhere the reports were coming in, of families that had never even owned a horse suddenly deciding to "indulge in automobiles costing several thousand dollars"; of the motoring mania that had "taken hold of the suburbanites . . . as never before"; of "hundreds of clerks and small businessmen . . . going to and from their work" in their new machines.[47]

Where other auto makers glowed with the expectation of big years that might triple or even quadruple a preceding twelve months' record, Durant's projections winged far above theirs. "Durant sees — actually sees — 90,000,000 people just aching to roll along the roads of this country in automobiles,"[48] a Detroit newspaperman reported after an interview, "and he wishes to fill that void." That was what lay behind the hasty snatching up of properties into arms already too full. "I figured if I could acquire a few more companies like the Buick, I would have control of the greatest industry in this country."

To dub automaking the nation's greatest industry was still a rare and bold vision in 1909 or 1910, but the distant future always presented itself to Durant in a blazing glow, as his contemporaries realized. It was the immediate present that flung itself into his full-tilt path and tripped him up before a third year of expansion could begin.

VI The reckoning came early in 1910, with a sudden drop in the sales of new cars. The cause was mainly a readjustment in the market; the costly makes had finished skimming the cream of the luxury buyers, while the manufacturers were reorganizing themselves to meet calls for lower-priced machines. But even a temporary slackening of demand shook the insecurely financed business to its roots. In 1909, a good year, eighteen new firms had tried their luck. In 1910, eighteen old firms were forced out of the game, and only one entered. Ben Briscoe, his hour come round at last, was able to borrow thirty millions from Anthony Brady and two other traction magnates, and buy a few bankrupt wrecks at fire-sale prices, and float his own consolidation, United States Motors. But he was not properly gifted by the stars for more than transient glories. In two years United States Motors also went onto the reefs and was broken up.[49]

In spite of being on the way to a record production year, Buick Motor Company was not immune to the virus that brought the strong as well as the weak to bed. William Durant was getting his comeuppance for having aspirated $4.5 million out of his best company's rainy-day vaults. This time he could not go on making and stockpiling Buicks. There was nothing on hand to meet due bills. Valiant efforts were made. Loyal dealers like Harry Noyes shipped suitcases full of cash to Flint. Money could not be transferred through ordinary bank channels, since it would have been seized on to pay off overdrafts in Buick accounts. The Durant-Dort Company gave some temporary help. Loans were floated, and climbed to eight million dollars—nearly as much as all of General Motors had reported in profits the preceding year—a heavy burden, even for a front runner. New construction work at the Buick complex came to a halt, men were laid off by the thousands, an approximate 4,250 of them, and the surest sign of how deeply Flint was shocked was that it elected a Socialist mayor that year. The revolution was brief and modest. John C. Menton was a respectable cigarmaker, and he was ousted at the polls the next year by Charles Stewart Mott, but few events could have better shown how strongly Flint was now bound to react to any threat to the automobile's future.[50]

The banking community's attitude was unhelpful. It did not necessarily believe the case to be terminal, but it was convinced that the patient would have to learn to live within sensible limits. Bankers did not think that the automobile was a morning glory, but they did underestimate how quickly it would become a mass craze. They believed that, for the average worker, an auto worth a year's wages was too big an item to handle, and they were blind to the ability and willingness of modest-income buyers to make adjustments and sacrifices for the sake of a car. Caught in their elitist view, they assumed that there was only a limited "class" market for autos, and that it would soon reach saturation. Accordingly, they would back only those auto makers who had very limited expectations. What they thought of Durant was that he was a wild man who would destroy everyone's chances by glutting the market.

It was in the face of this coolness that Durant had to play the beggar's role, the more galling because he was convinced that the corner would soon be turned. He had managed to borrow Buick's eight million in dollops of $200,000, $100,000 and even less, spread over a great number of country banks which had once financed his buggy and wagon dealers. He had another seven millions of credit in the form of inventories advanced to him by suppliers against notes of his own and of the Durant-Dort organization. With that much in hand, he was convinced that only a little more "accommodation" would see him through. His bitterness rose to overflowing when some small banks began to call in their loans to him; he was convinced that they had been propagandized to the effect that the auto industry was "unsound," and that a financial conspiracy had stripped Buick of "every dollar of working capital—the life-blood of our institution— which brought about the complete stoppage of our business with a loss to us of more than $60,000 a day."[51]

Still, there was nothing for it but to go to the major investment houses, for by the beginning of May he was in desperate straits. Friends secured him a contact with Kuhn, Loeb and Company, which was a Morgan-like pillar of New York's German-Jewish banking establishment, and he wrote to its head, Otto Kahn, first suggesting that they take "a considerable block of the preferred stock of this company." But that idea never jelled, and in mid-August he wrote again, his words honeyed and humble, his pose as prudent as any loan officer could wish. "I shall be very pleased to take up with you, should you care to do so, any feasible plan which you may have to propose for a secured loan of sufficient size to enable us to develop our business along conservative lines for the next season with safety and profit to all concerned."[52]

In vain. The circle of creditors tightened around him. He had a friend, John H. McClement, a General Motors director, making approaches to Lee, Higginson, in Boston, and in the meantime, as the lengthy summer days of pressure flicked off the calendar, he juggled expedients. He gave consideration to a five-for-one stock split to throw more shares on the market for cash, then decided against it as too slow and too inadequate. He begged his stockholders in a circular letter not to sell; big things, he told them, were in the wind. "This for your protection in order that valuable securities held by you may not be sacrificed at this juncture." From a small stock-selling office on lower Broadway he issued flyers from what was called General Motors Securities Company, calling attention to *Terrific Shrinkage in Industrial Stocks*, and pointing out that while U.S. Steel, International Harvester, General Electric, American Car and Foundry, and other major issues had floundered and dropped 6 to 10 points in June, "during the same period General Motors Common *advanced* 5 points."[53]

And he continued traveling to midwestern centers in search of money, taking Wilfred Leland with him to lend the prestige of Cadillac, General Motors' other major earner, to the quest. One night he met Hardy and Arnold Goss, a Buick executive, in Chicago. They had been to Kansas City and St. Louis looking for a loan and, like their chief, come back empty-handed. The three of them boarded a late train for Flint. Some hours later, there was a halt in the middle of a downpour. Durant looked out the window, streaked with glistening runnels, and at the end of a Stygian vista of deserted street, saw an electric sign proclaiming in fire the holy word, BANK. He shook Goss, who was dozing next to him. "Wake up, Goss," he said. "There's one we missed."[54]

There were flares of hope. A Chicago bank was almost ready to lend $7.5 million, and later $9.5 million, but backed away. Part of General Motors' problem at that point was that it lacked the centralized bookkeeping to know its exact needs. By the time $7.5 millions were offered, the debt appeared to be $9.5 millions. When a loan of that size appeared fleetingly possible, new estimates put the requirement at $12 million.

When the directors met in September, they had reached that terrible moment in the storm when the weak had to be sacrificed in order that the rest might survive. The Michigan Auto Parts Company, the Welch-Detroit Company, and the Marquette Company were all sold at a sacrifice. The two-year process of building began, before Durant's pained eyes, to reverse itself.[55]

Then, finally, rescue came, but at an inordinate price. Long afterward, Wilfred Leland told the story in a way that made him appear to be the last-minute savior. Since he and Durant had parted in bad blood by then, and since no one was alive to question or confirm his account, the truth could never be known. But as he told it, there was a meeting in New York in September, at the offices of the Chase National Bank. On one side of the table sat Durant and his operating company heads, and on the other, a jury of bankers. All afternoon the men with the money listened and interrogated and shook their heads, and finally told Durant to return the next morning.

Leland said that a Chase vice-president plucked his sleeve as the others were leaving, and extended an invitation to a private session that evening at the Belmont. There, the bankers told him that they would finance Cadillac alone if he wished, since it seemed a sound proposition. They saw nothing else to salvage. But then Leland said, in the very words that Durant himself had probably used already, that General Motors as a whole was not really badly off. It had earned nearly $10 million in a single year, Cadillac contributing $2 million all by itself, and "surely fifteen million was not such a great sum to loan to a business earning at that rate." And, Leland's version concluded, at 2:30 A.M.. the stay of execution was granted.

Next morning Durant, who knew nothing of the evening's work, was informed that the New York house of J. and W. Seligman and Boston's Lee, Higginson and Company would organize a $15 million loan for him.[56]

Whether or not Leland's story was correct, those two firms did actually arrange a loan in that amount. The terms were, in Durant's eyes, "outrageous." General Motors issued $15 millions' worth of 6 percent five-year notes, secured by a mortgage on all of its properties and assets, which were valued by bank auditors at $37.7 million, much less than the 1909 year-end statement claimed. The banks took these notes in exchange for $12.75 million in cash. In addition to this $4.25 million commission, they demanded a bonus of an additional $6 million in stock — $2 million in common, and $4,169,200, to be precise, in preferred.

And there was one other consideration. The wild man could no longer run the company. A majority of the outstanding GM stock would have to be deposited in a voting trust for the five-year life of the loan. The shareholders would receive in exchange certificates that were negotiable on the market, but the only voting power would rest with five trustees. Durant was to be one of them, and still a director — they granted him that much. But there were four others: James N. Wallace of Central Trust of New York; Albert Strauss for J. and W. Seligman; James Storrow for Lee, Higginson; and Anthony Brady, now heavily involved in motors. These four, plus several other bank representatives, would have to join the board of directors, and to make way for them a number of Durant supporters would have to retire. Among these were Dr. Campbell, Curtis Hatheway, Wilfred Leland, and two warm personal friends, R. S. McLaughlin, the Canadian maker of Buicks, and John T. Smith, a New York attorney.

It would be a banker-run operation, and General Motors would have to pay more than $8 millions in cash and securities for the privilege of having its founder and director submit his neck to the yoke. Durant writhed at the prospect, but knew that he could no longer wave away his dilemma with a hopeful pronouncement or two. "I was forced to accept," he later wrote, "to save my 'baby,' born and raised by me, the result of hectic years of night-and-day work, diligence and application."[57]

The wounds smarted worst afterward. Within a few weeks of receiving the banks' cash, Buick alone had 14,000 new orders, proving to Durant's satisfaction that nothing was amiss that a few timely infusions of money would not have straightened out. But the new masters of General Motors publicly proclaimed that they were the redeemers of a corporation that was a wreck, a position that naturally justified their generosity to themselves as only a fair reward for acute risks. Lee, Higginson sent out a circular to those customers whom it hoped to interest in buying General Motors' notes (which came with a bonus of two shares of GM common for every $1,000 taken). "This business comes to us in a rather peculiar way," it began, using a first-person-plural voice that sounded more royal than editorial. "At the request of one of our friends who had some Buick Motor Company paper, we started to look into the affairs of the company for him."

The voice went on to say that it had ordered an independent audit and done everything conceivable "to get at the real facts of the case," which, the implication was plain, had been disguised, but which actually showed quite reasonable profit potentials even after setting aside an annual sum to repay the loan. And so Lee, Higginson's utterance swept to majestic conclusion:

The meat of the situation is this. Here is a concern which got into trouble, not from lack of earnings but from lack of management. We now take the business up, put in an able board of directors and an able finance committee and become part of the management during the life of these notes.[58]

A final dash of humiliation was added in November by *Motor World*.

To say that every thinking person identified with the automobile industry is breathing more freely now that the banking interests have stepped in . . . on W. C. Durant, the prime mover and directing genius of the General Motors Co., is but to describe mildly the feeling that exists.

The feeling is . . . that an element of real peril to the entire industry has been circumvented and chastened.

Having a bit and checkrein placed between his teeth must saw sorely on the mouth of Durant himself. . . . He now is in the toils of Wall Street, so to speak, and must do its bidding.

And so he was, after two years of shooting-star progress across the business skies. But he would not be for long.

The Comeback

I Unhorsed, he returned to Flint to touch the soil around his roots again, and warm to the needed sympathy that did not even have to be verbalized. Flint would naturally feel, as he did, that he was the victim, not the creator, of the tempest of 1910. It was inevitable that he should lose little time in planning new beginnings there. Theoretically, he had the choice of accepting things as they were, of playing a gadfly's role as minority voting trustee and director, of simply enjoying whatever dividends the new management might cause to sprout from the considerable block of shares that he held. But the whole force of his character thrust away that choice.

The transition had gone with irritating efficiency. As crisply as they might have counted out new greenbacks, the bankers, headed by James J.

18.
The assembled Chevrolet cast unveils the Six in Detroit, 1912. Cliff Durant at the wheel. W. C. at the front fender. Tall, cap-wearing William Little to his left. Louis Chevrolet in smock, W. W. Murphy peering over his shoulder, A. B. C. Hardy at Murphy's left

19., 20., 21.
OPPOSITE:
(Top) The Chevrolet "Baby Grand," 1913

(Middle) W. W. Murphy driving a "Royal Mail," a 1914 Chevrolet hit

(Bottom) Proud sales manager Richard Grant with the 1915 Chevrolet 490

22.
Boston financier James J. Storrow, who ran GM during Durant's 1910–1915
"exile"

23.
Charles Nash, GM's president under the Storrow regime

24.
Walter Chrysler, third from left,
peering at a "Cyclecar" invented
by Walter Marr, who is at his left.
Charles Nash is the derby wearer.

25.
A confidant Durant, at GM's helm
around 1920

Storrow as interim president, began to lop off excess baggage. Into the darkness of writeoffs went Elmore, Cartercar, Ewing, Rainier, other acquisitions, and thousands of dollars' worth of useless inventory accumulated for them. Every slash drew blood from Durant. The new directors saw themselves as a salvage crew on the deck of a sinking vessel, the water pouring through dozens of leaks that needed mending. The wages of debt were insolvency, and the captain who permitted insolvency deserved disgrace. Durant was cut out altogether of another American business mold. Credit was the lifeblood of growth, which could be fatally stunted by shortsighted usurers frightened at temporary clouds. He did not necessarily know that this conflict between the promoters' and lenders' viewpoints had echoed through generations of American history, but he felt the insult implied in the new watchword, "liquidate and pay." It was as well for him that he never saw a letter that Storrow wrote early in 1911 to a friend of a creditor:

It may have taken some manager somewhere along the line a little time to get into the spirit of the new organization which is to pay bills promptly. . . . I should consider it a favor if he would call the matter to my attention, as we are trying to eradicate totally the old slack habits.[1]

Even without the inward burning of anger, Durant was not a man to sit in board sessions, arguing the merits of new ideas, cultivating support after hours from friends like McClement. "Opportunities that should have been taken care of with quickness and decision [were] not considered," he lamented, and the path of corporate politics led away from swift commitment.[2] He needed to act like lightning, alone. One New York banker saw the central appetite that the new arrangement starved.

Durant is a genius, and therefore not to be dealt with on the same basis as ordinary business men. In many respects he is a child in emotions, in temperament and in mental balance, yet possessed of wonderful energy and ability along certain other well-defined lines. He is sensitive and proud; and successful leadership, I think, really counts more with him than financial success.[3]

It was, however, exactly leadership that the other trustees were determined to keep away from him. They were, in the assessment of his Canadian friend and purged board member "Sam" McLaughlin, "afraid he was too much of a plunger. Mr. Durant was in durance vile; he had nothing to do."[4]

For Durant's active mind that torture could not be brooked. There was only one solution; to leave General Motors to them and begin a new ascension of his own. That course led him not only back to Flint, but to the great, walrus-moustached figure of Louis Chevrolet. "He was planning a comeback," Chevrolet reported afterward, "and told me, 'We're going to need a car.' "[5]

Chevrolet was a curious choice for a designer. The Swiss-born Frenchman was one of three brothers — Gaston and Arthur the other two — all of them enthusiastic track drivers. Louis and Arthur had shown up in Buick's early days to apply for jobs with the speed team, and the story was told that Louis drove faster and less cautiously, so that Durant hired him for race work but kept Arthur as his own chauffeur. Little was known of their personal histories, except that Louis had good mechanical aptitude and had invented a wine pump, which was not the equivalent of actual experience in creating a new passenger car. Nonetheless, when Louis crowded his 210-pound bulk into the driver's seat of "the Bug," a powerful, specially built Buick racer with a ram's head painted on the hood and an engine that poured flame through the exhaust ports and roared like Niagara, he could shatter records. And before and after races in whatever cars he drove, he delighted to tear apart the engines, thrusting knowing hands deep into their slippery, oily guts with a surgeon's pleasure, and reporting what he learned in a manner that impressed the master of Buick. Durant, therefore, sent him off in the middle of 1911 to a small rented loft in Detroit to design a six-cylinder touring auto. Durant, it was understood, would incorporate a company to build what Chevrolet came up with, and Chevrolet would accept his remuneration in 100 shares of its stock.

That was only one step in a more complicated design. It was still important to have a base in Detroit, where the builders, the buyers, the bankrollers, and the connivers of the world of wheels still crowded up to the bar of the Pontchartrain, behind whose green marble three perspiring bartenders worked the lunch hour every day, and where the cloths of the dining room tables were "covered with sketches: crankshafts, chassis, details of motors, wheels, and all sorts of mechanisms."[6] But there were to be two other new firms set up in Flint. One, supervised by William Little, would put out a light, low-priced car bearing his name. The other, under Arthur Mason, father and devotee of the early high-speed engine, would make the power plants for both the Little and Chevrolet products. Durant was especially anxious to get into the inexpensive car market. Of all the new General Motors policies that galled him, one of the worst was that which wiped out the Buick Model 10 and abandoned the under-$1,000 field to Ford.

All three of the new creations — Mason Motor Company, Little Motor

Car Company, and Chevrolet Motor Car Company — were incorporated in a three-month span beginning late that 1911 summer, and at the end of it, on November 28, Flint turned out to honor its leader in what came to be called "the Wizard's Banquet." The Flint *Journal* explained it as a festival of anticipation as well as gratitude. "While he has declined thus far to disclose his plans," it told readers, "they appear to have been so framed as to take particularly good care of his home town." One hundred and fifty people gathered in the Masonic Temple, and then sat, full-bellied after a calorie-unconscious meal in the spacious style of the times, listening to Durant's praises sung by every civic notable. The air was rich and blue with the smoke of free, Flint-made cigars proffered to the male guests, from boxes bearing Durant's portrait and the mock-Cuban label *El Capitan de Industria*. At the end of it all the Man himself gracefully responded with a long tribute to his associates, in which he declared: "Do not think that I have left Flint and am coming back. I never have been away from this city."[7]

But there were more than emotional assets in Flint. Durant could repeat his early Buick sequences there, letting friendship and credit substitute for hard cash. Mason Motors and Chevrolet were capitalized at only $100,000 each initially, and little of that was paid in, perhaps $10,000 for Chevrolet. The Little Motor Company was an even more impressive piece of sleight of hand. Its announced capitalization was $1.2 million. Only $823,200 worth of stock was actually issued, for which a total of $4,827 was deposited in its accounts to start with. In the long run it proved to be virtually a Platonic ideal of a shoestring operation, turning out nearly 3,000 automobiles with only $36,500 of "outside" cash being put in, and all else financed by sales receipts.

The feat was made possible by Flint's other great resource of 1911, the physical properties of the expiring wagon and buggy companies, which were at Durant's disposal. The Flint Wagon Works was ready to cry quits at the end of 1910, and its owners sold to Durant their entire property for $200,000, for which they accepted his personal note. The deal embraced their factory, the remaining inventories of wagons and wagon parts, and the rights, patents, inventories, and orders belonging to the Whiting automobile, a small effort to enter the car-making field, launched the year before and far too late. William A. Paterson tried to make the conversion to the new order of things with a car bearing his name, too, and so did Dallas Dort eventually, and for both of them the hour was long past for any hope of success.

The purchase gave Durant a "free" factory, and he used it in the best possible way by making it a theater for a fresh display of the talents of A. B. C. Hardy. Little was sent to Detroit to help out Chevrolet, and Hardy was given charge of making, from the designs Little left behind, a four-cylinder runabout to sell for $650 to $690, with electric lights and self-starter as optional extras. He was to do this in the former wagon works, likewise to build Mason motors there and fill out all uncompleted orders for the Whiting and for horse-drawn vehicles. The man who had built 52 Flint Roadsters in a slightly enlarged blacksmith's shop was equal to the task. In 1912 he produced 3,000 Littles, enough motors for them and a surplus, as well as "several thousand buggies, many thousand sets of wheels, and a raft of miscellaneous carriage parts and accessories." He neglected to mention any Whitings in his summation, but advised, "We made all of our bodies and most of our sheet metal parts."[8]

The next year Durant-Dort "sold" its founder more work space for $200,000, almost certainly paid in stock. The plant involved was the now-unused Imperial Wheel factory in Flint, an uncanny repetition of the deal nine years earlier that had set Buicks to being assembled in the empty Imperial Wheel buildings in Lansing. The Durant-Dort directors, who had seen their profits drop by over $100,000 in the single year between July of 1910 and 1911, were eager to convert their assets into the stock of Durant's new companies as quickly as they could. All of the surviving investors in wagons and carriages knew that the end had finally arrived, and it was the last moment for redeploying their capital wisely. The timing was perfect for the "wizard's" approach to his old friends.[9]

But whatever public professions he might make, Durant had not personally come back to Flint. He would continue to borrow and enlarge its wealth and to make the town his sentimental and psychological home, but he was moving on an eastward-bound tide, first to Detroit and then New York. On Christmas Day of 1911 Rebecca wrote him a gently reproachful letter:

Wish you were here to enjoy the merry time with us. Great fun in making ready. I can't say which enjoyed it the most, children or the aged! We were up early, breakfast over — a bugal [sic] sound from the third floor gave a signal that lights were turned on — everything ready — Santa had been and gone. Up over the stairs we went, maids and all, laughing and anticipating. The tree was beautiful, and around the room were tables covered high up. Such mysterious looking packages. Such surprises. Even the bird in his gilt cage piped up a sweet song, and with our smiles and tears we were happy, but we missed you so much — so very much. You needed a change, a rest — in a way we are glad you are able to take the time — 'all work and no play' — you know the old saying. . . . Margery just comes with her message. Tell Papa "for twenty-five years past he has been with us at Xmas time" and we have missed him. So do the children. She is happy supporting [sic] a diamond bracelet which she calls "Doctor's extravagance."[10]

He would never live in Flint again. Throughout 1912 he was in Detroit much of the time, where he often stayed in the residence that Margery and Dr. Campbell occupied there, near the factory on West Grand Boulevard where the first Chevrolet was taking shape. The location was convenient for both men, Campbell now being one of Durant's full-time assistants, but with Margery's removal from Flint another personal tie to the city whose growth had paralleled his own was dropped. For Margery, to gravitate toward her father's center of activity was more than the result of Campbell's involvement with him; it was an answer to a command within her. She was herself a mother of two after six years of wifehood. William Campbell had been born in the spring of 1907, and his sister Edwina two and one half years later. But the daughter in Margery was still a powerful challenger to the other roles that life gave her. On her birthday, May 24, 1912, in response to a gift of which no record was saved, she wrote in a flush of emotion:

Dearest Pops:

There are some things which come to us in our lives, even in twenty-five years, that we feel so deeply, we cannot talk of them, and *this* is one of them.

I just can't find words to tell you how much I thank you and how *much* I appreciate your doing such a great *big* wonderful thing for me. You have always been so good to me and mine, and so generous with us, but this is so *much*, Pops. I just can't believe it, but still it is just like you. Surely no one ever had such a father before.

I wish that I might *do* something for you, in return, but I have no opportunity. If one ever comes, I hope I may show in some way how much I appreciate all you have done for me. In the meantime, I shall try all the harder to make myself worthy of such a trust, and to be as unselfish as you. Surely it will be a great pleasure in being able to do for those who are unfortunate.

The day has been so happy, just as my whole life has been, and the dear children had dinner with us tonight. William had a big cake which was a *great* surprise, and we had a beautiful time. I wish you might have been here.

There is one thing, Pops, which is sure, I haven't learned in this twenty-five years how to express my thoughts on paper. Let us hope for better luck in the next twenty-five. However, you *know* that your *little* girl is very grateful in her heart, don't you Pops dear?

With a great deal of love,
Margery

P.S. I am not going to have any more birthdays.[11]

When Durant read the letter it was a reminder of how fast the birthdays passed. His own fiftieth behind him now. And Clifford's twenty-first gone by, too, and he grown and married and with a start in life to make. Durant did not see much of him, but there was a visit in Detroit that year under memorable circumstances. Cliff had finished Pennsylvania Military College and was described by classmates in the yearbook for 1910 as "a musical genius." They had little else to say about him, except that on the line where it was customary to put some uplifting motto or slogan the editor had merely inserted: "Get a Buick." After graduation he had gone out to California to be with his mother, who was living pleasurably on her settlement, and there he had shown an informed taste for fun, drinking, and fast automobiles. Somewhere along the line he met and courted Adelaide Frost of Grand Rapids, and with her as his pretty young bride, he came to Detroit in time to pose in the driver's seat of the first car that Louis Chevrolet produced. Durant and the rest of the staff were in the photograph, too, standing alongside and looking proudly possessive, and the car itself almost seemed to be rather haughty-looking — high, deep-bodied, shiny, and throwing off a sense of the power under its hood and of its high price tag, $2,150. Its very name was a boast: the Classic Six.

And rarely was pretension so quickly deflated. The car was a market disaster. Louis Chevrolet, oddly for a racing man, had produced something ponderous rather than whippet-like, although he might have offered in defense that only a few of his ideas had survived changes ordered by Durant, Little, and others. Whoever was at fault, the Six had only a scattering of sales after its introduction at the 1912 Auto Show. Except for the small amount of profit being earned by the Little, the wizardly conjurations of the preceding year were producing nothing but deficits.

Durant responded with moves that proved that his gambler's nerve had not been destroyed in the cleanout of two years earlier. He announced, with the confidence of a leader who knows how to bring fainthearted followers to their feet yet another time, that he had great new ideas to execute. He would create a new combination to outshine even General Motors. This one would be named Republic Motors. It would be incorporated in Delaware, which had now become the favored home of holding companies, and would be capitalized at $65 million. Its nerve center would be in New York, and from there Durant would orchestrate the work of eleven companies, nationwide, each serving a different regional market, and all of them together eliminating, in one brazen stroke, the entire problem of transportation costs. Durant put it this way to the Flint *Journal*.

The motor car is rapidly nearing perfection. The problem today is not that of production, but of distribution. The enormous waste and extravagance in the marketing of automobiles, if continued, must result in the undoing of the industry. Regardless of high commissions, the majority of dealers are unable to make a profit. Under the plan outlined by us, the cost of distribution is materially reduced, and each district is given the type and style of car best suited to its local requirements. Our trademark will be, "Built on the Spot."[12]

As if putting his master plan into immediate execution, Durant bought a tract of land in Highland Park, a small political enclave entirely surrounded by Detroit, where Henry Ford had recently built the world's largest and most up-to-date factory to manufacture the Model T by the tens of thousands. Durant's purchase was across the road from it, and carried a billboard that could not be missed by any executive, any workman, any supplier or dealer going in and out of the Ford offices. The billboard's message was that a Chevrolet factory was to rise soon on that spot.

Then Durant, who "could not think in small terms," put some of the dwindling money supply of his three companies into the purchase of a plant on the west side of Manhattan, at Twelfth Avenue and Fifty-sixth Street, to assemble Chevrolets. Having just explained to the *Journal* how his new competitor for General Motors was going to cut the waste of shipping cars from region to region, he now committed himself to an operation that required motors and parts made in Flint and Detroit to be sent to New York, united there in autos, and dispatched thousands of miles again to midwestern customers.

But economic feasibility was not his aim at that moment. The new move was what Chevrolet's advertising director called "stagecraft." There, in the heart of the lucrative markets of the mid-Atlantic states, Durant would be proving that his resurgence was no myth by actually making cars. "Grown-up people are very much like children in certain respects," he summed up at another time; "they like to see the wheels go round." At a moment when the business was still youthful and buyers and investors often were won over by taking them to watch the factories at work, he was placing another bet with reasonable odds of success.

The New York plant introduced him to problems unknown in Flint. The district in which it lay was one of the toughest in the city, known as "Murderers' Row." Juvenile toughs harassed workers in storage yards and gateways with barrages of trash. Durant bought them off by finding a portable merry-go-round operator and providing free afternoon rides twice a week. A more serious problem occurred when hoodlums beat up an engineer on the way to his lunch. Durant found out that the local political boss had his "office" in a saloon adjacent to the plant. He sought him out and made it clear that the Chevrolet Motor Company would, with pleasure, buy tickets to barbecues and rallies and make "a few other contributions." Thereafter, in the master persuader's words, "peace reigned."[13]

He had far more serious preoccupations in Flint, for these bluffs would come to nothing without emergency money and a winning product. For the first of these needs, he went once more to Durant-Dort, of which he was still the treasurer. The Chevrolet corporation was recapitalized at $2.5 million, and the Durant-Dort Carriage Company bought half the issue, Dallas Dort becoming a vice-president. Then, most probably to give at least the appearance of spreading the risks around, Durant spun into being another company, Sterling Motors. The incorporators were the familiar cast of himself, Dort, Little, Fred Aldrich, and the New York connection, Curtis Hatheway. And Durant-Dort took $75,000 worth of Sterling securities.

For the auto that would send him high enough to make the bankers crane their necks watching him, Durant could only go on pressing the engineering staff. It was slow, discouraging work. The Classic Six was scrapped. Another experimental model emerged from the Detroit shops, but even as the last parts were bolted in place, they knew it would cost too much to be competitive. Into the discard it went. A third prototype was born in Flint, and ordered by the commander to be racked with grueling road tests. It was "driven to its death in less than 25,000 miles," he remembered. Durant kept his smile, but the pile of chips was getting lower.

And then, in the middle of 1913, there was a major and disheartening shake-up, forever unexplained. What was said between old friends behind closed doors was never revealed by either of them, but "Dallas" and "Billy" parted. Dort resigned all his posts with Chevrolet, and Durant did likewise with those he still held in his first corporate creation. Perhaps Dort finally lost faith. Or perhaps he felt that it was time at last for him to step outside "Billy's" shadow; he did follow the breakup almost immediately with the manufacture of the short-lived Dort automobile. Whatever the reason, the twenty-seven-year partnership was at an end, though it did not carry the personal friendship down with it. They would go on saying kind things about each other, and a family story among Durant's cousins had it that when they met in a downtown Flint office shortly after the separation they hugged, and Dort walked Durant over to a window and pointed down to bustling Saginaw Street and said: "Everyone here owes everything to you, Billy." And Durant answered: "That's not true, Dallas, they owe it all to you."[14]

But all the same, 1913 was half gone, and the new enterprises nearing a second birthday, and the money from the carriage and wagon companies would no longer be coming in, and there was still darkness ahead. Then, in what was not a major loss, but all the same appeared symbolic of things unraveling, Louis Chevrolet quit. In his own recollection, it was because he was a stubborn oak, unwilling to become a corporate reed. Durant, he told someone, had tried to tell him that he should give up cigarettes in favor of cigars, which were more fitting for a corporate official. In an outburst that blended Gallic temper and mechanic's roughneck independence he snapped back: "I sold you my car and I sold you my name, but I'm not going to sell myself to you. I'm going to smoke my cigarettes as much as I want. And I'm getting out."[15]

More than likely the cigarette reprimand, if it took place at all, was a last straw. Chevrolet's car had not worked out. He felt underappreciated if not ignored by the other designers. "You know the jealousy between those engineers some time," Win Murphy commented.[16] And so Louis Chevrolet departed, not too gently, into the peculiar night that enveloped David Buick. Both men would have their names mentioned literally thousands of times a day throughout the United States and parts of the world, but those who spoke the names would rarely have any idea that they once belonged to men.

The year 1913 moved toward its end. There were new moves on the chessboard that were efforts to tighten up, maximize the use of remaining capital, and thrust for a breakthrough in some sales sector. Chevrolet was reorganized, buying a part of Mason Motors and swallowing up Little and Sterling. Talk of Republic Motors was dropped, its purpose served and its moment past. Chevrolet's business headquarters would move to New York. Its Detroit operations would end, and Michigan-made Chevrolets would now come entirely from the Little factory in Flint. The Little itself would cease to exist.

That was happy news for Hardy. He had insisted that a salesman was at a deep psychological disadvantage in selling a car named "little." He was not very pleased with Chevrolet, either—too uncomfortable for American tongues to pronounce correctly. But Durant overrode him. Too much was already invested in publicizing Chevrolet for a change now. And he had come up with a nice little device for the auto's nameplate, two parallelograms, one vertical and one horizontal, intersecting like a bow tie. There was more good news for Hardy, too, in the form of promotion from general manager of the expired Little works to a vice-president of Chevrolet.

Then the best news of all came from the engineering department. They had two cars ready to show as 1914 models, both four-cylinder machines, one a touring car called the Baby Grand, which could be sold at $875, and the other a roadster, the Royal Mail, priced at $750.

The season opened, the year's new automotive creations were displayed. And finally, in the nick, after the three dark and doubtful years since 1910, the wild chances and the improvisations and the bold strokes flung in the teeth of discouragement miraculously justified themselves overnight. The Baby Grand and the Royal Mail were instant successes, their sales zooming almost vertically upward from the moment of their showing. As he had known all along in his heart that he would do, Durant had hit a gusher.

II The delicious truth dawned with 1914 that Chevrolet could sell every Royal Mail and Baby Grand that was delivered by the hard-laboring machinery in Flint. "So great was the demand," a historian of the company was told years later, "that if a shipment was not taken off the railroad track promptly by the consignee, someone else in the community could be depended upon to lift it without delay."[17] Ecstatically, Durant announced a sales goal of 25,000 for that year, whereupon Hardy kindly but firmly, and with utter accuracy, told him that he had no chance of producing more than a fifth that many. But even 5,000 sales were fuel enough for a fresh expansion drive.

From the beached wreckage of United States Motors, Durant bought the old Maxwell-Briscoe factory at Tarrytown that twice before had been just out of reach of his fingertips. It supplemented the Manhattan facility both in volume and as a continuing object lesson to what Hardy called "these Eastern bankers." Here was a second site at their doorstep where, "even if it were only an assembly plant, they would be impressed by seeing the actual automobiles being turned out."[18] Another assembly operation was launched in St. Louis under Russell Gardner, and one in Oakland, California, headed by Norman de Vaux. Both were buggy-making friends of bygone days, and both helped raise local capital to put into their plants, which were regional subsidiaries rather than mere divisions of the parent corporation. Working with De Vaux as a sales executive was Cliff Durant, becoming more fascinated each year with race driving. In 1915 a Chevrolet factory rose in Fort Worth, this one wholly financed by the company's still-recuperating treasury, and in the same year the McLaughlin brothers in Oshawa began to assemble Canadian Chevrolets.

To dispose of the growing stream of Chevrolets, regional sales organizations flowered everywhere that pools of auto buyers' money were waiting to be siphoned — Chicago, Philadelphia, Boston, Atlanta, Kansas City. In the second year of Chevrolet's successful existence, Durant pitted his marketing forces against the challenge of Henry Ford (though the tract of Highland Park land flaunted in Ford's face in 1912 had long since been sold). He announced that Chevrolet's 1915 line would be built around a car called the 490, intended to go head-to-head against the Model T, which had been selling for exactly that number of dollars since the preceding July. It did not come close to doing so, and when it finally came off the line it had to be priced at $550, the price of a Ford a full year earlier. Nevertheless, Durant claimed that over 46,000 orders for it poured in almost immediately, and before 1915 ended, the factories were able to fill 13,605 of them. The 490 insinuated its merits to the purchaser so winningly that Durant was able to tailor a new slogan: "A Little Child Can Sell It."

To a friend Durant happily predicted that total Chevrolet sales of all models would total 60,000 in 1916. For a rare single time, even his optimism fell behind the facts. Americans bought 70,701 that year—each 490 earning the company a profit of $78, each of the others bringing in $112. And when the columns were summed at the end of 1917, Chevrolet's sales force, hailed by Durant as "second to none in the industry," had put on the road 125,882 autos carrying the double parallelogram, most of them 490s, altogether about 14 percent of the total national output for the year.

The dazzling prospects for the industry which had flashed on Durant's inward eye alone in 1909 were in luxuriant fulfillment. He had said then that in ten years there would be an annual output of a million cars. That threshold was actually crossed in 1916, and doubled in 1922. National production increased almost twenty-five-fold in the eight years after General Motors' founding, from 63,500 yearly to 1,525,578.

It was true that Durant could not surpass Ford, whose dominance of the century's second decade was complete. Unheeding of the protests of his stockholders, unyielding to intimations of profit in diversity, Ford continued to plow revenues into cutting the costs of the single model that he produced. In the year ending June 30, 1915, he sold 308,213 "Tin Lizzies." In 1916 he cut his price to $360 and disposed of still more. In 1920, Fords accounted for literally half of the 1.9 million autos sold in the United States.

Yet there was plenty of room left for others, because the automobile had assumed its major role in American life. The assembly lines were developing their full potential for turning out better and cheaper automobiles. A good 1916 model had an array of visible improvements like electric starters and lights, demountable wheel rims to make tire-changing much easier, a manageable gearshifting apparatus, and quite often a closed body. Many or all of these features were on the modestly priced cars, which were now the norm; those costing under $1,400, which had accounted for only one-third of the 1907 market, comprised 90 percent of it in 1916.

Less dramatically evident, but equally critical, was the growth of a supporting texture for the automotive revolution. Under the hood and chassis of every car were dozens and more of mechanical improvements available to all manufacturers through a system of cross-licensing of patents that preceded the development of individual companies' research divisions. The Society of Automotive Engineers, born in 1905, was pressing on with a program of standardization so that ordinary and little-thought-of parts would be interchangeable from car to car and could be purchased anywhere, meaning that one could buy on the road, if necessary, a spark plug, a bolt, a bulb, or a belt that would get an auto safely moving again, or be certain that a purchase of fuel or oil from a strange source would not destroy the engine. The adventure might be going out of motoring, but the driver's seat was open to women and in fact to all those who lacked mechanical aptitude and brute strength.

The Selden patent's invalidation in 1911 had ended the life of the A.L.A.M., but it was reborn two years later as the National Automobile Chamber of Commerce. Together with the eleven-year-old American Automobile Association, it lobbied effectively for enlarged programs of state and federal highway building and improvement. The whole network taken for granted by later generations was woven in these years—the highways, the fuel and service stations, the mechanisms of registration, insurance, and policing—all simply enlarged upon and refined in the following half-century. "Humanity had never wanted any machine as much as it wanted this one,"[19] said Alfred Sloan, and the field was now clear for the manufacturers to satisfy superabundantly the appetite of at least that part of humanity maturing in the United States at the time of the first World War.

Such was the world in which the young Chevrolet Company and the young General Motors Company prospered. Durant, adventurer though he was, for the moment had his feet more solidly planted in the economic and social truth of his times than his conservative detractors did. Dreaming of mythical kingdoms, he had made an actual landfall on a business continent as fertile as any starving explorer ever fantasized.

Even as he emerged from the pioneer years, however, Durant clung to a private self-portrait in which he was a hometown boy, operating a local enterprise. Informality was a strong element in his personal charm. In the midst of the most frenzied schedule he would evoke a cracker-barrel atmosphere by pulling from his desk a small, miniature checker set and challenging whoever was with him to a game. He played devotedly and victoriously with salesmen, plant executives, or a handyman or elevator operator summoned for the purpose if no one else was on hand. "The minute you met him you were friends,"[20] said Murphy, and Murphy himself or other old intimates could often have his attention while callers of greater wealth and consequence sat waiting in anterooms.

If he thought of the Chevrolet undertaking as simply another Flint business at root, Durant had cause to do so as late as the end of 1915. The stockholders' list began with all the recurrent names—Begole, Ballenger, Bishop, Fox, Hardy, Hatheway, Little, and Mott, to say nothing of Crapo relatives and Durant-Dort worthies. And those who had actually put the company together had a special intimacy rooted in shared memories of early struggles, particularly those of cash-poor 1913. Working in the New York office around that time was the teenaged son of a Pottsville, Pennsylvania, Buick dealer; his name was John Bergen, and Durant had given him a summer job. Sixty years afterward, Bergen claimed to remember carrying suitcases full of stock certificates to the nearby Gotham National Bank to use as collateral for small loans to pay the help. When it came to buying parts that year, Chevrolet often submitted orders through the Little Company, which was at least selling cars and had a credit standing.[21]

There was a sense of family about the whole operation, a lingering echo of the days when the directors set aside money for baseball admissions for employees whom they knew by first name. Arthur Mason's case exemplified the feeling. Mason Motors was only partly bought out by Chevrolet in 1913 because it was assumed that Chevrolet would need only part of its output, and Arthur Mason could be left free to market the rest independently. But by the spring of the next year, Mason was behind schedule, short of cash, and bowed under personal debts. Durant and Arthur Bishop had a lengthy correspondence about him. At first Durant was demanding. The company was at last ready for "motors in quantity," and Mason should, with Bishop's help if need be, pay off his obligations and accelerate his efforts or else be dropped. Bishop temporized, trying to soften the importance of Mason's "'inclinations' that would not go to strengthen the credit of the company," and Durant snapped back that it was vital for everyone to "get squarely into harness before starting in on the 1915 situation." Then the picture was changed. In October, Mason came to New York to help work on the 490, and Arthur Mason down in a shop a few blocks away was a person and not a problem. By December, the old, neighborly "Billy" Durant was writing to Bishop that he was pleased with Mason's "good ideas regarding axles, transmissions and spring suspensions, as well as motors." The upshot was that Durant suggested to Bishop, his fellow controlling stockholder in Mason Motors, that Chevrolet buy the remainder of the concern for stock, and put Mason himself on "a salary of $7500 which would enable him to live reasonably well, also take care of the interest on his personal indebtedness. Mason would be entitled to and [they] would expect to give him in addition a block of stock in the Chevrolet Motor Company to compensate him for what he [had] done in the past." Now it was Bishop's turn to grumble that Mason ought to "stick to his original and sole proposition," but Durant had his way finally, and the two old friends had settled the problem of a third.[22]

The same year, Bill Little came to Durant and revealed that he had somehow or other found time to get himself $35,000 into debt, and wondered if his chief could endorse his note. Durant reported this to Bishop, vowing that "endorsing notes years ago was [his] middle name, and got [him] into difficulties. . . . Nothing doing!" But, he added, Bishop was a banker, and Little was no deadbeat. "I do not think you would be taking any risk in advancing the additional $5000 or even $10,000 to tide him over."[23]

A family proposition, Chevrolet was — close and quarrelsome, affirming restraint and support in the same hug. Even the dealers were considered to be embraced within it. Late one year, Durant wrote to Bishop that he was concerned over a yearly winter problem that his distributors faced. They could get no loans from cautious bankers to build up an inventory of cars during the slow, snowy months — "a great hardship is imposed at the most trying season of the year," Durant said, since layoffs and slowdowns in the entire flow from factory to showrooms were the result of the slackening. He proposed to change the cash basis of the business, and run off a small number of autos to be sold in the winter for dealers' notes due on March 1, with a sixty-day renewal option. In turn, he wanted the parts makers — Mason Motors included — to take the Chevrolet Company's notes on the same basis. Naturally there was a risk of loss if spring sales were poor, but Durant added that the plan would be offered only to "dealers of the preferred class (past record and honesty being the standard)" and got directly to the root of the matter.

Under this arrangement, the greater part of the load will be carried by us in any event, but we feel that we would be justified in making this arrangement, which really means financing our good dealers who cannot get from their banks at this time all of the accommodations that they are entitled to.

"Our dealers," the small businessmen of a hundred Main Streets, were as "entitled" to a helping hand as Mason or Little when times were a little hard.[24]

A family proposition for some subsidiaries, too. Chevrolet of Canada grew out of a lunch-table conversation with Sam McLaughlin, who liked to drop in on Durant when he visited New York. On a rainy autumn Saturday of 1915 he and Durant and Dr. Campbell sat eating at Pabst's Restaurant on Columbus Circle with another General Motors stockholder, Nathan Hofheimer, a warmhearted immigrant success, who had made money in distilling and then in electric illumination, and poured a good share of it into the motor holding company. Durant asked after Sam's brother and partner George, and then came to mention that he was searching for a Canadian Chevrolet assembler. Hofheimer spoke up in his heavy accent. "Vy don't you giff that to the boys?"

McLaughlin and Durant looked at each other. They both knew the reason the proposition had not been made before. The McLaughlins were not only making Buicks for General Motors, but still carrying on the carriage business founded by their father, and in the same facility. It was understood that they had no space for additional commitments. Yet now Durant felt obliged to follow up Hofheimer by asking: "Sam, do you want it?"

Sam wanted it very much, and further table talk suggested a solution. If he and George could talk "the Governor" into ending the carriage operations, there would be space available. Before the day was out, tentative contract terms were set. Before another night fell, George was down from Oshawa to go over them and agree. On the day after that, Sam sat down nervously with his father, trying to find words to tell an old man that his life's work was obsolete. It turned out to be unbelievably simple. "Sam, I am about through," was the response to his opening probe. "Do what you please." Ten minutes later, R. S. McLaughlin was on the telephone selling out to a competitor. Four weeks later the last carriage materials were cleared away. Inside two months, the first Canadian-made Chevrolet was ready for showing.[25]

A family proposition, almost every day with its awakening of common experiences, its communications whose unvoiced overtones were richer than words. Alex Hardy in and out of the office from Flint, talking to Durant as he had been doing for eighteen years. "They were chums," said Murphy. "They understood each other; they talked the same language."[26] Hardy and Durant going to engineering conferences with Mason and Little and Alfred Sturt, designer of the 490, another old Flint boy, son of a wagon maker, mechanical prodigy, installer of the first home telephone in Flint, autotrained on the Buick and the Paterson. Mason and Little and Sturt arguing shop problems when there were kinks, and voices rising, and Durant finally bringing calm with: "All right, all right, it's a bad situation—we all know that—but what are we going to do about it?" And then things being done about it. The word getting back to Charley Wetherald, a Buick veteran and an incorporator of Mason Motors, that the tight-fitting pistons of a new engine generated more power, but seized up when hot. And Charley Wetherald hand-filing slightly elliptical pistons that solved the matter, and his pal Bill Notman developing a special cam for the grinder, which mechanized the process and became standard.

"We didn't even take the trouble to find out if we could apply for a patent," Wetherald told a questioner when it was all behind them. "That's how we used to do things in the old days." Talk it over, work it out, move on to the next knot, the next day, the next scrap, the next joke, the next drink.[27]

And yet, for all of that, there was an increasing discordancy with fact in

Durant's cherished belief that he was simply reenacting, a third time, a folksy saga of local achievement. As Chevrolet and the automotive culture blossomed together, Durant was being drawn into a new universe of power, a world of multiple millions and those who used them. His involvement was not innocent. He actively pursued ambitions for Chevrolet that far outran mere success, and as the profits piled up he began to incubate expensive intentions of restoring his rights in General Motors. He made his moves consciously. His only innocence was of the ultimate consequences of his new direction.

Inevitably, now, he was becoming a New Yorker. So were they all. The location of Chevrolet's headquarters there demanded a constant management presence, and by 1914, Durant had settled there to live, with his personal entourage coming to rest around him. Win Murphy took an apartment in the city, and two years later a bride, and settled into the pattern of commuting from uptown to the Chevrolet offices on Fifty-seventh Street. Margery, too, came to New York, and settled in 635 Park Avenue, at Sixty-sixth Street, "to be near my father who lived a little further up the avenue," as she put it. Hardy also rented living quarters in New York in 1915, though he still spent one-third of his time in Flint. But the surest sign of Durant's new rootage—though he continued to be on the road extensively—was that in 1916 he took an apartment at 565 Park Avenue, where Rebecca lived with a maid much of the time, with intervals in Flint and Pentwater. With Catherine at his side, Margery to call him daily, and the chance to drop in frequently for lunch with his mother, he had finally rebuilt the domestic life that had vanished a long time before in another city.

The time now came as well for fresh approaches to the New York financial world. His experience with it had never been encouraging, but his need was great. Chevrolet's explosive takeoff was going to require money for expansion more quickly and on a larger scale than even the utmost good will of Arthur Bishop, the deepest trust of all Flint could furnish. Durant discussed his problem with associates including Nathan Hofheimer, and Hofheimer made an introduction of far-reaching reverberations when he presented his friend, William C. Durant, to his friend, Louis Graveret Kaufman, president of the Chatham and Phenix National Bank.

Kaufman was young for his position, influential, self-made, self-willed, and proud. He was forty-two and hailed from the iron-mining town of Marquette in Michigan's upper peninsula. As a boy he had gone straight from high school to a job shoveling ore, and within a short time had risen to the superintendency of a mine. Then he left manual labor for a post with the Marquette County Savings Bank, in which his father held an interest. At thirty-five, he was its president. He descended on New York to take over the Chatham National Bank, merged it with the Phenix National, and developed the then-novel concept of opening branches within the same city as the main office. As 1915 approached, deposits were near $300 million. He boasted of the fact that he had gotten special governmental permission to keep the headships both of Chatham and Phenix and Marquette National; he liked to talk of his million-dollar collection of rare gold coins; he let it be known that one of his directors was the brother of Mrs. Woodrow Wilson.

Durant won Kaufman's admiration by his nerve and directness in a scene reminiscent of his meeting with George W. Perkins. Hofheimer led him into the velvet surroundings of Kaufman's suite in the Ritz-Carlton, where an elegant lunch was served, its purpose to impress as much as to nourish. It was early in 1914, the full potentiality of the Chevrolet was still to be revealed, Durant's corporate pockets were as yet empty. Yet when Kaufman finally got around to asking how much he thought he would need, his answer was unhesitating.

"Eventually, we can use many times the capital and surplus of your bank. But for the present, five million will do."[28]

It was precisely the kind of statement to please a man like Kaufman, who said he thought he could work something out with his friends at the brokerage house of Hornblower and Weeks. Within a short time, they underwrote an issue of 50,000 shares of Chevrolet common stock with a par value of $100. Their help came dear; they took the shares at 55, but it was as much as could be hoped for then, and the $2.75 million poured into Durant's outstretched hands bought the Tarrytown plant and guaranteed a start on others. Gratefully, he deepened his friendship with Kaufman, and there were mutual favors and gracious notes, and, when it was learned that Durant and Mrs. Kaufman shared the same birthday, an annual exchange of flowers on December 8.

In the summer of 1915, Durant went to Kaufman for help again. This time his plan was to merge the three operating Chevrolet companies — one in Michigan, one in New York, and Mason Motors — into one, capitalized at $12.5 million. They signed an agreement under which the new consolidation would issue $5 million in preferred and $7.5 million in common stock. Kaufman would handle the sale of $4.75 millions' worth of the preferred, and would himself take $1.9 million of the common, plus a commission of $475,000 in cash. The remainder of the stock would go to the owners of the constituent companies in exchange for their original shares. The date of execution of the contract was to be in September.

That month held profound meaning for Durant. It would mark the seventh anniversary of General Motors' founding, the end of the five-year voting trusteeship, and the time for an election of new directors, with all shareholders once more enfranchised. Since Kaufman was now not merely a friend but on the way to becoming an important partner in Chevrolet, Durant felt ready to share with him his plan for an appropriate celebration. He was going to try to take back control of General Motors by purchases of his own and by lining up enough friendly proxies to win a majority on the new board.

Kaufman's reaction was supportive. He would try to win allies, he promised, among General Motors stockholders and potential holders who did business with his bank. He had a special candidate in mind, one of his directors whom he knew to have some GM stock in his personal portfolio. The man he was thinking of was Pierre S. du Pont. Ten years later, Kaufman would crow to a financial journalist: "I got the du Ponts in."[29]

Pierre du Pont would not have corroborated that claim. As he recollected it, his first dip into the ownership of General Motors securities came at the suggestion of John J. Raskob, his chief financial assistant in E. I. du Pont de Nemours and Company, the country's best-known manufacturer of explosives. Raskob was an enthusiastic investor on his personal account, with a special taste for industrial stocks and a sharp eye for technological progress. In 1914 Raskob knew that the automobile was neither a fad nor a luxury, but both the symbol and substance of an entire new way of life. He bought 500 shares of General Motors at 70, and then talked his employer into a 2,000-share purchase. Du Pont expressed some concern about the low price, but Raskob, a careful reader of annual reports, understood what was going on. The bankers who ran the voting trust were plowing every cent of profit into debt retirement and reserve-building. They had yet to pay a dividend on the common stock, which temporarily depressed its marketability. But when the retrenchment period ended, there would be a marked change, he insisted.

Pierre's brother Irénée, too, bought 400 shares as a private flyer, independently of (in fact, in ignorance of) Pierre's purchase, and at the same persuasive instigation. "It was a minor investment in a company that I knew comparatively little about," he afterward asserted, "but it had been talked up a great deal by John Raskob and I had certainly enough faith in him to take a fling. . . . He just simply was such a bull on the future of the motor industry that I thought it was worth buying."[30] Both brothers insisted that, busy as they were with their own company's war work, they had no interest in helping anyone to the ownership of a controlling interest in General Motors, least of all themselves.

However that might be, Pierre du Pont was destined to play a key role in the events of the autumn of 1915, one that stamped them with a meaning that Durant missed. When he dreamed of reconquest, he thought of a return to the old ways, himself unquestioned at the controls, secure in the loyalties of those who believed in him. But men who dealt on the scale of Kaufman and the du Ponts saw any help they might render Durant as primarily a way to assist in the achievement of long-range objectives of value to them. Whatever they felt personally about Durant, reinstalling him in power was to them an avenue, not a destination.

What was more, Durant was thinking of a reunion with his "baby," but he was a preoccupied parent who did not know how much the child had grown in his absence. The loosely knit 1910 patchwork of companies gathered in haste had been evolving, while he was immersed in Chevrolet's affairs, into something more complex, more contemporary, and much less in harmony with his methods.

III The responsibility for initiating the modernization of General Motors belonged to James Jackson Storrow. His part was forgotten because he held the title of president only briefly, and he was so identified with the fiscal conservatism of the banker regime that his image came down through the years as a penny pincher, sired by thrift and nursed by denial. He was much more than that.

Storrow was as Bostonian as the Common, the State House, the Old North Church. He was born in 1864. His mother's ancestors included Oliver H. Perry, one of the naval heroes of the War of 1812. His grandfather on his father's side, a civil engineer, had taken to wife Lydia Jackson, whose family was the very marrow of the Bostonian mercantile and manufacturing aristocracy. From his first outcry, Storrow was ticketed for Signor Papanti's Dancing School, Harvard, a profession, a home on Beacon Hill. And he was faithful to his genes and his cultivation. At twenty-one he had completed a career at Cambridge which lacked academic distinction, but he had been in the correct clubs and he had captained the varsity crew as a senior.

He chose as a career the law, the calling of his father, who had won a major patent case for Alexander Graham Bell. At the Harvard Law School he lived like the young Yankee milord that he was, sharing a house with a small group of fellow students comfortable in their money and position. They were all waited on by a Scottish couple, and they did not hesitate to invite to dinner family friends like Professor Charles Eliot Norton, or the chief justice of the Commonwealth, Oliver Wendell Holmes. On weekends and vacations, Storrow liked to get away for solitary rural tramps, climbs, and canoe rides, dressed in cap, tweed knickers, and stout shoes. There was no distinction in his classroom work, but a knack for leadership was emerging. Assigned to coach the undergraduates in the crew, he recruited, on his own, an expert who trained the eight in a new stroke that brought them to the most important finish line of the year, twenty-five cheering lengths ahead of Yale.

On graduation he clerked for Storey, Thorndike and Hoar, then joined the paternal firm, Fish, Richardson and Storrow. He passed all the expected milestones — marriage, a child, the acquisition of a winter house on Beacon Hill and a country place in Lincoln. The partners assigned to him much of the work with the investment house of Lee, Higginson and Company, a leading client. Frederick Fish told Henry Lee Higginson that Storrow would become Higginson's successor as the first citizen of Boston. After watching the young man for a time, Higginson agreed. In 1900 he invited Storrow in as a partner, and watched approvingly as his new associate climbed the toilsome slopes of civic leadership.

Forward-looking minds in the young century warmed to an array of new ideas that formed a design broadly called Progressivism. One part of Progressivism's pattern was loosely socialistic and talked of restoring government to the people, humanizing the conditions of work, liberating the oppressed, curbing the arrogance of wealth. It was not generally well regarded on Beacon Hill. But another aspect of Progressive belief was that there was virtue in efficiency. It called on voters to modernize, reorganize, purify, and enlarge the tasks of the rusty, patronage-befouled machinery of urban management. That appeal enlisted even "conservative" bankers like Storrow. Between 1900 and 1912 he led a campaign to turn polluted stretches of the Charles River, full of tides, traditions and sewage, into the tamed and healthful Charles River Basin. He served on Boston's school committee, and was "stroke oar" in a crusade to upgrade professional educational standards. He became president of the City Club and the Chamber of Commerce. In 1910 the nonpartisan Citizens' Municipal League nominated him for mayor. His opponent was a popular Irish politician, "Honey Fitz" Fitzgerald. Storrow lost by just 1,402 votes out of 95,193.

At Lee, Higginson, too, he opened windows, let breezes blow Boston dust out of the pigeonholes. When he entered the firm it was fifty-two years old, and its oldest member, George Cabot Lee, had begun work there the year after Daniel Webster's death. The next senior member, Higginson, was still called "the Colonel," in deference to his service in the Civil War. The partners had made money primarily in securities of western railroads and copper mines, basic Boston investments in the nineteenth century. They had just begun to shift some funds into electrical and communications equipment. Storrow urged and got even larger purchases of municipal and industrial securities; pushed for the opening of branch offices in New York, Chicago and London; created a statistical department and another that specialized in foreign exchange. Under his prodding, the house geared its plans to the scientifically studied functioning of the contemporary world economy.

This was the man who took over General Motors' undisciplined regiments late in 1910. He threw himself into learning the new job with customary energy. For two years, he boarded a train to Detroit almost every Monday afternoon, and returned to New York or Boston only late in the week, in time to struggle to catch up with the rest of his work. He frequented the plants as well as the offices, firing question after question at the production men. Once he made them take a Buick apart and lay out every one of its components on sheets spread over the floor, so that he had a clear mental picture of what it actually took to put an automobile on the road. He was not merely looking for knowledge that would let him evaluate cost sheets with intelligence. He wanted to start organized research programs to replace the rule-of-thumb methods carried over from the industry's fumbling infancy. Invited to a dinner of the Harvard Engineering Society, he had to decline, but answered eagerly:

You might tell the men at the dinner, if it is sufficiently informal, that in the reorganization of the General Motors Company I am looking for anywhere from two to six sound, level-headed mechanical engineers. The output of the company last year was $58,000,000, and this was almost entirely accomplished without the advice and assistance of technically trained mechanical engineers. We also need a few managers and superintendents of factories. If some of the Harvard engineers have developed along administrative lines, you can say privately to some of the chaps at this dinner . . . that if they know of the right men for any of these positions we are in sore need of them. . . . We have just voted to expend a large annual sum on an engineering laboratory for making mechanical, electrical and other tests which we hope will prevent most of the defects which have developed in the production of automobiles, and at any rate cause these defects to appear in the laboratory tests rather than to first be discovered in the factory, or, worse yet, in the field.[31]

Storrow also nursed a strong suspicion of one-man rule. His distrust rose from the same impulse that led to battles against "the boss" in City Hall. He became a forceful spokesman for administrative decentralization. As he once told a group in an exposition of his management philosophy, "I have always tried to work out a division of responsibility from the top to the bottom." As the head of a large organization, he was responsible for overall profits. But his first step was, he said, "to get some men under me who are responsible for the profit and loss of the different departments or units. If I can get into these men a lively sense and keen interest in the game, there is nothing for me to do at the top."[32] In practice, that meant giving a long leash to the heads of operating companies. Storrow let them keep independent bank balances to register their scores, and on at least one occasion when the central office needed money badly, he reported, "We went out and borrowed several million dollars rather than interfere with the pride and joy of some of our managers in the balances that they had succeeded in building up for their companies." But the expectation in return was for teamwork above all. His managers were not to compete with other General Motors divisions, and to share information and resources fully. Each year he had a statement read to them like a proclamation to the troops; it ended: "We are of the opinion that there is no permanent place or advancement in this organization for the man who is not imbued with the spirit of helpful cooperation."[33]

Storrow was in luck in finding, within a year and a half, two men who could carry out his conceptions with dedication and brilliance. Each was a self-educated individualist, but each was able to make the jump to organization man and earn a fortune in doing so. The gods of Beacon Hill smiled on Storrow when they offered him Charles Nash and Walter Chrysler.

Nash had been superintendent of Durant-Dort operations during the early years of General Motors, but was anxious to move into the vacuum of leadership at Buick caused by Durant's absorption in the holding company's affairs. At the time of the bankers' assumption of power, "Billy" obliged him by submitting his name to Storrow for the post. The problematical mating between the Harvard lawyer and the bound boy from Illinois turned out to be a match that delighted both parties. They met on the common ground of their abhorrence of waste, their diligence, their orderliness. The economizing talents that had lifted Nash from the bottom were soon at work, slashing inventories, squeezing extra productivity out of the facilities, and compressing costs. Storrow relished the spectacle of Nash at the head of columns of black-ink figures marching up out of Buick's valley of debt. He liked the man personally, too, and it is likely that the friendship was deepened on hiking and sporting weekends at Lincoln, where Storrow would bring executives to size them up outside their offices. Nash, on his side, penetrated Storrow's New England reserve to find

an extraordinary man. I doubt if a man ever lived who had a warmer, bigger heart than Mr. Storrow, and who, on the other hand, was so unable to show it in his daily contact with men. A great many men felt that Mr. Storrow was of the "banker" type—rather cold-blooded—which was entirely contrary to his real makeup.

He was the largest man that I have ever met. . . . If he found he was wrong in his diagnosis of any problem, he did not hesitate to immediately acknowledge that he was wrong and place the credit where it belonged — to the man that was right.[34]

In mid-1912 Storrow nominated Nash to become the president of General Motors. "I picked him to be head," he summarized later, taking another backhanded swipe at Durant as he went on. "In five years he turned a wreck into a concern having $25,000,000 in the bank."[35] At last, Storrow could go back to spending his whole week in Boston. As he wished, there was nothing for him, at the summit, to do.

When Nash assumed Buick's presidency, he found himself so swamped with budgetary and administrative details that he needed another man exclusively to supervise the mechanical operations. Storrow had a candidate in mind. As a director of the American Locomotive Company he had heard how a new superintendent at its Allegheny plant, a troubled and deficit-ridden operation, had turned it into a moneymaker in remarkably short order. Storrow had not met the man, but he put through a call to Pittsburgh and left a message requesting that Mr. Walter Chrysler call on him at his earliest convenience at Lee, Higginson's New York offices. The next day he found himself confronting a sturdy individual with wide cheekbones, receding hair, a blunt way of talking, and an air that suggested a slight eagerness to get back to the shops which had been the theaters of his life for most of his thirty-six years.

Chrysler had seen, at first hand, the old, physical frontier close and the new industrial one open. He was born in 1875 in Ellis, Kansas, on the Union Pacific line, for which his father was an engineer. It was a hardworking place, still crouched in the shadow of danger and want. Fear of Indian raids was real. On an occasional Saturday night, liquored-up cowboys would spray bullets at storefronts. Ellis stretched aspiringly toward civilization however, and herded its girls and protesting boys into a rudimentary but demanding school system. After hours and after chores at home, Walter peddled milk and calling cards for pocket money, held his own in the obligatory fistfights, and poked around the town, especially the rail yards, where he could gape at the great fiery engines that his father, enthroned in the cab, forced to obey with a gloved hand on the throttle.

He could hardly wait to finish high school and go to work for the line as a janitor earning a dollar per ten-hour day. That job was simply a way station, putting him first in line for an opening that let him become a machine-shop apprentice at five cents an hour. The slash in pay meant nothing to him. He wanted to become intimate with the powerful creatures that were fed and doctored and honored in the shops. He learned, with a lover's importunate disregard of hours, everything that he could possibly learn in his apprenticeship, starting with the root proposition that when a machinist needed a tool, he made it himself, by hand. Even his passion left some time for other things, however — to play tuba in the town band and second base for the town team, to walk Della Forker to Big Creek Bridge on Sundays, to acquire the forbidden manly skills of smoking, beer-drinking, and card-playing from the older apprentices.

His training done, he was ready to wander for a while. Pride and high temper already were personal earmarks. His first foray into the world took him to the Santa Fe shops at Wellington, Kansas. He told the hiring boss there that, although he was a beginner, he expected the top rate of pay. He would work for two weeks to show what he could do, and then be raised to the limit or quit. "You're a cheeky young fellow," the man told him. "No," said Chrysler. "I'm just a good mechanic."[36]

He drifted through his journeyman years along the lines that webbed the mountain West, riding the boxcars from job to job in Pocatello, Cheyenne, Laramie, Salt Lake City. At twenty-six he put it all behind him. Ellis had imparted the basic lesson: fun was fun, but a true man was ambitious to settle down and make his mark. He came back and claimed Della. After the wedding they went to Salt Lake City, three dollars a day to live on, the hard work of raising two small children for her, and for him the job all day and correspondence courses in electrical engineering at night, when bones ached and eyes smarted, but the dream of success was an unwavering light to follow. Slowly he went up the ladder to roundhouse foreman, shop superintendent, and division master mechanic, living in three of the towns strung like beads on the tracks that ran from metropolis to metropolis through stretches of nowhere — Trinidad, Colorado; Childress, Texas; and Oelwein, Iowa.

It was while at Oelwein, in 1908, that he met the auto. He was a master mechanic with a $350 monthly salary, $700 in the bank, a frame house with a porch and garden. He went to Chicago on business, and dropped in at an auto show, and there saw a Locomobile touring car that was ivory white with red cushions and trim, a khaki top, and a toolbox and tank of gas for the headlamps on the running board. And he went mad.

The car cost $5,000. He spent four days hanging around and mooning over it, aching at the thought of his mere $700 in savings. At the end of the four days he found a bank that would take his note, with a cosigner, for $4,300, paid his money, and had the car shipped to Oelwein. He had never driven and did not know how. "I did not simply want a car to ride in," was his explanation. "I wanted the machine so I could learn all about it. Why not? I was a machinist, and these self-propelled vehicles were by all odds the most astonishing machines that had ever been offered to man."[37] His imagination could not have escaped the lure of those early autos for long.

They were so triumphantly mechanical. Their smells and noises were not yet disguised, as if they were infants or elderly relatives whose mortal failings were an embarrassment. They shuddered, belched, sweated oil, and carried their spare parts in shameless exposure. But they also advertised what made them so fascinating to so many people of Chrysler's generation — their cunning adaptation of part to purpose, their preciseness, their power, their immunity to fatigue and confusion and emotional, unreasonable judgments about whom they served.

For three months he worked over that car in his spare time, going from astonishment to exploration to mastery. He took it apart as an anatomist does a cadaver, repeatedly laying out the secret kernels of its life. Piston, connecting rod, valve-stem, valve-lifter, tappet, spring. Point, plug, coil. Gear, crank, fitting, and knuckle. Gasket and pedal, cam and belt, drum and blade and housing. Until he knew each one and could, if asked, reproduce each one, and improve each one, and calculate to the decimal the probable cost of each one or ten thousand duplications of each one. Only then did he get behind the wheel for his first drive, a wild career through garden and ditch and over boulder, ending in a near-collision with a cow.

Though he might not have realized it, that day sealed his departure from railroading, though not for a while. Soon after buying the Locomobile he quit the Chicago and Great Western in a row with his boss, and went from there to the American Locomotive Company's job in Pittsburgh. He was a maker, finally, not a repairman, and he exulted in it. "There is in manufacturing a creative joy that only poets are supposed to know," he was to say later. "Some day I'd like to show a poet how it feels to design and build a railroad locomotive."[38]

All the same, the automobile was the future, and when Storrow outlined what he had in mind, Chrysler's interest was immediate. Storrow arranged for him to meet Nash in Pittsburgh. The two men liked each other from the moment that they lit their first cigars. Chrysler was invited to Flint, prowled the works, and returned to Nash's office with his mind made up. "I'd like to come here," he said. "I'm anxious to get into this business and with this company."

Nash asked him what salary he was getting. "Twelve thousand a year," was the answer. Nash, shaken, stared off into vacancy, then turned back to Chrysler. "In this business," he announced, "we don't pay such salaries."

"Mr. Nash, what will you pay?"

"Mr. Chrysler, we can't afford to pay over six thousand."

"I accept it, Mr. Nash."[39]

Shortly thereafter, Chrysler walked into the Buick plant, beckoned a foreman over to him, and asked: "Where's the piecework schedule?" No one knew what he meant. There were conferences, scurryings, and finally someone proffered a sheet of paper with scribbled figures on it. Chrysler crumpled it up, called the men together, and explained that at the locomotive works he had just left, when they bid on a job they had to know to the penny what it cost to drill a hole or make a casting, even the tiniest; that they then had to schedule hundreds of operations with a slide rule so that those costs could be maintained, if not reduced.

Step by step, he began to institute that kind of rationality at Buick. "Every minute," he said, "we were figuring out further ways to adapt carriage-craft operations to automobile building." They cut out a third coat of paint on the chassis and dried the two coats faster by raising the drying-oven temperature, and so saved half the time needed to get the chassis ready. They retrussed the factory roof to get posts out of the men's way. They began to prepaint some of the parts, move the gradually growing unfinished car more rapidly along its tracks, swing more components into place from overhead conveyors. Like all the successful car makers, they were increasing the tempo of the dance of men and machines. "Starting with the assembly line, we worked backward through the plant until everything was tied in. Every new thing was an invention. We were making the first machine of considerable size in the history of the world for which every human being was a potential customer."

Durant would have understood that Promethean pride. His joy in selling objects equaled Chrysler's in making them. His trouble was in accepting the hobbles that a disciplined approach to mass production placed on his instant inspirations. Storrow and Nash, however, knew and appreciated what Chrysler was doing, and he forced them to prove it. When Nash became General Motors' president, Chrysler inherited the presidency of Buick. He walked into Nash's simply furnished office, rested his hands on a flat-topped table, and said: "Charley, I want twenty-five thousand dollars." Nash screamed, argued, pleaded. He could not break the cheeseparing habits of a lifetime, no matter how strong was his sense of Chrysler's value. But Storrow had no such problem. Called in on the matter, he patted his new head of Buick as if he were an overexcited horse. "You're going to get your twenty-five thousand dollars," he told him. "Thank you," was the answer. "And by the way, next year I want fifty thousand." Chrysler went home from that meeting and began to enjoy his raise. He was forty. His second apprenticeship was over.[40]

Storrow, Nash, and Chrysler perceived, each in his own way, that the instrument of mass production on the gargantuan scale that the auto makers believed their machine merited was a new kind of business organization, the supercorporation. It would operate on the basis of experiment, analysis and constant supervised readjustment, a "giant enterprise" too large for anything but committee management, with responsibility at the apex. The General Motors they saw might have been born thanks to Durant's genius and adventurousness, but it could live only through treading the pathways measured out by accountancy and engineering.

These visions were neither completely formed nor fulfilled before 1915. Other hands than theirs would finish the work. But the bankers' administration, overall, showed signs of the ultimate transformation. They did not confine themselves to dismemberment. They increased their shares of control of Weston-Mott, A.C., General Motors of Canada and Brown-Lipe-Chapin, their gear-train supplier. They consolidated some of the pre-1910 acquisitions into the General Motors Truck Company, and saw it prosper. The groundwork was laid for the administrative transformation of 1916, in which General Motors was turned from a holding into an operating company, with the subsidiaries becoming divisions — the step from industrial feudalism to nationalism. While doing all this, the trustees made money. In the year preceding September 30, 1910, General Motors' output was just under 40,000 cars. In the year ending September 30, 1915, the total was 76,068 and the profits were $14.5 million. Building on the foundations already in place, they would almost double these next year.

But their caution had cost them something. "Your board," the 1915 annual report primly stated, "does not believe in running into debt," and that principle helped to drive down General Motors' share of the total volume output of autos from the 20 percent of 1910 to 7.8 percent five years later. One of the directors, who remained anonymous, chastised the bankers as "too skeptical about the future of the automobile industry. . . . They didn't take advantage of the opportunities." Durant, in his opinion, might have had some temporary financial troubles now and then, but the corporation would have grown faster and earned more.[41]

Durant felt exactly that way. And as the days of the voting trust waned, and the season of ingathering came on, he was ready to leap back to where he and he alone could "take advantage of the opportunities."

IV   The drama of an approaching proxy battle now began to unfold. Durant had been accumulating shares and proxies for months, and not finding it especially difficult. Much of the GM stock that had gone in exchange for Buick was in Flint hands. Other thousands of shares were owned by the heads of companies bought by Durant, and his impulsive generosity in dealing had disposed them to be his friends. Luckily, few of these holdings had been dispersed through sale, since the low price of the issues on the market discouraged any disposition to unload. GM fluctuated between 35 and 51¾ in 1911, between 30 and 42⅞ in 1912, and between 25 and an anemic 40 in 1913. It had climbed to 99 as a 1914 high, and was back to 82 on the first day of 1915. The only problem would come when the date of the meeting grew close, and both sides would begin to buy openly. Then the price would rise steadily, and the temptation would be keen to take long-deferred profits. When that danger point approached in August, and daily GM quotations started a climb that would take them over 500 by the year's expiration, Durant was kept busy exhorting his supporters to be steadfast. "Don't sell any part of your holdings" was his message to cousin George Willson late in August. "I will protect if necessary," he added, the meaning of which was a promise to buy at the highest market price himself, no matter if there was a later decline. A week later he called once more for Willson's constancy: "Hold every share you have regardless of price changes." To William Ballenger he sent word that was repeated over and over again to others in Flint: "Do not let any of our crowd sell any stock. You will hear something that will please you within thirty days."[42]

The accumulation, the calling in of longstanding debts of personal gratitude, went on at a stepped-up pace as the meeting date of September 16 neared. Stories made the rounds at dinner tables for years afterward of old friends like A. M. Bentley of Owosso, Michigan, showing up at the Chevrolet offices with a briefcase stuffed with voting trust certificates representing the stock he had got for his Reliance Motor Company. Wilfred Leland claimed to have been in New York on the thirteenth, where Durant had actually shown him a safe crammed with the precious pieces of paper that "would control the outstanding stock."[43] Another tale that emerged mistily from some unidentified source was that Durant and three others sat up through the entire night of the fifteenth, passing the certificates from hand to hand, calling out and inscribing names and numbers. All of these fragments of a saga might have been true, but they were sometimes stitched together with a culminating scene of satisfying artistic power, but also of demonstrable untruth. In it, Durant strode into the meeting followed by assistants carrying bushel baskets full of certificates, and quietly announced: "Gentlemen, I control this company."

It did not happen so, although there was enough tension in the atmosphere on the eve of the showdown to satisfy those followers of events who enjoyed suspense. It was evident in the letters that were exchanged among Durant, Dr. Campbell, and McClement, who was leading the pro-Durant forces on the board. Campbell wrote to "Dear Pops" from Bretton Woods, New Hampshire, where he was spending September, alone, to find surcease from a severe case of hay fever.

I am very glad you are taking the position on Storrow that you are. I hope you have absolute control and can rely on it. You and McClement must not miss a meeting for fear they will put something over on you. Say, it will be happy days in the village if we ever can get in position where we can even up old scores with some of the sons of ——es.

He added a private joke to the effect that Whiting could be induced to go along if promised a directorship. "He could even be a vice president, as he writes a good hand."[44]

But he found nothing to laugh at in a letter from McClement that he enclosed along with his own. Its burden was that Storrow's allies were whispering that McClement and Durant both lied about the number and identity of those who had entrusted them with their votes. McClement added that he held the proxies of several members of the Rockefeller clan, and they informed him that a Lee, Higginson representative had called on them and made "serious representations in regard to Mr. Durant's character."

Campbell's anxiety was aroused as well by the evident alliance between Storrow and their old neighbor, friend, and partner, Charles Nash. If Durant did regain the upper hand, he must be sure, Campbell warned, not to leave Storrow on the board. "He controls Nash absolutely and the only way you can get along with Nash is to take his prop out from under him." Urging his father-in-law to "pay back a little of the humiliation you have gone through," Campbell ended:

Nash certainly is a "He-pup." I hope you are sure of the control. . . . Every share will help. My, you must not lose. If you get control and can hold Chrysler, it would not make any difference about Nash going. "Keep a stiff upper lip."

Durant's answer, written on the very morning of the meeting and enclosing a wad of blank proxies, was intended to reassure.

Dear Doctor:

Nash is acting like a baby and Storrow is so disconcerted that he is willing to resort to blackmail to secure even decent representation. It is clearly a matter of conspiracy between the two and an attempt on the part of both to save their faces.
We are sawing wood.[45]

The formal meeting, when it finally took place, was empty of any rhetoric, attitude, gesture, or display that in any way suggested a clash of wills. McClement arrived at its scheduled location, the Belmont Hotel, at two o'clock in the afternoon, and found only a scattering of directors on hand, not even enough for a quorum. One of them, Thomas Neal, explained that there was no hurry. Something was happening downtown—a private conference among Durant, Nash, Storrow, and "certain other parties." As was so often the case, the real arena of decision would be a closed-door encounter among principals, who would then present themselves to the other participants behind a facade of harmony. Men might be driven to suicide or bankruptcy in boardrooms, but never with raised voices that might carry abroad to disturb the public's confidence in its business leadership.

McClement was an old hand at the game and understood the rules. With neither excitement nor frustration, he went down to the dining room to consume a leisurely lunch. As he ate, an anti-Durant director, Jacob Wertheim, joined him and made a last appeal. Did McClement realize, he wanted to know, that his support was vital to Durant's hope of victory, and that Durant's first act as a winner would be to oust Nash, the proven success? McClement answered calmly that Durant already had enough votes without him, according to his own claim, and since he was a "truthful" person, there would be "no contest and it would only be a question of compromise." That point having been disposed of, the conversation became amiable and a proposal was made to pass the time with a little auction bridge. McClement and Wertheim joined Nicholas Tilney and C. S. Mott, and the minutes slipped undemonstratively away, and then it was 5:30 and Durant walked in, unruffled, and said that Storrow and Nash would be along in a short while. As he sat down by invitation to take a hand, he made it clear either by word or manner that it was all settled. Just as McClement had predicted, the end result was a compromise.

The three of them—the founder, the president and the chief moneylender of General Motors—had got together around noon for a preliminary probing before the formal proceedings. With them were the "other parties" mentioned by Neal; these were important friends of each side, including Kaufman, who had brought along du Pont, who had brought along Raskob. Storrow and Durant were the chief antagonists. Curiously enough, they had been born within three years of each other in Boston, and Durant, in his own way, was as much a son of New England as his rival, but two men more widely separated by temperament would have been hard to find. One rumor that escaped from the closed session later, and was a somewhat subdued version of the bushel-basket-of-certificates legend, reported that Storrow asked Durant coldly if he expected any trouble at the forthcoming meeting. Durant answered in his usual low tone: "There won't be any trouble, Mr. Storrow. I'm in control of General Motors today."

That was precisely the point in question, however, and the fact was that neither side had enough certain votes to claim a majority, so the only real choice was to settle or risk humiliation in the final count. Each side named six candidates for the eleven-man board, and was informed that they were unacceptable to the other. The deadlock continued through the afternoon hours.

Then Storrow broke the ice. During a brief recess he came over to where du Pont stood chatting with Kaufman and expressing some surprise at the turn of events since Kaufman, like McClement, assumed that Durant had things completely in hand and had told du Pont as much. Storrow broke into the conversation with a new plan. The board would be expanded to seventeen members. Each faction would name seven. Storrow would be satisfied if du Pont, who was himself one of the Durant side's nominees, chose three more. Durant readily agreed to this, provided that "the new comers should not be connected with either faction." Du Pont accepted this role, and submitted the names of Raskob, of his own brother-in-law, Lammot Belin, and of a longtime du Pont corporation executive, J. Amory Haskell. Raskob rushed out to telephone the other two, but was unable to reach Haskell, who learned of his new post, much to du Pont's embarrassment, by the next morning's papers.

Those were the decisions that were already on record when the leaders got back to the Belmont at six o'clock. At last, the formal meeting that had kindled such dire anticipations got under way, and it was, in McClement's words, "a regular love feast." Nash first spoke with the happiest news of all. The debt was retired, and the long fast of the shareholders was to be erased from memory in a flood of abundance. There would be a dividend of fifty dollars on every hundred-dollar share if the board approved, which it did with acclaim. Next, Nash introduced Storrow, who, he said, would explain a compromise that had been reached through the cheerful willingness of "Mr. Durant" to make sacrifices. Storrow rose to spell out the details of the agreement just concluded, and voiced his regret that some of the directors currently serving would have to be dropped. A proxy committee of Nash, du Pont, Kaufman, and Durant would vote in the new nominees at the full stockholders' meeting of November. And finally Durant himself took the floor, "thanked Mr. Nash for his kindly remarks and assured him that we were all working together for a definite end and the success of the company."[46]

And so it was done, the trusteeship ended and a new crew installed on the bridge. Yet a cloud of ambiguity overhung the outcome. The fact that Storrow had chosen du Pont for the middleman's role could be used to argue that the balance of power was in genuinely neutral hands, with neither faction entitled to rejoice. But since du Pont had been introduced on the scene by Kaufman, and Kaufman was tied to Durant through Chevrolet, it was possible to believe that Storrow's approach to du Pont was merely a face-saving surrender to the inevitable—that the game had gone Durant's way.

It was in character for Durant himself to see it so. And what Durant thought, the Flint *Journal* thought as well. Exulting in the fact that the new board would contain four local heroes—Durant, Nash, Bishop, and Mott—the editor proclaimed: "William Crapo Durant has come into his own."[47]

But the final phase of the battle was yet to be fought.

In Pierre du Pont's mind there was no uncertainty whatever. He had played the honest broker in order to help out a company in which he now had some interest. The day after the meeting, he wrote to Haskell explaining how they had both come by their new positions. "It is my judgment that the Directors will now work together, having decided upon a policy," he confided, "and that we are not entering a Board full of friction. . . . It will be my policy to try to be informed and I hope that you will take the same position. I have no intention of being a 'dummy' director."[48] There was no hint of displeasure, either, in Storrow's thank-you note to du Pont, admitting that the preceding day's work had been "an irksome job," but adding the opinion that "the stockholders are much better off than would otherwise have been the case."[49] And if there was any dissonance between the du Pont and Durant views of what had happened, it was unheard in Durant's brief message: "I think you have handled the matter splendidly."[50] Du Pont could easily convince himself that he had preserved rather than tilted a balance.

But Durant's friends knew nothing of these exchanges. Their information came from the newspaper accounts, which rendered the affair as the colorful promoter's return from limbo. "Long live the King," wrote Kaufman to him, enclosing one such clipping.[51] In Flint especially, and throughout the hinterlands where he had spent thirty years making friends, there was an upwelling of affection that came from deeper springs than mere pleasure at the leap of GM's quoted market price from 250 to 340 in the single week after the meeting.

From the chemical laboratory of Albion College in Michigan came a letter signed by Delos Fall, who had instructed "Willie" in the sciences in Flint long before.

My dear Friend:

The world loves and applauds a winner and you have my sincere congratulations on your great success.

However, *I* loved you before your successes came, ever since our High School experiences.

May the dear Lord bless you, Will, is the earnest prayer of your one time teacher.[52]

Durant had that to savor, and also a pungent letter in Fred Smith's wry, staccato style.

My dear Billy:

More power to you. An old friend of both of us told me this was "due" some time ago—but this is the first "straight goods" I have happened to see.

The fact that you and I haven't always drilled in the same spread doesn't keep me from sending on my sincere congratulations at carrying thro' what you set out to do, and doing it brown. You may bet on one thing—that a whole lot of people who have no more axes to grind than I have—which means none at all—are genuinely pleased to see the outcome. . . .

Your success pleases a lot of people who admire a well-scrapped scrap and an ability to bide the time till the other pup has chewed himself tired.

Inasmuch as I have always known it was the "game" that held you and not the money, I can only hope that you have the usual 28 hours worth of jobs to pull off in 24, and only a half—or say one third the required help to do with. This, I figure, is as near Heaven as you are at all likely to land.

I wonder if you would have a hard job to believe that if you had gone—or *when* you go BUST—I shall still be

Very truly yours.[53]

And there was Hardy's letter, sent from Flint, following up a telegram that said he was "proud to serve under a General who wins out by such fair methods and patient persistence as yours." Even with more space at his disposal, Hardy found himself at a loss to say everything.

The only trouble with the English language is that it does not enable me to express all I feel toward you, not alone in the General Motors fight but in any other fight which you have made or are making or will make in the future, but I know you will believe me when I say again in this letter that I am always yours to command, and am ready as in the past to serve you to the limit of my ability.[54]

And there were more letters, far more. "You deserve it all and anything more you want. Please accept my last shirt." That was Arthur Mason. "Congratulations, you did it! Permit me, the next time you are in Detroit, to buy the chop suey at two o'clock in the morning." That was Harry Shiland, the Buick service manager of early days. "Five years ago when the gang had you with your back to the wall, I prayed that I might live long enough to see you clean their clocks. . . . My prayer has been answered." That was a Flint neighbor, W. P. Cook. And W. W. Mountain, whose Flint Varnish Works had mixed the paint that sent thousands of Durant-Dort buggies gaily into the world, knew exactly how to reach Durant's heart.

I think possibly there may be just one person in Flint more pleased than I am, and, without doubt, she could find no possible way to express her happiness unless she would have the opportunity of putting her arms around her boy's neck and just telling him that way.[55]

There were dozens of them, perhaps hundreds, a chorus of affection sung in the stock phrases of men less handy with words than with tools and numbers, who had to make commonplace words do. "I want to shake your hand, and just whisper 'Forward march to greater things.'" . . . "I think you are the greatest genius in the line of business since the days of the late E. H. Harriman and a far better man than he was, for you do it all with a smile." . . . "To work with you is to love and esteem you." . . . "There is something about you that after one has been your friend or identified with you in a business way . . . expands the friendship ties and increases admiration."

And a simple "hearty congratulations" from a friend who had recently been golfing at Bretton Woods with Dr. Campbell and Dallas Dort. He was a district manager for R. G. Dun and Company, whose Boston books still carried the fading ink-tracks of William Clark Durant's toboggan ride to disgrace just fifty years before.[56]

Though he tabbed these tributes "personal flattery," Durant believed in and lived by his faith in the reality of the fondness expressed by the writers. In his own conception, they were the people on whose behalf he had won. How deeply he felt this was unveiled when a disturbing chill of speculation suddenly blew out of the warm skies over Flint. Talk went around that with Durant once more in an inside position at General Motors, the Chevrolet Company would be ingested by the combine, perhaps relocated, at the very least the power of Flint men in its councils diluted. Hardy voiced such fears to Durant, who wired back:

To set your mind at rest for all time, there is not enough money in this country to buy Chevrolet, or consolidate Chevrolet, or take from our little crowd control of Chevrolet. The Chevrolet is my newest, latest and best Prize Baby dedicated to and controlled by the men who built it up against terrific odds.[57]

What he had in mind for his "little crowd," his happy few, was something special. It was true that he planned to join his two creations, but in a way that exalted poetic imagination over business logic. He intended to have Chevrolet, where his mastery was absolute, take over General Motors, where it was still shaky. The infant child would lead the tamed behemoth on a leash.

V Only a week after the General Motors board convened, Chevrolet's directors met, and under Durant's baton, proceeded immediately to put into effect an enlarged and modified version of the agreement that he had concluded with Kaufman in July. The Chevrolet Motor Company was reorganized as a holding company in the friendly shelter of Delaware, its capitalization now $20 million. Thirteen million, two hundred thousands' worth of its new stock would be traded for that of the constituent companies which it was taking over. The other $6.8 million of par-$100 shares would be sold through Hornblower and Weeks, to raise the money needed to triple Chevrolet's 100-auto-per-day production. Of those 68,000 shares, Durant set aside 10,000 to be allotted, at $75 each, to those who had earned their reward in the proxy campaign. The list included the usual stalwarts from Flint, favored outsiders like McClement and the McLaughlins, suppliers who had trusted Chevrolet in its lean years, possible future investors to cultivate, kinsmen like George Willson, and Mrs. W. C. Durant.

The beneficiaries were invited to send checks for their allotments at their convenience. None had cause to feel burdened. The shares were quoted at 97 and going up within a few days of issue, and theoretically could have been sold at once and paid for entirely out of the profits; Durant urged anyone who was so minded to give him the first option. But the great boom in demand for Chevrolet cars kept carrying Chevrolet stock aloft on its wings. It made no sense to sell. The clamor for shares was unceasing. "I am simply swamped with applications," Durant wrote to Kaufman in a petition for a few extra hundreds from those in the banker's control, "and am attempting to retain a few of my many friends." He managed, nonetheless, to take care of himself. On his 1916 birthday Kaufman's card read: "I regret that I cannot give you Chevrolet stock, as I understand your strong-box is not big enough to hold any more. So I am sending you a few roses. . . ."[58]

Ninety days after the issue of $20 millions, the moment had come for the jump-off into the second stage of the operation, the one begotten out of pure audacity. The directors recapitalized anew at $80 millions. What Durant intended to do with the fresh $60 million in stock was explained by Ballenger in a letter to Curtis Hatheway:

The idea is that the Chevrolet Motor Company, the Delaware corporation, will take over all this [GM] stock controlled by Mr. Durant and his associates, and for each share of General Motors common they will issue five shares of Chevrolet common; for each share of General Motors preferred one share of Chevrolet common. . . .

There has been a terrific fight on as to who should eventually control General Motors Company, but Mr. Durant seems to have the upper hands of it at this time. Only those people who have been working with Mr. Durant and have given him, or his associates, their proxies to vote at the meeting of the General Motors, are being allowed to come in on the proposition of five shares of Chevrolet for one of General Motors.

. . . It would be a wise thing for you to get in touch with him as you probably will want to play the game with him.[59]

The temptation to play Durant's game was almost overpowering. A part of the arrangement was that a syndicate would be formed to protect the price of Chevrolet at 140, a point beyond which it had already risen. Any drop below that level would trigger automatic buying from a pool of money contributed by the syndicate's subscribers and kept in reserve. The result of a five-for-one trade would be the acquisition of at least $700 in Chevrolet stock for a share of GM, which, even at its highest 1915 threshold, was 558. Even when the trade-in offer was made public in January at the reduced rate of four shares of Chevrolet common for one of GM, it was still a profitable step to take. And even if General Motors prospered and the price of its stock rose, those who had traded it were protected, for the inevitable results would be dividends on the GM shares, which would pour millions into the Chevrolet treasury that held so many of them, and which would be transmuted quickly into dividends on Chevrolet stock.

As Durant had no doubt anticipated, there was a rush to take advantage of the offer while it lasted (it was gradually reduced and finally withdrawn by May), and in one great inhalation Chevrolet, his fiscal other self, drew in enough GM securities to put the issue of supremacy beyond doubt. "Durant Again Holds Control of General Motors" ran a New York *Times* headline. "'Wizard of Automobile' Ousted In 1910 Now Holds Majority Of Stock." The *Times*'s estimate was that Durant and his associates held the voting keys to 100,000 of the 165,000 shares of GM common outstanding, and that Durant alone owned 90,000 of Chevrolet's 200,000 shares of common.[60]

There was a flicker of potential discomfort late in November. The new General Motors board of directors had chosen Pierre du Pont as their chairman in November, and while he was on a subsequent visit of inspection to Michigan Nash, Leland, and Emory Clark, the Detroit banker who was one of the 1910 additions to the board, had warned him to beware of Durant. Clark followed up his attack by mailing to du Pont a news clipping that appeared to quote Durant as saying that his latest triumph owed much to du Pont backing. Du Pont was concerned about the loss of his noncombatant status and wrote back that any such implication was "hardly fair." To raise himself higher above reproach, he made it clear that neither he nor any du Pont executives holding GM shares would take advantage of the trade-in.[61]

It was not a moment to alienate the new board chairman, and Durant was prompt in mending the fence, for the doctor wrote him at Christmastime, just a few days after the offending news interview had taken place, saying: "I am glad you saw the du Ponts and put your side of the case to them." Campbell was still nervous about counterattacks. Learning that the Detroit directors had been in New York, he urged Durant to have Kaufman keep an eye on them, "so that they can not put anything over on you." Depression gnawed at Campbell's confidence and what should have been his pleasure in the growing value of his own portfolio. He was in the midst of a growing estrangement from Margery. "It hasn't been a very pleasant Christmas time," he concluded, apologizing for adding "this trouble" to Durant's "other burdens."[62] But Durant's buoyant nature was incapable of sustained sadness, and in any case he was busy preparing to repel the last charge of the bankers, who were still unwilling to believe that they had been routed by a country boy.

General Motors' stockholders opened their mailboxes the first week in January to find the pro-Storrow directors' answer to the trade-in maneuver embodied in a blunt circular, signed by eight of them, that deplored any arrangement under which control would be vested "in any other corporation." Their remedy was to propose a new three-year voting trust to begin in November, when the existing board's term would expire. Seven of the eight represented investment houses in Boston, New York, and Detroit. The final and surprising name on the list was that of Charles Stewart Mott. His enlistment in the counterrevolution added to it the weight of an operating executive's opinion. On the first of March a second circular arrived, this one over the signatures of thirteen stockholders who denied any "aspiration to become members of the Board" or to take part in the corporation's management.[63]

After this disclaimer of self-interest, they argued hard for the stockholders to pause and reflect. The existing leadership, they pointed out, had written off over twelve million dollars of bad assets and retired the fifteen million dollar debt, and still managed to pay regular dividends on the preferred stock. It had just begun to declare them on the common as well, and had scored a thirteen million dollar profit in the final half of 1915. The corner had been turned. "We believe," the thirteen declared, "that the continuation of the present conservative management is especially essential during the next few years, and that those who have been largely the creative influence of the great success of the Company should be retained." They held for the last what they thought of as their most telling argument, a guarantee that the "creative influence" of the preceding five years would be preserved. They had, they said, secured the names of six directors who would willingly become the new voting trustees—Storrow and Strauss of the original five, Emory Clark, Albert Sabin of Guaranty Trust, Mott—and Charles Nash himself, enfolding the cause in his own long and faithful record. What they asked of the recipients was to sign an enclosed form, an unofficial advisory ballot, favoring the trust idea.

But the field was lost to the conservatives. Nothing could overcome the power of profit, and even GM stockholders lukewarm to Durant's methods set their misgivings aside for a chance to earn hundreds above the market price of their shares in a four-for-one Chevrolet exchange. Pierre du Pont later observed that "the sale of stock by interests that might otherwise have been averse to Mr. Durant" was a major force in his tightening grip.[64] Durant faced down the threat with a confidence that edged almost into contempt. Late in March he wrote Campbell, then in Pasadena, that he had on three occasions come to the office at 4:30 A.M. to write him, but each time fallen instead into dealing with other matters, "which, thank Heavens, have nearly all been disposed of. The principal item . . . has been the General Motors proposition which is now well in hand. Emory W. Clark's latest attempt to organize a new Voting Trust was somewhat of a joke."[65]

Durant was not laughing, however, over the appearance of the name of Nash as a possible new voting trustee. He did not react to the presence of Mott on the list. Mott was primarily a business acquaintance, whose conduct openly proclaimed his intention to do what he thought best for the company without regard to personal attachments. But "Charley" Nash was bound to Durant with invisible but sturdy fibers of association. He was a Durant-Dort old-timer, one of the few to call the man "Billy." Their children had grown up together; they had shared sickness and discouragement along with success. Durant had apparently entertained no objection to Nash's working harmoniously with the voting trustees. "Charley's" dedication to the job at hand was an asset that he had used before and planned to use again, something he had tried to hint to his old friend long before September of 1915, without revealing his plans.[66] But for Nash to join now in a plot, as he saw it, to deny him his hard-won victory was beyond forgiveness.

For Nash, the events of the 1915–1916 winter were an agony. He knew better than anyone what he owed to Durant. But he also had moved into a limelight of his own under the bankers, and he was aware of the adamant will behind "Billy's" smile. Durant's return would mean a plunge back into subordination. To support Durant was to deny his own ego; to fight him was betrayal. Impaled for once on problems that hard work and common sense could not solve, Nash squirmed in equivocation.

For all of his celebrated amiability, Durant could be a figure of ice and steel when he chose. The moment he learned of the circular of March 1, he fired a telegram to Nash, then on a business trip to the West Coast. "Was this circular prepared with your knowledge and is your name being used with your consent?" Nash responded: "Had advice before leaving of circular. Wrote letter refusing use of my name."

Durant's telegram was waiting for him the next morning. "Kindly advise to whom you wrote letter refusing use of your name in order that full and complete correction can be made." Nash answered that he had received a letter asking for the use of his name from Howard Bayne, one of the circular's signers. Revealing his growing misery, he explained further: "Replied would not want my name used as stockholders would think I was trying to insure my job. Do not want this impression to prevail as am fast becoming discouraged and losing interest in whole proposition."[67]

Durant ignored both the emotion and the explanation and pressed in. "I understand from your telegram that you wrote letter refusing to use your name as trustee in voting trust plan. Am I correct?" Nash avoided a direct answer. Either he had to accuse Bayne and his sponsor Emory Clark, behind whom Storrow probably stood, of being liars or admit that he was their accomplice against Durant. "Have wired you for your personal information only," the words came over the telegraph line. "Do not use me in any controversy you may have with others."

Durant ignored Nash's implicit pleas once more, and refused to let the matter drop. Thirteen copies of a letter went from his office to the signers of the circular, each one asking the identical question: "Will you kindly inform me . . . if . . . you received a letter from Mr. Nash refusing the use of his name?" From the array of answers ranging from hostile to indifferent denials, Durant pounced on the one that had the answer he expected — Bayne's. "Mr. C. W. Nash at first stated that he preferred not to be named as a voting trustee," Bayne wrote, but went on: "Mr. Emory W. Clark subsequently discussed the matter with him, and wired: 'Nash will serve as trustee if named.'"[68]

So it was Clark who was behind it all, as Durant had been inclined to suspect. On Nash's return from California, Durant confronted him in a furious mood that he had described to Campbell on March 26. "I am through with side-stepping and four-flushing and expect to . . . have the atmosphere cleared once and all." The clarification cleared Nash of lying and convicted him of spinelessness. He produced his original reply to Bayne's draft of the circular, which damningly declared: "I can see nothing wrong with this statement," but explicitly did reject service in any new voting trust "as I do not want to get mixed up in any way in this scrap." But when this refusal reached Emory Clark's ears, he had gotten on the telephone to Nash and said that he "could not understand why if [he] were elected by the stockholders of the Company as a Voting Trustee for them [he] would refuse to serve." Nash repeated once more that he "did not want to be mixed up in the thing." But then, as his final letter of explanation recorded, Clark had bluntly asked him if he really had any choice but to serve in case he should be elected. "I replied, 'Well, that would be a different proposition,' and the matter dropped."[69]

He had said no to Bayne, and Clark had blustered him out of it, and there was no face-saving way left for Charles Nash to stay in Durant's company. Torn between loyalty and his judgment of what was best for his future, he had elected not to be ruled by a quarter-century of friendship. And he had discovered that in corporate wars there were no bomb shelters for the highest ranking officers. On April 18, Nash submitted his resignation to Du Pont as chairman of the board, asking that it not be publicized immediately. Durant's reaction was crisp. "I am not at all surprised, and, in view of the circumstances, think it is the honorable thing for him to do."[70]

In his official biographical statement of later years, Nash said that Durant had offered him a huge salary to stay on. That could very possibly have been true up to March 1, 1916. After that the likeliest version of what Durant said to him at their last meeting was the one reported by Murphy: "Well, Charley, you're through."[71]

Now it was May of 1916, the best of Durant's springtimes so far, and almost every day a new bough blossomed for him. The doctor still fussed at him, this time urging that he take the presidency vacated by Nash, forsaking his usual preference for power without title.

You are the only one who can hold the different companies together. There is no one else who can do this job and don't lose sight of it. . . . The other chaps have been in power for six years and of course have their friends in power and this situation will have to be handled very carefully and you are the one to do it, so don't make the mistake of putting a figure head in for president; it must be you and you only. It will give you back all your lost prestige. *Now don't let anyone talk you into doing anything differently.* I hope Storrow and his bunch of wolves resign also. . . .

Don't get up so early. Don't take cold. Don't work so hard. Don't see
so many people. Keep cheered up, for the promised land is in sight.[72]

Durant listened serenely, said nothing yet about his presidential plans,
and laughed. "If they stab me again, it will be when I am looking right
straight at them."[73] The promised land was all around him. In the middle of
May he announced without challenge that he controlled some 450,000 of
the outstanding 825,589 GM shares. And in the middle of May, too, his
mail was filled with fresh notes of thanks and congratulations for another
shower of prosperity that he had called down from the clouds. From the
year's beginning until the last of April, he had managed the syndicate that
was propping the price of Chevrolet shares. He had bought 29,000 shares
at an average price of 110. When the period of need had passed, and the
syndicate contract expired, he had sold them at an average price of 160.
Even after deducting interest on a loan and a small loss on 3,000 additional
shares, he had a melon of approximately $1,212,000 to divide pro rata
among the subscribers.[74]

The largest checks—for over $100,000 each—went to heavy investors
like Kaufman, Hofheimer, Coleman du Pont (Pierre's cousin), and Elbert
Gary, the president of United States Steel. Their appreciation was no less
keen than that of smaller plungers. "Let me throw you a bouquet," wrote
Coleman du Pont. "I take my hat off to you." Kaufman's response to his
check was the statement: "I regard this . . . as a donation absolutely. There
was never a time . . . when you required the support of the syndicate to
accomplish what you accomplished."[75] In the general rejoicing among the
affluent, even Pierre du Pont was swept into the conviction that it might
now be within the bounds of propriety for him and his lieutenants to join the
Chevrolet family by at last exchanging their GM stock. The offer had
actually expired, but Durant knew when it was time for magnanimity.
Lammot Belin turned in 100 shares, Raskob 1,200, du Pont 2,235, and
Haskell an unrecorded number, and all received the five-for-one terms
reserved for insiders.

And in addition to the large checks from the syndicate operation, many
smaller ones went to brokers and bankers and acquaintances both old and
new who were often unaware of their good luck until they received the
money, since Durant had simply bought stock in their names, laying any
deposits out of his own pocket. The general sales manager of the Chevrolet
Company was one such beneficiary. "I can assure you," he wrote fervently,
"that I more than appreciate your thoughtfulness."[76] Once more, Durant
had played the part described by a supplier who knew him well as "the
egocentric with the fairy wand."[77] John Bergen said it in simpler words. "If
he liked you, he made you rich."[78]

Finally, that May, there was one last, well-relished opportunity to discomfit James Storrow.

As he heard the advancing footsteps of Durant's march back to power, Storrow made his plans to leave General Motors. He had, however, enjoyed his taste of the automobile business too much to forsake it. His idea was to set up Nash and Chrysler in a new enterprise, the three of them to improve on their past performance in a more concentrated area. Storrow found a suitable property, the plant at Kenosha, Wisconsin, where Thomas Jeffery had gone into bankruptcy producing a car named the Rambler. He arranged its purchase for $5,000,000.

But as the final days of the Nash tenure at General Motors were being counted off, the door of Walter Chrysler's office at the Buick factory opened to admit William C. Durant, with a soft-spoken offer to promote him from general manager to president if he would remain, with a natural upward salary adjustment.

"I cannot hope to find words to express the charm of the man," Chrysler said, looking back. "He could coax a bird right down out of a tree." Chrysler found himself liking Durant as they talked, but clinging to his own tree. He explained that he had a new position in the process of development, and would probably be leaving. At the very least, he needed some time to consider. Durant smiled. "This is a great company. You've been doing a splendid job. I'll be in Flint thirty days. When you make up your mind, you call me."

When Chrysler finally made the call, Durant asked briskly when it would be convenient to talk. Chrysler was one of that breed of men whose day began before others got their blood circulating. He offered seven o'clock in the morning. Wordlessly, Durant appeared on his doorstep "at seven sharp." Within minutes he offered Chrysler $500,000 a year, ten times what he had just begun to receive, and over eighty times his salary of four years earlier. "He just sprang it on me that way," the ex-machinist marveled. "He didn't bat an eye." Instinctively, sympathetically, Durant understood what Chrysler's last barrier was, his desire to move out on his own. "Give me just three years of yourself," was his clinching plea.

When he left the office, the terms of the three-year contract were set. Chrysler could draw $10,000 a month, and the balance of the $500,000 at each year's end, in cash or stock. The stock would be figured at the price of the day on which they signed the pact. If Chrysler helped it to climb, he profited directly. It was impossible for him to pass up such a challenge. Before a friendly good-bye, he added one last condition.

I don't want interference. I don't want any other boss but you. If you feel that anything is going wrong, if you don't like some action of mine, you come to me; don't go to anybody else and don't try to split up my authority. Just have one channel between Flint and Detroit, from me to you. Full authority is what I want.

Durant beamed, another sale closed. He touched his fingers lightly to the table top for emphasis and uttered with joy the three incantatory words that had raised the curtain on so many scenes for him: "It's a deal."[79]

June 1, 1916, arrived. Charles Nash left to produce the Rambler, which would be renamed for him, without the assistance of Chrysler. And Durant, taking his son-in-law's advice, stepped into Nash's vacant place as president. He still felt modestly apologetic, as he told an old friend:

None knows better than you how little I care for official position or title, but I have always insisted that the General Motors Company should be in the hands of motor car men, and I am amply compensated for any of my efforts by the expressions which have come by telegraph, phone, mail and personally, all to the same effect, that there is general happiness over the fact that the great industrials, like General Motors and Buick, are now in the hands of those who organized and builded them.[80]

The ultimate victory warmed him to his center. Nothing could match the pleasure in his simple statement to Catherine over dinner. "I took General Motors back from the bankers today."[81] On that soft June evening he could not have believed it possible that he would ever lose. Once more he had shown an amazing capacity to create much from little in a short time, to persuade others to be willing instruments in the execution of his dreams, to succeed by pressing on in deliberate blindness to the possibility of misfortune.

He was back at the top, ready to reassume command. What it meant for General Motors was best expressed much later by Alfred Sloan. "The big show was on again."[82]

7)

Second Empire:

the Best of Years

I Before the end of June, 1916, he had four new scalps to dangle from his belt along with that of Nash. Storrow and Emory Clark resigned as directors, and so did Samuel Pryor and Albert Wiggin, two other bankers on the board who had signed the first manifesto of resistance to the Chevrolet takeover. With the struggle for control behind him, Durant was free for fresh bursts of creativity. He felt no need to share his plans with his new directors as a group. A session of the board was due July twenty-fifth, and he informed its secretary, Standish Backus, that it might as well be canceled, as he had "no particular business" to bring before it at that moment. Pierre du Pont, as chairman, chose to react with polite bewilderment to the president's lack of interest in internal communications. "As I have not heard from you," he wrote early in September, "I fear that through

(203)

26.
Durant demonstrating the ill-fated "Iron Horse" at a 1919 state fair in Trenton

27.
Durant and Catherine, in the
height of 1919 fashion, chatting
with A. B. C. Hardy

ELEUTHERIAN MILLS HISTORICAL LIBRARY

28.
Pierre S. du Pont (left) and John
J. Raskob, Durant's allies, later
successors at GM

29.
Past and future GM executives at Kenosha, Wisconsin, around 1916. Alfred P. Sloan at left with Charles S. Mott's arm around him, a shirtsleeved Charles Nash, and H. H. Bassett

MR. GREGORY SMITH

30.
Durant's attorney at Chevrolet and GM, and lifelong friend, John Thomas Smith

31.
The "great bull," Durant, in his sixties

misunderstanding I have failed to communicate with you as to a convenient date of meeting. Am I wrong in waiting for advice from you relative to General Motors matters?"[1] Du Pont would learn, in time, that while Durant was not intentionally discourteous, pinning him down to a conference table at a precise moment was a task that demanded unusual patience.

Durant was hard to reach that spring and summer because he had once more been hunting for live specimens in the corporate game preserves and was busy arranging for the care and feeding of what he had bagged. With the help of Kaufman he built a new consolidation of parts and accessories manufacturers, calling it the United Motors Corporation, and gathered into it within a few months five widely scattered concerns — the Perlman Rim Corporation of Jackson, the Delco Corporation, the Remy Electric Company of Anderson, Indiana, the Hyatt Roller Bearing Company of Newark, and the New Departure Ball Bearing Company of Bristol, Connecticut. To this nucleus, intended to guarantee supplies of wheels, electrical apparatus, and bearings, he subsequently added factories producing horns, radiators, and steel subassemblies.

The method of acquisition was the usual exchange of stock for stock. There were no fewer than 1.2 million shares of United Motors authorized, with no par value. Riding on Durant's resurgent reputation they quickly reached a respectable market value, were being sold to individual subscribers at 62 and to bankers in wholesale lots at 50, and could be expected to go higher as the combination developed strength. As he completed one of the purchases, Durant reported cheerfully to Kaufman: "Your latest baby — a weak, struggling infant, which I adopted and which has cost me to date somewhere between $4,000,000 and $5,000,000 cash — with careful nursing begins to show signs of strength and will in time, I believe, become a very healthy child that you will be proud of."[2] To make certain that the child did not escape their control, Durant and Kaufman saw to it, in incorporating United Motors, that only 5,000 of its shares of stock, firmly grasped by the two of them, had voting rights.

The creation of United Motors was a step timed to the accelerating beat of integration of the auto-making process. It repeated Durant's early experiments in enfolding Mott and Champion into his operations on a scale appropriate to the industry's growth in the succeeding ten years. But it would take some time after 1916 before its greatest importance, which was not reflected on a balance sheet, emerged in clear outline. That happened to be the eventual drawing of Alfred P. Sloan into the framework of General Motors' leadership.

At forty-one years of age, Sloan was already an "old-timer" who had moved through practically the entire history of auto manufacture, accumulating success, yet full of an Alice-in-Wonderland bewilderment at the strange creatures inhabiting the topsy-turvy world in which he had to function. For in its primitive era the business was dominated by plungers and roisterers, and Sloan was above all serious and rational, a man whose mind delighted in the orderly gathering and classification of facts, followed by analysis and scrupulously weighed decision. One could see that in a picture taken shortly after his graduation from the Massachusetts Institute of Technology in 1895—a rather long face, large and slightly protuberant eyes held unblinkingly on the center of the lens, full lips solidly pressed together, obviously not moved often or easily to a smile.

He had gone straight from there to a $50-a-month draftsman's job at the Hyatt plant (founded by the inventor of celluloid), a small brick building on a lot that was half ash-heap, half junkyard. He left it for a time, but when it was on the edge of bankruptcy in 1898, his father—a tea and coffee importer in Brooklyn—put up $5,000 that enabled the young man to return and take it over. With his friend and associate "Pete" Steenstrup, he went about building up the business, more and more of which was going to fill auto-making demands. Their first encounter with the new era came with the purchase of a car for the company, a Buffalo-made machine called the Conrad, painted bright red. When it was delivered to the plant, it refused to start. A call to the factory produced the manufacturer's son, a sporty character, as Sloan remembered him, with a silk handkerchief in his breast pocket. He removed the handkerchief, stuffed it into the carburetor, swung the crank twice, and miraculously the engine roared into life. Then he swaggered off, leaving the handkerchief as a gift.

For years Sloan and Steenstrup did what they needed to for survival among rough-hewn types like Ford, the Dodge brothers, the body-making Fisher brothers, their self-trained production engineers, their boisterous buyers. They ate with them, drank (reluctantly) with them in alternating shifts, played with their children, submitted to their practical jokes in order to bring in orders that frequently came on paper "mottled with the stains of oil and graphite" from the workbenches on which they were written.

> Pete Steenstrup was the perfect salesman. If he was playing cards on a train on the way to an auto race and became aware, through the hubbub and the chatter, that the person who was fastening his shirttail to the car seat was Henry Ford, he would enter into the joke, feign an errand, and get up with a jolt that would tear his shirt. . . . If someone monkeyed with his Autocar so as to make only two of its four cylinders fire, he would never let on that he suspected the source of the trouble.[3]

What bound them all together, melting down the differences in temperament and training, was a common fascination with their products. "Our minds moved together as sympathetically as meshed gears," Sloan realized. "We'd talk shop until we could not stay awake." And then they would plunge back into work, caught up in their other shared experience, the sheer excitement of keeping up in the race.

You would use every dollar you could get to put into bearings to make more dollars to buy more machinery to make more and more bearings. . . . Whether you made axles, engines, wheels, bodies, lamps or hardware, it was the same story. . . . I saw nothing of the mining camps of the West and nothing of the booms that happened where oil was struck, but I did see Detroit.

In the course of time, however, the engineer was becoming paramount over the sport. More sophisticated autos demanded greater precision of components. Sloan found himself increasingly confronted with demands from designers for bearings to do special tasks. More of his own company's resources went, with his blessing, into planning, model-making, and testing. But all of it was done within a relentless time schedule. The rationality necessary to mass-produce high-grade machines put everyone in a lockstep. Suppliers were as dominated by the pace of the assembly line as any worker. "Literally," Sloan noted, "it was a capital offense to hold up a production line." A laggard delivery of parts meant that the entire, intricate process stalled, and everyone from the president of the hobbled company to the lowliest idled hand knew what was wrong and who had sinned. "You would not dare go into the plant the next time you set foot in Detroit."[4]

To Sloan it was a challenge to master this game with reason. Like John D. Rockefeller plunging into the wildcat-haunted oil trade fifty years earlier, he was fired by the energy that roiled around on every side, and smitten by the prospect of what it could achieve when tamed, harnessed, cleansed of its wastefulness, and shorn of its appalling risks. Laboring relentlessly, he had, by 1916, turned his own company into a thriving testimonial to his planning. Hyatt Roller Bearing's factory boasted 750,000 square feet of floor space, its own powerhouse, its own heat-treating department with a 3,500-horsepower gas plant, its own three sidings on the Pennsylvania line, and even its own fire department and 300,000 gallon reservoir. The company had three separate sales departments: one in Detroit for the auto trade, one in Chicago for tractor companies, and one in Newark to reach manufacturers of general machinery. Each of these had a research staff available to cooperate with manufacturers. All of this had been accomplished without falling into the hands of moneylenders. The owners were still Sloan, his father, and two Newark lawyers.

Such was the prize and such the leader on whom Durant's eye had fallen early in 1916 when he was planning United Motors, and the meetings between himself and Sloan that led to the purchase stripped bare the styles and thought processes of the two men. One of the Hyatt staff in Detroit carried to Sloan an invitation to lunch with Durant, who lost little time in getting to the point once the opening pleasantries were past.

"Mr. Sloan," he asked, "have you ever considered the sale of your company?"

No one who knew Durant's history could be surprised at the proposal, and Sloan was ready with an appropriate answer. "After all, Mr. Durant, it's a business."

"If you thought of selling, about what price would you have in mind?"

Sloan replied that he would have to consult his partners. Durant showed no sign of impatience. "His was the manner of a gentleman striving to be harmonious with the world." As he had done with Chrysler, he told Sloan to take his time and think it out.

Sloan was actually grateful for the offer. The same shrewd sense of the industry's direction that had underlain the growth of his company now prompted him to sell it. A few strong concerns were inevitably going to dominate automaking. Already, Hyatt depended heavily on two giant customers, Ford and General Motors. It could easily occur to either of them to save costs over the long pull by manufacturing its own bearings, leaving Sloan with a plant capacity far in excess of what he could sell. Consolidation had put his lifework out on a limb. Far better the shelter of a conglomerate's roof than such precarious freedom.

Sloan put the case to his co-owners in much these terms. They were less farseeing than he was, but agreed that, for testing purposes at least, they would set a figure which one of them frankly described as "crazy."

"Well, Mr. Sloan," said Durant pleasantly when the pair met again, "have you got a price in mind now?"

"Yes, Mr. Durant. I think about fifteen million dollars."

The smile never left Durant's face. "I'm still interested, Mr. Sloan." His teeth, it struck the younger man, were very white.[5]

Sloan was sent over to see Kaufman and Durant's New York lawyer, who together showed an interest $1.5 million less intense. The bargain was finally struck at $13.5 million. Sloan's minority partners hesitated over a provision that called for the usual heavy proportion of stock to cash in the payment, so he personally bought them out and converted their Hyatt holdings to United Motors holdings, with the result that he wound up the possessor of 135,000 shares in the combined enterprise, and was named its president. He had, at last, an enlarged sphere in which to apply his conceptions.

Durant's capacity to keep smiling was severely tested in the purchase of the Delco Corporation by the man who was its key figure, Charles F.

Kettering. It was Kettering's caprice to go through life pretending to be "just a mechanic" as he accumulated a fortune based on inventive ability and a solid foundation of professional training. He was the son of Ohio farm-owning parents, who had him ticketed for the ministry. He was already embarked on the abstract tides of theological study at Wooster College when he convinced his father and mother that he might serve God as acceptably through his true love, engineering. He transferred to Ohio State University and graduated in 1904, aged twenty-eight because of his late start and several recesses forced on him by a struggle with bad eyesight. He went to work soon afterward for the National Cash Register Company, designed a number of profitable improvements in its products, and became a co-founder, with Edward A. Deeds, of a corporation to develop, test, and market electrical and mechanical inventions. Kettering's breakthrough was the self-starter which he created in 1912, after which Delco moved quickly to a commanding position in automotive starting, lighting and ignition equipment.

Durant's terms for Delco were $5 millions in cash and $3 millions in stock, to be equally divided between the two owners. The stock was to be figured at the bankers' price of $50 per share — 30,000 in all. As always in such arrangements, there was a provision requiring the recipient of the stock to wait for a prescribed time before selling it at the higher market price and possibly forcing it into a temporary dip. On the day that the official papers were to be signed, Deeds alone appeared for a meeting with Durant, and explained that he was representing both partners and that Kettering fully understood all the terms.

A few hours after the delivery of the United Motors stock, the New York Curb Exchange received a large offering of it for sale from Kettering's broker. Durant tried to reach the inventor, failed, and finally got through to Deeds, whom he reproached angrily. Deeds waved it all aside. "Ket" was no businessman. He was away on a trip, had probably let the agreement slip his mind and left word at the broker's for an automatic sale at a certain price level. Durant had no choice but to settle for this excuse. In the fullness of time, Kettering would prove to be an asset well worth some momentary unpleasantness. The chain of events set in motion by Durant that spring brought him into active and profitable research activities for General Motors some three years afterward, but his failure to observe his agreement was one of the few unpleasant surprises for Durant in that otherwise resplendent season.[6]

Still, it could not diminish the promoter's pleasure in the fresh evidence of his powers. Durant was now both maker and master of three complex economic organisms, Chevrolet, United Motors, and General Motors. The transformation of the last-named into the General Motors Corporation of Delaware simply gave him more shares of stock, the chips of his game, without diluting his control. Five shares of new, "corporation" common were issued in exchange for every one of "company" common, and one and one-third of preferred for each preferred share in the old New Jersey–based concern. But the majority of them all remained in the grip of the Chevrolet organization.

From Kaufman came immediate suggestions that the three combines be united under a single, efficient sovereignty. But Durant held back. His overt reason was that he might then run afoul of the new Clayton Antitrust Act, passed in 1914. But beneath that there were emotional needs being served. Tidy administration held no attractions for him at best, and he was especially reluctant to see Chevrolet lose its particular identity. It was the project of his exile, endeared to him especially by its early ordeals. Jacob Newmark, its advertising chief, took note that even when he was back in command over all of General Motors, when he had "an engineering problem, or an advertising or sales angle he wished to discuss or have worked out which would be applicable to any of the . . . divisions, he would rely on Chevrolet executives."[7] Natural enough when so many of them were part of the old "family"—Hardy, Bishop, Hohensee—and Chevrolet's attorney, John Thomas Smith. Smith was the firmest of the friends made outside of Flint, and the closeness between him and Durant was an element of a new pattern of cosmopolitan life that layered itself around the person who had once been "Grand Pa's Willie" and then a promising young bachelor salesman in a sawmill community.

John Thomas Smith was born in 1890 to a New Haven gentleman who devoutly named his three sons John, James, and Joseph after the sons of Zebedee who became apostles. He grew up brilliant, and at college time was sent off to Omaha for supervision by an uncle while he attended Creighton College. He sailed through courses there, absorbing languages with special pleasure and filling a thick notebook full of classroom and other essays on the many topics among which his curiosity leaped and somersaulted: "A Plea to Catholic Journals and Their Readers"; "Judge Taney on Slavery"; "Imperialism"; "The Sun"; "Evolution"; "Buddhism and Brahmanism"; "The World Self-Existent and Eternal or No?"; "Oedipus"; "Lord Baltimore"; "Resolved: That Protection Is Against the Public Good." These and many more. On graduation he was offered a newspaper job in San Francisco, and prepared gratefully to accept it at a salary that was "more money than he had ever heard of," according to his own son's later recall. But he was commanded to return and attend Yale Law School. At twenty-one, he was a bachelor of laws, working for the Wall Street firm of Alexander and Greene. Before long he had opened his own office at 10 Cedar Street, barely big enough to accommodate a discussion among three people.[8]

Durant may have met him during his own period of explorations in the financial district. The acquaintance was formed by 1910, since Smith was then on the General Motors board of directors. And by 1916 Durant and "John Thomas" and their wives were fast friends, and Smith was becoming progressively more important and affluent as counsel to Chevrolet and General Motors, though still in his thirties.

The comradeship was curious. Durant was short of formal education, raised in a midwestern Presbyterian home, too busy for most of the first half-century of his life to develop much appreciation for the pleasures of the senses. Smith was a Roman Catholic, an omnivorous reader and fluent speaker in several tongues — he argued cases for Latin-American clients in Spanish, and was to conduct foreign negotiations for General Motors in French and German — an informed and appreciative consumer of good wine and good food, and a savant of comely things. He was an impressive figure later in life to the young attorneys who worked for him in General Motors' legal department, and one of them, David Sher, recollected that it was impossible to spend five minutes in Smith's compelling presence without realizing that he was "a person of the highest order of intellect."[9]

What drew Smith and Durant together was partly the chemistry of friendship that defies analysis. But an element of the attraction for Durant was, in all likelihood, an innate response to the unexpected encounter with someone of such breadth in the world of contracts, titles, notes, and shares. Wrapped though he might be in business concerns, Durant was rarely reached and stimulated by fellow industrialists and executives. Powerful people without imaginations like his own clearly bored him. His behavior showed plainly that he preferred his own desk, his phone lines to brokers, his anonymous checker partners or his old chums over their company. Smith was unique in his experience. And Smith, for his part, was tuned to certain emanations of sensitivity that were thrown off by his most unusual businessman-client. Their mutual regard probably prospered on the basis of each man's reaction to what was special about the other. It was strengthened rather than weakened by Smith's reported willingness to disagree with Durant when so minded. Social hours spent with the Smiths became part of a fresh setting for Durant's life, as his surroundings started to reflect his wealth.

For he was really rich now. Money had never been a personal problem for him. It was only corporate bankruptcy that he had scrambled so adeptly to avoid for years. But in 1916 there was an outpouring of dollars from almost every investment, and he began at last to spend them on himself and Catherine. He reported a gross individual income for the year of $3,419,835. Of this, seventy dollars was in "salary" as a Chevrolet director, $629,039 had been received in dividends, and $2,769,331 cleared in stock dealings — against only $266,958 in market losses, which were deductible.

He also deducted approximately $170,000 in interest payments, $48,000 in state and local taxes, and slightly more than $40,000 in miscellaneous business expenses. Altogether he and Catherine had a net income of $2,891,189.72. In that fourth year of collection of income tax, he paid a total of $356,217 on his $2.89 million earnings, a figure arrived at by combining a 2 percent tax on net "ordinary" income with a special surtax. His return for 1917 did not survive among his papers, but in the following year he received $2,104,954 in dividends, scored profits of $2,602,101 from "business, trade, commerce or sales," and earned interest on war bonds, premiums for shares of stock loaned to others, and royalties (amounting to $117.29) from the What Cheer Mining Company of Flint, for a gross total of $4,996,765. From this sum, however, he deducted nearly four millions in losses incurred through the sale, for $5,872,476, of stocks and bonds that had originally cost him $9,755,799 to acquire. From the remainder he also deducted $415,668 in miscellaneous expenses and other items, which included $15,385 in gifts that ranged from $10,000 to United War Work of New York down to $15 for the First Presbyterian Church of Flint. When the computations were complete, his tax bill this time was $377,374. The modesty of the figure was due to the operation of the internal revenue code at the time, which separated income into categories taxable at different rates. Dividends were not taxed at all. Thanks to his deductions, therefore, Durant actually had a negative net income for regular taxing purposes, and was only charged a surtax on $678,000 of his total earnings.[10]

Some of his losses, like some of his gains, were no more substantial than columns of figures in ledgers. But when the bookkeepers had finished their year-end dotting and underlining, he had anywhere from a third of a million to over two million dollars to dispose of in a period when a dollar's purchasing power was still lusty. In 1917 he moved into an apartment whose annual rental was $16,500, at 907 Fifth Avenue, on the corner of Seventy-second Street. It overlooked the green preserve of Central Park, along whose margins there flowed, in regulated spurts, the annually thickening stream of motor traffic that was Durant's river of gold. The clamor of brakes and horns did not penetrate deeply into the well-draped and beautifully decorated rooms for which they paid. Here, amid an elegance of carpet and carving, statue and tapestry, figured silk and glowing silver, the Durants made their New York residence for a decade and a half. For the purposes of the tax code, at least on the 1918 return, it became a deductible place of work, a stopping place in town that was handy to the office as well. The basic Durant home, after November 9, 1917, was on the seaside at Deal, New Jersey. On that date Durant bought from the heirs and executors of Regina Rothschild, widow of Jacob Rothschild, a white stone villa of thirty-seven rooms designed some ten years earlier by an architect named Arthur P. Gottlieb, and known as "Raymere." It sat on a lot of five hundred by two hundred and sixty feet, was surrounded by hedges, gardens, lawn, fishpond, and fountain, and was referred to in local guidebooks as a mansion in "French style."[11]

Durant paid $115,000 for the property, $60,000 of it in a three-year mortgage. Raymere stood at the western edge of Ocean Avenue, a north-south road that ran just inside the shoreline down to Asbury Park, a few miles below. Shortly after he bought it, Durant acquired additional lots that stretched from the back of the house westward to the right of way of the New York and Long Branch Railroad. Later he waved his checkbook and gathered into his grasp still more lots across Ocean Avenue, down to the water's edge. With a domain that ran from the tracks to the breakers, dominated by his castle, he had put the days of boarding with his son-in-law far behind him.

Except in winter, Durant would commute from Raymere to New York. It was an especially good time to be successful in the great city, which was reaching its height of development. Its energies had bored underground subway tunnels through solid rock and were flinging office buildings as much as an eighth of a mile into the sky. Its separate cultural provinces were already bursting with vitality or on the threshold of their golden ages — Wall Street, the lower East Side, Greenwich Village, Broadway, and Harlem. The few blocks south of Columbus Circle where the motor, tire, and oil companies were settling their command centers shared in the electricity. They were called the auto district. In the city at large Durant was a minor prince. In that little but potent zone a few minutes from his apartment, he was a sovereign.

He could scarcely have felt at that moment that any strain would threaten what newspapers inaccurately called his "alliance" with the Du Ponts. He was no longer dependent on their goodwill, and the relationship was less that of parties to a treaty than it was a honeymoon. Nothing portended changes, or suggested the sobering thought that any connection with a house so powerful might have aspects more complicated than anything he had handled in dealing with Flint's wagon companies. Time would have its own way of dealing with this self-confident attitude.

II No more than Durant did Pierre du Pont anticipate any difficulties in the collaboration that he believed would naturally arise between the president and the chairman of the board of the General Motors Corporation. He saw the man who had raised Buick from the dead and produced Chevrolet from emptiness as a brilliant manufacturer who had unluckily run on financial shoals in 1910. He, Du Pont, would bring his own financing and organizing skills to the game and free the creator to concentrate on operational problems, a favor that he innocently expected Durant to appreciate. To an automotive engineer who wrote in search of a job, Du Pont replied: "Beg to advise that my connection with the automobile industry is largely administrative and financial,"[12] and he scrupulously passed along to Durant letters beseeching his attention to new inventions or prospects, with little covering memos: "I dislike to bother you." . . . "I am sorry to again trouble you." . . . "Can you give this passing attention?" Deprecation of his own importance came naturally to Du Pont's pen. When Durant urged him in the spring of 1917 to help resist a measure for a wartime excess profits tax on auto sales, Du Pont wrote to both of Delaware's senators and its lone representative and so informed Durant, adding the modest and unlikely comment: "I have not much hope of consideration, but it is worth while trying."[13]

There were the usual exchanges of high-level courtesies. Durant was asked by Raskob to put in a word to expedite the delivery of a Buick to Du Pont's brother-in-law. Du Pont got a request to intimate the virtues of General Motors trucks to a subsidiary company in his organization. Both men promptly complied. Seemingly the joints between their enterprises were smoothly welded. But in fact the underlying relationship was complex. The real point of contact between General Motors and E. I. du Pont de Nemours and Company was John J. Raskob, and Du Pont and Raskob were a strangely mated pair. The two of them and Durant formed an even more unusual triad of leadership.

Du Pont himself belonged to a rarity in the United States, a hereditary elite. He was the descendant of a refugee from the French Revolution who, at the nineteenth century's outset, had established on a branch of the Delaware River a successful powder mill and a dynasty. For the following century the children and the children's children of Eleuthère Irénée du Pont and their kinsmen had bejeweled the upper reaches of the judiciary, the armed services, and the legislatures of Delaware and the nation. Pierre, born in 1870, matured in the semifeudal atmosphere of an estate on the Brandywine, mantled in its slow-moving, protective expectancy. The curtain of security was rent violently just after his fourteenth birthday, when an accidental explosion at the factory killed his father, but the flow of life closed around the tear and carried him on through Penn Charter School, and then to Massachusetts Institute of Technology, where he was five years ahead of Alfred Sloan. He posed for a college-boy snapshot there, showing the world a young, moustached face under a funny fraternity hat. He had a beer mug in front of him. He was said to be a good man with a poker hand. But it was understood that after graduation he would put away childish things and go to work. At thirty he was accumulating business seasoning as the operator of a family investment, a brace of street railway systems—one in Ohio, one in Texas.

In 1902 there was a crisis. The explosives business, which was still an important source of fortune, had fallen on hard times. The clansmen responsible for it were ready to sell it, leading to the unthinkable possibility of its passing out of family hands. With two cousins, Coleman and Alfred, Pierre bought the firm. Its separate plants were consolidated in a new holding company. It prospered on the advancing century's demand for explosive materials to mine, to quarry, to dredge, to clear, to excavate, and to destroy. It came to a position of dominance in the industry in America, and had strong links to foreign cartels.

Pierre slowly worked his way toward leadership. In 1915 Coleman retired. Pierre and his younger brother Irénée bought out Coleman's interest, and Pierre became the corporation's president. The talents he brought to the job were a formidable will to order, and a sense of the need to diversify. He enlarged the organization's research activities and its worldwide search for nitrate and other mineral deposits, and began to turn it in the direction of manufacturing chemicals and synthetic products created from them. In that way E. I. du Pont de Nemours, Incorporated, would be doubly safe, from changes in the market and from antitrust prosecution. Ironically, World War I interrupted this program and simultaneously assured that there would be plenty of money to carry it on in the long run. From 1914 to 1918 it was estimated that the firm furnished a billion and a half pounds of explosive material to the Allied armies, and made 40 percent of all the smokeless powder fired by their guns. Millions in munitions profits piled up in the Du Pont treasury.

Even before the boom, Pierre built a management structure that reflected the military staff model emerging as a necessity in the coordination of large enterprises. At the top were a finance committee that concerned itself exclusively with funding and cost control, and an executive committee for operations. Under these were the neatly labeled divisions: manufacturing, sales, purchasing, appropriations, development, legal, employees, reports, development. The ultimate idea was to channel, dam, and direct the flow of information upward, execution downward, with the minimum of imprecision.

It was not merely engineering logic that was built into the firm's corporate bones. The tidiness of Pierre du Pont was a force that made itself felt in whatever he touched. He had abandoned the moustache with his youth, measured the world through rimless glasses, dressed in conservative colors, and ventured out with his thinning hair covered by dark derbies. At Longwood, his private estate, life was regularized by a thick book of instructions, which servants had to learn. There were schedules for serving the three-course breakfasts and the seven-course dinners, for cleaning and polishing the tableware weekly, for inserting fresh candles in the candlesticks each morning. The gardens were Du Pont's special delight. A botanist by hobby, he loved to collect, trim, prune, train, align, and improve the plants that surrounded the home and filled his greenhouses. He gave a fitting amount of time to civic endeavor, especially to the modernization of Delaware's school system. His charitable donations were large, consistent, and thoughtfully adapted to long-range objectives.[14]

That so scrupulous an arranger of particles of life should have befriended John J. Raskob was a fresh proof of the heart's inscrutability. Raskob had swum into Du Pont's ken as a youngster of twenty-three, hustling to support a widowed mother and three siblings. His father had been an Alsatian immigrant cigarmaker in Lockport, New York. He died just after Raskob graduated from high school in 1898, an event that forced his son to leave business college and go to work for a pump company at $7.50 per week. Young Raskob had no wish to remain in a dead end. He asked around and learned by luck that a Mr. Pierre du Pont, who operated the streetcar line in Lorain, Ohio, needed a stenographer. Raskob applied, got the job, and jumped to an annual salary of $1,000.

Du Pont soon found that Raskob was no ordinary secretary. He had an outstanding grasp of financial subjects. When Du Pont moved on to Texas, he took Raskob with him as treasurer of the traction company there, and then brought him back to Delaware as a fiscal advisor to the reorganized explosives corporation. "Money multiplied and developed in his hands,"[15] a reporter later wrote of Raskob, and so it did—both Du Pont's and his own. Not only could he devise intricate, skillful arrangements for raising and transferring capital, but he had a fine eye for the industrial future and what it offered a canny investor. A natural optimist, he not only kited his own savings into a substantial fortune, but was certain that the miracle of compounded dividends was available to anyone who had his faith. In a memorable peak moment of bullishness, he was to write a magazine article entitled "Everyone Ought to Be Rich." It explained how anyone who began early in life to put only a few dollars weekly into "good, sound common stocks" could hardly fail to make a fortune by middle age. The date of publication of this piece of advice was 1928.

In 1917, however, he was the embodied verification of the success legend, and he enjoyed it, though unobtrusively. He had a country place with ample room for his eleven children near Wilmington, a summer retreat in Maryland, where he indulged in Chesapeake Bay sailing and golf, and a suite at New York's Carlton House, where he stayed when on business there. He went out little in society, walked to work in New York, and gave large sums, without publicity, to Catholic charities.

Inside the dove-colored world of the Du Pont executive offices he was a colorful figure. He enjoyed wearing what were described as "gay shirts," and it was his habit to shed his jacket to show them off, and to scribble notes on the starched cuffs in shorthand. Stocky, energetic, and quick-tongued, he would bounce into the head office with an idea, "wanting to get it into action by waving a magic wand; he would want the whole organization to come to a meeting right off." So said Alfred Sloan, who observed the performance at General Motors headquarters. His "aggressive, impatient intelligence" seemed misplaced among neat charts of organization, but Sloan divined that that was his strength. "Mr. Raskob was brilliant and imaginative, where Mr. du Pont was steady and conservative." The short, pushy Raskob complemented the tall, reticent Du Pont in some needed way.[16]

Raskob's optimism should have vibrated in sympathetic harmony with Durant's, and to some extent did. Both men were expansionists in their business outlook, but with significant differences. Raskob was interested not in new ventures but in building on existing foundations. He did not enjoy Durant's contacts with the production process itself; his pleasure came from manipulating the financial symbols that kept the assembly lines moving. Above all, there was a limiting streak of prudence in him. He was not a loner; he worked for the Du Ponts, and whatever he undertook would not jeopardize that shelter. He had a feeling, absent in Durant, for boundaries.

Still, the two bulls initially hit it off, though the friendship was complicated by Durant's constant motion and Raskob's own shuttling between Wilmington and New York. Throughout 1916 and 1917 Raskob's letters to General Motors' main office sounded a consistent theme of encounters just missed—calls made or wires sent as Durant was bounding off to Detroit, to Pentwater, to Chicago, to the West Coast, to Oshawa, to Washington. Once Raskob himself, freshly back from a winter rest in Palm Beach, almost plaintively asked for a meeting "at some hotel where we can talk without being interrupted by telephone and otherwise," suggesting that he, like others, had trouble getting Durant's unbroken attention for more than a few consecutive minutes. Once he sounded desperate: "Have been trying all afternoon to reach you on telephone but the operator seems unable to get your number to answer." Once he tried ingenuity: "Please call me twelve o'clock tomorrow[,] Saturday[.] Sending Special Delivery letter to you tonight."[17]

But he never sounded irked. On a day in 1917 when he did get to see Durant, he handed him a book of prepaid mileage coupons on the Pennsylvania Railroad, and shortly afterward got it back with a check for $2.75 and a notation that 109 miles had been used. "I meant that you should accept this with my compliments," answered Raskob in mock despair, "and must now try some other way of getting even for the many courtesies shown me." About a year later he requested "that photograph of you which you forgot to promise to send me. I have intended for a long time to ask you for this." Durant absently pocketed the letter, found it again in three months and gave it to Murphy, who sent the picture.[18]

Perhaps these darting passages back and forth across the map disturbed Du Pont from the beginning. A friend of Durant's in his later life thought so; Durant, it was his belief, was "mercurial . . . you couldn't catch him. [He] did not fit into the concept of capitalistic rationality."[19] But there was no sign of unease so far as operating policies were concerned. For at least a year and a half Durant had his head, and in the middle of 1917 he strengthened his grip on the car-making divisions by firing the Lelands. His feelings toward them were scarcely cordial after the hard bargain to which they had held him in 1909, and for their part they claimed that Durant, on his return to power, backed out of a promise to compensate them for salary cuts imposed under the banker regime. Through the 1916–1917 winter, Durant apparently complained that they were disorganized and slow, and denied their requests for more inventory and larger production schedules. "Not interested in GM. Interested in H. M. & W. C. Leland," Durant penciled on the margin of a letter from Wilfred after one angry exchange.[20] Finally, canceling his own pledge to leave them alone, he told them they would be replaced after August. The episode would have remained a purely private in-house quarrel if the Lelands had not struck back a year later. In the full, febrile glow of wartime patriotism they testified to a Senate committee that they had been fired for wanting to undertake military contracts — that Durant was a pacifist who had no sympathy with the war or what he called their patriotic "platitudes." The story was untrue on the evidence in the company files, but it required quick public relations counteraction to avoid serious damage to sales.

The Lelands were replaced at Cadillac's helm by Richard Collins, a smalltown Illinois product whose friendship with Durant ran back to the days when Collins was selling farm equipment for the John Deere Company at the same rural exhibitions where Durant-Dort buggies were being promoted. Collins was brought into the Buick sales department, rose to be its general manager, and was nicknamed "Trainload" for the quantities that he was responsible for shipping out.

Over at Oldsmobile in 1916 the head man was Edward Ver Linden, a former Buick master mechanic. At the Oakland plant was Fred Warner, likewise a former Durant-Dort salesman. Collins, Ver Linden, and Warner all had private salary and bonus arrangements with Durant. Their fealty was personal, not institutional. With a friendly management at General Motors Truck, with Chevrolet firmly in hand, and with Buick under Walter Chrysler, who was independent-minded but grateful, Durant could count on firm support from any council of the men who actually ran the factories.

Even had Du Pont been otherwise minded, there were sound tactical reasons for not challenging Durant's rulings with regard to production.

It was in the areas of funding and structure, predictably, that trouble began to appear as Wilmington discovered that the wizard of Flint was not amenable to guidance.

III On a wintry January day in 1917, Raskob dictated a letter to Durant, the buoyancy of its mood reflecting his own pleasure at a forthcoming Palm Beach vacation. The first six months of the new presidential regime at General Motors were showing splendid results in the sales and profit statements. A new year was starting, and it was time, he suggested, to think constructive thoughts about the many forthcoming tomorrows. He and Du Pont agreed that the moment was ripe to adopt a policy of paying a regular annual 12 percent dividend on GM's common stock. Whatever Du Pont's reasons might be, his own were tied in to bright plans for growth. If the rate of improvement over 1915–1916 earnings should be maintained, the company could expect to earn something in the neighborhood of $108 million over the five years ahead. Supposing that slightly over half that amount, about $59 millions, were put back into an expansion plan, then General Motors' assets could jump from an existing $73 millions in value to $132 millions by the middle of 1921. And— Raskob's mind enjoyed playing with such possibilities—if more investment money from outside sources should be needed, a regular dividend record would guarantee that any new issues of stock for sale would be snapped up. GM common had settled to a level of 200 after the galvanic leaps of the proxy war, and was worth every penny of it. With a guaranteed yield, it would have an allure certain to produce fresh money in any moment of need.

Having demonstrated, with tables, that these anticipations were glimpses into a very palpable future, Raskob ended with the genial flourish of asking Durant to come along with Catherine and join him and Helena for some relaxation in the sunshine. Whether the invitation was taken up went unrecorded, but a few weeks later Raskob was back, refreshed and bubbling with the great prospects of an idea he had long been advocating—the merger of General Motors, United Motors, and Chevrolet. "This would make a magnificent company," was his prediction, "with a splendid organization and would result, I am sure, in elimination of a great deal of waste and a savings of large amounts of money."[21]

Yet Durant held back. *Magnificent* and *splendid* were words that appealed to him, though he was usually the one to use them on others. Raskob had an odd way of turning him from a salesman into a prospect. But he had already brushed aside Kaufman's suggestions for the three-part fusion of his companies. And whatever the virtues of regular dividends, they would pin him down to sharing profits with the stockholders at a time when he might have other, more inventive uses for them.

As it was, his cherished freedom had already been slightly pared down the preceding summer. When Du Pont finally got to see him he had pressed for more director participation in decision-making through subcommittees of the board. The founder had yielded a little; he would settle for a three-man executive committee. Not enough for Du Pont. He wanted a finance committee as well, and now it emerged that in some way, though the control fight was over and Pierre du Pont was still only a small stockholder, he had enough influence to get his way. The finance committee was created. In a loose sense it did not threaten Durant. He and Du Pont sat on it, and the other three members were Raskob, Kaufman, and McClement. The latter two were his friends and allies, though the terms meant something different in their cases than it did with men like Bishop and Hardy. The committee would meet monthly to review expenditures. It had to approve any ordinary outlays of over $300,000 a month, and any new appropriations of more than $150,000. Twice a year it was to set up a capital expenditures budget for the following six months.[22]

The committee had not yet been troublesome. It had authorized an expansion in plant and equipment from about $24.3 million to slightly over $40 million, which pleased Durant, and even after financing that out of retained earnings it would have $11 million available for dividends, which satisfied Du Pont. Durant still kept on top of day-to-day operations undisturbed, helped by a small private staff consisting of John Thomas Smith; the company's treasurer, Herbert Rice; and its comptroller, Meyer Prensky. So at the midpoint of 1917, there was as yet no conflict between himself and the quiet board chairman who was taking his job with such seriousness.

And yet. There were small shifts in the wind, a different hue to the waves, signs that experienced business pilots could read. The New York headquarters of General Motors, clustered in the United States Rubber Building at 1764 Broadway, were slightly expanded to make room for visitors from Wilmington. The first to show up was J. Amory Haskell, looking kind and elderly with his white, colonel-of-the-Lancers moustache. "Just looking around," he said amiably, but then settled into a full-time desk in the export division. Office space was also set aside for Raskob and Du Pont to use when they came up from the south. A few blocks away in the Chevrolet offices at Eleventh Avenue and Fifty-seventh, there was another new face from Delaware at the conference table. Du Pont's Chevrolet holdings entitled him to a seat on the company's board, and he filled it with Hamilton Barksdale, president of the American Nitrogen Company, one of his subsidiaries. By the time these settlings-in were completed, Jacob Newmark observed, "the 'old-timers' knew that there was a 'new deal' in General Motors, and that although Mr. Durant was the chief, there were others who had to be taken into consideration."[23]

But success has a way of keeping potential conflict safely sealed in the bottle. There were no shocks to test the distribution of power under the "new deal" so long as the profits kept flowing. All was well—until, in spite of prosperity, the price of General Motors stock suddenly began to slide down, and then further down, dragging William C. Durant's liberty of action with it.

The slump began in April. By June GM was quoted at 115 on the board. It dropped to 86 by the middle of September, and in the closing week of October it was languishing at 75. It was an unpredictable and puzzling drop. "The ability of General Motors Company to earn large returns on its capitalization does not appear to have been impaired by any developments affecting the automobile industry to date," reported Hayden, Stone and Company in a September market letter.[24] Nonetheless, buyers were turning their backs. Durant was certain he knew the answer. It was the work of "professional speculators of Wall Street," the short sellers, the destructive "bears."

Ordinarily, Durant's sunny mind had few dark corners where imaginary enemies could lurk, but in times of market distress, he saw bears everywhere as readily as mad kings saw plotters. What a short seller did was merely to contract to deliver shares of a stock on a future date at the price prevailing when the agreement was signed. His hope was that the market would fall in the meantime, and he could pick up what he needed to fulfill his bargain cheaply and pocket the difference. In effect he placed a legitimate bet (at that time) on a market decline.

Durant was convinced, however, that the mere act of entering a short contract was itself a vote of no-confidence that depressed prices. More-over, he suspected many of the bears of deliberately forcing them down by fictitious sales, or the spread of damaging rumors about the company whose stock was involved. He himself always bet the opposite side of the wager, buying at the quotation of the moment for receipt on a day to come, when, if the price had risen as hoped, he could resell profitably. That this traditional "bull" position could also be called speculation, and that a stock's market value could be temporarily inflated beyond its real earning potential by the same maneuvers as the bears used, was something he never admitted. He could not believe that it was possible to exaggerate the growth potential of any securities he supported, especially if they came from a company of his own. He almost seemed to endow the mechanics of a trade with magical significance. A future purchase was an act of belief that by itself could transform an ordinary share into a more valuable one. A short sale was an enchanter's curse that turned an Exchange beauty into a toad.

Therefore Durant put the blame on an organized and unreasonable campaign.

This drive was without rhyme or reason. It was not because of any inherent weakness in the financial position of the Company or the Company's business outlook. In fact during that period our business was never better. The demand for our products continued; our production increased steadily over the same period of last year, which year was the record in the history of the industry. . . .

So these things financial could not have been made the foundation by the speculators for their drive against our common stock.

Such was the diagnosis, but what was the remedy? For the long pull, Durant framed a scheme that was to captivate him for years to come, and be an important force in several of his moves at critical moments. The answer was to disperse holdings so widely that large transfers were harder to bring off. The mechanism to effect this was to be a forerunner of a mutual investors' fund, specializing in automobile stocks. Holdings would be limited, and a partial payment plan would open the doors to buyers of small means. The project might be launched with an appeal to General Motors' employees, then its stockholders, and finally, perhaps, the public at large. Durant explained it in a draft circular letter of November, 1917, soliciting applications.

The management of General Motors corporation believes that the prevention of another such attack must be found in obtaining a wider distribution of the shares with investors seeking permanent lodgement of their funds. . . .

It would truly be ideal if our shareholders were made up largely of investors owning not more than twenty shares each; these scattered from Maine to California and from the Gulf to the Great Lakes. That is what we shall ultimately effect. . . .

In this manner the amount of General Motors common stock available for the operations of the speculative element of the Stock Market will be materially reduced. . . . This because the volume of transactions at any time will then be governed largely through the buying and selling in small amounts from investors instead of being controlled by the heavy transactions of the professional operators.[25]

The quixotic and the imperial mingled inseparably in this proposal. An army of small stockholders strewn nationwide would give a new and liberal dimension to corporate ownership. It was a fresh and intriguing conception in 1917. But it was also true that under such an arrangement no large single holder could threaten Durant's control. The vision of a democratic host of installment-plan investors, battling the speculators with their modest accounts in country banks, had a Jacksonian ring to it, but it was always plain that they would have a leader and that Durant would be his name.

In any case, such a mobilization would be a long-term undertaking. His short-run answer to GM's decline was to be a move in the exact opposite direction; to wit, heavy transactions by professional operators; specifically, a Durant-led buying syndicate. He proposed this to Du Pont and Raskob, convinced as he always was that a massed phalanx of purchase orders could stem and reverse any downward thrust. They turned him down, repeating that the surest way to stimulate general interest in GM was to promise regular dividend checks.

Thwarted, he took a step that rapidly worsened his position. He began to buy on his own account, and as the price continued to topple, he was caught and squeezed in the harsh mechanics of buying "on margin" in a falling market.

The rules allowed a buyer to put down as little as 10 percent of the cost of a block of stock. The brokers carried him on their books for the amount above this "margin," which was simply Wall Street's name for a cash deposit. In effect, they were lending the customer the unpaid balance — at interest, of course — secured by the stock itself. Thus far it was like any installment purchase, except that the value of the object that the lender could "repossess" was subject to sudden sharp drops in value. When that happened — when the price of the stock fell to where its sale would not cover the loan — the brokers called for more margin.

When Durant's margin calls exceeded his available cash, he could borrow from the banks, but he often had to pledge as collateral other shares of stock, including GM, that he fully owned. As GM shares went on shrinking in value, he needed to lay hands on more of them to put up, which meant borrowing shares, or stripping his own reserves, and starting fresh rounds of purchasing. A steady drain was set up, and at the end of the road, if the nosediving stock did not level off, lay the final horror of default; of being sold out by the brokers and bankers for what cash they could get, and left with nothing.

No one was ever to know how close Durant was to this precipice in 1917, but the situation was bad enough for him to take a drastic step. At the end of October he turned to the directors of General Motors, with Pierre du Pont at their head, and asked them to open the company treasury and give him help with his personal finances. He wanted a loan of a million dollars.

He did not shuffle or clear his throat apologetically when he approached the finance committee. His market operations, he said, were aimed only at supporting GM, and were therefore of direct benefit to every stockholder in the concern, so that his request was entirely reasonable. His own shares would secure the loan, repayment would promptly follow the inevitable recovery on the Exchange, and he would be freed from worries that were "absorbing his time and attention to the detriment of the Company's interests." It was a self-assured, eyes-straight-ahead statement, as much like a proposition and as little like a supplication as it could be made to sound, but for all that it was not what the committee might have expected from a man who had been hailed eighteen months earlier as a financial genius.

On November 9, the five of them refused the loan. They had been inclined to go along at first, but then McClement, whose experience they all respected, had pulled back. The idea of a corporation lending its own president funds for market operations, he said, was possibly illegal, and if not that, might well invite a civil suit by stockholders in which individual directors could be held liable for losses. The others agreed, and Durant's petition died, and with it, more importantly, at least some of McClement's confidence in him. But the need to help Durant remained real, because a public airing of his distress could be lamentable for General Motors. So the finance committee hit on a temporary solution. They voted the president an annual salary of $500,000, retroactive to the beginning of 1916. He would have his million, and not as a loan but as payment justly earned. Ostensibly, it was a victory. But it was conceded by the committee, not wrested from them, and it was clear evidence that the weight of influence in that crucial body was shifting away from Durant and toward Du Pont.[26]

The course of history was accelerating that transfer. While Durant labored in his difficulties, every month of the war was making the Du Pont interests richer. That was the central truth on which an entire new control arrangement was built as a final containment of the problem of the 1917 break in GM's stock-market standing. The money bestowed on Durant averted his possible financial collapse, but the problem of restoring the healthy price levels of early in the year remained, seemingly beyond a temporary fix. Initiatives were weighed and discarded in hasty high-level conferences. Then John Raskob came up with the kind of idea that had earned him his reputation. The Du Pont Corporation was sitting on a fifty-million-dollar surplus. Let it use half that sum to buy General Motors and Chevrolet stock. That would raise prices well beyond the power of even a strong syndicate to achieve. And it would put the house of Du Pont solidly into the country's fastest-growing business at the very moment when its old munitions mainstay was about to vanish, for the world conflict was clearly entering its final stage.

Du Pont was presented with this in private conclave, nodded, frowned, made a reservation. Yes, but. It must be spelled out this time that Durant would leave financial control absolutely in Du Pont hands. And as a token, the symbolic single annual peppercorn or red rose of feudal submission, the merger of General Motors, United Motors, and Chevrolet must be pushed through.[27] When this was put to Durant, whatever he may have thought, he assented. The brink was too close.

The matter could not simply end there. The Du Pont Corporation had its own board of directors who would need to be won over to a sudden leap into an alien, competitive field. On the weekend before Christmas in 1917 they gathered in Wilmington to listen to the arguments. Pierre du Pont was expectedly low-keyed. The company, he pointed out, was giving up none of its interest or expertise in the business of chemicals. But surplus engineering and research talent was going to be available when peace was restored, and it would benefit everyone to redirect it into motor-car development. They all knew that there were slack times when new chemical products were in development, and in such seasons a flow of General Motors dividends would be a very significant comfort.

Raskob then advanced to center stage to present a paper that came to be known as the Raskob Memorandum. He was in a promotional efflorescence that might, under other circumstances, have won Durant's professional admiration. There would be no problem with competition, he promised. "The General Motors Company today occupies a unique position in the automobile industry and . . . with proper management will show results in the future second to none." Its prospects were as boundless as the horizons of the land of the starry banner. The proposed purchase offered "an attractive investment . . . in what I consider the most promising industry in the United States, a country which in my opinion holds greater possibilities for development in the immediate future than any country in the world."

And what of the directors' pride in their organization, their duty to the stockholders?

During the past two years our Company has been doing big things. After the war it seems to me it will be absolutely impossible for us to drop back to being a little company again and to prevent that we must look for opportunities, know them when we see them and act with courage. . . .

Rather than have a coterie of our directors taking advantage of this in a personal way, thus diverting their time and attention (to some degree at least) from our affairs, it would be far preferable for the Company to accept the opportunity afforded, thus giving our directors the interest so desired through their stock ownership in the Du Pont Company.

If pride and patriotism combined did not urge the step loudly enough, there was profit. The money would simply roll in. The new General Motors, which would include Chevrolet, would earn at least $65 millions in 1918. Even after war taxes and the preferred stock dividend, there would be $43.8 millions to be split up, a sum that was about 40 percent of the value of all General Motors stock then outstanding. Where else would a comparable return on investment be found?

These points alone might have carried the day, but Raskob, in full flight, sang lyrics whose echoes would haunt the corporation many years afterward, when the Department of Justice replayed them. To woo the chemicals-oriented skeptics, Raskob dangled the prospect of a closed market for Du Pont–made auto enamels and synthetic upholstery fabrics: "Our interest in the General Motors Company will undoubtedly secure for us the entire Fabrikoid, Pyralin, paint and varnish business of those companies, which is a substantial factor." Even more fatally, he hinted at a total Du Pont engorgement of General Motors over a period of time. Durant was not present at the meeting. Nor, to anyone's knowledge, did he ever see the Raskob Memorandum. There can be little question that its contents would have astonished him.

Mr. Durant . . . is very desirous of having an organization as perfect as possible to handle this wonderful business. . . . Mr. Durant's association with Mr. P. S. du Pont, Mr. H. M. Barksdale, Mr. J. A. Haskell, Mr. Lammot Belin and the writer has been such as to result in the expression of the desire on his part to have us more substantially interested with him, thus enabling us to assist him, particularly in an executive and financial way, in the direction of this huge business.

Perhaps it is not made clear that the directorates of the motor companies will be chosen by Du Pont and Durant. Mr. Durant should [sic] be continued as President of the Company, Mr. P. S. du Pont will be continued as Chairman of the Board, the Finance Committee will be ours and we will have such representation on the Executive Committee as we desire . . . , and it is the writer's belief that ultimately the Du Pont Company will absolutely control and dominate the whole General Motors situation with the entire approval of Mr. Durant, who, I think, will eventually place his holdings with us[,] taking his payment therefor in some securities mutually satisfactory.[28]

So, in fiery epilogue, Raskob outlined his supertrust, and won his point. Two Du Pont family stockholders held out, but the plan was adopted. Legal and taxing requirements for one corporation to invest in another had to be met, and the mechanism created was a special holding company known as Du Pont American Industries, which bought 97,875 shares of General Motors common — about 24 percent of the outstanding total — and 133,690 shares of Chevrolet, enough for a very audible voice in its direction. The price was $25 million, provided by the parent company. $22 millions' worth of the stock was bought on the open market, an action that did, as predicted, lift and stabilize the price. $1.8 millions' worth were purchased from Nathan Hofheimer, and the final $1.2 million in shares came from Durant himself.[29]

By the end of January, 1918, it was all accomplished, and words were weak to carry the full freight of meaning in the changed picture. In June of 1916 the Du Pont connection had been through the small, if critical, number of shares personally owned by Pierre. Now the firm of E. I. du Pont de Nemours, Incorporated, was the second largest stockholder in General Motors, next to Durant. The finance committee, moreover, more or less officially became a Du Pont organ. Pierre took over its chair. McClement and Kaufman resigned, and were replaced by Irénée and Henry F. du Pont. The three of them and Raskob would keep watch over the money chest. The departures of McClement and Kaufman were not forced. Durant was no longer their golden champion. "If there is anything else I can do to strengthen your position in this situation," wrote Kaufman to Du Pont in submitting his resignation, "do not hesitate to command me."[30]

Everything was handled with great tact. Du Pont went on excusing himself for taking up Durant's time by forwarding "motor projects I have promised to send for your 'waste-basket.'" He explained very carefully to the originators of such projects: "E. I. du Pont de Nemours and Company . . . have purchased a large interest in General Motors Corporation and the Chevrolet Motor Company, but do not control, although working in harmony with Mr. Durant, the other large interest."[31] Even the press releases were marvelously sensitive. When the union of General Motors and Chevrolet was announced, the nuptial headline read: "Du Ponts Prepare for Auto Expansion. Durant's Vision Realized."[32] And a year afterward, when the Flint Chamber of Commerce, at its third annual banquet, honored Durant, the 550 pairs of applauding palms included those of John J. Raskob, who was present to testify to Wilmington's respect for Flint's favored son.[33]

Yet the essence of things was altered. There was another official dinner, a formal affair, held at New York's Metropolitan Club late in February of 1918. Du Pont set it up in order to present Durant to the new members of the finance committee and "our friends among the bankers of New York." The friends included the heads of Chemical National and Chase National, of Guaranty Trust and Bankers Trust, of Irving National and National City, of Empire Trust and the National Bank of Commerce, and Chatham and

Phenix, naturally. There were even two who had come from Philadelphia, representing Philadelphia National and Fourth Street National. They were grandees of the purse one and all, and if they had dressed to show their rank and power as men did in the Renaissance, the room would have been aflame with velvet capes and silver dagger hilts. As it was, they sat back in their black and white dinner clothes to appraise Durant, comfortable in the knowledge that any money they might put up for him to spend would be supervised by three Du Ponts and their lieutenant, which was the evening's basic message.[34]

Now at last, it seemed, with the finance committee imposing order on Durant's turbulent creation, there would be a reign of peace and prosperity at General Motors. Enjoying these pleasant intimations of things to come, Pierre du Pont left the bankers' feast to march on into a future that would be full of surprises.

Second Empire:

the Collapse

I Outwardly unshaken by the dilution of his control, Durant soared into 1918 on the lift of two new undertakings, still sure, in spite of everything, of his gift for choosing winners. It was put to the test almost as soon as the year started, when he was called on in his Detroit office by one of two young brothers named Murray. Together with their father they owned the Murray Body Company, a subcontractor supplying General Motors with fenders, body stampings and other sheet metal parts.

Into Durant's ear the small businessman poured a distressing family tale. The father, it seemed, had got himself the kind of distracting toy that early senility sometimes endows with a fatal glitter. No, it was not a young mistress that J. W. Murray had taken into his life. It was an invention. Father had found a man named Alfred Mellowes, who, with a partner, had invented a — a, well, an electric icebox. He called it a "Frigerator," the Guardian Frigerator, and since 1916 he and some friends, having organized a company, had been struggling unsuccessfully to produce the device in quantity. Father had gotten interested, poured some money into the cripple, was taking precious time from body parts affairs to nurse it, and was about to lose his shirt and his senses together. Would Mr. Durant, who was an old friend, try to talk him into some sense?

Durant liked nothing better than to chat with the comradely members of his nationwide constituency of dealers and suppliers. He arranged an interview with Murray, and Murray, in an eruption of enthusiasm, turned the dialogue in a wholly unforeseen direction. He ticked off the deficiences of the existing method of preserving food — the unsanitary blocks of ice, covered with dirt from the delivery wagon, against which unwrapped groceries were cradled; the heavy pans of sloppy melt-water beneath the box that housewives had to empty frequently; the difficulty of guessing needed quantities; the delayed deliveries; the waste, the expense. In contrast, electric refrigeration would be clean, available for pennies daily, a helpful, brightening presence in the kitchen, a homemaker's friend.

By the time he was finished Durant had forgotten his mission of discouragement. Here was another self-seller thrusting itself at him. He immediately agreed to go with Murray to the abandoned organ factory that was Guardian Frigerator's workshop.

Up dark stairs they climbed, into a warm, smelly clutter of bags of sawdust and charcoal insulating material, sheets of fiber and metal, compressors, radiators, wires, pipes, coils, hinges, all gangrenous organs of a dying enterprise. Durant looked, and was once more young and happy, certain that he knew how to quicken those morbid members into life. Writing of it later, Sloan understood what happened that day.

He possessed rare ability to sense an opportunity in some inventor's attic. The Buick car had been scarcely more than an engine in an improvised body when it was first shown hopefully to him. In Boston, in 1908, a stranger said to Durant: "I can make spark plugs out of porcelain." . . . So when Durant accompanied the elder Murray up two flights of stairs into the disorder of a loft factory, he was having the excitement for which he seemed to live and for which he was temperamentally suited.[1]

Quickly Durant, by consent, took over the leadership. New money and organization were needed. The company should be reorganized with a capital of $100,000; Murray and his partners would keep a quarter of the stock, and General Motors would take the rest for $75,000 of working cash. Durant had no intention, however, of subjecting Murray's tacky assets to the finance committee's scrutiny. He laid the money out as a personal expense. Later, he bought out the other 25 percent of the concern.

He moved the operation to an unoccupied building on Cadillac property, and sent in the indispensable Hardy to set up the nonstop process of getting ready, a whirlwind of calculating, ordering, contracting, hiring, measuring, installing, and transporting. On trips to Detroit, Durant would often burst in at 6:30 A.M. to prod everyone along, having just descended from the overnight New York train at the nearby depot. It was too much for Alfred Mellowes. Like David Buick, he could not work harnessed to a bolt of lightning. He quit one night late in the year, despite Durant's promises to turn his brainchild into millions, and said later that he would have stayed if offered, instead of riches, a few weeks of vacation.

As the date for going on the market approached, Durant searched about for a name that would explain as well as sell the new product. Mellowes's original choice did not satisfy him. He announced a contest for its replacement, then made it unnecessary by thinking of the answer on his own during a morning ride to the office. They were going into the business of providing coldness, he thought to himself—cold air, frigid air, *Frigidaire!* The name was registered quickly, and became one of those trademarks that was almost too perfect, like Kodak, Victrola, or Thermos. Millions of customers, in time, used it as a generic name for any refrigerator, instead of associating it with a single maker.[2]

Inside of a year Frigidaire was off and doing so well that there was no trouble whatever in securing board approval, on March 31, 1919, to buy it from Durant for $56,366. The sum, Sloan was certain, "was probably a great deal less than he had paid into it out of his own pocket."

Finding four aces in a Detroit attic was Durant's kind of game. His success with Frigidaire encouraged him to put down a pile of General Motors chips on another hand, but with far different results.

It began with what seemed a reasonable decision of 1917, which was to go after the tractor business in competition with Henry Ford's Fordson. To replace the horse on the farm as he had been replaced on the roads was a last, fast-opening frontier for motor manufacturers. Durant, with full authorization, bought, mainly for its good name, the long-established Samson Sieve-Grip Tractor Company, located in California. He added to it almost at once the Janesville Machine Company, farm equipment makers in Wisconsin, and subsequently another small machinery plant in Doylestown, Pennsylvania. With an "agricultural unit" in hand, he set his engineers about creating a new Samson tractor. In a relatively short time they had produced one, dubbed the Model M, equipped with a four-cylinder Mason motor and a special design that cured it of a fault common to rival

Fordsons of toppling over backward when the implement they were pulling got stuck. Three thousand of them came out in 1919, along with 56,000 machines of various kinds, for a promising start.[3]

But meanwhile, Durant's eye had been caught by something more daring. An Illinois inventor approached him with a patent for an unusual tractor that could be literally managed like an animal with a pair of reins, connected to control levers, that stretched out behind it. There was practical sense behind this seeming caprice. Thousands of the farm machines still in use in 1919 were designed to be guided and operated by someone who rode upon them. A solitary farm owner could do this, binding, raking, mowing, or planting while his horse drew him through familiar furrows, managed by an occasional shout or flick of the reins. If he had to move up to the driver's seat of a tractor, however, he faced the expense of hiring a hand to take his abandoned place. The new device promised to give him all the advantages of a machine while sparing him this necessity. Durant eagerly bought the idea and had a small tractor designed around it. It employed a Chevrolet engine and was known as the Samson Model D, but that name yielded to a catchier label, the Iron Horse.

Newmark watched Durant's eyes sparkle as demonstrations were conducted for them. His chief seemed to believe that he had another natural on his hands. The name itself had sales poetry, and the little, almost personal, tractor seemed to fit into some subliminal plan to uplift and modernize farm life by putting Delco electrical appliances in every barn and kitchen, and in each garage an Iron Horse, a Samson Truck, and a nine-passenger Samson car, with removable seats, to accommodate the large rural family or serve as a pickup at need. (Only a few of the trucks were ever produced; the car never got past a prototype stage.)

Durant could hardly wait to bring the new discovery to birth. He ordered a production run of 30,000, and hired a specialist in advertisements to the farm trade named Bill Galloway, from Waterloo, Iowa. For $60,000 a year Galloway produced copy of the kind that supposedly made him a prize barker among countryfolk. "Of all the inventions of modern times," one of his efforts ran, "including the electric light, automobile, telephone and airplane, the 'Iron Horse' is the greatest invention up to date for the farmer." The newest Durant promotion was also described as "powerful, efficient, easily controlled, and economical."[4] Brim-full of anticipation, Durant watched the first demonstration model's showing at the Milwaukee State Fair in August, 1919, a location rich with memory, for it was there in Wisconsin, thirty-two years earlier, that he had astonished his elders with the Flint Road Cart.

Durant especially enjoyed the reestablishment of his connection to the earthy people who had been his first customers. Stumping the county exhibitions, he seemed to be transformed into old Mr. Paterson, beguiling his potential buyers with turkey drumsticks and slices of pie. One scene enacted at the Trenton, New Jersey, fair of 1919 summed up the essential Durant style, the paternal generosity and showmanship that were evoked by his return to such surroundings. A gloomy, cold day. Bursts of rain spattering from sullen, gross clouds. Knots of dealers stand about, blowing into hands, hunching shoulders, squinting skyward, paying no attention to the Iron Horse stepping through its sputtering but gilded paces. Action of some kind is a perceived need. Suddenly, the magician Durant appears, derbied, velvet-collared, impeccable, unperturbed. He makes passes with his hands. A truck is dispatched, returns. One hundred and twenty-five raincoats are produced for one hundred and twenty-five dealers, courtesy of the General Motors Corporation. Grand sensation! Curtain.[5]

Unfortunately, the spell-casting power did not extend to the Iron Horse itself. There was incurable trouble with the transmission belts. They stretched unevenly with wear, or under the wrong atmospheric conditions, and sent the creature into senseless meanderings. The few models that made it off the line had to be recalled, and eventually a halt was called at fewer than 200. Meanwhile, the familiar and cheaper Fordson was outselling the superior Model M. In the end, despite heroic efforts by J. A. Craig, president of the Samson Division, the whole operation was written off early in 1920. Estimates of loss ran as high as $33 million, though after taking from that figure the money recovered from sale of inventory and saved by the conversion of the Janesville works to a Chevrolet factory, the figure of $12 million was more realistic.

Yet the loss came at a time when General Motors was particularly hard beset, and grieved by any kind of bad news. In the economy of ingratitude prevalent in the world, Durant's failure with Samson was not charitably wiped out by the recollection of his success with Frigidaire. Instead, Newmark suspected, it "probably confirmed the early fears of the du Ponts that Durant took long chances, that he did not safeguard stockholders' money, that he was hasty in his judgments."[6]

In actuality, anyone who, after January of 1918, saw Durant as a lone, careless expansionist inflating General Motors' structure to the bursting point was not only unfair but outdated. The days of 1909 and 1910 were past. Now, energized by wartime demand, General Motors began to grow with an almost uncheckable momentum of its own. Its rush to gigantism was not merely a Durant conception. It was fully endorsed by all the directors. Ironically, the supposedly gentling hand of the Du Ponts encouraged some leaps that gave pause even to a hell-for-leather rider like the founder.

It began with the decision to increase the capital stock to $200 million, $150 million of it in a million and a half shares of common. With this in hand, Chevrolet was bought in May. The actual process was an exchange of 282,684 shares of GM for all of Chevrolet's assets, except for the 450,000 GM shares in its treasury. For a time at least, though it ceased to be an independent car-making concern, Chevrolet remained a stock holding company, dowered with those shares by its father, Durant. But there was a major change; no longer did they represent a majority of all GM's outstanding stock. (Cars bearing the Chevrolet insigne continued to appear, but were now produced by a division of General Motors.) The curious arrangement was a point in Durant's favor; it meant that, as the head of Chevrolet, he still had leverage in General Motors beyond what his personal holdings entitled him to, and he was in need of all he could get.[7]

The United Motors consolidation came next. The cost was $44 million, paid mostly in General Motors' preferred stock. The owners of United Motors certificates now became, through exchange, the owners of General Motors certificates, and one of the largest blocks went to Alfred P. Sloan, who became by virtue of them a director of General Motors, a vice-president in charge of its accessories division, and a member of the executive committee of the board. He boasted of never selling a single share.

The deal for United Motors put a terminal chill on the cordiality between Durant and Kaufman. Kaufman was unsatisfied with the price offered. Durant, for reasons to which he gave no tongue, pushed the union nonetheless, reversing the positions that the two men had occupied for a long time. "Mr. Durant came out in the meeting enthusiastically for making the purchase," Pierre told Barksdale, "although he has been holding back for some time."[8] He discreetly did not add the reason, well known to him, for the change of heart: namely, his own insistence.

After swallowing United Motors in June, the directors and Durant continued their foraging. In the remainder of 1918 they bought another car-making operation, the Scripps-Booth Company; they put money into Samson Tractor; they snapped up a steel plant in Lancaster, Pennsylvania; took a partial interest in a die-casting firm of Brooklyn, and added to their holdings the remainder of the McLaughlin-owned firms in Ontario, so that General Motors of Canada was now wholly owned. The year-end reports amply justified so much growth. The sales of all "units" — cars, trucks, and other machines — totaled 246,834, and brought in just under $270 million. This was achieved while filling out $35 millions' worth of government orders, including 5,000 ambulances and trucks, 2,360 Cadillac staff cars, 2,528 Liberty aircraft engines, and large quantities of kitchen trailers, artillery tractors, mortar shells, and shell caps. War work, instead of canceling out civilian production, only fed it with extra profits. Quarterly dividends of 3 percent were promptly paid, and General Motors' stockholders and its 49,118 employees enjoyed happy and optimistic Christmases, looking forward to great things ahead in a coming year of peace.

The only negative note from the point of view of Raskob and Durant was that inflated operating costs, as well as dividend payments, consumed too large a share of gross profits to leave enough for reinvestment. In November the company's capitalization was increased again, this time to $370 million, split among 200,000 shares of common, 20,000 of preferred, and a million and a half of a new, 6 percent debenture stock, which, like the preferred, had priority on dividends but was limited to no more than the percentage imprinted on its face. This outpouring of new shares was intended to provide a payment mechanism for acquisitions already authorized. It still left the promoters considerably deficient of their estimated needs for the 1919 program. That would include the building of new factories, the completion of additional mergers, the formation of credit companies to help dealers finance their customers' purchases, and — Raskob's idea, basically — a great new central office building in Detroit.

Raskob advised the finance committee that he calculated the total bill to be about $52.8 million. Of this sum, $24.7 million could come from earnings. To raise another $21.6 million he proposed to sell 180,000 shares of the common stock to a syndicate at a price of $120. The finance committee of E. I. du Pont de Nemours, at this point, came to the assistance of the finance committee of General Motors in the handling of its problems, which was not surprising, since the two bodies had overlapping memberships and were mutually dedicated to the interests of Wilmington. The Du Ponts had found their first year of heavy investment in GM profitable indeed, and were willing to double the stake. They would buy the 180,000 shares of common. In addition, they would pay for the remainder of the McLaughlin properties by paying the brothers $6.5 million in cash, and taking off their hands a large block of stock that they had been given, and that at the moment was less desirable to them than dollars in hand. In effect, Wilmington would put up $28.1 millions, and when the accounts were balanced out, Du Pont American Industries would be holding 206,472 shares of GM and 159,115 of Chevrolet.[9]

It was an unlooked-for ending to a year in which the Du Ponts were supposed to cool the enthusiasms of the venturesome ringmaster of the big show. The Wilmington directors had sanctioned an acquisition binge that reduced the two- and three-million-dollar purchases of 1909 to relative ten-cent-store transactions. And smilingly. Their annual report of 1918 declared: "We feel fortunate in our partnership with Mr. William C. Durant, president of the General Motors Corporation and the father and leader of the motor industry not only in the United States but in the world today."[10] Durant responded graciously. Over his testimonial victuals in Flint he told old friends that the name of Pierre du Pont was "one of the best and safest, one of the fairest and most considerate, one of the most generous in the country."[11]

And in an atmosphere delicately perfumed by such mutual flattery, the growth program of 1919, the year of big money and release from wartime constrictions and the shedding of the world's old skin, thundered ahead at full throttle. In February the board invested in companies to build housing for the mushrooming General Motors work forces in Detroit, Flint, Pontiac, Lansing, and Bristol, Connecticut. In March it purchased Frigidaire and also the Interstate Motor Company of Muncie, Indiana, scheduled to become the producer of an automobile called the Sheridan. In April it spun off a corporation to rear the Detroit building of many wings and many stories where the directing brains of General Motors would be sheltered. The structure would, against his will, carry Durant's name if the plans went through.

Then General Motors bought a surplus war plant belonging to the International Arms and Fuse Company, which they would convert to the fabrication of auto parts. The price tag on that was a million. Then they bought the T. W. Warner Company of Muncie, manufacturers of gears, for five millions. And another bodymaking firm in Pontiac. And in Dayton, Ohio, they showered stock like manna, giving 35,000 shares of the common worth $3.5 million for the Domestic Engineering Company, and 21,000 shares of common plus 25,000 of 6 percent debenture — five millions at the going market, there — for Dayton Metal Products, and 11,000 more shares of debenture for a foothold on the future in the form of the Dayton-Wright Airplane Company. They also bought the Delco Light Company, which had not been part of the original United Motors package, and it was this step that finally enfolded Kettering in General Motors' grasp. Before he had been on the staff very long, he was off with an impressively credentialed delegation, consisting of himself, Sloan, Mott, Champion, and Chrysler, to visit France and see if it might not be a good idea to purchase the Citroën auto factory, but on that proposed acquisition, at least, the recommendation was negative. There would be other ways to penetrate the European market, the committee said, that would be more economical.[12]

But that appeared to be almost the sole moment of self-denial to which the Durant-Raskob regime could bring itself. They dispensed more dollars to set up the General Motors Acceptance Corporation and the General Motors Export Division. And in September they reached a landmark for a single purchase when they spent $26.7 million to buy 60 percent of the capital stock of the Fisher Body Company, putting $5.8 million of it down in cash and the rest in five-year notes. That was one particularly desired by Durant. The seven Fisher brothers had been known to him since early times, when they were the rising sons of an Ohio blacksmith and he a wagon and buggy entrepreneur, writing Durant-Dort checks for the orders they filled for him.

Along with all these ingestions of entire plants, more stock was bought that increased General Motors' share of ownership of Goodyear Tire and Rubber, and Dunlop Rubber, and General Leather, and Doehler Die Casting, and Brown-Lipe-Chapin, and Ball Brothers Manufacturing Company. Some of them had names that were meaningless to the general public, but every auto maker knew who they were and why it was important to have a voice in their management. For every day, the assembly lines had to be fed with thousands of parts and subparts that were buried anonymously in the recesses of cars that only mechanics knew—parts that ranged from heavy truck differentials to tiny fuses, bulbs, and switches, instrument needles, and mounting screws for mirrors and wipers. Parts as simple and vital as belts and hoses and hydraulic lines, and as delicate and hard-used as the armatures of generators and the needle valves of carburetors. They had to be available in quantity and quality every day for any successful auto maker, because the appetite of the assembly lines was unrelenting; because cars could not roll out fast enough for a United States at peace and at last, finally, unreservedly, without second thoughts or backward glances, committed to having cars, buying 1,650,625 of them in 1919 and 1,905,560 the next year and sprinting toward the two-million-car year of 1922. These parts were made by the unknown factories in the uncelebrated little industrial towns and neighborhoods through which the finished cars sped on their way to the open road and the clean suburbs. And buying a guaranteed share of the output of those unnoticed factories in the ignored parts of cities was among the most important things that General Motors, in its surge of growth, could do.

Midway through the year, the issue of more stock became a necessity, and when the directors nodded approval to it they crossed a historic divide. President Durant asked for five million shares of common, and five million of debenture, and 200,000 of preferred, and when he had it in hand, General Motors had become, like United States Steel, a billion-dollar corporation, only the second such corporation of the century. Yet once more the year-end figures seemed to justify the step, for net sales were over half a billion—$509,676,694, to be exact. There were $60 millions of net earnings to divide, of which $22 million went out in dividend checks and $38 million to pay for some of the new investments, more than $13 million in excess of even Raskob's bright projection, the year before, of what would be available. There was even a little money to bestow on old-timers, as

$1,077,650 was paid out in bonuses to veterans. Arthur Mason acknowledged a $1,500 check and a Blue Ribbon Certificate in a letter to Durant, but confessed a problem. "What is worrying me now, you will have to tell me just what to do so I can earn the money."[13]

It was another genial New Year's season. John Raskob, in his office, had the balance sheets for every year since 1916 folded into an envelope and sent to Durant. They showed, he wanted his friend to know, that the company had been using $58 millions' worth of capital three and one half years earlier, but was now the owner of assets totaling $452 million.

In other words, the General Motors Corporation of today is eight times as large as the company which the bankers were managing.
This is indeed a fine tribute to your foresight.[14]

In actuality, the company had expanded beyond even the furthest foresight. It had put nearly $50 million into plants, equipment, and real estate and another equal sum into partly owned subsidiaries, more than Raskob's early estimates and enough to use up all the available retained earnings, and the money put in by the stock purchases of Du Pont American Industries, and another $25.4 million raised in 1919 by the sale of a large block of debenture stock through four underwriting houses. With its size came obligations as well as strength. Its fixed investment was up to $153.8 million, on which charges such as taxes, depreciation, and maintenance ran in good years and bad. Its inventories were huge, running up storage and control costs whether used or not. Its payroll was 85,890, and could be shrunk only so far by temporary layoffs if needed. If its new acquisitions were to be integrated and harmonized and brought up to the tempo of high-quantity production, they needed changes and enlargements. General Motors Corporation was committed to pouring out a golden flood to contractors, designers, engineers, and suppliers. It owed interest on its $20 million in notes to the Fisher brothers and on many short-term borrowings. It really needed to continue dividend payments if it was to enjoy any standing in the investment world. "Facility for future financing," Raskob once wired Durant, "will depend largely on reputation of our securities."[15]

It had come an unmeasurable distance from the dawn hour of 1908 when William Crapo Durant bought the Oldsmobile Company and created the nucleus. After that the process of multiplication had gone on under Durant's rule of 1909 and 1910; it had paused, but never really halted under the bankers; it had resumed in the first year of Durant's return from exile, when he had a free hand; it had accelerated when the Du Ponts moved in. The original dream had been Durant's, but the growth, seen in perspective, seemed to be something uncontrollable once he had started it, as if he were not the sorcerer that others took him to be, but the sorcerer's apprentice, helpless before forces that he had unlocked.

The expansion of 1916 to 1919 was not a mere repetition of that of ten years earlier. Its result was the emergence of the essential, modern General Motors, the supercorporation that was no longer recognizable as his "baby." It was now far beyond his powers of management aided by the support of his "little crowd." As that fact became clearer and clearer, the strains on the relationship with Wilmington grew stronger with every passing month.

II Ironically, the stresses began to show in a surprising pattern of disagreement with Raskob that had Durant playing the conservative role. Raskob upset the balance of the presumed equation in the finance committee that counterweighted Durant with three Du Ponts and himself. Henry F. du Pont lacked any deep interest in General Motors affairs, Irénée was fully occupied with his own job as president of the Du Pont Corporation, and Pierre had entered what he thought of as an early semiretirement, devoting much of his time to the nurture of green plants, classrooms, and public responsibilities. It was therefore up to Raskob to rein in Durant, and he himself was, if anything, fond of a gallop.

It was Raskob who was pressing hard for the Durant Building, and Durant who objected both to the cost overruns that began to recur as the work got under way and to the very concept of a maze of offices to shelter corporate bureaucrats. "What on earth do they want it for?" he groused to Hardy. To Bishop, to Edward Ver Linden, to an official of the construction company putting up the structure, to the secretary of the board of directors he voiced a string of complaints — it was a Du Pont idea, it would divert money from more critical projects, he did not want it to carry his name. But at voting time he undercut his own position by going along with Raskob.[16]

There was trouble, too, in the executive committee. Its members, the operating division managers, were eager to set production records. They would overspend the appropriations allowed them in their individual areas of responsibility, then, sitting together in committee, jointly recommend extra allotments of money from the central treasury. The finance committee reviewed these requests and was supposed to be stern. But in fact it was often confused by disagreements among the supposed production experts on the executive committee, and not immune to the prevailing optimism. At the end of October, 1919, as an instance, the executive committee was divided on the question of a request by Sloan for development funds to be used by the New Departure bearing plant—so divided that Durant actually left its chair to argue against the appropriation, as well as to oppose new funds for the Durant Building. The executive committee's resolution was to back its president by voting against the building money, and to comfort Sloan by recommending one-third of the sum he was asking for New Departure. The finance committee now weighed the issue, and the action it took was to send Raskob as its emissary to the next executive committee meeting. There he explained that there would be plenty of money coming along, since a plan was in the making to raise another fifty to a hundred million dollars by stock sales. Relieved of the burden of choice, the executive committee promptly approved in full of all requests before it, and broke up in harmony.

Durant found himself disturbed by this pattern of living, like an expectant heir, on anticipated revenues. He wrote as much to Raskob.

I do not wish to annoy you, but I feel that I should call your attention to the enormous expenditures and capital commitments which are being authorized by the Finance Committee against Prospective Earnings—a method of financing which I do not think is either safe or sound and which, in the event of industrial disturbance or paralysis, might seriously impair our position. Frankly, I am very much worried and I know that many members of our organization in the managerial and operating divisions are much concerned.[17]

Sloan, too, was concerned, though for reasons that went beyond simple fear of overcommitment. Since his entry into the corporation's decision-making center in 1918, he had kept an appraising eye open for General Motors' structural weaknesses. He was unmoved by any associations with early company history, which was a closed book to him. He did not know who Hardy was; he seemed not to have heard of the Heany fiasco;[18] neither old loyalties nor memories of blunders past colored his judgment. What disturbed him was the planless, politicized nature of the executive committee's decision by horsetrade. He called it "management by crony," and though he might himself be able to play the game, it was no system for making sound judgments. He noticed, too, that Durant's favorite advisors and appointees were often without formal technical or business training. They were what another contemporary onlooker referred to as "men that would come up as some of the automobile men had by working in the shop. . . . They had done it by cut and try, and some of them did a very good job; a lot of them didn't."[19] Sloan succeeded in getting from the committee, as 1919 ended, a unanimous vote for a study to recommend some policy to the finance committee for dealing with the contingency that no one was ready to think about—"should a serious recessing in business occur, or should plants be suddenly shut down due to serious strikes extending over a period of several months." These were exactly the possible troubles that Durant had mentioned to Raskob, "industrial disturbance or paralysis." For a brief and rare moment the views of these two coalesced.

Pierre du Pont gave no clues to his feelings about the lavishness of General Motors' 1919 spending, leaving others to guess whether silence signified approval, indifference for the moment, faith in Raskob, faith in himself to check Raskob in time, or a simple vow of nonintervention. But there was evidence both in his behavior and in his files that he was becoming uncomfortable with Durant's managerial methods, and that his concern ran back at least as far as the autumn of 1918. From that time onward, he had begun to have reservations, not only about the financial responsibility of the man from Flint, but about the operational brilliance that he had been taking for granted.

Some months after the first $25 million of E. I. du Pont de Nemours' money was put into the automobile business, the company's engineering department was requested to send an observer to Detroit to evaluate General Motors' operations there from an efficiency standpoint. The man entrusted with the job was named E. L. Bergland, and his appraisal, submitted in September, was passionless in tone and devastating in substance. Its key paragraphs read:

Mr. Durant, apparently, has complete charge of all of the planning and dictates largely the policies to be followed. His opinion is consulted for final decision in a great many cases as there seems to be no one else in the organization who is the final arbitrator for the various plants or for the new developments. . . . A very large amount of detailed work seems to be brought to his attention for final decision . . . and I have even heard of a case where details or designs for electric wiring were referred to him for decision, as controversies had arisen which no one seemed able or of sufficient authority to decide. . . . His offices are in New York but he takes periodic trips to Detroit . . . and there meets either jointly or separately the various managers of the plants . . . and final instructions are issued at those times, as well as various points discussed relative to problems which may have arisen. His time is necessarily limited and it is, therefore, impossible, I believe, to properly consider all of them, and men frequently are not able to see him so that decisions are, therefore, postponed for weeks. . . .

When new plants are to be built Mr. Durant often personally supervises the letting of the contract and the engineering details with the engineering and contracting firm, but the details of the design receive very little attention and very little detailed information is apparently known by the members of the organization. . . .

There is no system similar to our work order system for making suggestions, or no central engineering organization. . . . There is, I think, also a certain lack of co-operative spirit between the different plants. These plants are practically independent as regards their purchasing, accounting and other organizations, and as they were independent operating organizations before the General Motors Corporation was formed, and have been more or less functioning ever since as independent organizations, it is very easy to understand a feeling of this kind as there is no central organization directing them, except in the most general way. . . .

The General Motors Corporation have in mind the expenditure of millions of dollars on future construction, and the future success of the business will depend largely upon the proper planning, design and execution of the work, and, therefore, the necessity of having the advantage of the du Pont Company, Engineering Department, or of developing an able Engineering Department of their own, seems to me very great.

Du Pont could not have been profoundly disturbed by Bergland's report, since it did not deter him from agreeing to invest another $28 million in General Motors at the end of 1918. Untidy Durant might be, but he was likewise successful still, and there was no edge of urgency to the problem of improving his machinery of command. Not until the summer of 1919 did Du Pont send over a Wilmington man, Frank Turner, to become comptroller of General Motors, replacing Durant's appointee, Prensky, who became treasurer. Turner's mission was to "bring about a uniform standard system of accounting and eventually to effect a centrally controlled financial accounting organization." At about the same time John Squires, of the Du Pont personnel office, was sent to New York to give some lessons on centralized record-keeping, assignment and supervisory procedures affecting employees. Meanwhile, Du Pont had set up within his own company's development section a three-man motor development team, headed by his brother-in-law, R. R. M. Carpenter. In 1919 one of the duties of a member of the group, John Lee Pratt, was to go up to New York monthly in order to discuss and sometimes initiate research projects with the president.[20]

Durant had no objection that anyone knew of to these steps. In the case of Pratt, especially, he was actively pleased, since they had already met and struck up a good relationship. Pratt was an easygoing man who rambled in conversation, dressed simply, and liked to call himself a "dirt farmer."[21] It was a guise that was useful in putting others off guard when Pratt was boring into a situation with keen and well-trained powers of observation. He was a 1906 graduate of the University of Virginia's Engineering School, well-enough thought of there to be offered a teaching job immediately. He turned it down, saying he could not afford it, and went to work for the Du Pont Company. After various travels he had become an assistant, in 1917, to American Nitrogen's president, Hamilton Barksdale. Barksdale often took Pratt on business trips to New York with him, and stopped in at the offices of the Chevrolet Company on director's business. There, the soft-talking engineer in his early thirties had met Durant, who liked him at once, and one week suddenly asked him if he would go out to Flint and find out why General Motors was having trouble selling the houses that it had built for its workers there.

Pratt's report was prompt and concise. The houses had been built too expensively and were priced out of reach of the intended buyers, for whom some subsidy would be necessary. Durant was so pleased that he asked then and there if Pratt could be assigned to his office, as well as the personnel expert Squires.[22] Pratt's immediate boss, Carpenter, was so devoted to the team concept that he reacted with a blend of pride and annoyance. What allowed Pratt to make such a "fine impression," he said to Pierre, was "the organization for which he works."

For example, aside from being a good man himself, Mr. Pratt had access to all the information in the Engineering Department, and knew exactly where to get this information quickly. . . .

A very analogous case might be that of a man who heard an extremely good orchestra and immediately sent for the leader of this orchestra to come to his house and play for him individually, believing that he was going to get the same music.

. . . You might have an opportunity some time to impress this on Mr. Durant.[23]

Durant was disappointed at not getting Pratt on a permanent basis then, and pleased when he began to show up at the office once more. Pratt liked the mission, too. He was impressed by the breadth of the head man's mind, the way it ranged far ahead of the day's line of march, reconnoitering over the horizon. In 1919, William C. Durant was worried that the motor industry's buildup would result in a petroleum shortage. He wanted that looked into. And what about aluminum? It was so marvelously light, strong, useful, and so damnably expensive. Could that problem be cracked? How about plate glass? Should General Motors go into its manufacture to make sure of future supplies? Then there were storage batteries. Replacements were too expensive, perhaps discouraging buyers. Should General Motors be thinking of entering the battery business?

Faithfully, Pratt did his legwork and reported the best answers he could get at the time. The oil men said there would always be plenty of oil. Aluminum was just basically expensive to make; better to get the best deal available from Alcoa, the monopoly in control of production, and "design away from it" as much as possible. Belgian plate glass factories, stopped by the war, were getting back into full production; best leave that alone for a while. Storage battery prices might come down by themselves fairly soon. Pratt enjoyed the assignments and relished Durant's uncanny anticipation. Durant was equally pleased, and brisk in reaching out to get what he liked. He asked Pratt to move to New York permanently in May of 1919. Pratt held off. He and his wife both enjoyed Wilmington, he said. Durant let the matter rest for six months, though he seemed to lose interest in starting Pratt down fresh tracks thereafter. Then, suddenly in October he pounced again: "I have got a wonderful job for you up here." It was to be one of three general assistants to the president. Pratt began a series of slow-talking objections, and Durant shook them off and propelled him out to a lunch table at a Childs' Restaurant on Columbus Circle. The old talents were not entirely lost. "He sold me," Pratt recounted, "on the idea that I should come to General Motors."[24]

From an office diagonally opposite to Durant's, Pratt became a front-row spectator of the drama going on at the highest executive levels. His fondness for Durant did not keep his comprehensive glance from taking in the worst of the leadership habits on display. He was one who observed the chief's fondness for "cut and try" types. He noted that Durant's reluctance to give up direct dealings with plant managers meant that forty or fifty individuals could go directly to him for decisions.[25] He was aware not only of the division presidents' back-scratching on the executive committee, but also of how each one, trying to build a good personal record, liked to stockpile supplies and thereby overload inventories. And he knew that Durant, quietly ignoring the rules, sometimes gave verbal permission for a plant expansion not yet sanctioned by the finance committee.

These were hard things for a good engineer to swallow. Like others of Durant's friends that year, Pratt had to make the best sense he could out of a perplexing sheaf of self-contradictory traits in the man he admired.

Durant could match his conceptual powers to the new scope of General Motors' operations. The sharp questions he put to Pratt emerged from a species of prophetic engagement with things still in the womb of time. But in those trances he seemed to lose track of the meaning of immediate time itself, and in that state he lost his grip on the first principle of self-organization, which is the management of hours and minutes. He had always been indifferent to priorities on his attention, and he delegated almost nothing. Both Newmark and his daughter recalled that he would fuss endlessly with a letter or a piece of advertising copy, hounding it through a dozen drafts, staring at it, rearranging, excising, often throwing out an entire idea if it was not in perfect pitch to his ear.[26] And he would fall into this paralysis over a trivial matter as readily as an important one. His checker breaks were part of his charm; his chats with old friends while executives waited to see him were part of an oddly "democratic" arrogance that inconvenienced the lordly and the commonplace associate impartially. But their end result was to pile unfinished business higher on his desk and bind him more firmly to it. "He was inhuman in his capacity for work," Chrysler believed. "He was striving to make completely real his vision of a great corporation."[27] But in another sense he was too human to adapt himself to a great corporation's powerful reordering of the lives of those who served it.

He had always had moments of egocentric insensitivity to subordinates' needs. He would suddenly command an all-night or holiday session on some crash project, which would then be dropped. Or he would swoop into someone else's area of responsibility and undo weeks of work with a decision whose rationale remained hidden within him. Yet he was forgiven again and again because he was transparently without malice. "We loved the man," was Newmark's explanation. "We seemed to enjoy being humiliated by him."[28] Even when interference "struck as a lightning bolt into your own department," said Sloan, "you did not protest, because he was so sweet-natured, so well intentioned. It was just Billy Durant's way. You accepted it, and perhaps liked it because you liked him."[29]

But there were limits, and as the claims on his concentration multiplied throughout 1919 and into 1920, Durant began to exceed them. Those who came to him with problems found it a trial to get his ear for more than fleeting moments, as he broke off conversations to answer a battery of telephones—Chrysler counted ten, Sloan thought there were as many as twenty—linking him to plants, offices, and his brokers. There was scarcely a moment when a receiver was not in his hand. "In the same minute he would buy in San Francisco, sell in Boston. . . . It seemed to me he was trying to keep in communication with half the continent."[30] So ran the testimony of those who saw him. His voice stayed calm, his smile ready, but frenzy seemed disquietingly close.

Forgiveness came harder and harder. He would summon people to the office on Sunday morning and talk to them while his barber, Jake, shaved him in the portable chair he kept there. Or worse still, he would call an executive meeting of ten or fifteen officials in Detroit. Some, like Sloan, would arrive overnight from New York. Walter Chrysler would have risen at dawn to drive the sixty-five miles from Flint. And they would wait and wait while Durant telephoned or fussed with minutiae, his mind away in some Emerald City of automotive wonders. The session might not start until four in the afternoon, according to Sloan's testimony, and would drag on through short-tempered, dinnerless hours. Once Chrysler, on whose time Durant himself had set a price of nearly $10,000 a week, waited to see his boss for four days, then gave up and went back to the factory.

He was going beyond the boundaries of an important code. His lieutenants lived, as he did, for their work. It was their compass, their purpose in life, their true religion. By forcing them to stand idle he was devising for them a torment worthy of a Caligula. They understood that he was unconscious of what he did, and held their patience. But it would later become manifest that they began to worry about what was going to happen to General Motors, and those worries could not fail, in some form or other, to reach Wilmington.

Engrossed in his plans, receiving only those signals from outside his own consciousness that he chose to heed, Durant was getting himself into the posture of a man about to be rebuked by the gods. Nineteen-twenty would be the year of the thunderbolts.

III In all of Pierre du Pont's dealings with Durant that year a courtesy prevailed that suggested only profound satisfaction. If the idea of a replacement at the helm of General Motors ever crossed his mind, he gave it no slightest outward expression, and he would deny to the end of his days any consideration of trying to end Durant's rule. Yet he kept moving in directions that he knew would provoke disagreement with Durant, exhibiting a patient confidence that things would go his way. He was himself a calculator, and calculators who deal with plungers know that eventually the plunger will run one risk too many.

So Du Pont was the portrait of serenity when he sat down to a chat in January with his friend Seward Prosser, the president of Bankers Trust. Prosser was frank in expressing the concern of some members of the financial community that General Motors was overextended. That was not the case at all, Pierre assured him. Everything was going well, and he was so certain of it that he was about to indulge in a vacation in Hawaii, where he would collect some choice specimens for his greenhouses. He would send Raskob around to answer any detailed questions.

Raskob appeared in due time and, as always, outlined only sunny prospects. By 1928, he advised, General Motors would have capital assets worth $1.5 billion, and would have raised 40 percent of what was needed to acquire them through the sale of "senior securities." Whether or not he was reassured, Prosser dropped a cordial *bon voyage* note to Du Pont, urging him to look up a brother in Honolulu who could show him around, since he had been there twenty years and "[knew] the game thoroughly."[31]

Raskob and the finance committee were in the middle of a fresh drive for dollars as Pierre took ship. They planned an issue of new 7 percent debenture stock, which holders of the old 6 percent debenture and preferred certificates could trade for on an attractive basis. One share of the old would bring in two of the new, if accompanied by half the price of a new share in cash—sixty dollars. There were a million and a half shares of the 6 percent issues outstanding, and the committee believed that an exchange so tempting would result in most of them being converted, with a net yield of as much as $85 millions. The common stock, too, was to be transformed by a ten-for-one split. In place of the five million authorized shares of "old common" whose par value was $100, there would be fifty million shares of no-par "new common." The theory was that this move would stimulate and satisfy a latent appetite for GM common and bring more money into the treasury without requiring any actual increase in capital assets.

Buoyed by the hopes that these decisions of January raised, the committee gave its approval to new production schedules of runaway optimism. In 1919 the corporation had sold some 397,000 units. It planned to manufacture more than twice that number in 1920, a total of 876,000 cars, trucks, and buses. The sales estimates, Sloan was convinced, were reached "by rule of thumb, of the division manager's ambition."[32] A scramble to accumulate inventory began, and supply orders gushed from division offices. The board itself continued the drive to expand, though at an abated pace. It bought out the undigested remainder of Chevrolet of California, and the balance of the stock of the Klaxon Corporation, makers of horns, which had been a partly-owned appendage of United Motors.

While these confident sallies into the new decade were being launched, Durant was experiencing a winter of discontent. To begin with, there had been a discomforting sequel to the split of the common stock. Suspecting that General Motors might be facing corporate indigestion, short sellers had made contracts for heavy deliveries of the old, $100-par common at the end of March. As that date approached, they were horror-struck as the price, instead of dropping, began to rise under steady buying pressure. Almost certainly it came from Durant. One February evening he had asked Pratt over to his apartment, where they had spent a long night going down the list of GM stockholders. Under the president's direction, Pratt had sorted the names into three categories, each of which then got a separate message from Durant. One of them read: "There will be something happening in our stock; don't sell yours until you get in touch with me." Another announced a "favorable" picture developing on the Exchange and counseled: "Buy all you can afford." The third asked for an option on the recipients' GM shares at the market price.[33]

The last week of March began, and GM was being quoted at 350. The next day it reached 409, and with the thirty-first imminent, it touched 420. The bears were faced with the ultimate disaster, for them, of a "corner"— one buyer, or a group coordinated by one buyer, holding most or all of the shares they needed to fulfill their contracts or be ruled off the floor. There was no alternative then but to pay the corner's price, however ruinous.

But at the brink, the governing committee of the Exchange stepped in to the rescue. It ruled that ten shares of the new stock would be considered a "good delivery" against one of the old. The new stock was superabundantly available. Inside half an hour from the announcement of the decision, GM "old" had dropped seventeen points. The corner was broken, and the shorts had been spared, in the *New York Times*'s words, "a real catastrophe."[34] The fateful effect for Durant went beyond a missed opportunity to pinch the paws of the bears. If he had in fact been behind the corner, he was now left with a heavy load of the new stock, whose value steadily declined from the 42 of its peak in a melancholy diminuendo that appeared to have no ending as the year grew older.

While this had been taking place, the directors had finally written off the Samson Tractor venture, in what was a personal defeat for Durant. He admitted to some adverse field reports, conceded that there had been losses, but in the free-spending atmosphere of the finance committee's meetings it seemed a special rebuke to his judgment to deny the Samson division a little more money until its problems could be worked out, as he was convinced that they would be. He had some positive evaluations to prove it. Then, however, Kettering shook him up. On a train trip that the two of them were sharing from Dayton to New York, Kettering furnished irrefutable proof of something that he had learned through a chance tip from an old friend. Two agents sent by Durant to report on field tests in Kansas had never gone there. Instead, they had faked a set of laudatory telegrams and arranged to have them sent at intervals to the head office.[35]

That was not quite the end. There was a trip out to Janesville—Sloan, Kettering, and Durant—for a firsthand look, and a great deal of arguing, and only reluctantly at last did Durant accept the verdict of the other two against his vision of bringing the godlike fires of internal combustion to agrarian mankind. The Samson line was taken off the market.

Finally, there was the really immeasurable loss of the young year, the irreplaceable human write-off of Walter Chrysler, lost to the company by a resignation for which Durant was squarely, damningly responsible. Chrysler had proven to be exactly the precious human asset under Durant that he had been in the days of Storrow. He kept Buick in top form, the breadwinner of General Motors, bringing in as much as half its earnings. As he laid away his $380,000 worth of stock each year, he moved up to become a vice-president and director, his voice respected by everyone who sat around the conference table, Durant most emphatically of all. The two of them seemed a perfect match at first. Both were direct, undevious, unhesitating in their pursuit of what they thought would help the corporation. "When we saw something we wanted," Chrysler remembered, "we would go, or send, and get, generally, just what we wanted." To transform desire into fulfillment Durant simply "waved a wand of gold," and improvements in Buick's productive apparatus flashed into instant being.

The trouble was that Durant would sometimes use the same impulsive generosity to unravel a design that Chrysler had painstakingly wrought. He was constitutionally incapable of keeping his promise to yield "full authority" to anyone, and his frequent interference in Buick affairs, combined with his inaccessibility, finally overdrew his account of goodwill with Chrysler. It began when "Trainload" Collins informed Chrysler one day that Durant had sold him what was referred to as a "branch operation" of Buick in Detroit. Bursting into a temper that was celebrated in railroad repair shops throughout the Far West, Chrysler stormed down to Detroit and made it clear that he would have no partition of his kingdom without his consent, much less without his knowledge. Durant backed away and the clouds lifted temporarily. But before long the superintendent of Buick's vitally important drop-forge plant walked into the office one day to say good-bye to Chrysler. "Mr. Durant," he explained, had hired him, at a 50 percent increase in his $8,000 annual salary, to do the same job at a Detroit location.

This time Chrysler let matters rest. He had been a workman himself; he was not going to stand in the way of a man's chance to get ahead. But he pleaded with Durant for firm ground rules. He did not want to undermine but to execute with a free hand. "For heaven's sake," he begged, "just tell me what your policies are," and for answer he received "Billy's" casual statement that he believed in changing policies as often as the office door opened and closed.

The back-breaking straw was laid on during a Chamber of Commerce luncheon in Flint one day in 1919. The wartime boom had strained the city at its seams. Housing, skilled labor, and building materials were all scarce and expensive, and at that very moment Durant chose to play fairy godfather once more. As Chrysler sat at his table he was astonished to see Dallas Dort rise with an announcement. "Boys, I've got great news for you. Here's a wire from William C. Durant! He says he has just authorized the spending of six million dollars to build a General Motors frame plant in Flint." Choking on his food, Chrysler waited until it was his turn to speak. Heedless of public relations, he spelled out an unmistakable intention. "Not so long as I stay here will General Motors have a frame plant in Flint."

At a board meeting in Detroit the next day Chrysler snapped angry questions at his president. Were there any cost estimates on the new plant? Who had made them? Where was the layout? Did Durant have any idea that it would take two years to build the factory, three to learn how to run it, even longer to staff it really well? Did Durant know that he, Chrysler, had just concluded a deal for frames with a Milwaukee firm that would not cost as much in ten years as the new plant would in five? Durant reacted with rare anger. For the first time he was being challenged openly on his methods, and what was more, on a grandiose gesture in Flint, whose applause was his by divine right. Whatever was said, the situation became sufficiently strained to need a moderator, and it was Haskell who stepped into the role. He proposed that the three of them, as a subcommittee, look more carefully into the matter. They did, and in the end, Durant pocketed his pride and there was no frame plant in Flint.

But the board meetings continued to be the battlegrounds of a crisis-stricken relationship. Chrysler literally loved Durant as a man, and would remain a lifelong friend, but he was becoming frightened. One afternoon the Samson affair was on the agenda, and the voices rose, and finally Chrysler was shouting, in front of everyone, that it had been a terrible idea, that Durant had paid far too much for the Janesville plant, that they ought to have left the farm business to the corporations that were ready for it. He had worked himself up to a pitch, and someone tried to calm him down by pointing out that in any case Janesville was outside his area of responsibility; what on earth was he roaring about?

"What am I roaring about? I'm roaring as a stockholder, if you really want to know. Everything I have in the world is in this company. I don't want to lose it." And he stamped off when it was all over to fume in his office. After a while there was a knock at the door and the gentle, patriarchal face of Haskell looked in.

"You just flew off the handle today," he said soothingly. "We all do that. So did Billy. He wants you to forget it."

But it could not be forgotten so long as Durant's ways remain unchanged. And one day, Chrysler walked into the head office and laid on the desk his letter of resignation, to take effect on March 25, 1920. Others had done their best to deflect him; they all would have been "happily grateful if he had changed his mind." But it was too late.

"Now, Billy," he said, "I'm done."[36]

So the fourth spring of his presidency approached, and brought no cheering blossoms for Durant. He had failed to slay the bears, he had lost out on Samson Tractor, he had driven away Walter Chrysler, and the end was not yet. General Motors' ongoing voracity for capital was forcing him to admit new and demanding copartners from the world of high finance. The secret of his early strength had lain in his capacity for "trading on the equity of the uncontrolling stockholders," the friends who questioned none of his dealings with their property. Step by step in this unblessed year, he was shorn of that power, so that by midsummer it was reduced to a fraction, though still a large one, of what it had been.

Like an offensive bogged down far short of its objectives, the campaign to raise new expansion money by splitting up and revaluing old stock had been a failure. By the middle of May, only $12.5 million had been picked up from this source. How far short that fell of what was needed was clear to anyone familiar with the minutes of the executive committee. At one early-year meeting alone they approved $10.3 millions in cost overruns.

Contemplating these disheartening figures on his return from the Pacific, Du Pont could not fail to be struck by an imbalance. The public offerings of 1919 and 1920 had netted a total of $37.5 million. On the other hand, the Du Pont company by itself had put up nearly $55 million, counting the major purchases at the conclusion of 1917 and 1918, and another of some 6,000 shares in the spring of 1919 which, Du Pont told Raskob, he considered final. He was not minded to increase the approximately 29 percent share of General Motors that was now within his clasp. Yet it was evident that there would have to be other heavy individual purchases if any really helpful inflow of money was to be expected soon.[37]

While he considered which of his friends might be approached, Du Pont was willing to collaborate with Durant in the formation of buying syndicates whose purpose was to acquire and hold GM stock temporarily, bidding up its price and making it more alluring thereby to other long-term investors. There were several of these. The legal agreement formalizing one of them, known as Number Six, empowered Durant, as manager, to buy GM "at prices considerably less than its actual and prospective value," and turn it over, within a fixed period, at a "reasonable profit" if possible. Durant himself had put a million into it, and so had Du Pont, and there were half-million-dollar contributions to the pool from the Fisher brothers, and Albert Wiggin of Chase National, and Coleman du Pont, and other very well-endowed subscribers. The total amount available was ten million.[38]

Perhaps less important, but dearer to Durant's heart, was Syndicate Number Five. This one aimed to raise only between $1.25 million and $5 million, but its customers were the old crowd—Fred Aldrich, Arthur Bishop, Harry Noyes, Norman de Vaux, Ed Ver Linden, Dr. Campbell, "Trainload" Collins, and others. The form letter asking for subscriptions contained the phrases that needed to be only half-heard to bring on the old, familiar glow as he sang the "advantage of a syndicate operation . . . against individual purchases and sales during a very feverish market."[39] With warm recollections of 1916 they sent their checks to "Billy," who knew how to make the money breed, often enclosing cheery notes like that of General Leather's James Smith, writing from Palm Beach's Royal Poinciana Hotel: "I hope it will make some money, as this place absorbs it like a sponge."[40] And, harassed as he was, he could chirp back to the

Chevrolet dealers and Buick dealers and in-laws and tribesmen. He had from mid-February to mid-May to buy and then sell out and split the pot, or, in the dread event of a drop in price, to split the stock itself, leaving it to individuals to wait in hope or to liquidate and take their beating. But they did not expect to lose, and neither did he. Writing to a Mrs. L. T. Hollister in New York, where she was awaiting embarkation on a pleasure cruise, he made the playful gesture of a man comfortable in his element.

In view of the fact that you are leaving tomorrow for an extended trip to foreign fields and will probably be inclined to purchase large quantities of rare and expensive works of art . . . of which you are a great admirer, I felt that you might use to advantage your profits in the syndicate, and am anticipating the distribution in your case.[41]

Enclosed was his personal check for $1,040.

So the syndicates swam through the financial seas, those of the big fish and those of the $25,000 and $50,000 investors around their flanks, hoping to catch the morsels that were dropped. And even these were not enough. Raskob computed that they would need $60 million more for the year, and late in April, he and Du Pont knew where they wanted to go to get it.

The first candidate was Sir Harry McGowan, head of the Nobel Company, a British explosives combine allied with the Du Pont interests and, like them, in search of uses for its wartime earnings. McGowan was told that General Motors planned to market 3.6 million shares of its new common stock, which then stood at 27. Durant and E. I. du Pont de Nemours between them had the right to subscribe to 60 percent of the issue at $20. The Nobel enterprise was offered the remaining 40 percent, or 1.44 million shares, at the same below-market price, and accepted. In addition a jointly owned subsidiary of the Nobel and Du Pont firms, Canadian Explosives Limited, took another 300,000 shares at $20. The conclusion of the purchase contracts in June brought $34.8 million of fiscal reinforcement to General Motors, and also two new corporate partners who would be represented on future boards of directors.

But that still left Raskob short of his $60 million, and the time had come to turn to the biggest banker of all. The house of Morgan would have to be asked if it would like to take up the subscription rights to all or part of the 1.86 million shares yet untaken. Few developments could have been more painful to Durant. It was twelve years since they had spurned his first request for help in creating General Motors. The elder Morgan was gone. George Perkins, too, slept with his fathers. Francis Stetson would die that very year. But "the Corner" still drove a hard bargain, still exacted a price in freedom as well as percentages from those whom it helped.

But Durant was overborne by argument, or else found the need for money too exigent for scruples. The dose had to be swallowed. The Morgan offices behaved much as he had expected. They took up 1.4 million shares, which they would distribute to associated banks at $20. For these partners they demanded an aggregate of $1.34 millions' worth of stock as a commission. And for themselves, 60,000 shares at $10—a $600,000 fee. In effect, General Motors paid some $2 million to raise $28 million. The figure was not exorbitant, though in view of the eventual value of GM stock the ultimate return to the bankers on the shares bought at distress prices was stunning. But the usual Morgan demand for board seats for themselves and those who worked with them claimed a price that was beyond recording in ledgers. On June 3, 1920, almost four years to the day after assuming General Motors' presidency and boasting privately that he had taken it back from the bankers, William Durant had to issue a press release listing six new directors. They were Edward R. Stettinius, a member of the Morgan partnership; Seward Prosser, the Bankers Trust president to whom Du Pont had spoken so confidently five months earlier; George F. Baker, a vice-president of the First National Bank of New York; Owen D. Young, a vice-president of the General Electric Corporation; William H. Woodin, president of the American Car and Foundry Company; and Clarence M. Wooley, president of the American Radiator Company. Two of the three men representing industrial companies, Young and Woodin, were financial rather than production experts.

"In addition to the underwriting, Messrs. J. P. Morgan & Co. and their associates have acquired a substantial interest in the Corporation."[42] So the news story of the transaction ended. The General Motors of 1920 now had as little resemblance in its financial structure as in its physical size to the holding company of 1908 with its Durant-handpicked board.

There was once more a discernible change in the atmosphere at 1764 Broadway. Durant accepted the Morgan intervention as a bitter exaction of necessity. The Du Pont group went forth rejoicing and dancing to meet their new partners, as if they had achieved a longstanding intention. "I think it would be very nice," Raskob wrote to Pierre in July, "if you would write a letter congratulating J. P. Morgan & Company on the success of our stock offering and in particular, paying some little compliment to Mr. Stettinius for his untiring efforts." Du Pont willingly complied.

My dear Mr. Stettinius:

I fail to express to you in words my deep appreciation of your interest in General Motors affairs and the satisfaction that comes to us in knowing that our views of the motor industry are supported by the house of Morgan and your associates. The industry has assumed such large proportions that I have felt for a long time the necessity for having our group more closely connected with large interests, in order that harmonious action should be insured. We wish you and the other new directors to feel that General Motors is an open book to you; that all questions will be considered by all of us; that no criticism or suggestion will be received in an unfriendly way.[43]

Comparable letters of welcome went to the other newcomers to the board, and that to Prosser ended with a special flourish: "General Motors is too large a factor in industrial life to remain even a partly closed book to the great financial people of New York."

Stettinius's reply to Du Pont contained one specially revealing sentence. Cordially acknowledging the offered embrace, he said of the deal: "It would not have received the support we have given it had it not been for your active connection with and interest in the company."[44] The translation of which was that without Du Pont, Durant would still have seen no Morgan money. From the moment of their involvement, Durant was in jeopardy. The collective judgment at 23 Wall Street was still that he was an irresponsible speculator. The partners saw in him what they most despised, the egotist and anarchist, resistant to the indispensable claims of economic order. Their new position offered them a potential for acting on that judgment that could be aroused by any slip.

The new relationship had been in effect only a few weeks when there was a small, violent quarrel. The Morgan concern was now joined with Durant and others in still another syndicate to shore up GM, which, by the twentieth of July, was down to 25. One week later, Durant's phone rang, with one of his brokers on the line. Someone had dropped 100,000 shares of GM common on the market, badly breaking the price. It was at 21½ at that moment, and sinking. Stock transactions are supposedly anonymous, but Durant had contacts who, in response to his probing, assured him that the shares had come from Stettinius.

Boiling, Durant waited until some business brought the new director to the General Motors building, whereupon he called him into his office, and in his presence dictated a memorandum that accused the fifty-five-year-old banker of deliberate bad faith. Stettinius, he charged, had agreed to buy as necessary to keep the price above 20, and gone back on his word. The implication was that the Morgan group had cheated, was bailing out to cut losses and leave others to suffer, was further destroying confidence in GM.[45]

Stettinius made no immediate record of his answer, and its tone could only be guessed at from a reprise of the incident that a journalist got from him some years later. But he was apparently far from abashed, and did not disclaim the sale. He had only recently finished a tour as Assistant Secretary of War, advising the government on purchasing matters, and the experience had ripened that sense of infallibility that was the essence of the Morgan approach to any problem. He seems to have made three points. First, he flatly denied any agreement to hold the price at a particular level. Then he counterattacked. Durant, he said, was buying on his own hook, and it was impossible for a syndicate to work if its members carried on outside operations. The accusation was a stark presentation of the typical Morgan distaste for independent action. To it, Stettinius added in conclusion the official Morgan viewpoint of that summer. Strong forces working in the economy at large were depressing the stock, and it would be impossible to halt the plunge until a natural bottoming-out occurred. Before that point was reached, it might make sense to unload some GM and pick it up again later at a lower figure.

The battle of the Stettinius memorandum changed nothing and left both sides locked in their mutual distrust. But the stalemate left Durant still without the buying help that he needed. Once more, using Raskob as an emissary, he petitioned the Corner to step up its GM purchases. Once more the answer came back that the time was not right. If J. P. Morgan and Company had any inkling that the prolonged downslide was pushing Durant toward a personal disaster, it may only have confirmed them in their refusal and even spiced it with a little pleasure.

IV August came on, hot and discouraging. The telephones on Durant's desk were as insistent as ever, the course of GM still inexorably downward. One day Alfred Sloan, after the usual difficulties, got in to see the chief and found him, predictably, on a line to someone. Durant looked up at him with a fleeting smile. He was never, Sloan noticed, too tired to be kind.

"What is it?"

Sloan asked if he might go away for a while; he was not feeling too well.

"Certainly. Get some rest." And back Durant went to his conversation, unaware that the sense of impending trouble at the top had permeated Sloan's thinking as it had Chrysler's. He wanted time off to think about how he, too, might abandon ship.[46]

Back at the beginning of the year, Sloan had carefully drafted three long reports suggesting ways of landscaping and cutting roads through the administrative wilderness that he believed was all around him. They contained plans for centralizing engineering and research functions, setting up strict procedures for approval of capital expenditures, spelling out operating policies and creating an interdivisional billing system. Durant had praised them and filed them away and continued in the old practices, and Sloan was chilled by the growing feeling that under a real shock General Motors might collapse and bury his life savings in its ruins. Or so, at least, it seemed to him in recollection afterward.

During his month's holiday in Europe, he came to his decision. He would say good-bye not only to General Motors, but to production itself, with its tangible achievements but its endless struggles with changing tastes and needs and prices. Lee, Higginson and Company had offered him a job as an investment analyst; evidently James Storrow had kept his eye on the talent showcase at General Motors. He would come home and accept it; slowly liquidate his proudly accumulated GM holdings as best he could without loss; let others take the risks, protected by such advice as he could give them. He ordered a Rolls Royce for future delivery, and prepared himself to taste the good life.

And if he had any doubts about the wisdom of his resolution, the news from home was enough to dispel them. For in early September the institutional crisis, the business "recessing" that both he and Durant had anticipated, struck with sudden fury. "We were sailing along at full speed," were his words; "the sun was shining and there was no cloud in the sky." But the 1919 boom had been artificial, resting on the persistence of inflated wartime prices, on easy credit and flushed expectations. In mid-1920 the reaction set in. A wave of liquidation, price breaks, and layoffs rolled over the economy. The auto makers would learn that they always felt retrenchment first and hardest. "Before it was realized what was happening, this great ship of ours was in the midst of a terrific storm."[47]

The strength of the tempest was measured by cataclysmic sales figures. In June 47,000 cars and trucks had been sold, a number in itself far short of the monthly target needed to justify the year's 876,000-unit schedule. In November the figure was 12,700, one-third of the preceding year's output for the same month.

Unsold cars crowded the factory lots. The huge inventories of supplies ordered in enthusiasm continued to roll in amid despair. The great warehouses full of radiators and axles and motor castings and tires and gear trains and gasoline tanks and plate glass and the hundreds of other elements that became alive when joined together on the assembly line were now expensive mortuaries, full of dead materials that were not being turned into cars or dollars. In October the value of inventory on hand was $210 million, $60 million over the allotment, money imprisoned. The well of working cash was being sucked dry. Eighty millions were borrowed in short-term bank loans, setting up another drain on future revenues.

The entire industry was staggering. The Lelands had gone into the manufacture of a new car called the Lincoln. They started the year with $8 millions in cash on hand, and ended with $11,000 in the till and $6.25

millions of debt. Even Ford was hard hit, cut his prices by 30 percent, and finally shut down altogether in December, as did Willys-Overland, Packard, Dodge, and Studebaker.[48] General Motors suspended production at all divisions except for Buick and Cadillac. Its total sales for January of 1921 were 6,150. The auto-making world itself, a great machine whose human "parts" were hundreds of thousands of workers and suppliers and creditors and families caught in an interlocking motion, slowed to a virtually total halt.

At General Motors hard but belated decisions were made in the executive committee. In October, Durant set up an inventory control team of Pratt, E. F. Johnson and a longtime assistant named Henry Barton, and gave it sweeping powers to freeze divisional purchases until stocks on the shelves were reduced. But it was only a desperation measure, taken to avoid foundering while the rampage continued.[49]

In the midst of all this, Sloan returned, ready to resign, and found something unaccountably different in the air. The feeling was not merely one of crisis, but of something in the wind. Durant himself was away on a rare rest break. There were no comments from the finance committee on what future steps it had in mind to cope with the changed circumstances. Sloan did have an occasion to see Pierre du Pont, in the course of which he mentioned his January reports, and was invited to send copies over. He did so, and received a pleasant note of acknowledgment. Du Pont would read them at the first opportunity and then see him for a talk.[50]

Sloan decided to wait with the resignation, at least for a while.

And almost day by day, the price of GM on Wall Street dropped. Seventeen on October 27, 16 on November 3, 14 on November 10, down and down.

And William Crapo Durant was giving what attention he could to the fate of General Motors while the auto-making depression was wiping him out personally. The price slump was murdering him, because he had self-destructively challenged the market singlehanded. The secret of his year was that in addition to the syndicate operations of which he was part, he had been buying, buying, buying on his personal account. By the autumn, every drop of a point was costing him as much as two million dollars. And still the phones jangled daily with the calls for more margin and more collateral, and at the midpoint of November he had thrown in the last of his reserves and was looking straight into the wolf's jaws.

Outwardly he gave no sign of any wounds. He was more attentive than ever to Catherine. "Darling Muddie," he wrote to her once, using their special pet name, "I love you more and more every day. Willie."[51] He stayed in Deal on Wednesdays and weekends to be with her and to "rest," though there was always a briefcase of work with him, and the telephone rang there, too. On the other days he commuted by train, or train and ferry from Atlantic Highlands, not far north of Deal, to lower Manhattan, looking into the waters of Sandy Hook Bay and The Narrows to find the answers. He probably visited Margery, too, in the new home that he had helped her to buy in Westbury on Long Island. It was finally all over with her and the doctor, a Paris divorce in 1919 following her recovery from a severe bout with influenza during the epidemic of the preceding year. The change in her situation was sad but not devastating. She had plenty of money from a trust fund that her husband and her father had agreed that she ought to have, and a zest for enjoying it. She was still devoted to "Pops." For that matter, so was Campbell, who continued to function as a Durant assistant.[52]

It would not have been in character for Durant to have confessed any anxieties he might feel to Catherine or Margery or Rebecca. His code did not allow for the sharing of business problems with women. He would not have been likely to confide in Cliff, now thirty, and busy with his own investments, his own marital conflicts, and his passion for the auto track. In 1919 he had qualified for the Indianapolis 500 and dropped out with steering gear trouble after 54 laps.[53] A wealthy young man with his hobbies and his problems, and, blood kin or not, no one to choose as a confidant.

There were no confidants, so far as anyone ever knew. Any fears lurking in dark corners were not admitted to the oldest friends, the closest associates. Not even, it is likely, to William Durant himself. But his silence not only walled him off from possible helpful advice; it left unanswered the question of why so experienced an operator kept struggling to prop the collapsing market for GM all by himself, an effort that Sloan compared to standing at the top of Niagara Falls and trying to stop it with a hat.

His own explanations, to the end of his days, were strictly businesslike. He had done it for the company, trying to keep the stock viable and a good choice for investors—trying to keep McGowan from backing out of his commitment. He had simply stayed alone at the post of duty, fighting while others fled.[54]

But there were clearly other reasons. The optimism of a lifetime, fed by successes the most recent of which was only four years behind him. And loyalty and pride and a reluctance to be shamed. How could Durant let down those Flint friends whom he had invited into Syndicate Number Five? What could he tell Arthur Bishop if he lost money for him, after Bishop revealed that his $100,000 in the pool was a sum he had borrowed and it was "like pulling teeth to get it"?[55] How could he admit to them all that he had run out of miracles? He was bound hand and foot by his own reluctance to disappoint those who trusted him. In a multimillion-dollar market he clung to the obligations of good fellowship. On three separate occasions John Lee Pratt sat in Durant's office when visitors from Michigan walked in and told the same story—they had bought GM on their old business advisor's prompting, and now they were facing ruin.[56] In each case, Durant had reacted identically—called their brokers and told them that he himself was taking over the stock.

He was still trying to preserve a personal grip on the industrial giant that he had helped to create and which was moved by energies indifferent to the solitary human unit. His last gesture was a new attempt to rally a grassroots militia to take on the armies of the speculators. On October 15 he announced the formation of the Durant Corporation. It was an outgrowth of the General Motors Stockholders' Services Division, the earlier effort to encourage widespread small holdings of GM stock. But the new organization was entirely Durant's, unconnected with the motor combine, and was to deal in securities of every kind. At the start, however, it was making a special offer to people of modest means "desiring to become permanent investors rather than speculative buyers." They could have GM common at $18 a share, a low price made possible by the Durant Corporation's heavy purchases of "the past few days when stocks were being thrown on the market at ridiculous prices, with the consequent demoralization aided by the speculative interests." As he explained it to the press (the headline report was "William C. Durant Enters Investment Field"), he expected to have 300,000 holders on the rolls inside of five years and be on the way to purifying the market. There would be a fifty-share top limit, a time-payment plan, even passbooks to allow the nonspeculative investor to keep track of his progress, coin by coin, to ownership.[57]

The Durant Corporation's officers were a far remove from Wall Street. One of them was an obscure person named P. D. Wagoner, and another, H. W. Alger, Durant's nephew by marriage. In future time the project would have some use for him. But in that desperate week it was a move that backfired. Its very nature was suspect, for no matter how he might explain it in long-range perspective, Durant was doing what he had bitterly denounced others for doing—selling GM, adding to the downward pressure.

A reaction came almost at once from Pierre du Pont. He sent Durant a letter whose ostensible purpose was to protest a minor embarrassment. The Durant Corporation had sent out circulars to Delaware schoolteachers. Since Pierre himself was on the state school board, and since it might not be clear to everyone that he had no part in Durant's new enterprise, it could appear that he was improperly using his position, pushing stock on public employees over whom he had some authority. Behind his plea to desist, however, was a question that bit deeper. Did his partner really think it was a moment to recommend purchases of GM to anyone not well enough off to hold out for the "long pull"? Stripped of the occasionally confusing circumlocution that Du Pont's politeness made habitual, the letter was asking what Durant thought he was up to, selling GM at this of all possible moments.[58]

Yet if Du Pont felt any uneasiness about Durant's behavior on the market, he took an almost simultaneous action which in that case was hard to explain. On a date late in October, he agreed to a request by Durant for a loan of 1,307,749 shares of GM common from the Du Pont Corporation's treasury, against which the borrower would deposit 95,000 shares of Chevrolet as collateral. Though he was shortly to claim utter innocence of Durant's situation, Du Pont had clear evidence that the man with whom he had been working since 1916 was involved in some transaction requiring huge quantities of GM stock. Moreover, he was willing to help furnish the needed shares.[59]

The birth of the Durant Corporation, meanwhile, created a genuine furor at 23 Wall Street. Dwight Morrow, another of the Morgan partners, expressed their anger and concern to Du Pont and Raskob. Was Durant beginning to unload a personal oversupply of GM, while spurring his syndicate allies — the Corner included — to keep buying? Was this merely the tip of the iceberg? Was Durant secretly arranging, through others, to keep up the mysterious selling waves that accounted for the long decline? Morrow put bluntly to Du Pont what Du Pont had insinuated softly to Durant: What was the man up to?

Du Pont's answer was to arrange for a meeting at which the air could be cleared. He, Durant, and Raskob would sit down with Morrow and George Whitney, another of the seemingly innumerable Morgan men. The conference took place on November 10, and set in motion a three-week-long chain of events, at the end of which William Durant was left for dead.

V On the appointed day, a Wednesday, Durant once more sat across the table from a Morgan representative who was mistrustful of his motives.[60] Morrow, who took the lead in speaking for the firm, was of the younger generation that had succeeded the likes of Stetson and Satterlee, and he manifested identical qualifications — legal brilliance, golden connections to the highest levels of government, and arrogance. He had graduated from Amherst in 1895, Columbia Law School in 1899, joined the Morgans with a stunning reputation in 1914, and been advisor to the Allied Transport Council during the war. Ahead of him lay an ambassadorship and a Senate seat, as well as the chair of blue-ribbon financial and legal commissions.

Only Pierre du Pont left a full record of the events of that busy November, and he pictured himself as a moderator at the outset, gently defending Durant against Morrow's suspicions that the engineer of the great takeover coup of 1915 was once more speculating—that was Morrow's word—in GM securities. The dangers of a company president gambling with his own organization's stock were self-evident. If he collapsed into liquidation, he took the concern down with him. If it were big enough, the widening circles of its distress could embrace the entire economy. Wall Street had seen more than one panic start in just that way.

Du Pont claimed that he had, in private discourse, assured the Morgan people of his own conviction that Durant was merely holding on to his personal investments, and neither buying on margin nor borrowing. All the same, Morrow bored in with sharp questions, starting with the Durant Corporation. Was it linked to some larger purpose? Durant answered that it was not; he merely hoped to get more participation in General Motors' ownership, particularly by dealers and employees of the automobile business. Then, Morrow wanted to know, was the Durant Corporation his only connection with the market at that moment? Durant gave what appeared to be a straightforward affirmative answer. And finally, did Durant know of any "weak accounts"? The answer was no.

Morrow then changed his tone and offered a soothing summary. General Motors was a sound organization. Its market position was not out of line with other unfortunate developments in the economy, and was sure to improve soon, provided that no one had borrowed heavily on GM stock and was in trouble. Any routine selling could easily be absorbed by the "stabilizing syndicate" in which they were all involved. He concluded by asking that Mr. Whitney be shown the accounts of the Durant Corporation for a detailed study on Friday, and won ready consent.

So they parted. The next morning, Durant was on the telephone to Du Pont, asking if the two of them and Raskob could lunch together. It was a memorable meal. Durant's nerve was shaken, and in a state of agitation he confided that he was being pressed by nameless adversaries, whom he described simply as "the bankers." He was, he said, in their hands. They were demanding his resignation. He would have to "play the game." His partners assumed his meaning to be that General Motors' creditors wanted to be rid of him. They made efforts to calm him, pointing out that no bankers were at that moment pressing the corporation. In the general surprise and stress of the hour, a remark by Durant to the effect that he was "worried" about his personal accounts slipped by.

Only later did that fleeting reference suddenly strike Pierre, he said, as troublesome. He sent his squire, Raskob, over to Durant the next morning, Friday, for elaboration. Raskob asked, in a tone that must have been jocose, considering the range of the figures involved, just how much Durant owed. Was it six million or twenty-six? The answer was in dead seriousness, and wiped out any laughter. "I will have to look it up," Durant said.

Look it up? Nothing could have bared the distinction between Du Pont and Durant more than such an unnerving response. Pierre du Pont was the kind of man who, when the General Motors treasurer once sent him a check for $38,502, representing a $3 dividend on 12,834 shares, answered immediately and correctly that he was returning a $3 overpayment, being certain that he had only 12,833.[61] Over a long weekend at home, he came to a firm determination that his first priority of the following Tuesday in New York was going to be the discovery of exactly what was Durant's debt and, more importantly, how much of it was secured by GM stock.

He checked with the Morgan offices the first thing that morning, and got a cheering report. George Whitney and Thomas Cochran had reviewed the Durant Corporation's books, and while they believed that Durant had "behaved foolishly" in his advertisements for the undertaking—they were probably annoyed by the implied references to malign and nameless financial powers—there was no sign that he was personally entangled in any threatening situation.

This pleasing illusion lasted only until the afternoon. It was a sign of the moment's gravity that Raskob and Du Pont personally came knocking at Durant's office door, and of his own harried state of mind that he kept them waiting, tapping their expensively shod feet as had hundreds of others, while he dealt with the inescapable phone calls. They finally got in at 4 P.M., an hour after the market's close, and he began to give them figures from rough penciled notes. Finally, he presented a harrowing approximation. He believed he owed some $34 million to brokers and bankers, secured, as Pierre wrote to Irénée, by about 3 million GM shares of his own, and 1.3 million owned by "others."

In that offhanded reference to "others," Du Pont left a whisper of suspicion that he was dissembling somewhat in his statements, obviously written with an eye for the archives; that he was not quite the guileless friend, shocked by his partner's transgressions, that he purported to be. For the Du Ponts were the "others" who had handed over those 1.3 million shares only days earlier. In the long, unhappy aftermath of the crisis Durant's friends would murmur, but show no evidence, that the Du Ponts and the Morgan interests conspired to entrap Durant. It was clear enough from his history that he was entirely capable of ensnaring himself, but the possibility of some small, final help from others cannot be completely ruled out.

In any case, the magnitude of Durant's revelation made it an earthquake. If he was about to be sold out, then up to four million shares of GM could be tearing the floor out of the market within a matter of days, ruining everyone who held GM stock or who relied on its value in any way—all in one red-ink burial blent. And to avoid his being sold out, he needed to raise almost overnight a sum far beyond the power of even a solvent individual investor.

Plainly a full emergency was on. Though Du Pont's memoir contained no hint of any harsh words, it made clear that Durant was told firmly to get his brokers' statements in complete order by the close of the next business day. Du Pont and Raskob then retired, and Irénée was summoned to take the first available train and be in New York next morning.

That very night, Tuesday, Durant had a margin call for $150,000 due the next morning, which he somehow managed to scrape together. But on Wednesday GM dropped to 13½, which meant that all that day his switchboard was jammed with more such demands. As he struggled to cope with them, the two Du Pont brothers and Raskob, in one of their offices, sat and wondered not only how one man could amass a total of $34 million in I.O.U.'s, but what could be done about it. For it was clear that, whatever anyone thought, Durant could not simply be left to take his medicine. For General Motors' sake and all that went with it he would have to be extricated.

Raskob was called on to devise one of his expedients. His first was uncomplicated. The Du Pont Corporation would have no trouble borrowing the $34 million Durant needed and even more. They could buy out his three million shares at $12, only a point or two under the market, thereby increasing their share of control as a happy by-product. Durant was called in and offered this solution. It must have taken a stellar effort to keep his composure, but he did, saying that such a forced sale would ruin him. Hard as was his position he knew, too, that the alternative of letting the creditors have their way with him was unacceptable. His one card left was that he could pull the temple down around everyone's ears by consenting to nothing, and he played it with as much coolness as he could to the very end.

Undismayed, Raskob reached into his bag of tricks again, and drew out a more complex device. A new holding company would be formed, issuing stock of its own, which the Du Ponts would buy for a relatively modest amount of cash. The holding company would then give its own notes to the brokers for Durant's unpaid-for shares, which would become its "assets." It would turn over its cash to Durant to enable him to pay his more immediate debts, in return for ownership of part of his shares. What was at the core of the plan was an exchange of collateral. The brokers would now have Du Pont–backed promissory notes to protect them, and the major goal would have been achieved of "lifting this great mass of stock out of the extremely critical and threatening position in which it then stood."

The consideration of this scheme occupied the balance of Wednesday, and Thursday the eighteenth, which was to prove a marathon day, opened to the demented concert of Durant's telephones signaling new ultimatums from the Wall Street offices holding his paper. By the close of trading on the Exchange, he was without any recourse except for a final, humiliating step of begging the Morgans in person for help. Late in the afternoon, he rang up George Whitney with a question. Would Syndicate D, the current stabilizing pool, buy 1.1 million shares of GM from him at 13?

Whitney passed the request to Morrow, who called back promptly. Durant, he said, must surely know the rules. Syndicate members did not buy from each other; their job was to place purchase orders in the open market. He wanted to know the reason for the request. Was Durant in some kind of trouble?

Here again the account of the conversation came from Du Pont, whose entire chronicle of the proceedings was carefully purged of any passion, but in this instance claimed truly extraordinary detachment. For according to Pierre's version of events, Morrow was surprised by Durant's call, since he did not yet know of the appalling debt. Pierre and Raskob had not told him. Nor did they tell him until after Durant had confessed to Morrow on his own. Nor did they begin to work jointly on the problem with the Morgan people until after a chance Thursday night encounter. All of which, taken together, seems to be protesting too much that there was no prior collusion, no putting of Morgan and Du Pont heads together to consider W. C. Durant as a problem. Nonetheless, Pierre's is the only surviving indisputable firsthand account written close to the time, and according to its testimony, Morrow's question as to whether Durant was in trouble initiated some brief sparring.

No, Durant said, not personally. But he had loaned some of his stock to friends to help them "margin their accounts." Morrow followed up with a good, hard attorney's question. Would Durant himself be involved in the profits or losses of those accounts? "Well, in certain conditions, yes," was the reply.

Morrow suggested that Durant come down and talk to him. He was leaving at six for a long weekend in Amherst, but there was still time to discuss things. Durant hesitated. It would take him time to get his papers in order, he protested. It would be much easier if Morrow came to his office, where he would have the assistance of Russell Briggs, the secretary of the Chevrolet Company, John Thomas Smith, General Motors' counsel, and Dr. Edwin Campbell, his personal assistant, all of whom were "very familiar with the entire affair." Morrow thought briefly, and decided the situation was serious enough to warrant a little delay in his plans. He said that he would come over, with Cochran and Whitney, at six.

Durant now called Pierre, said that he had a meeting set up with the three Morgan officials, and asked that he and Raskob join in. The response, frosty in its virtue, gave him an undoubted shock. Du Pont said that it was clear that Durant had been untruthful with Morrow at the meeting a week earlier, and he could not be a party to any conference in which the deception was continued. Durant would have to admit to the Morgan partners what he had admitted the day before yesterday to him and Raskob, or they would not participate.

Until then, Durant seems to have operated on the assumption that he and the Du Ponts were partners in the motor business, fellow industrialists who would handle their problems with as little disclosure as possible to the bankers, the strangers, the moneylenders who did not understand the joys and the challenges of creation. But as Du Pont addressed him from that plateau of rectitude where he habitually dwelled, the bitter truth must have broken at last on Durant that he himself was the outsider now, and that the Morgans and Du Ponts spoke the same language. His immediate reaction was to stiffen his own back. He would accept no conditions of that kind. Let Du Pont and Raskob stay out of the parley if they chose.

Yet within an hour he caved in on his own. Perhaps in the short time it took the three financial experts to ride uptown he had gotten more duns. In any case, when they were in his office, he began:

I wish to explain an apparent discrepancy between the present condition and what I replied to your question a week ago when you asked me if I knew of any weak accounts, to which I answered "No." The stock was then selling at $15, and the depreciation in the stock from $15 to the present level of $13 has changed the whole complexion of the situation.

Morrow cut him short. There was no point in discussing what was past. If the Morgan firm was to help, Durant had better give them all the facts at once. Whatever Morrow's specific words, his manner was charged with an anger which was still hissing two years later in his question to a financial journalist: "Why didn't Durant lay his cards on the table?"[62] It outraged him to think that so many fortunes were imperiled by these actions and held as hostages to a liar's ego. Under Morrow's steely scrutiny, Durant got as far as acknowledging partial truth: that he was carrying about 1.5 million shares on margin, on which he owed $15 million, and had "interests" in other accounts also secured by GM shares in quantity. His most crucial problem, however, was only fifteen hours away. He needed $940,000 before the Exchange opened next morning, or the dam would give way, the flood of liquidation roll.

The banking men knew that matters were critical. Morrow would have to bid good-bye to his plans for a pleasant autumn Friday in Massachusetts. They left Durant's office at seven, telling him they would be back at nine and hoped to find his accounts ready. And as they stepped out of the elevator on the way to a hasty dinner, whom should they run into but Pierre, Irénée, and Raskob, returning to their hotel. So all six went back up to Raskob's office to compare notes, now that they were all in on Durant's disgrace, and then, according to Pierre, the three from Wilmington and the three from Wall Street went separate ways to eat and to make phone calls canceling their evening arrangements. There would be no return to home or bed for any of them that night.

At nine o'clock the hosts gather again in the General Motors building. It is another of those scenes that crop up in Durant's life in which he reaches some turning point during an encounter with other men who represent forces and elements of his past and future. Sitting at his side are the doctor, John Thomas, and Briggs, three of the Chevrolet "crowd." Confronting him are the three plenipotentiaries from the kingdoms of high finance. And the two brothers from the distinguished eastern family, with their assistant who is much like Durant, and yet now cast as one of his rescuers and judges. Ten men, three groups. Durant at the center, the cause of this convergence and its victim.

As they enter the conference room a figure sits waiting in Durant's antechamber — a partner in a brokerage house, waiting for more collateral. Only a few lights burn in the corridors. Charwomen push their buckets and mops. Horns sound faintly as traffic pours to and from the amusement district a few blocks south on Broadway.

Heedless of the clock, probably with jackets off (though they are all very formal men), with pencils flying, they probe and arrange and compute. Who owns this? Who paid for that? How much? Where did these shares come from? And so on in a process that Thomas Lamont, of the Morgan firm, who is not there, will later describe as "corkscrewing it out of him."[63] When the corkscrewing is finished, the totals are found to be not quite as bad as expected. Durant owes $27 million.

The groups separate. The judges and rescuers withdraw to one office to think of how to raise almost a million before breakfast time, now rushing toward them as the sky lightens over Central Park, and another twenty-seven million soon after. Durant and his friends go to another to await the verdict and retrieve what they can.

Messages pass back and forth. The rescuers agree on a modification of

Raskob's plan. There will be a holding company to take over Durant's stock. But it will buy it outright from the brokers, with money borrowed from banks. The Morgans believe that keeping the brokers involved as lenders, with a changed collateral, is too cumbersome. And Durant will have a share in the holding company; it is his stock and he is entitled to something. They offer him 25 percent. He holds out as best he can, using his remaining power as president of the Chevrolet Company, which will be called on to help raise money, and his implicit power of financial suicide. He gets them up to 40 percent. Finally, red-eyed and stubbly, they all agree to basic terms. The sands have run out of the glass. The twelve-year relationship of Durant with his "baby" has finished its course.

The final arrangement was this. The Du Pont Securities Company was to be created, capitalized at $17.5 million, represented by 100,000 shares of stock. The parent Du Pont Corporation would receive 40,000 of them in consideration of $7 millions in cash. Another 20,000 would go to J. P. Morgan and Company, to distribute to whatever bankers it would use in arranging a loan of $20 millions to Du Pont Securities — a commission of 17½ percent. Durant would receive the final 40,000 shares in return for turning over to the holding company all of its assets, to wit, 2,546,548⁹⁄10 shares of GM common, figured at $9.50 per share. The Morgans would handle the matter. They would establish a credit balance for Durant; pay his bills and charge the outlays against it; then deposit the GM stock with Du Pont Securities as it came in. There it would lie, no longer endangering anyone, until disposed of at some happier time. In the meanwhile the Du Ponts, as a side arrangement, would also lend Durant an additional $1.17 millions immediately — $640,000 by morning, and another $530,000 before the day was out.

Stripped to its essence, the contract meant that Durant was giving up 60 percent of his stock at 4½ points below the market — 40 percent to the Du Ponts for their $7 million, 20 percent to various bankers for their loan. And the 40 percent that he was "keeping" was not in his control; he was merely entitled to the profit on it, should there ever be any.

At 5:30 A.M. on Friday, the nineteenth, the signatures went on the draft document. The salvation committee was enfolded in a glow of self-congratulation over a good night's work, an impermissible ugliness averted. One of the Du Ponts expressed the opinion that the Morgans were "splendid" to pitch in so willingly without any thought of commission for themselves, and their expansiveness was matched, on the Morgan side, by a voiced gratitude at the way in which the Du Ponts sprang forward to "contribute" $7 million to the operation. "There are two firms in this country who are real sports" was Cochran's jovial pronouncement — "du Pont and Morgan." He chose, in the exuberance of the moment, perhaps the last characterization that anyone would have ever applied, ordinarily, to either house.

There remained only one awkward piece of business to get through. That was, of course, Durant's resignation from General Motors. The Du Ponts would always insist, with customary delicacy, that they had never raised the matter. It was the recollection of both brothers that the idea came from Durant himself (which he denied), and of course it seemed a good idea under the circumstances. No one from Morgan even spoke to the matter, but Morrow in particular made no secret of his conviction that Durant was unfit to run the company. Perhaps a wordless message was exchanged, like the "suicide" gun handed to the officer who has lost his honor. Whatever was said or suppressed, when they all went down into the morning chill, it was understood that the resignation would take effect on the thirtieth.

Only when the bookkeepers at 23 Wall Street neatly totted up the final columns did the depth of the pit into which Durant had fallen become manifest. He owed huge sums to at least seventeen brokers, those financial provisioners and supercargoes of the great argosies that sailed corporate capitalism's oceans. To these companies J. P. Morgan and Company counted off hundreds of thousands at a time, a guardian paying storekeepers for the misdeeds of a naughty ward. To J. S. Bache $543,000 as the balance on 77,600 shares; to S. B. Chapin $649,623 on 73,000 shares; to Arthur Lipper $1,091,851 to complete the purchase of 154,274 shares; to Dominick and Dominick $1,385,131 for the 120,723 they held for Durant on his margin; to Van Emburgh and Atterbury, and Hornblower and Weeks, and fully a dozen others, amounts that equaled several times over the entire capitalization of Flint banks in Durant's youth.

Banks had to be paid, too. He owed $4.3 million to them, all told, and for every ten dollars lent him they had demanded one share of GM as collateral, 430,000 pledged in all. Eleven banks, the biggest debt of all to Chatham and Phenix for $2.2 million, and half a million from Chase National, $300,000 from Empire Trust, and then a string of $200,000 borrowings from around the country—from Irving National in New York, and Chicago's Continental and Commercial, and Detroit's Peninsular State, and even $100,000 from the Fourth Atlantic National Bank in his Boston birthplace. He had been, as he said, "in the hands of the bankers," especially those who had come to the Metropolitan Club in 1918 to meet him as Du Pont's protégé, and who now held out their "Past Due" notices in accusation.

The total value of his shares at $9.50 was $24,045,185.45—they figured it all to the penny—and the sum of money advanced on his behalf was $24,037,319.61. In the end, his credit balance left on Morgan's books was

$7,865.54. Seven thousand in cash left from an investment whose cost could not be calculated, because the 2.5 million shares had been acquired at many different times and prices. If he lost an average of $10 a share he lost $25 million, and the stock had dropped thirty points in 1920 alone. His own estimated figure of what he sacrificed was $90 million. No one disputed it.[64]

Somehow, the last week was gotten through, the appropriate rituals performed. He kept his smile, honoring the good gambler's code that forbade whining. The newspapers were informed, and so were the directors at his final meeting with them. "You knew he was grief-stricken," said Sloan, "but no grief showed in his face."[65] Margery, who was accused of adding an excess of artistic detail to her stories, said that he did come to see her one day, and as she hugged him, she could feel his body trembling and tears on his cheeks.

Contradictory legends enshrouded the final days. John Lee Pratt, nearly a full thirty years after, would claim to remember a special farewell dinner that Durant had held for some of his favorites — Harry Bassett, Collins, Hardy, Fred Hohensee, Fred Warner of Oakland, Tom Warner of Warner Gear, Karl Zimmerschied (a new man at Chevrolet), and Pratt himself. But Catherine Durant, still very much alive then, said she recalled no such thing and it would not have happened without her knowing.

Nonetheless, true or not, it was Pratt's testimony that Durant's mood was mellow, even humble. He explained to them all that he had become "overextended" in the market while trying to support GM.

> I am telling you this because you will hear rumors that the du Pont Company took advantage of me and forced me out, and you will find possibly some people will show resentment in General Motors because I am out. But I want you to know that the du Pont Company treated me as fine as anybody could treat me. If they hadn't gone out and borrowed money . . . to take over the brokerage holdings, General Motors stock would have gone to practically nothing. I would have been broke and you boys who have your money in General Motors would have been broke.

He was going to retire on what he had left in the world, he said, and begin to take his pleasures with Catherine at his side, now that he was almost sixty. The best thing they could do for him was to work hard for General Motors so that his "equities" would rise in value. He concluded when midnight was past, and Pratt said that his parting words were: "Boys, it's another day, anyway, and tomorrow there'll be another."[66]

Thanksgiving Day came and went, a festival charged with irony if the Durants paid attention to it that year. An earlier age, used to seeing "visitations" of heavenly providence embodied in human events might have made something of a happening of that afternoon. For nearly eight years, whenever the name Chevrolet had appeared in the press, it had usually been in connection with some triumph of Durant's. On this holiday, it was Louis Chevrolet's younger brother, Gaston, who created the story. He was driving in a 250-mile race on the Los Angeles Speedway. On the one hundred fiftieth lap he turned out to pass another machine, struck it, shot to the banked top of the track, tore out twenty feet of fence, and rolled down the incline. He was dead when they pulled him from the wreckage.[67]

And then, finally, it was Durant's last day. The Goodrich Tire Company had offered him temporary office space in their own building a few doors from General Motors, at 1780 Broadway. He came into his old quarters, cleaned out his desk, looked around brightly at the somber faces of his personal staff. "Well," he smiled, "May first is National Moving Day, but we seem to have made it December first."[68] And then he was gone for good.

The New York *Evening Mail* was one of the many papers stunned by the resignation, and it predicted that his company would suffer without him. General Motors without Durant, it said, like "U.S. Steel without Gary, the tobacco industry without Duke and the oils without Rockefeller do not appeal to the ordinary investor." Clearly the editor was a man who, like Durant himself, could not yet understand that the persistent vitality of any modern corporation exceeded the lifespan of its creator. He wanted to inject an appropriate note of tribute to the departing leader, and he finally emerged with a thought that the founder himself might have approved. "Durant was overloaded with stock," was the summarizing sentence, "but at any rate it cannot be charged against him that he was afraid to invest in his own company."[69]

King of the Bulls

I His fifty-ninth birthday followed his farewell to General Motors by a
week. He spent it at the Homestead, in Hot Springs, Virginia, finally
giving a rest to nerves strung too taut for months. He went through the
gestures of play and relaxation, restoring his energies on the resort hotel's
gingerbread porches that looked out on the Appalachian ridges. He may
have played some golf, a recreation that he had finally allowed himself
during the good years at General Motors, when division heads came for
weekend visits to Deal, and there were foursomes and tournaments with
prizes consisting of four-figure checks. He was, Murphy observed, not
much of a player, except on the putting green, where he had "the velvet
touch."[1]

He left no trace of what passed through his mind in the calm after the

MR. JOHN ANDERSON

32.
Son Clifford Durant, ample and
at ease, 1928

33.
When the good times rolled. Durant and Catherine off to Europe, 1928

34.
Raymere, the Durant pleasure dome in Deal, New Jersey

35.
Catherine as a Jazz Age queen, with Pekes

36.
A Durant Four rolls along a Lansing assembly line in the twenties

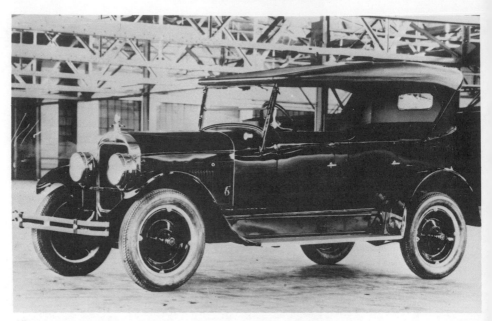

37.
The Flint Six, last of Durant's hometown-made cars, about 1924

38.
The creator embracing the 1922 Star, destined-to-fail competitor of Ford's Model T

THE MOFFITT COLLECTION

39.
A 1929 Locomobile town car, an elegant, gleaming Durant Motors bid for the
luxury trade, too late to help

debacle, but his actions gave the clearest possible indication that his thoughts were, as always, on the still-pliant future, not on the irrevocable past. If he really had announced to Pratt and his old comrades a resolve to retire, its life span was no more than a matter of weeks. He was incapable of rest yet; the machine that had run for four decades at high speed could not slow down without corrosion. In the last week of December, he was back in New York, launching a new automobile company.

He had ample encouragement from the family to go on. "You are still young in spirit," Dr. Campbell had wired him on December eighth. Rebecca, like any parent, was blind to the accumulated years that set their mark on her child. "My love and blessings to my boy, Willie," was her greeting. Even Cliff, aware of the value of support at that moment, sent a telegram couched in the unconscious accents of a Ring Lardner parody:

Arrived home today. Full of pep and the old fighting spirit that is bound to win. Sorry I am not with you to offer congratulations but want you to feel that not only myself but all the boys are with you heart and soul. We are all counting on you to pilot the ship and we will deliver the goods. Am writing you tomorrow. Love to Catherine.[2]

Uncle William, too, the family patriarch in his nineties, sent kind words through Rebecca some time later. Having outlasted almost a century of crashes, panics and depressions, he had strong convictions of what was due to the survivors of business wars.

My dear Beckie:

Why cannot I go to New York and join in celebrating your 88th birthday? Sally Ross [another sister] goes and why cannot I do the same? Well, it is just this way. I am old and blind and deaf and sometimes fall down and generally unable to care for myself. Sally Ross however is young and spry. She is only 85 or 86. She runs around and flies about like a butterfly. You can't do that.

I see much in the papers about my nephew, W. C. D. I hope his difficulties are not serious. His faithful and hard work and the comfort and happiness he has freely given to others deserves some reward. Give him my hearty and kind regards.[3]

Warmed by such currents of affection, there was good reason for a naturally sanguine man to believe that a second resurrection was not only possible but could be even easier than it had been in 1911 — that the intervening years would have no weight when set in the scale against his reawakened hopes.

The immediate business of his return to the Goodrich Building was the settling of accounts with the Du Ponts after the four and one half years of a corporate presidency conducted with Durant's usual financial insouciance. He had paid the salaries of some staff members out of his own funds; he had worked out with his loyal cut-and-try division heads private profit-sharing arrangements (which the Du Ponts promptly terminated and did not fully honor); he had bought some properties for company use; he had, even in his extremity, failed to collect his salary for 1919 and 1920. On the other hand, he had loans of both stock and money to repay. Audits and adjustments would be necessary, but there was another issue beyond clearing the books. Durant had no intention of remaining a partner in the Du Pont Securities Company, which he now regarded as the jailer of "his" stock. He wanted to liquidate his 40 percent interest and reclaim those languishing but precious shares.

There was, in short, to be a divorce, and two things quickly became evident that usually characterize divorces — first, that initial good manners were rapidly strained, and thereafter that the party under greater monetary pressure was the less resistant negotiator. On the morning of December 30, John Thomas Smith, who was remaining with General Motors, walked across the street to report to Durant on the finance committee's deliberations concerning what was due him. The substance of his message was put into a memorandum by Durant on the instant, in language possibly more vigorous than Smith himself might have used. Durant's version of Smith's advice came to a blunt conclusion:

The position taken by Mr. Raskob was so manifestly unfair — with reference to the adjustment of my claims against the company and the carrying out of the agreement (written and implied) which led to the turning over of my stock to the Du Pont Securities Co. — that it would not be to my best interests to rely upon him to continue the negotiation, and that I should employ counsel to represent me.[4]

The specific source of the alleged unfairness, which Russell Briggs later confirmed to Durant, was the committee's demand that Durant not only waive any future claims against General Motors forever, but agree to an unchangeable official version of everything done and said in the pressure-cooker of those final hours. He held out strenuously against this requirement, but at a growing cost to himself, since not all of his debts had been purged away in the fires of liquidation. In impolitic distress he urged Pierre du Pont, his successor as president, to expedite matters. He needed resolution "as early as possible, as there [was] considerable pressure from certain quarters at the moment, which, by reason of not being able to state definitely when the obligations [were] to be met, [was] exceedingly embarrassing."5

The basic compact was reached as January ended. General Motors agreed to pay its begetter $1.5 millions in cash to dispose of all outstanding claims that he held against it. He also surrendered his 40 percent equity in the Du Pont Securities Company and got back 230,000 shares of his ill-starred GM common. He was given the right to subscribe to an additional 65,000-odd shares whose ownership had been in contention since finding their way into the hands of the Durant Corporation.

On paper this left Durant with the elements of a modest, but secure, income. But as always, rich tendrils of obligation entwined themselves around the trunk of his fortune. He owed the company $540,000 in taxes that they had laid out for him, and just under $250,000 for sundry other disbursements on his behalf. Even when reduced by small credits in his favor, including the pitiable $7,865 balance on the Morgan books, these subtractions left him with $817,704, far short of his immediate needs. He immediately repledged 140,000 of his shares to secure a half-million-dollar loan from Du Pont Securities. Another 95,000 were passed out to "certain interests which he [owed]." Apparently this left him unable or unwilling to repay the 1,307,749 shares borrowed from the Du Pont Corporation's treasury the preceding October. He elected instead to keep them, or what was left of them, yielding up the 95,000 shares of Chevrolet that had been the collateral. Their full value, with GM still hibernating at 13, would have been some $17 million. The Du Ponts, perhaps because of this transaction, never did sell off the GM stock they held through the Du Pont Securities Company, and when, later on, outstanding Chevrolet shares were finally converted into GM shares in a procedure of overpowering legal complexity, they remained beyond dispute the largest and controlling stockholders in General Motors.6

Nothing ever dislodged the Du Pont brothers from their view that they had been benefactors who not only extracted Durant from his own folly but left him with the means of comfort. He, on the other hand, was plagued for years afterward with the recollection of sums advanced by him for which he had made no claims. "There were many things I had forgotten," he told an interviewer, "and so when I really cleaned up and protected everybody else I had nothing left."7 The gap in how the two parties viewed the end of the affair extended to their versions of the resignation itself. In reading the annual report of E. I. du Pont de Nemours & Company for 1920, Durant was disturbed to find this explanation of his departure: "He desired to resign and sell his interest in the Corporation to liquidate his personal indebtedness, which was very large and pressing."

He wrote immediately to Irénée, the author of the report, presenting his first recorded summary of the crucial week. His mood now was crisp to the point of combat.

On the evening of November 15th a personal friend of mine, representing the du Pont interests, called at my apartment and informed me that my resignation as President of the General Motors corporation was desired and would be accepted — the reason given, that I was not in sympathy with the policies of the controlling interests and would not cooperate. I must and do plead guilty to the charge.

Two days later, he continued, he had first revealed the acuteness of his emergency to Pierre and Raskob (which would have been six days after they had dated his confession), and his own mind now held no shadow of recollected panic. He had described his debts, he maintained, as "burdens which [he] had assumed in attempting to correct the mistakes and errors which had been made, for which [he] was in no way responsible." And, he finished, pounding the assertion home with capital letters, "FROM THAT POINT we started to work out a plan which would relieve me of my embarrassment and which resulted in the Du Pont Securities Company taking over my General Motors holdings." Somewhat discordantly he expressed a concluding confidence that, even under "new conditions . . . nothing [would] occur to destroy [their] friendship."[8]

Irénée was no less cordial, but unyielding. He checked with Raskob, and retorted, "It seems that none of us had asked you to resign. . . . So far as I can determine, the suggestion that you 'step out' of the presidency came from you, though, of course, that was the most satisfactory solution under the circumstances."[9] There the conflict of testimony rested, misted over by ambiguities that would baffle curiosity forever. Durant had not said whether or not he accepted the alleged request to quit that was conveyed by the mysterious emissary. Nor did he clarify why it mattered from what "point" the discussion of the rescue plan began. And Irénée, for his part, was far from explicit about whom he meant by the "us" in "none of us," or just how he "determined" that Durant had offered, on his own, to leave as president.

What mattered in 1921 was not that the question of whether Durant jumped or was pushed remained beyond verdict on the available evidence. It was, rather, what the exchange showed about his frame of mind. He would enter his next comeback attempt having drawn no lessons in humility or caution from his experience. He would go on, as before, following only the fatal, alluring guidance of his own inner voices, those bewitched compasses of the unique and the doomed. Before the first month of the new year was gone, before there was time for reflection or serious preparation, he had organized a company to build his new car.

II The year 1920 was not yet gone when, with one unavoidable, crestfall-en acknowledgment of the failure behind him, he stepped off into the new venture. Within four days of each other, in the last week of December, he sent out two multiple letters. One went to all the members of Syndicate Number Five, explaining to them why the GM stock they had shared in buying was being returned to them on a pro rata basis, lamentably shrunken in value since the time of purchase. There had been no magic this time to make their money multiply and be fruitful. "I know that you will appreciate how keenly disappointed I am," the failed necromancer confided to them, adding that "the only satisfaction that I can derive is that no human being could forecast the present financial and industrial disturbance which, I think I am safe in saying, has no equal in the history of this country."[10]

A subsequent message followed to at least some of the syndicate members, driving right to the point in its opening lines.

While I am not ready just at this time to make the announcement (for which reason I will ask you to treat the matter in confidence), it will probably not surprise you to know that I am still interested and a firm believer in the motor industry and that I am organizing a company, controlled by myself and several of my good friends, which will be in active operation August 1, 1921.

There was to be only one kind of stock, with no special prices to insiders, and "no commissions, bonuses or reservations to myself or associates issued for experience, ability or past performance." Those who chose to trust Durant anew could have an alternative to reclaiming their GM stock. He would, if they liked, set aside seven shares in his new enterprise for every five of GM they would like to exchange, valuing the GM at $14 and the new issue at the subscription price of $10. This would still leave them with an average loss of approximately $12 per share of GM on their earlier investment, but he reminded them that it would be "a proper deduction for purposes of taxation in making [their] report for the year," provided they turned the GM shares over before the thirty-first of the month. He closed with the gentlest of urgings, the sure sign of a salesman's confidence in the prospect's goodwill: "I believe when the project in all its details is explained to you that you will be well pleased."[11]

There was no announcement of how many responses there were to the offer, but the mere news that Durant was exchanging stock in a new organization for GM stock immediately reminded financial observers of the coup five years earlier that made the Chevrolet corporation General Motors' master. The rumors of hidden meaning in the trade-in proposal were strong enough to disturb Pierre du Pont. Was Durant, though wounded, still dangerous? He wrote to him directly, saying that a nameless friend had advised of a "definite plan of securing control of General Motors Corporation" through such an offer. "Would it not be wise," he suggested with what seemed a touch of nervousness, "to set such stories at rest forever?" There was no hint in Durant's reply of any possible pleasure at Du Pont's anxiety, which was groundless for a reason known to both men — that the number of outstanding GM shares had grown from 800,000 at the end of 1915 to more than fifteen million. He simply shot back a crisp retort: "Your friend was not correctly informed and the idea is too ridiculous for words."[12] The very fact that the question could be raised, however, was another psychological asset, a demonstration that the market's respect for Durant's supposedly awesome powers had outlasted his topple.

The new company was formally launched with a temporary New York incorporation in mid-January. In at least two respects it mirrored changes in Durant since he had first burst upon the automotive scene. Now he was willing to involve his own ego more visibly in his creation. No more discreet wirepulling from the financial area behind the curtain. Durant was the name to be blazoned on the hood emblem of the four-cylinder car that would be the first product, the letters slashed diagonally across a quartered shield under the claws of a heraldic griffin. And Durant Motors, Incorporated, would have as its owners the loyal legions of modest stockholders who had crowded into the incorporator's imagination in his hours of trouble. The initial capitalization would be $5 million, and the first million shares of stock, as he had forewarned in his prospectus, would be sold at a single low price, with no reserved special blocks.

In other respects than these two, Durant Motors would, in its first years, consciously recapitulate the early patterns of Buick and Chevrolet. There would be the promises, the fanfares, the creation of subsidiaries, the optimistic contracts, the hinted and actual mergers, the sudden sprinkling of the map with sales agencies. The jinn would rub the lamp, and the palace would gleam once more on the skyline. The very act of creating a new enterprise in the face of the still-lingering auto depression was dramatic. It shouted a rebuttal to the diminishing band of skeptics who believed the slump to be a sign that at last the industry was reaching the edge of the world, the legendary "saturation point" of the market. Durant still knew how to make the most of his old starring role of unterrified leader, scoffing at such tremors.

The first step was the almost ceremonial promise to Flint. Palsied by the hard times, the city was eager for the healer's touch, and word of the new Durant undertaking was hardly hours old before the Chamber of Commerce had sent a telegraphed petition for a share in the great work, with Dort entraining for New York to add personal emphasis. The answer arrived by wire and blazed on the front page of the *Journal* on the very day of Dort's return. "You may say to the good people of the best little city in the country that one of the plants of Durant Motors will be located in Flint." From the podium at a Chamber luncheon, Dort added details of his interview, and a coda that set off a storm of applause: "They say Billy is coming back home to Flint. He never left Flint."[13]

But Flint would wait. Durant was on the lookout for a factory already in existence and available, where he could install Alfred Sturt to design and Fred Hohensee to produce the Durant Four, and he found what he wanted in March just outside New York. It was a two-million-dollar facility of the Goodyear Tire and Rubber Company in Long Island City, which had originally been an eastern assembly plant for Fords. While the news announcements of its purchase by Durant Motors were taking effect, he turned to General Motors, armed with his insider's knowledge that they would be liquidating excess inventories to cure their unrelenting cash flow problem. From them he bought the works in Muncie that he himself had helped to bring into the fold in 1919 to produce the Sheridan. Its function now would be to serve as the hatchery of the Durant Six, his entry into the growing field of higher-powered cars. A separate incorporation created a subsidiary, Durant Motors of Indiana, and those who bought its 300,000 shares at $10 were assured not only that the Six would make their fortune ("I predict at Muncie a repetition of the Buick success,"[14] was Durant's personal word on the subscription-seeking letters that went out), but that in time they could, if it proved advantageous, turn the shares in for those of the parent company.

In May the reinvigorating showers of promises fell on parched Lansing. Durant Motors of Michigan was summoned into being, armed with the authority to issue stock worth five millions, and it prepared to build another plant for Durant Fours, under the supervision of Edward Ver Linden, well known in town as the president of the Oldsmobile Division of General Motors, who was following his old commander in new adventures. The factory would engage 2,500 to 3,000 employees, which the Lansing press immediately calculated would add to the city's population by 15,000. At that prospect, "real estate strengthened, the employment situation took on the brightest aspect in several months, business houses turned thoughts to the definite promise of the immediate future, and prepared to handle the business of a greater city." Ver Linden, who was "always known as a fast worker," left General Motors' payroll on the morning of the twenty-first, and was on Durant's the same afternoon, helping to light the lanterns of a carnival of boosterism.[15]

Through the summer the intended display of unexhausted creative power continued to dazzle. Durant Motors of California was launched, with Norman de Vaux and Clifford Durant on the bridge. And then Durant Motors of Canada. And meanwhile, Richard Collins left Cadillac to found a company that would market a car under his name, but everyone who knew him as a Durant loyalist assumed that, like the old Little Company or Mason Motors, it would in time be absorbed into Durant's fold — that it was a colony, set up for political reasons under an independent flag. Then Durant Motors gladdened the hearts of the business districts in the lean and hungry parts-making towns by a series of multimillion-dollar orders: engines for Fours from Continental Motors of Muskegon, Michigan; engines for Sixes from the Ansted Engine Company in Connersville, Indiana; axles from the Adams Company of Findlay, Ohio; an entire year's worth of tires from Fisk Rubber in Akron.

On November 19, 1921, exactly one year after the nightlong ordeal that ended the Durant era at General Motors, a New York investment publication ran a banner headline over a story describing how more than 30,000 orders for Durant cars had already been placed. "Durant Motors," the large type called out, "Created Out of an Idea by Wizard of Automobile Industry, Now Prosperous Enterprise."[16] He had regained his old title and vindicated the high roller's credo that he announced to an interviewer three months after his disaster. "Forget mistakes. Forget failures. Forget everything except what you're going to do now and do it. Today is your lucky day."[17] His apparent second comeback at sixty was even qualifying him to become one of the official spokesmen of the business civilization of the 1920s, the impending golden age. The incongruousness of speaking at one moment like a gambler and in the next breath like a senior statesman disturbed neither him nor his contemporaries who read, in *Commerce and Finance*, one of the first of many statements, almost all identical, that he would make as the good times began to return and expand.

> The automotive industry is and will continue to be an essential factor in the development of our whole civilization. It has gone through the period of reconstruction. It has reorganized its policies and methods to meet the new order of things. . . .
> A liberal expansion of credit will hearten our businessmen and will create a new confidence. Confidence will bring back prosperity. Prosperity means an expansion of transportation facilities. The burden of transportation expansion will fall on the automobile. The automobile will meet the demand on it.[18]

He was a ruler of dominions again, his headquarters in the New York offices of Durant Motors (reincorporated, however, in friendly Delaware), his plants in at least four states of the Union, his former satraps like Ver

Linden, Hohensee, Tom and Fred Warner, and Jake Newmark gathered around him. He was so content in his proven defiance of time and chance that he easily forgave the lieutenants who did not join him now, but remained with General Motors, most importantly Hardy, John Thomas Smith, and Pratt. Staying on had, according to Pratt, been Durant's own advice to them just before his departure. In the buoyancy of the hour it was undoubtedly easy for him to be tolerant and hard to understand how much the poorer he would be for their absence or why, friendship aside, they had decided that the future with him was not quite safe.

The sources of capital for these beginning acquisitions were somewhat murky, and even susceptible to sharp questioning in later, less sunlit moments. What was providing the initial assets? There were no longer any friendly horse-drawn vehicle companies with plants to convert and savings to invest, and there were no publicized angels of generous means. Durant was to say, in time, that some sixty-seven friends had answered his first appeals with a total of seven million dollars, an actual excess of two million over his seed money requirements.[19] He had also possibly committed unstipulated resources of his own that survived the wringing-out process. But the mystery cast over the prospects of the new empire shadows that would deepen as it grew.

Yet one acknowledged source of funds as the structure of Durant Motors took shape was the Durant Corporation, the desperation bid of his last weeks at General Motors to fight off the encroaching control of the Du Pont allies. Freed of that impossible battle assignment, the organization became what Newmark labeled a "money collecting machine of huge proportions."[20] Within two years, he claimed, it had branch offices in thirty-five states, three thousand salesmen, and a clerical staff occasionally swamped by an influx of up to a million dollars in small checks in a single day. By the end of 1922 there were 146,000 participants in its plan of buying stocks — primarily Durant Motors shares — in lots of no more than twenty shares per person, with payments as small as three dollars down and three dollars monthly. The ultimate number of subscribers was 350,000 and the value of all sales during the corporation's lifetime approached $100 millions, a powerful figure, but not one beyond Durant's capacity to spend.

The popularity of Durant Motors stock in the company's early years was more than a matter of marketplace economics. True, the shares were attractively priced, the more so as salesmen frequently offered them at a few points below the market rate. Moreover, Durant Motors seemed to have genuine promise. Just as Durant had planned, his swift-paced early strokes sounded an exciting overture that created rousing expectations of the performance to follow. And there was still reason to believe in the magic of Durant's name. His market troubles of 1920 were not necessarily proof of any taint in his instinct for nurturing automotive winners, and it was only eight years since the sensational debut of Chevrolet's Royal Mail and Baby Grand models, followed by the 490—best sellers all.

But there was also a social testimony in those thousands of small remittances to the Durant Corporation that went further than the logic of breeding new dollars from old. By tempting small investors to put their pin money into a game once confined to the lords of Wall Street, Durant Motors placed itself at the head of a major development of the 1920s, the broadening of the base of the stock market. The white-collar employees and employers with extra savings in hand, knocking for admittance to the halls of speculation, wanted to believe that the paths to at least some of the big money were still open to them; that even in a highly organized and controlled economy there was a residue of individual mobility. They hungered after the fruits of large-scale capitalism without total submission to the dominance of the large-scale capitalists. Durant was an attractive figure as one of the "givers" of the automobile who seemed not to have lost the common touch, and who was actually inviting their participation in the feast. The popular perception of him as a victim of the bankers became one of his strengths. "News had gone far and wide," according to Newmark, "that he had been crucified by his General Motors associates and people were inclined to lean toward him, for to them he was the underdog, who had been wronged by the big financial interests."[21] He was gathering the rewards of two contradictory symbolic roles—master industrialist and champion of the average man.

And so, spellbound by him, the subscribers flocked in, and the quotations for Durant Motors stock on the New York Curb Exchange, the only place where it was listed, climbed from the $10 initial offering figure to $27 by the close of November, 1921. For those who had bought early, the trip to the Big Rock Candy Mountain was underway. Rumors of impending new spectacular exhibitions flashed like heat lightning as the concern's first anniversary approached and set off fresh surges of purchasing. One of the more electrifying of the murmurs had Durant about to merge Studebaker, Pierce-Arrow, and the Collins Motor Company into Durant Motors, thereby forming an unconquerable rival to General Motors.[22]

So he continued to rise, almost too swiftly for his own good. In a rare moment of self-assessment he had virtually admitted to Pratt, early in 1921, his problem of overextension at General Motors. "His trouble," he was quoted as saying, "had been that he expanded too far, and he couldn't look after the business." Now, however, it would be different. He was reentering the auto world because he was "too deeply wed to it, he couldn't get out of it," but he had "made up his mind to just build a real good car. . . . He was going to limit his production to 50,000 a year." The succeeding months, however, proved that he was incapable of clinging to that resolution. He was taking too literally his own advice to "forget mistakes, forget failures," and once more discarding experience, the nurse of maturity.[23]

III The dramatic moments continued to pile up. On New Year's eve, December 31, 1921, a single train of 100 steel freight cars rolled out of New York amid the best fanfare that Newmark could devise, loaded with five hundred Durant Fours from the Long Island City factory, all of them ordered by a single California dealer. Statistics were mobilized to cram the press release that was headlined "Durant Breaks World Records." The "Prosperity Special" was carrying the largest single shipment of automobiles ever sent to a retail agency; the largest single shipment ever made from a plant in operation less than six months; the largest-ever single shipment of any one commodity from coast to coast. That the figures were essentially meaningless did not discourage editors in a nation hungry for good news of the economy. They were glad to help the Prosperity Special leave a transcontinental trail of clippings behind it.[24]

Fewer than sixty days later, Durant's name bestrode the business pages once again. This time, as in 1915, he would assault Henry Ford's position of dominance. Mid-February saw the announcement of a forthcoming Durant auto to be named the Star, a five-passenger, four-cylinder vehicle to retail at $348, the price of a Model T. When the first model was shown in Washington on March 10, 1922, thirty thousand people lined up to file past it as if it were a touring celebrity or a national relic. Similar throngs snaked into the showrooms of its subsequent unveiling in New York, Boston, Philadelphia, Detroit, and Houston. Their admiration was boundless, for the Star appeared to be a far better buy than Ford's car, which belonged to a now-primitive motor age. The Star was fitted with modern components, and offered sliding-gear transmission, demountable rims, and a self-starter. It was, in fact, so relatively sophisticated that it could not possibly be sold in competition with the Model T except at a loss, especially when Ford responded with a fifty-dollar price cut. But that was not manifest in the buzz of the curtain-raising, and the first million shares of stock in the Star Motor Company, priced at $15, disappeared in one swift stampede. A second million were taken up with the speed, in Newmark's comparison, of peanut sales at a circus.

With orders cascading in, the Star would need an adequate production home, and Durant found and bought one in still another spotlighted high-wire performance that also brought his career once again into intersection with Walter Chrysler's. A June morning found him in Elizabeth, New Jersey, gathered with others at the entrance to a three-story-high factory that loomed like an industrial temple on the flat and bare surrounding acres. It was the largest such building in the world, a third of a mile long, spreading its several roofs over thirty-five acres of floor space. Its incoming railway sidings could receive 80 carloads of raw materials for it to digest, while simultaneously, at other platforms along its brick walls, 125 outgoing boxcars might be taking their fill of finished goods. Its cafeteria was able, with the same planned efficiency, to fill 1,200 stomachs at a sitting. Its own power and refrigeration plants helped to make it an almost independent city of mechanical creation.

And it was a white elephant. It had been built for John N. Willys, head of the Willys-Overland Corporation, who had plunged not wisely but too well in the 1919 boom and ended $50 million in the red. The great plant, along with all his other assets, was now up for auction at a receiver's sale.

Chrysler entered the picture through being summoned out of a brief retirement in 1920 by the bankers who held Willys's notes, and given a two-year contract at a million per year to see if vitality could be restored to the patient. He had worked hard and mercilessly at slashing budgets, but put most of his hopes in a fresh entry in the sweepstakes, a middle-priced car to be powered by a new engine of superior smoothness and power. To design it he hired three talented young engineers trained by Ohio State, Michigan, and Stanford—the days of cut-and-try car-making were now gone the way of hand-cranking—and set them to spending laborious but enthusiastic days and nights in a corner of the mighty plant, translating his idea into an actual machine. Before they were quite finished, however, Chrysler was forced to give up the revival of Willys's concern as impossible. He removed his trio of Fred Zeder, Carl Breer, and Owen Skelton to an office in Newark to await further use, and bought a controlling interest in another casualty of the 1920 calamity, the Maxwell Motor Car Company, once run by Ben Briscoe's partner. Under existing rules, however, all the blueprints and specifications of the dream car remained Willys-Overland property, and went under the hammer with the Elizabeth factory.

Chrysler was eligible to bid on the entire property as an outsider, and on the sale day he had a representative on hand to try for the recapture. General Motors was likewise interested, and despatched a real estate agent. But William Durant was on the scene in person, his prodigality undiminished by the years and excited by remembrance of things past. Chrysler dropped out at $3.125 million, General Motors stayed until $4.465 million, but Durant topped all bids and became the owner at a price of $5.25 million. His victory proclamation declared that in almost no time at all his superplant would be producing 400 Stars and 150 Durant Fours each working day.[25]

As for the dream car and engine, Chrysler's final inadvertent gift to him, Durant had other plans. The Star was intended to jostle Henry Ford. The

Durant Four was competition for the Chevrolet. The newcomer's mission would be to challenge the Buick. And where could it be better built than in the very city where, long ago, Marr and Mason had created superior power plants for their day that lifted Buick to the heights. At last, Flint would have its turn.

Early in July, hard on the heels of the Elizabeth sale, Durant announced that the Flint Motor Car Company was in process of birth. With its five millions in starting capital, it would produce the Flint Six just south of the city on a hundred-acre site, bought from Durant's longtime friend Edwin Atwood, an amiable-looking, bespectacled businessman popular enough to have served a term as mayor. The news unleashed a celebration on the twenty-fourth that became a panorama of the Harding era. As it paid festive tribute to Durant for what proved to be the last time, just fifty years after his arrival in town as a small boy, Flint perfectly executed its self-portrait. Its official joys furnished a permanent record of its folkways and creeds as it stood in the vestibule of the 1920s.

Conceive the scene that hot July evening of inauguration. At the four corners of Atwood's former farm, on which the factory will rise, bonfires are burning. As early as 6:30 P.M. the Dixie Highway is filled with an eel-like column of vehicles, exhaling fumes, that inches toward the site and there breaks up into individual metallic creatures that straddle, with their rubber feet, a crop of oats not yet fully harvested. Policemen vainly try to protect the green shoots, while the traffic jam increases until it is backed up for a solid two miles into the center of town. There are already too many cars for the old streets to handle easily as Flint pours out of its garages to celebrate the coming of still more cars.

Finally, however, the Dixie Highway is cleared and down its length march the Lions, the Kiwanis, the Exchange Club, the Rotary Club, the Genesee County Dental Association, the Genesee County Bar Association, and four companies of the National Guard, which only recently tramped down Saginaw Street to signalize victory over the Kaiser. There is music to spare from the *Journal* Boys' Band, the Chevrolet Band, the Salvation Army Band, and one left nameless by the reporters. At the site itself, as night falls, the Flint Community Music Association's director is there, leading communal singing. The strains of "America" and a song called "Let the Rest of the World Go By" rise into the humid air, audible for miles, since it is guessed that thirty-five thousand people, one-third of the entire population, have driven or walked or taken streetcars to the farm.

The packed crowd would, of course, welcome words from the hero of the occasion, but Durant is not there because, incredibly, the entire affair is almost spontaneous. It has been organized on a day's notice after the announcement. Motion-picture cameras will record the scene for him, and at a later day he will show up to turn the ceremonial first shovelful of earth, dressed in a straw skimmer and a perfectly pressed suit.

But now he will be praised in absentia. What a *Journal* correspondent calls the "old saw" about prophets without honor in their own country is suffering a "knockout blow in the first round." Durant is "idolized." Mayor William McKeighan takes the improvised platform to recite anew the Homeric legends of how Durant created the Durant-Dort Corporation from a handful of road carts; how he pulled Buick forth from the cave of failure; how he summoned General Motors from his brain, was overcome by his enemies in 1910, and rose from the grave bearing Chevrolet; how he has escaped the mausoleum a second time to enrich the world with Durant Motors. And if Durant can do so many wonders, then Flint can surmount recessions and grow, and grow. "I do not believe," the mayor says, "that some of the dreamers who said that Flint would be a city of two hundred fifty thousand by nineteen-thirty were so far wrong in their predictions."

Cheers reverberate; fireworks skewer the air with lances of light. Then the occasion's chairman, William E. Holler, adds his testimony and draws the appropriate doctrine from "Billy's" saga. "Let's all work together for the good of Flint. Let's cut out kicking and knocking and all become boosters."

Then it is the turn of the Reverend Howard J. Clifford, who is the official representative of the Durant Corporation in Flint, and has already sold quantities of stock to many members of the audience. His present secular employment is the outgrowth of almost a decade and a half of friendship with Durant. The two men met when Clifford was a captain in the Salvation Army, and Clifford (as his son will later affirm) worships the ground Durant walks on. Durant hired him from a Presbyterian pulpit for a few years' work as head of a Personal Service and Employment Division at Buick, doing elementary social work, supervision, and grievance-reporting among the employees. Durant took him from the church again in 1920 for a similar role of institutional paternalist under General Motors, but when Durant was dropped overboard, so was his friend, in spite of the founder's strong letter to Du Pont recommending Clifford as "a real human being, a forceful speaker, a splendid influence."[26]

Though he has traveled the road from divinity to salesmanship, the Reverend Mr. Clifford is still basically concerned with inspiration. He addresses the thoughts of the gathering to higher realms than are encompassed by the promise of dividend checks.

Mr. Durant's purpose is deeper than the financing of motor car companies and the construction of automobiles for mere gain alone. He has expressed himself as desiring to get interests in great manufacturing concerns of the United States in an effort to help the great multitude of

workers. He has a desire to help people to earn and save money and
invest it. He has said to me time and again "I would rather help
hundreds of thousands of people to independence than to place a library
in every city in the United States."

To the credit of Flint we have one man who stands out in the industrial life of our country as a man who puts the helping of the people above
the making of millions.

Then he reads a poem by Berton Braley, entitled "The Thinker," dedicated
to Durant. Its concluding verse is:

> *Might of the roaring boiler*
> *Force of the engine's thrust*
> *Strength of the sweating toiler*
> *Greatly in these we trust*
> *But back of them stands the Schemer*
> *The Thinker who drives things through*
> *Back of the Job — the Dreamer*
> *Who's making the dream come true.*[27]

And as the last sparklers and bonfire embers fade to dull red, and
hundreds of engines clear their throats and prepare to carry the tired but
jubilant people of Flint home, Durant is enshrined as a hero of the
machine-intoxicated culture of his time, which is triumphantly unshaken
by the laughter and the railing of bohemians and radicals. Even a man less
inclined by nature to challenge the odds would have been hard pressed, at
that point, to cling to a modest resolve of producing no more than 50,000
examples annually of "just a real good car."

In the ensuing nine months Durant sped through the final stages of a
reenactment of the creation of General Motors, with only a few scenes
missing, as if he were on a schedule set by some private urgency. He
bought the struggling Locomobile Corporation of Bridgeport, Connecticut,
from whose plant there had rolled, over the years, autos whose buyers were
"a roll call of the financial elite." The cost of a single Locomobile, liberally
decorated with bronze and endowed with many handmade parts, could
reach $12,000. With this presumed competitor of Cadillac for the luxury
trade, the passenger-car line of Durant Motors was complete, though a car
to be called the Princeton was announced and never produced.[28]

Then there were the incorporations and purchases of the Mason Truck
Company, producing a workhorse known as the Road King; the Hayes-
Hunt Body Company, which was given a fiefdom in part of the giant
Elizabeth plant; the American Plate Glass Company; the New Process
Gear Company; the Warner Corporation specializing in ignition apparatus;

and the Electric Auto-Lite Company. By the middle of 1923, Durant Motors was a complete, vertically integrated enterprise, employing 50,000 workers in ten factories with a combined capacity of over 650,000 cars and trucks a year. There were four thousand Durant dealers to market them, calling for credit on the Durant Motors Acceptance Corporation.

For a final flourish, the untiring builder added an organization that was an attempted fulfillment of a fantasy—a bank uncontrolled, in theory, by bankers. It was in April of 1923 that Durant took over the charter of the Liberty National Bank from its former owners. It had no direct relationship either to Durant Motors or the Durant Corporation, but like them both it was a manifestation of the man's will not only to prove himself undefeated, but to eliminate for all future time the enemies who had twice undone him, the money barons and the speculators. Durant wasted no time in publicizing his determination to run the bank on new principles. "It is intended that this bank shall be owned by the people at large" was his manifesto, and "established on the principal of business comradeship."[29]

What that meant specifically was that the capital would be provided by a corps of 300,000 shareholders, each restricted to the possession of one share, priced at $150. The directors would be unpaid, as would be their chairman—Durant himself—and the president. No commissions, fees, or bonuses in cash, goods, or stock would be charged for any loans—merely the "legal rate of interest" and "management fees." No investment company would operate as part of the bank's work. No loan would be made to any company with which an officer or director had an official connection. It was to operate with a purity that would be a standing rebuke to the rest of the fiscal community.

It was also to be, in practice, still one more of the chairman's many corporate incarnations. Its directors were described by Newmark as Durant's "trusties of many years' standing," and its first president was a thirty-nine-year-old bank examiner from Virginia, Robert W. Daniel, who was shortly to become Margery's second husband. The initial prospectus was sent out to every Durant Motors dealer and stockholder, and it was from these loyal ranks that $5 millions were raised of the $45 millions theoretically attainable under Durant's structural plan. The first offices, at 256 West Fifty-seventh Street, were only a few steps away from Durant Motors' headquarters. Even more than the companies that bore Durant's name, the Liberty National Bank was a personal testament, an almost pure expression of how his business improvisations molded themselves to his quirks in the way that works of art reflect their creators.

The apex of Durant Motors' initial climb was reached on a January day in 1923, when 300 guests gathered at tables specially set up amid the pillars, pipes, and wires of the Elizabeth factory for a special luncheon. Its formal purpose was to honor Durant's thirty-six years of association with Fred Hohensee, and its underlying goal to demonstrate "that the physical assets of Durant Motors were real." During the flow of speechmaking Benjamin Block, head of the brokerage firm of Block, Maloney and Company, stage-whispered to Durant that the shares of his new "baby" stood, at that moment, at 84 on the Curb. He was overheard by Newmark, the toastmaster of the occasion, who owned 10,000 of them, and found his eloquence miraculously enhanced by the news.[30]

But the thrill was only momentary. Within a few days the stock had broken back to 64 and was soon down to 47. The decline continued, remorselessly exposing a truth embedded in the balance sheets. The trappings of empire might remain the same, but they were a facade. There was no genuine comparison between the early achievements and their subsequent imitations. Durant was not paying for new plants with stock in 1921 and 1922, but with the cash swept up by his financial children's crusade, and the outflow was in no way balanced by returns. The Durant, the Star, the Flint, and the Locomobile, struggling in a more developed and difficult market, did not begin to equal the sales records set by Buick, Chevrolet, and Cadillac ten and fifteen years before. The occasional earnings of one constituent of Durant Motors were quickly devoured by the losses of the others, and there were no dividends. Durant, in his sixties, believed that he was reliving the old days, but no more than anyone else could he go home again.

There were flickering intimations of personal changes, shifts in his emotional center of balance. For the first time in a career that had resounded mainly with praise, he began to encounter critical slings and arrows that shook the good nature he had shown when life yielded him his expected quota of admiration. B. C. Forbes, a well-known business writer, asked for an interview on which to base a series of syndicated columns for the Hearst press. Durant gave his consent, expecting a friendly invitation to the dance of public relations. Instead he was plied with sharp questions about assets, capitalization, actual revenues, and plans for managing operations of such "staggering magnitude." Forbes blended the replies with information from other sources and produced articles that made no secret of his belief that Durant Motors was a shakily financed and weakly organized company, whose stock was dangerously overpriced.

Durant's answer was an enraged letter, demanding an apology and a list of Forbes's informants. He charged the columnist with intentional distortion and said that *Forbes Magazine* was a "General Motors publication." As always, the journalist had the last public word, but a growing querulousness on Durant's part crackled through the episode, and was not confined to it.[31] In one public statement he blamed business "paralysis" on high interest rates imposed by the "greedy money vultures."[32] On another occasion, he picked up a rumor that Clarence Barron, of the *Wall Street Journal,* was attacking him at the behest of the Chase Securities Company, supposedly resentful of the Liberty National Bank. Instead of dismissing it, he tried to fish a confirmation out of the *Journal*'s financial editor, saying that it would be a "wonderful addition to my already large collection . . . having to do with Wall Street methods and the operation of the Money Control."[33] These were utterances in a strange tongue from someone who had usually been described as soft-spoken and smiling. The experience of 1920 had not left him unscarred, after all. A sense of paranoia hovered. In spite of his suspicions of Barron, he granted him two interviews, repeating in full detail his entirely self-exculpating account of his last days at General Motors. As the second ended one August evening in 1925, Barron's secretary asked Durant if he would mail an envelope on his way out, and later commented: "When I handed him that letter I saw his face had been relaxed and was now very hard. It was as though he had worn a mask of pleasantry all day."[34]

Looking into his immediate past, he saw betrayal. Raskob had thwarted him by turning "his" surplus at General Motors into a deficit through unwise expansion. The Du Ponts had pounced on him when he tried to support the market for GM securities. Misunderstanding had ensnared his foolproof designs.

Looking into the distant future, he was still possessed of his old powers of penetration. In 1922 he gave an automotive trade journal his preview of what lay ahead.

The next twenty years will witness an expansion of automobile making more marvelous by far than that of the two decades through which we have passed. . . . Most of us will live to see this whole country covered with a network of motor highways built from point to point as the bird flies, the hills cut down, the dales bridged over, the obstacles removed. Highway intersections will be built over or under the through lanes and the present dangers of motor travel, one after another, will be eliminated.[35]

Picking out of the dim unknown the cloverleaf intersection and the national grid of expressways — that was where Durant's intuition worked best, alone on the farthest shore of discovery.

And as always, the immediate present had little power to command his concentration from the moment he had fulfilled some plan. That was the seed of Durant Motors' downfall, fatally germinated in the founder's mind. Once his whirlwind two years of building had shown that he was still viable as a promoter, Durant's interest in his bantling industrial confederation's immediate problems waned. It needed his nurture even more than General Motors had at a comparable stage of its growth; it swam in rougher seas, and it was not as well supplied with loyal assistants to the begetter.

Yet it received far less of him. For Durant's pleasure in building was increasingly giving way to a passion for trading in securities. His personal rhythms coinciding with a national trend, he spent more and more time following the pulsations recorded by the tickers of the Exchange. Undeterred by his own calamity or by the recollection of his father's as he must have heard it, he was yielding more and more time to the market. Durant, the wizard of motors, was emerging in his seventh decade in a role of far different overtones, Durant, king of the bulls.

IV   Even when he sat in the command post at General Motors he was "frequently the subject of Wall Street rumor about large gains or losses in the stock market." But after the fall dealing in securities became "a passion with him, an obsession, it ruled his life, it ruled him." The judgment came from Newmark, colored a shade or two more intensely than reality, perhaps, because Newmark, like others who had followed Durant into his comeback venture, was dismayed that "it was impossible" for the leader "to give to his industrial pursuits the time and brain power they required." Yet even allowing for Newmark's anxiety, there was basic truth in his conclusion. Durant Motors, as soon as its elements were assembled, became Durant's new child and responsibility, but the market was an old flirtation kindled into an autumn love, to which he seemed eager to give all that was left in him.

He would sit in his office at the corner of Broadway and 57th and initiate a wave of buying which would reach from New York to San Francisco and every principal point between those two cities. He knew everybody of importance, everywhere, and his word was accepted absolutely. Not only that, but he was custodian for many accounts, and had unlimited discretion; he could do what he wanted with them, buy or sell as he willed. He made money for people, when the market-trend was right. But it was different when the guess was wrong.

. . . Durant stood firm and steadfast, like the "bull" that he was, ever believing that there could be no retreat and that the country was going constantly onward to greater heights of industrialism, to expansion, to increased corporate earnings. It is said that he never sold a share of stock short.[36]

He did sell from time to time on a falling market when it seemed necessary or prudent to him, but it was as a buyer that he dazzled the

financial press. His purchases were heavy and consistent, and his judgment of which companies were on the way up proved so often to be right
that the mere rumor of his investment in an issue was enough to stimulate
interest in it and create the very effect that he predicted. He bought
Studebaker at 50 and saw it rise to 100, and his profit was guessed to be $4
millions. He began to acquire the stock of the Fisher Body Company—the
40 percent of it not already owned by General Motors—and it climbed from
150 to 214. He reached out for shares of United States Cast Iron Pipe and
Foundry Company, a concern responsible for manufacturing three-
quarters of the country's gas and water mains, and from a soggy 35 it
wavered slowly upward to par, then to 110, and then accelerated to 138
late in 1924, while a news story estimated his winnings under the headline:
"Say Durant's Profit Is Now $2,000,000."[37]

Brokers' transactions were confidential, so that his moves were always
shrouded in a plume of rumor, as if he were in fact some Olympian bull,
glimpsed only fitfully but conveying intimations of immense, more-than-
mortal power in the flash of a gigantic horn or hoof. Twice in a sixty-day
period the *New York Times* made him the subject of a front-page story,
itself an indication of how the Exchange was becoming a focus of public
attention. "'Durant Put at Top of Wall Street Winners," the first of them told
readers, and related the triumphant bidding-up at various times of U.S.
Cast Iron Pipe, Southern Railway, Missouri Pacific, and RCA, with Durant
setting the buying pace. The follow-up article summarized its contents
almost completely in the caption. "Durant's Paper Gain a Wall Street
Wonder. He Wins $2,500,000 in Two Days by Forty Point Advance in
Cast Iron Pipe. $10,000,000 in Two Years." And still another report of
1927 fed the legend of his omnipotence: "Durant Snaps His Whip over
The Ticker."[38]

No one would ever fully grasp what was behind this manifestation of the
wizard of wheels in a new guise. His ultimate yielding to his addiction
could have served, in ancient drama, as the fulfillment of some doom laid
upon William C. Durant, senior, and transmitted with his seed. Such a
scientifically unrewarding explanation is not permitted to contemporary
inquiry, however. A more acceptable modern judgment might be the
psychological one that he was trying by mastering it to wreak revenge on
the market that had unhorsed him. Or even that he possessed a self-
destructive urge to risk his future on it again. Or—and this explanation is
most in tune with his past—his career as a bull may have represented a
new form of achieving power that was no longer in his grasp through the
processes of industrial creation. Despite the pyrotechnics of bringing
Durant Motors into being (and demonstrating his recuperative powers), he
may have realized inwardly that the competitive situation confronting a

new auto conglomerate forbade spectacular ascensions by newcomers. There was no way to create a fresh replica of General Motors in the nineteen-twenties, and the prospect of running a mere second-line organization was not enticing to Durant, whose imagination had always chafed at routine or small tasks.

No, he and the industry were both older. The age of miracles was behind them. The stock market, then, may simply have offered him, in his own mind, a chance to execute grand designs in a new realm. Yet it was hard to say; his own statements never articulated his deeper purposes.

The writers struggled with the handicap of a subject whom they described as "a silent man," who said "nothing about his views for publication and is seldom seen in Wall Street." They created what drama they could from scraps pieced together in suggestive collage. The "new market leader" was a "little man . . . gray about the temples, with a sharp, rather tired-looking thin face." He worked through at least fifteen brokers, or twenty, or perhaps it was twenty-six, sending his buying orders humming through the wires that connected their offices to a "banana stand" of telephones at his elbow. He stood at his private ticker almost steadily during each day's trading hours, making swift decisions on the basis of its staccato reports plus the information brought him by a "handful" of assistants. He was said by friends to have made unpublicized killings in oil, in steel, in communications. He was the creator of "Durant markets," which were "not easily pinned down . . . likely to be wild, tumultuous affairs."

The estimates of his power swelled as they passed from narrator to narrator, and would eventually credit him with handling as much as a billion's worth of stock in a single year, 1928. Though exaggeration almost certainly puffed that figure beyond truth, the few records of his market dealings that survived him show transactions of extraordinary scope. His accountants kept a 1927 analysis of his securities dealings that credited him as beginning that year in possession of 414,905 shares of various stocks. During the twelve months he bought 2,644,083 additional shares, for which he paid $284,210,700. He sold 2,255,957 shares, on which he realized $269,652,481, but these figures did not represent a loss, for the "unsold" shares went into his inventory, almost doubling it in size (to 805,012 shares) and adding to its value so that, on paper, he had a year-end profit of $7,511,105. In summary, he had dealt in nearly five million shares valued at over half a billion dollars.

He traded in seventy-five industrial issues that year, not counting bonds and the stocks of investment corporations. He had a predilection for the healthy areas of the economy — construction materials, motors, oil, movies, and radio. But there was no clear overall pattern. In seventeen of the issues he bought or sold more than 25,000 shares. The biggest single transaction was a 623,000-share purchase of General Motors, which he later sold, along with 71,000-odd from his inventory, at a profit to himself of almost $8 millions. He turned over 145,800 shares in a firm called International Combustion Engineering, which had plants in France, England, and the United States that were designed to extract gas, oil, tar, and other by-products from low-grade coal. He bought the shares for approximately $7.82 millions and sold them for $8.69 millions. He cleared a relatively modest profit of $214,000 on almost 70,000 shares of American Smelting and Refining, an even more modest one of $130,000 on the sale of 44,100 shares of Houston Oil. He paid for 67,100 shares of Hudson Motors and 179,700 of Hupp Motors, and in both cases sold some at a small profit and added the rest to his inventory, whose year-end value was $43 million.

He was not infallible, nor were his resources unlimited, and he often had to sell to cut his losses. He dropped over $200,000 on a fifty-thousand-share deal in American Safety Razor. He guessed wrong on 60,000 shares of Warner Brothers, buying them at some $2.5 million and selling them for a quarter-million less. He was beaten, to the tune of $380,000, on 34,000 of General Asphalt, and another $264,000 were wiped out when $21 millions' worth of U.S. Steel that he had ordered turned out to have fallen instead of risen by the time of delivery. Even faithful U.S. Cast Iron Pipe finally let him down, when he bought 26,200 shares at 218 and had to let 20,900 of them go finally at 212. Most significant of all, he bought a huge block of his own Durant Motors — 235,729 shares — for which he had no market at all as the year ended.[39]

Money in such quantities took on a shimmering, impalpable quality, lacking the literal impact of the smaller sums that he had spent his life raising and dispensing for real estate, parts, workers. It was true, some of the figures in the ledgers were translated into figures in a personal bank balance, against which accountants and secretaries wrote checks that produced tangible luxuries and services, a process to which a multimillion-aire had little cause to pay personal heed. But for the most part, the rise and fall of Durant's new fortune was measured in balances that shifted back and forth between black and red without immediate, visible conse-quences. "Payments" and "receipts" were simply transfers of credit among banks and brokers. The seven- and eight-figure numbers following the dollar signs only recorded his score for accuracy of judgment.

To some extent this was a by-product of the economy's steady move in the direction of a diminishing reliance on cash transactions, a trend that would become a landslide years afterward, with the birth of the computer and the credit card. But for Durant there was a deeper meaning in his paper debts and credits, for in themselves they represented his holdings of shares that were likewise only symbols of assets. He was now twice removed from the actual, gritty process of mechanical creation that he had once mastered to his advantage. He had come to manhood among Flint's workshops, and spent his successful middle years close to the actual producers, the Hohensees and Hardys, the Marrs and Masons, the Buicks and Chryslers, who literally supervised the cutting and grinding and hammering, the placement of machine tools, the conversion of lines on blueprints into living power. The satisfactions of the game for Durant had been in praises for his shrewdness, and in his ability to reward his entourage, and these came with money no matter what its source. But in addition there had been the special pride of selling the vehicles, the concrete end products of the process initiated by his faith and drive.

No good news from a broker could restore that to him. He kept some of his taste for products with the stamp of the future on them. He took directorships in only a few of the many companies whose shares he held, but among these were International Combustion Engineering and Industrial Rayon, vanguards of major developments to come in new energy sources and in synthetics, and American Cottonpicker, which was trying prematurely and with an inadequate machine to revolutionize agriculture in the South. Yet he knew little of the concrete details involved. He once innocently offered the use of some of his factory space in Elizabeth to Industrial Rayon, unaware that its manufacture called for enormous quantities of water and mandated a streamside location.[40]

In his own mind he was still a dynamic force in the nation's growth, for he took at face value Wall Street's self-portrait as a literal marketplace where corporations offered morsels of themselves to investors. To a luncheon club audience he explained that there were

thousands of industrial institutions that obtain capital for the development and extension of their business through stock issues. The demand for these stocks and the ability to distribute them regulates the extent of the development of these institutions and has all to do with the prosperity of the country.[41]

His role as a respected consultant, he thought, was to direct support to unrecognized merit.

Success in the stock market comes from finding out a stock selling at $50 that should be selling at $100, or one selling for $100 which should be selling at $150 or $200. . . .

Whatever my activities have been in the security market . . . they have been on the constructive side. I have tried to find meritorious stocks selling far below their real worth, and then I've backed my judgment.[42]

There was no room in his thoughts for consideration of whether even partial truth was to be found in a different, harsher judgment of the bull market, which held that stock prices were inflated far beyond any figure justified even by the undeniable boom in consumer goods — that the purpose of the Exchange had become, for many, not the mobilization of capital but the quick killing. Matthew Josephson, then a young writer freshly back from a brief expatriate's sojourn in Paris, took a job around 1927 as a customer's man with a brokerage house, and found himself helplessly involved in manipulation. Insiders were known to bid up quotations by false rumors, then sell out and leave the sheep to be shorn when the truth dawned. The market was a "great gambling casino . . . a jungle where each man's hand was turned against the other." When he expressed regret at unwittingly passing along a manufactured "inside tip" that cost a schoolteacher his life savings, he was told by an old hand to waste no pity; "they all come here to get something for nothing."[43]

Durant's eyes were closed, so far as the record shows, to that aspect of his new arena. Nor did he register any awareness of the changed texture of his associations. Some of his fellow heavy buyers were industrialists like the Fisher brothers, steelman Charles Schwab, or Walter Chrysler, taking an occasional plunge. But the full-time ticker followers like himself were, in many cases, mirages of the bull market, men who came from no discernible managerial, manufacturing, professional, educational, or regional background; men who faded into obscurity the moment prosperity's crest was passed. Arthur Cutten, a high-collared Chicago bookkeeper whose first great coup was a short sale of wheat futures. Redheaded Michael Meehan, an Irishman who had worked for a theater ticket agency and used the information dropped by his broker customers shrewdly enough to win himself a seat on the Exchange and a fourteen-room Fifth Avenue cooperative apartment. George Breen, who lived in winter at the Sherry-Netherland, and in summer conducted much of his business by telephone from the golf club at Rye. Benjamin Block, best known outside "the Street" for the ownership of Morvich, the horse that won the Kentucky Derby in 1922. Ruddy Jesse Livermore, ostentatiously fond of good cigars and yellow Rolls Royces.[44]

Their game was simply being rich, and in forsaking his own longtime milieu of car-making for theirs, Durant was losing touch with something that had been at his center since 1886 when he uncrated the first road cart made at his behest. As a builder, he was unique. As a speculator, however fabled, he might be outstanding in the scale, but not the substance of his operations. His dimensions contracted to those of mere affluence. And as he finally gave himself time, after 1924, to enjoy that affluence, he showed in his home life the limits to his imagination when it was severed from making and marketing.

VLuxurious as it might be, the New York apartment was fundamentally only a residence. But Raymere was more, a showplace and a seat of leisure for a man who had spent his first half-century of life in disregard of show and in flight from leisure. It had a visibly price-tagged scope and elegance, and it also had touches of improvisation in its grandeur. Its very location in Deal set it apart in the social geography of the twenties. The Jersey shoreline was in a different category from Westchester or Long Island, though a 1929 *Sketch of Monmouth County* swore that the oceanfront was dotted with an "unbroken string of brilliant and fashionable seaside resorts . . . palatial homes and magnificent estates of the nation's wealthy" and gathering spots for "the world's most brilliant personages—statesmen, scientists, stage luminaries and princes of finance and commerce."[45] Among the nobility of commerce in Deal and Long Branch, just to the north, were families of German-Jewish bankers, admitted there when they were still discouraged in other enclaves of wealth—Lehmans, Seligmans, Nathans, and Guggenheims. Their tastes ran to "villas" of Italianate demonstrativeness, profuse in white walls, red-tiled roofs, balustrades, full-length windows, lawn statuary, boxed trees. The Rothschilds, who had owned Raymere before Durant, had followed the pattern, and Raymere looked vaguely Florentine.

Yet even in this Renaissance setting, the touch of modernity was everywhere evident, most significantly in the fleet of cars kept in the huge garage (as many as ten, according to some memories). Guests who arrived by rail were picked up by one of these chauffeured vehicles; those who drove themselves arrived at the entryway along an Ocean Avenue then paved in yellow brick and locally styled the "Golden Road." When they stepped into the main hall, they encountered the first of displays that many of them found breathtaking. "I had never experienced luxury to compare with Billy Durant's house" was the reaction of Walter Chrysler.

But the luxury was curiously uneven. The furnishings were chosen by Catherine with the help of decorators and dealers of quality, and sometimes, it appeared, by the accident of inheritance. The total effect was powerful, especially for those whose tastes were formed in simple settings, but there were odd incongruities. On the walls hung Flemish tapestries, one of them said to have cost as much as $40,000. From their woven surfaces Venus, Adonis, Mars, Cupid, hunting hounds, a surrendering monarch, and animals grazing in a medieval forest looked down at their latest audiences of rich admirers. But in wall spaces between these masterpieces were oil paintings entitled "Barnyard Friends," "A Storm at Sea," and "Watchful Waiting," in the last of which a mother and daughter anxiously scanned a distant maritime horizon.

In various niches and corners there were Louis XV carved walnut benches, bishops' chairs upholstered in Genoese velvet, a walnut Renaissance chest with carved leonine feet, a carved and gilded screen with tapestried panels, and Ch'ien Lung glazed porcelain flower vases. These treasures of European and Asian culture shared space with several statuary groups by Frederick Remington. There was a Knabe Ampico baby grand piano on which Catherine, Margery, Win Murphy, and visiting friends played familiar melodies; it was also used, from time to time, by hired entertainers.

Most of the Durant guests seem to have been General Motors and Durant Motors sales and production executives. They found nothing ill-mated in a reception room that contained Sèvres vases, an Empire mahogany curio cabinet, a Persian silk rug, and a bronze equestrian group of an Indian war party. As they sipped drinks in Louis XVI gilt and carved wing chairs — the host himself joining them, according to various memories, in a martini, a Manhattan, or a weak Scotch-and-water — they enjoyed the contemplation of Meissen busts of a boy and a lamb, a girl likewise with a lamb, and King Henry IV in regal attire.

The dining room was slightly more coherent. Those who proceeded into it had their steps softened by the underfoot thickness of Wiltons and Axminsters, Kermānshāhs and Kāshāns. They ate from Cauldon porcelain, sipped from gold-encrusted etched crystal glasses, and inhaled the perfume of flowers that were grown in Durant's own garden and displayed in a huge crystal ormolu bowl in the center of the table, as well as in Limoges flower vases placed about the chamber, upon which Arabian girls were suspended forever in the movements of a dance, heedless of the hours announced by a great ormolu and marble clock, suspended on columns and crowned with a spread eagle and caryatids. This timepiece itself arose from a black marble base adorned with a chiseled plaque of "cupidons" disporting themselves among billows.

The living room offered an array of Gothic walnut cabinets, Chippendale benches, bronze lamps, gold cigarette boxes, and silver candy baskets. The recreations of the Durants and their visitors were traditional in essence while elegant in their trappings. In the billiard room there was a satinwood and rosewood parqueterie inlaid gaming table primarily for cards, or checkers (if anyone was bold enough to challenge the master of the house), though it did also conceal a roulette wheel. And, naturally, a Brunswick-Balke-Collender pool table.

Visitors who betook themselves to the library once again found a curious amalgam. The decorations included Doulton pottery jugs and jars, bronze inkwells and figurines, red silk drapes, terra-cotta bowls, and another ormolu clock. The books themselves ran a gamut of tastes. There were the acceptable giants of the ages and the century immediately preceding—the Bible, two sets of Shakespeare, and five volumes of Goethe's works, and Guizot's and Macaulay's histories, and sets of Carlyle, Victor Hugo, Balzac, Scott, and de Maupassant. But jostling them were the accumulations of various Yankee business families' stabs at culture. J. M. Barrie and O. Henry. *The American Conflict,* by Horace Greeley. The lectures of John L. Stoddard and the collected writings of Charlotte Yonge and F. W. Bain. Two volumes of *Godey's Ladies' Book,* two of the *Works of Henry Howland Crapo* (presumably bound speeches), fourteen of *Little Journeys Abroad* and three of *The American Nation.* And in addition, whatever was contained within the scope of *The Library of the World's Best Literature* and *Great Men and Famous Women.*

On afternoons of idleness there could be tennis or golf at the Deal Golf Club; sometimes a stroll or a drive about the area, with Durant pointing out the two dozen or so "cottages" that he had built on the tracts of land adjoining Raymere and which he called Deal Gables. Some were rented to strangers; others housed retainers and kinsmen such as his nephew Wallace Willett, superintendent of Durant Motors properties in Asbury Park; Win Murphy; Ted Johnson, a Durant dealer; John Bergen of the early Chevrolet days. Or Raymere's inhabitants might simply choose to sit in the garden and admire the marble urns, chiseled lions, the sundial whose base was all of carved lions' heads and spread eagles, the fountains in which the water purled from a conch shell carried by a bird, a fish held by a little girl, a turtle with a "cupidon" astride his shell. On some special evenings there would be musicians, and a gathering of as many as thirty or forty people would disperse to the guest rooms, yawning their goodnights and making plans for morning meetings in the breakfast room or the sun parlor.[46]

Raymere was unforgettable in the generosity that the Durants radiated, and unmemorable for any identifiable quality that bespoke an owner's character as loudly as Pierre du Pont's greenhouses, or old Governor Crapo's beloved demonstration farms. No single theme unified its attractions, no one collection established a dominant mood, no hobby dictated the use of a single corner of its spaces. What warmth it had bubbled up from Durant's unforgotten, spontaneous drummer's power to please. "In five minutes, he had me feeling as if I owned the place," said Chrysler.[47] Catherine, too, apparently welcomed people with visible sincerity into her pleasure in the setting that "Willie" had finally provided for her.

Yet she left no mistressly imprint on the place. She was not one to impose any strong individual pattern on her environment. In contrast, she was a shy person, seeking friendships among simple people and avoiding the cultivation of those who were socially or otherwise powerful. So retiring were her ways that John Thomas Smith's wife remembered how she would always arrive at a party a few minutes before the precise time of invitation. In that way she was certain to be the first on hand, and therefore not obliged to walk into a room full of strangers. She could be seated already, waiting for others to make an entrance, past appraising eyes.

Given their two natures — Durant's rapt absorption in business and Catherine's tendency to withdrawal — it was inevitable that no evident sovereign will should inform Raymere's sticks and stones. It became a palace whose major statement about its royal couple was simply that they could afford it.

It devoured money. In one single account that seems to have been used for personal expenditures, Durant deposited $315,796 in 1926, against which checks of $309,802 were written. The next two years saw more modest expenditures, but only by comparison: some $160,000 in 1927 and $99,000 in 1928. Ten thousand a month on living well — not all of it on the Deal residence, but every penny underscoring the one way in which the rich were undeniably different, their enormous power to spend. In 1928 the manager of the Star Motor Company's Philadelphia branch got $500 a month. Durant paid $572 in a single bill to the Tintern Manor Water Company. A wholesale salesman earned $300 monthly, which was $75 less than one ninety-day bill for heating Raymere. An accountant was paid $225 monthly. Catherine ordered $314.11 — or rather, Amanda Anderson, the cook did — in groceries from the Oxford Market in the same span of time. The mechanics who serviced the cars before they went out to the dealers were paid $80 a month, the same as a stenographer, while a single statement to the Durants for thirty days' worth of dairy goods from Sheffield Farms ran $85.70. The head of the parts and service department took home $140 monthly. The Durants had memberships in thirteen clubs, whose combined dues ran somewhere between $130 and $390 each month. Those were the facts of class in the prosperity decade. Every four weeks, too, payments of $75 to $125 went to the cook, and the kitchen maid, and Sigmund Tiefenbrunner the houseman, and Hilda Smith the laundress, and Margaret Short the parlormaid, and Anna Swanson the chambermaid, and Torvald Trulson the caretaker, and to Robert Hilliard and Thomas Wash and Hugh Brown, of unstated duties — around a thousand dollars a month to keep Raymere's attractions spotless, its guests protected from any moment of unfulfilled desire, its motor armada sparkling and ready to roll at the lifting of a telephone to the head chauffeur.

Those were, of course, the ordinary items of expense. Then there were the checks for the trips to Europe that became an annual event starting in 1926. A full $5,400 for a world tour on the *Homeric* for Catherine's mother, who lived with them; $8,754 for passages for the two Durants and guests to and from Europe in 1927; deposits for first-class cabins on the great, deluxe floating hostelries that plied the North Atlantic—the *Majestic, Paris, Caronia, Aquitania, Berengaria.*

The biggest single checks went to the jewelers, and dealers in fine furnishings and silver, and decorators and galleries who provided the special treasures that Durant loved to bestow on "Muddie." There was $67,500 in one payment to Black, Starr and Frost in 1925, then another lump sum of $50,000; $2,265 to the Deal Decorating Company, and $1,675 to the Rosenbach Company, and a scattering of payments over the years to bedeck those adored wrists and arms and hands fittingly—to Tiffany's $3,077 here and $3,216 there; to Cartier's $1,260 one April day, sums mounting up year by year to levels only hinted at when, in 1926, thieves managed to steal a portion of Catherine's gems, whose total value was estimated to be $75,000.

There seemed to be no end to the money coming in. Dividends alone, almost untaxed by Coolidge's benign Secretary of the Treasury, accounted for anywhere from a quarter to three-quarters of a million in spendable income each year. The golden deluge gave Durant a vocabulary of material expression of his love. He was grateful for the utterance of diamonds, the eloquence of silver. Yet in other forms of giving he was tongue-tied. Impulsive and generous as he was to his nearest, he could not think institutionally when it came to charity. Durant's gifts to good causes were sporadic and uneven responses to immediate solicitations. His check stubs showed him pinioned to a small-town, neighborly pattern of passing out donations to figurative and literal door-to-door collectors. There was a single large gift, in 1925, of $5,000 to the Salvation Army, and it seems reasonable to guess that an appeal from Howard Clifford might have lain behind it. Then there was a scattering of miscellaneous donations—fifty dollars for five tickets to a performance of some kind sponsored by the Italian Welfare League, and ten each to the Children's Aid Society and the Association for the Aid of Crippled Children, and five for the New York Tuberculosis Association. The largest single gift of the following year was $1,000 to the Mineola Home for Cardiac Children. In 1928 and 1929 more miscellaneous driblets—$15 to the Junior Society of Congregation Emanu-El, $250 to the Federal Council of Churches, $2 each to the League of Catholic Women and to St. Anthony's Guild, and $1 to the Friars of the Atonement, the tiny sums dutifully recorded along with the large in the total of claimed income tax deductions for the year. The big gift of 1929 was $1,000 to the National Radio Youth's Conference, followed by $350 to the Children's Village of Dobbs Ferry. The one with the most homespun ring was the $10 given to the Ladies' Auxiliary, Deal Fire Company Number Two.[48]

His skimpy handouts, dispensed at random, were hard to reconcile with his known generosity to friends and kin, and especially his unconstricted largesse in the business world. He could offer half a million a year to Chrysler, or fifteen million for a factory to Sloan without a blink of hesitation because he could see the effect of his decision in some overall pattern of motor development which his mind alone stretched to encompass. He could not make the same connections, or conceive of large-scale worthy objectives in private giving. He lacked a sense of money as maintainer of community, endowed with the power to perpetuate and enlarge instant pulses of goodwill. It was not surprising that he did not give, like a Du Pont, to universities, which were outside his experience, or to churches, museums, and research foundations. But he did not even follow the examples of Dallas Dort and Charles Stewart Mott in endowing Flint with parks, community centers, hospitals, auditoriums, municipal services. What he did for the city he did without thinking socially; he was diligent in his business, and it brought in money. Outside of that central fire, all else was shadow.

The contact with Flint's relative simplicities was almost totally lost by the end of the twenties. The strongest link parted, inevitably, on a February morning of 1924. Rebecca Durant, just short of her ninety-first birthday, and unconscious from the third stroke she had suffered within a year, slipped out of life as unprotestingly as she had lived it. Durant was there. It was Margery's testimony that he sobbed like a child at the funeral. IIis telegram to Catherine, who never seemed to accompany him to the place of his beginnings, held a revealing sentence from a man who had lost a sister, been divorced, and sacrificed a fortune and his dearest creation. "This is the first real sorrow I have ever known," he told her.[49]

Among the most touching of the condolences was one from poor, deaf, blind, stumbling Uncle William, who had outlived most of his wards. "Beckie was my baby sister," he dictated to a typist. "In childhood we played together and romped together, and in after life there was unabated affection and unusual confidence and esteem. . . . I shall remember, during the brief period left to me, her constant loyalty. . . ." Not long afterward he, too, was gone.[50]

All of Flint knew about the bond between Rebecca and her "boy," demonstrated for the last time as he kept her house empty and intact for four years, before finally accepting the finality of her departure and selling it. He had the furniture removed to Raymere to remind him of what had been, and Edwin Atwood sent him a thoughtful souvenir, a set of checkers made from a limb cut off one of the maple trees that grew in her yard. Atwood neatly completed the symbol by enclosing them in a box fashioned from the wood of an apple orchard on his farm, cut down to make way for the sheds and machinery of the Flint Motor Company; the gift and the container both fragments of a bygone time.[51]

Durant's son and daughter were as removed as he was from their childhood pasts in the town of their pioneer grandfather. Margery had shed the skin of the young matron who, in spite of being the child of the town's richest man, kept the books for her middle-aged doctor husband. She was, in the recollection of her own daughter, Edwina, enthusiastic about living the role of free-spirited woman as the twenties understood it. She loved music, entertainment, theater, and travel, enjoyed the casualness of short skirts, took laughing-aloud pleasure in cigarettes and cocktails, orange juice and gin being a favorite. Catherine and Willie would visit her in Westbury, where he was especially popular with the many guests who came to enjoy the scenery, the pool, the flow of spirit. Edwina was unable to recall, later, any content in his conversation that was unrelated to business, and yet for all that she kept an impression of gaiety that they shared when in each other's company—"a family of charmers," she called her Durant kin.

Margery had a sailboat, on which Win Murphy remembered being offered rides with his children; she would have, in time, a plane and a pilot to fly her on adventurous jaunts; and in 1923 she acquired a second husband and another estate. He was Robert Daniel, the once-divorced president of the Liberty National Bank, a handsome black-haired descendant of the Virginia planter-aristocrat John Randolph. He was only three years her senior. He owned an aging mansion on the James River, known as Brandon, and Margery invested a generous quantity of her trust fund's income in redecorating and renovating it. By the time the task was completed, unfortunately, the marriage itself had become dilapidated beyond refurbishing. They were divorced in 1927. Daniel kept his job at the bank and consoled himself with raising racehorses until he found another wife with money.

Margery was shaken into an impulsive third marriage in the autumn of 1928. Edwina learned the news through a surprise telephone call to her freshman dormitory at Vassar. The new husband was to last only a short time, and leave so little impression on the family and on the public record that his first name is lost to recollection. He was to survive in the Durant chronicles only as "Mr. Cooper, the ginger-ale king." His effervescence was brief, and by the next year Margery was once more being styled "Miss Durant" in the press, and seeing much of a new and distinguished escort. This was Fitzhugh Green, an intriguing and talented figure with a profitable appetite for adventure and an ultimately fatal one for alcohol. He was an Annapolis graduate of the class of 1909, and among other assignments had been given a part in an Arctic exploring expedition four years later. On his retirement to the Reserves in 1927, he had given full time to the development of what had begun as a sideline, writing about other discoverers and risk-takers. He had to his credit books on Admirals Bartlett, Peary, and Byrd, all of them conquerors of the polar regions, and had been a coauthor of Charles Lindbergh's first account of his transatlantic flight, simply entitled *We*. He and Margery were shortly to become husband and wife, and remain so until their deaths. In this second mating for him and fourth for her, both seekers were to travel a hard road in a search for emotional health and stability—a path that became steeper, more urgent, more painful as the years implacably advanced beyond the age when it seemed that the party had no end.[52]

Cliff Durant, meanwhile, lived in a steady condition of high combustion, neither finishing first in anything nor displaying any deep concern over it. Three times he tested himself against the Indianapolis brick oval in the "500," in modified Durants. He came in twelfth in 1922, seventh in 1923, thirteenth in 1924, then gave up racing. His work in California for his father's new enterprise left him with a surplus of time and energy that he poured into pleasure. Into a two-masted schooner on which he sailed and sported with Hollywood friends like Lew Cody and Mabel Normand, stars of silent comedy. Into airplanes when that fancy took him and he buzzed tiny biplanes in and out of grass strips, bought several for his amusement, and toyed briefly with the idea of entering aircraft manufacture. Into a 26,000-acre estate in Roscommon, Michigan, that stretched for ten miles along both sides of the Au Sable River, where he could hunt and fish and entertain visitors with the wares of his private bootlegger, who operated out of Canada, conveniently close.

The money that paid for the boat, and the sixteen-cylinder Marmon passenger car, the Waco and Stearman and Stinson planes, and the fairy castle in the Michigan pine woods that had started the first family fortune before there were buggies and Buicks—the money came from the market, which he played with a skill equal to his father's and with greater prudence. The two of them had an up-and-down relationship, warmed in spurts by affection, but they were at their most comfortable in exchanging market tips. "Can line up some very good purchasing if you think the stock will go through two hundred this week," Cliff would advise when Durant was forming a syndicate. And paternal counsel would go forth in such forms as: "Buy (would suggest) 3,000 General. Two shares for one at next meeting with six per cent on new stock and extras. Look for decided advance. Best regards, Dad." The market was their bridge between generations.[53]

Cliff did not watch the big board from New York, which he disliked. Instead, he had his own broker's clerk, a young man named John Anderson, authorized to work in Roscommon as a "traveling office" of Clarke, Childs, Inc., a firm with a seat on the Exchange. It was a one-of-a-kind arrangement for this whimsical heavy customer. Anderson would get ticker readings by telephone from New York or Detroit, then call in Cliff's orders, running up bills as high as $3,000 a month. He was paid by Cliff, and recalled him as a kindly and genial boss, who referred to him as "Jackie Boy," and peppered him with commands, always humorously couched, from the golf course, the auto track, Clara's home in California, hotels in Europe. Cliff, too, was one of the family of charmers. Years later, Anderson would still be gently rebutting widespread talk of Cliff's heavy liquoring. "He was rather sedate, but he did like a drink. Now and then he'd get a little on the high side." And Anderson was pleased to recall sudden bursts of intensity, like the occasion on which Cliff decided to cultivate a talent for music that his schoolmates had remarked long before, and bought a $50,000 Guarnerius on which to take lessons. He did well for a time, then abruptly dropped the project. Somewhere deep in that Yankee-ancestored nature there were currents of seriousness stirring that never found an outlet.[54]

Nearing midlife, Clifford Durant appeared as an oddly reversed image of his father, giving himself to the enjoyment of leisure as spontaneously as the older man plunged daily into work. Each was not quite at home in the other's realm, something that Cliff, like many sons of achievers, might instinctively have sought. As he grew pudgier and ruddier, and headed toward his fortieth birthday and second divorce, he seemed more than a mere three generations removed from the great-grandfather who had brought a pinchpenny history, a devastating capacity for work, and profound fears of idleness, drink, and gambling to Michigan some seventy years earlier.

In outgrowing Flint in his particular way, "Billy" Durant had made himself and his children overnight immigrants to the world of twentieth-century urban wealth, without ever troubling to prepare any of them for the journey. All three had trouble finding personal landmarks in those new surroundings.

The hollows in Durant's life were not publicly visible. He was a lord of the ticker, a special order of nobility under Coolidge. When he sailed for his annual vacations reporters gathered respectfully for the ritual of the shipboard interview and begged him to venture Opinions. He never failed to assure them, like Raskob, that industry was at its healthiest and the market bound to soar higher. His paper fortune furnished his credentials as prophet.

Yet his earlier strength had not been in the accumulation of dollars. It grew from his godlike power to say: "Let there be wheels," and to fill the void with transportation. That was the reward of the game, the joy that, as Fred Smith had guessed, meant more to him than money.

And it was dwindling. Durant Motors struggled, and the old Durant, who kept moving though broken parts screeched and howled, whose home was in his son-in-law's spare bedroom or a Pullman berth or a factory office lit at 3 A.M. or wherever he could tap his own center by rushing from merger to merger, was not fighting back. His hand wavered at the control panel. He moved in and out of command, promised undelivered miracles, scolded, launched diversions. He never articulated or even recognized the problem. It could have been that age had finally slowed him, or that the game was at last too complex, or that he had been wounded far worse than he knew in 1920.

Whatever the causes, the effects were plain. Durant Motors, between 1926 and 1928, began to go downhill as fast as the creator's reflex spasms of 1921 to 1923 had pulled it up. The phoenix was collapsing back into the ashes.

V I Death nearly ended it all a few weeks after Durant's sixty-fourth birthday. He was coming back from a holiday in the sun of Palm Beach, part of his new style, rolling northward in a private car. With him and Catherine were Randolph Hicks and his wife. Hicks, a lawyer with Satterlee and Canfield, had become a dedicated friend, his loyalty enriched by Durant's skillful management of his investment portfolio. It was a Sunday morning, January 11, 1926, when the Royal Poinciana stopped somewhere in Florida. The two couples toyed with their breakfast, stared out at sand and palms, speculated on the cause of delay. Then there was the screech of a whistle, darkness, appalling sounds of shattering glass and grinding steel, screams. Signals had failed somewhere along the line, and a following train had plowed into their car at full speed, telescoping it into the one ahead.

Miraculously, the four came out alive, though elsewhere on the trains there were three dead and thirty injured. Rescue workers found the women unhurt and the two men conscious but with head injuries. Blood poured from Durant's severely torn scalp. "I hit all four walls in that compartment," he told questioners. He was bruised over much of his body, and in shock, but a local doctor cleared him for travel to New York by a special nonstop express. "Somewhat bruised but still in the ring," he wired to Murphy, and on Monday afternoon swayed through Pennsylvania Station, porters at his elbows, his head mummified in bandages, staring glassily into the news cameras. Had he been killed, he would have followed Dallas Dort by just a year, his old friend falling to a heart attack on a Flint golf course in 1925. But the gods had marked him out for a slower end.[55]

Durant's first thought was for the market. The mere news of his injury had brought slumps to several of his favorite issues. Tuesday morning found him, gray-faced and in pain, propped up with pillows and on the telephone. His doctor, John F. Erdmann, came in, pursed his lips, shook his head, and ordered his protesting patient into the Post-Graduate Hospital, "to keep him from doing the work he insisted on performing at home." But the businesslike physician could impose only a few days of abstinence on Durant. A week and a half after the collision, working through Murphy, who relayed his messages to the Exchange floor, he was credited with rallying a sagging market and adding two to seven points in an afternoon to U.S. Cast Iron Pipe, Independent Oil and Gas, and Humble Oil. The bears, the *Times* reported in the combat metaphors that financial writers worked to exhaustion, "turned tail and ran when the word was spread about the street that 'Durant is back.'"[56]

Suffering and fear could not keep him from his addiction, but they could drive him from the directing role at 250 West Fifty-seventh Street. On February 18, freshly discharged from his bed, he announced that he was giving up the active management of all Durant Motors subsidiaries, partly on medical advice and partly to give more time to the care of his investments. Buried near the end of the newspaper story was the significant comment: "The companies which bear his name . . . have not been particularly brilliant earners."[57] The faith healer who supposedly could make lame issues run and skip by infusions of confidence could do nothing for his own, down 43 points from their 1923 pinnacle.

In the best of times, Durant Motors would have been struggling, but when the master turned the command over to a committee of his top executives, the situation was especially critical for new and weakly financed firms. Overall the industry had never done better. From 1925 through 1928 passenger car sales ran between 3.5 and 3.8 million each year, except for a slight slump in 1927 due to special circumstances. Henry Ford, after a losing battle to preserve the Model T, shut down for a year to retool. In 1929 there would be almost 4.5 million sales.

The new cars rolled, in the full pride of conquest, over a thickening network of roads and through a social landscape designed around their needs. They were lower and quieter, developed more horsepower from better fuels. Balloon tires softened their ride, meshed gears smoothed their acceleration under the clumsiest hand on the shift knob. Their bodies were closed, tinted, cushioned, warmed in winter. Best of all from the manufacturers' viewpoint, the annual model changeover had ended the fear of saturating the market. Planned obsolescence was to keep auto makers forever confronted with a self-renewing supply of customers, to whom a new car every few years was not a whim but a need.

That very fact, however, mandated a yearly expenditure of many millions in design, research, and advertising. No longer could a new car challenge the established makes on the strength of one successful year of production on borrowed money. The number of entering firms melted away. Only one new company began to manufacture automobiles in 1923—and fourteen were crowded out. Two tried in 1924, and fifteen fell into bankruptcy. None entered in 1925, only one in 1926, by which time the whole number of makers was 44. The gates were closed. And a merciless equation governed the relative standing of the 44.[58] Only the leaders could afford the constant reinvestment required, so that with each year the gap widened between their share of the market and that of the stragglers in the parade. The rich, as usual, got richer. In 1925 Ford and General Motors had half the total sales between them. Durant's "baby" was doing well. In 1923 Du Pont had yielded the presidency to Alfred P. Sloan, one technology graduate dedicated to order making way for another like him. In 1926 Sloan, after reorganizing freely, reported to stockholders: "General Motors has become an institution rather than a collection of individual units."[59]

Only a consolidation among some of the firms fighting to divide the remainder of the business could guarantee a possible challenge to the front runners. Durant saw as much, when he predicted with customary intuition that "the automotive industry will eventually be composed of three or four big combinations."[60] In 1922, he had obviously expected Durant Motors to take the third place. But in 1928, when he made his statement, it had been preempted by Walter Chrysler. Chrysler, after losing his first superior new auto to Durant in 1922, had got another one from his gifted engineers in 1924, marketed it under his own name, and swept to a position near the head of the column. The following year he dropped the Maxwell label entirely, and styled his concern simply the Chrysler Motor Company. In 1928 he bought out the twelve-year-old company of the Dodge brothers, the brawling mechanics who had once been suppliers and partners of Henry Ford. Both were dead, and their concern was in receivership. In that same year, the Plymouth was introduced as Chrysler's competition for Chevrolet and Ford in the low-priced line. The trio of Plymouth, Dodge, and Chrysler ended 1928 with 20 percent of the market. Walter Chrysler had reached the end toward which he had been moving since those long-ago days of breaking down and reassembling his new Locomobile over and over again in Oelwein. And some three and a half dozen independent carmakers now had 30 percent of the passenger auto business to cut in snippets among themselves. Durant Motors was merely one of them.

Not only that, but a particularly troubled one. The huge debts run up in the first whirlwind months of creation still burdened the books. Merely servicing them ate up promotion money. Nothing less than a torrent of sales could generate the power to lift the stalled giant out of the morass of obligation, and there was no prospect of that for any but the top three. There was truth in Murphy's observation regarding Durant's inability to match records with General Motors and Chrysler: "He'd made some pretty good competition for himself."[61]

Four months after Durant stepped down, the balance sheets of two subsidiaries told a chilling tale. Durant Motors of Michigan had a mere $175,000 in cash on hand and in the banks. The book value per share of its outstanding stock was $7.60. It owed $4.2 million, against $2 million in accounts receivable. Its only elements of worth were its inventories, real estate, and plants. Durant Motors of New Jersey was only in slightly better condition. It owed less and its physical plant—primarily the monster Elizabeth factory—was worth more, but it, too, had less than a quarter of a million in cash on hand and $2.5 million tied up in parts and materials that were languishing for lack of orders for cars to incorporate them.

A proposal of the management committee to merge the two companies did not win stockholder approval at that time. Cash had to be raised by selling off the great new factory in Flint to General Motors. The Flint car itself would be made thereafter in Elizabeth. Four years after the mighty celebration, Durant Motors' name died in the annals of local industry. And even that sale was neither saving nor final. Durant Motors announced that it would produce 94,000 cars in 1927, but as the year's early months revealed that that modest total, too, could not be sold, the managers began to dismantle the moribund Locomobile Company and sell off its properties.[62]

Twelve months after his first retirement, a desperate outlook brought Durant back into control. In March of 1927, he suddenly announced that he was "on the job" again, in third-person advertisements.

Now fully recovered from his serious illness of a year ago, he proposes to devote his entire time (with every other interest secondary) to a thoroughly constructive motor car program that will duplicate his previous and widely known accomplishments in this field. . . . Mr. Durant promises a statement on April 7 respecting his future plans that will startle the industry. . . .[63]

Two weeks would elapse before April 7. Durant's name still held enough power to compel a short daily story as the automotive editors waited. Durant flourished his cape, turned back his sleeves, rapped his stick on the table, displayed the empty top hat to them. On the appointed date the chords were struck, the snare drums rolled, he reached in and produced — nothing. The startling announcement was that he intended to form a new combination, called Consolidated Motors, built around a new, six-cylinder Star. As proof of good faith he was resigning his directorships in the Liberty National Bank and three other companies in whose stock he dealt heavily.

The market yawned. Durant Motors stock had heaved itself sluggishly up from 11¾ on the Curb in mid-March to 13⅜ in anticipation of the dazzling stroke to come. On April 8, 25,000 shares of it were dumped in disgust. The quotation collapsed to 11½. The house lights were killed, the curtain lowered, Consolidated Motors was heard of no more. Two weeks later, Durant Motors sold the Long Island City assembly plant back to Ford for a first-aid cash transfusion of $2.5 million.[64]

In November Durant tried one more pathetic fanfare. This time he announced an impending consolidation of Durant Motors' lines with several other cars — the Moon, the Chandler, the Hupmobile, the Jordan, and the Peerless. Every one of them was in deep trouble. What Durant was trumpeting was a new assault with fresh regiments, when in fact he would have merely a motley band of invalids, stragglers, and rejects at his heels. And he could not even bring off this last-ditch mobilization. One of the companies to be involved denied the entire story, and it promptly disappeared from sight.[65]

He became querulous, petulant as he had never been. When a preliminary annual report showed losses of over $3.6 millions in the first eight months of 1927, he fell back on the timeworn lame excuse of bad policy makers, the lack of positive thinking on the part of his followers. His covering statement scolded:

During the past few years many of our stockholders have manifested a noticeable spirit of criticism because of the failure of your corporation to progress to the point of giving them a return upon their investment and for other reasons. This feeling of unfriendliness upon the part of stockholders has exerted a hampering influence in obtaining new and better distributors and dealers for our products. It has slowed up the sales of our cars, it has furnished the basis for the disparaging statements of outsiders.[66]

That Durant should reproach those who had trusted him for expecting a return on their savings was a sign of how powerfully imbalancing a force exerted itself in him through frustration. His whole career had hitherto rested on arousing and cheerfully satisfying the hopes of others. But each monthly statement of Durant Motors confirmed that any hope of dividends on its stock was a fading mirage, and that every dormant share was an affidavit to his failure. The stoutest good nature could not indefinitely survive such constant, embittering reminders without flight into self-justifying attacks on others.

In October of 1928 there was a last attempted master stroke, characteristically in advance of its day. This time, Durant proposed the introduction of a small European import to the American market, through an agreement which he signed with the Société Anonyme Française d'Automobiles to sell their "Amilcar" in the United States. They, in turn, would sell Durant models in Europe, in effect creating a transatlantic distributing partnership of the two organizations.[67] But like the other projects that he had sired in hopes of jolting Durant Motors back into life, this one was not pursued. In any case the patient was in a terminal decline that was beyond injection, shock, or incantation, though some organs and members would twitch for another five years. The closing reports for the third quarter showed the Elizabeth plant "virtually shut down," with fewer than a thousand men turning out a handful of cars.

So a January day came, when Durant stood before an annual luncheon of his dealers that should have been especially festive because it marked the beginning of his twenty-fifth year in the industry. Waiting for silence, he asked a simple, dramatic question: "Do you believe in W. C. Durant?" There was a pause, and then the room resounded with applause, the men scraping back chairs and rising to their feet in groups, until the whole hotel banquet room was alive with one of those demonstrations of faith that had warmed his quarter of a century of automotive adventure. Having evoked his tribute, Durant then proceeded to abandon those who had rendered it. He announced that he was once more quitting an active role of leadership to attend to other demands which "must be heeded," a phrase embracing all of his market activities, and particularly Industrial Rayon and International Combustion Engineering. It was a strange farewell speech, half-apologetic and half-boastful. He was shocked, he said, to learn that "every form of misrepresentation" had been used to induce people to invest in his companies, but he swore to repay any losses they had incurred, with interest. He did not specify what the "misrepresentations" had been, or who was responsible for them, though he seemed to hint at those malign, faceless forces that he had earlier accused of making his name "a football in Wall Street." He excused himself for failure to bring off the expected victories with the explanation that he had been unbelievably busy in the preceding year, investing over a billion dollars for banks, trust companies, and individuals—enterprises "thirty-five times greater than Durant Motors, with all its plants," as if this would impress men whose entire livelihoods were tied up in the success of those plants. Nor did they need to be told that his attention was elsewhere. During the preceding three months they had followed, in the press, the course of a sudden aberration of their chief, a contest for the "best and most practicable plan to make the Eighteenth Amendment effective," with a $25,000 cash prize from Durant's own pocket.

He offered them final, placating crumbs. "Do not for one moment gain the impression that I am retiring from business or releasing control of the company bearing my name" was his assurance. "I am, however, delegating to the ablest group of men I could find the entire management of Durant Motors, Incorporated." This new directorate turned out to be four executives of the Dodge Motor Company, displaced by its absorption into Chrysler's corporation. He had signed a three-year management contract with them, paying a collective $150,000 a year to the quartet, and holding out what was, under the circumstances, a somewhat wilted carrot — options on a large block of Durant Motors stock, theirs to enjoy at a bargain if they could find some way to infuse it with value. Durant had closed a cycle. He entered the automobile business as the savior of a worthless firm, charged with the task of making the desert blossom. He left it, for all practical purposes, asking other men for the same miracle on his behalf.[68]

It was beyond them, beyond anyone. They did manage to dispose of 75,000 cars — under 2 percent of the total — in booming 1929, and they comforted the mourners in their annual report with the news that the gross profit of those sales amounted to $644,307. That reduced the net losses for the year to some $980,000, and the overall deficit of the corporation to $12.8 million. Meanwhile, Durant, having touched his lowest point as a manufacturer, reached the top of his highest bounce as a dealer in illusions. He rushed toward 1930 in an augmented frenzy of stock handling, still predicting wonderlands over the horizon, still insisting that the only threat to prosperity was doubt. If no one lost faith, storms would never break, and the dream would play endlessly on.

VII Still, he could not altogether disregard the bleats of the shorn sheep that broke through to his ears. There are no records left of any trips to Flint in 1929, when to go there was to be reminded of promises unkept. Howard Clifford, scraping a livelihood by the sale of real estate, endured with what fortitude he could muster the reproaches of neighbors and confidants to whom he had sold Durant Motors shares. His loyalty to the man did not waver; his creed, after all, taught him that pain was possibly a test of his commitment. Durant could not have been completely innocent of such woes, multiplied many times among his other Flint adherents. (He was later to hire Clifford as a manager of his own remaining properties in the town.) And besides the discontents of Flint there were the vocal complaints from around the country, voiced by the veterans whom he had drilled in "habits of saving," and led out to confound the speculators behind the banners of the Durant Corporation. Typical of them was the lament of one resident of Norristown, Pennsylvania, who wrote on the stationery of the Dixie Theater, the Show Place of Manayunk, featuring High Class Vaudeville and Photoplays.

My dear Mr. Durant:

Was sorry to learn through the press that you have relinquished the presidency of Durant Motors, Inc.

We felt sure when you took active charge of the Corporation's interests, that you would put it on a paying basis and feel that you should continue to supervise the concern personally.

Of course I feel sure that you know what is best for your personal interests, and feel sure that you do not wish to sidestep your responsibility to the stock holders of Durant Motors.

The 225 shares of the stock which myself and family hold is only a drop in the bucket but it is all we could afford and have paid for it out of hard earned money and not through speculation.

Besides I practically lost a good general Mdse [merchandise] business through being too active in the sale of Durant and Star Motor stock, which did not net me any profit for my time spent.

What advice can you offer a man who has done all in good faith whereby he might recover what is possible?[69]

A tough-minded answer might have been that the disappointed correspondent should, in the future, forgo expectations of getting something for nothing. But it was not in Durant's nature to be so blunt with himself or others. What he wrote back, if anything, was lost to history, but early in 1929 he drafted and set up in dummy copy an advertisement intended for the *Saturday Evening Post*. Its headline, next to a benign portrait of him, told readers that "W. C. Durant Wishes to Buy Certificates of Durant Motors, Inc." The text carried a long list of serial numbers of Durant Motors certificates. Any of the original holders of those particular shares might, if they wished, redeem them for the purchase price by mailing them, properly endorsed, to the Liberty National Bank. Durant later claimed that he had five million dollars set aside for this fund of conscience, but the offer never saw daylight because his lawyers advised him that partial redemption would not stand up to a court challenge from others who were not reimbursed. He had to stand ready to pay off all buyers if need be, a goal toward which he was struggling as the buying orders to his brokers continued to pour through the wires.[70]

It was consistent with his past behavior to attempt the impossible, particularly when his deepest sense of his own worth rested on his hope that he could go on, as so often in the past, taking bad investments off the hands of friends. He bought as if he were trying to accumulate hasty millions. He now had three dozen brokers, many of them with multiple accounts. One, "Pat" Cusick, alone carried forty-six—for Durant himself, for Catherine, for Margery, for Randolph Hicks, for old Buick and Chevrolet dealers, for "Trainload" Collins and George McLaughlin, for a vice-president of Durant Motors, for the heads of supply companies bought out by Durant Motors, for the president of at least one company in which Durant had heavy holdings, for the president of at least one bank that had lent him money—for a representative sample of all those to whom W. C. Durant was a fountain of plenty.[71] And to almost every broker, for each account, there were almost daily calls, buying here, selling there, juggling RCA and Columbia Graphophone, American Can and Industrial Rayon, Anaconda and U.S. Steel, a dazzling number of transactions, beyond any one memory to retain, but coalescing in a huge scaffolding of market "support" that somehow fitted inside Durant's consciousness. He was rarely identified as a specific buyer in any large turnover, but he was a known presence, sometimes figuring in public jokes about the market. When Michael Meehan had traveling offices set up on several ocean liners so that seaborne plungers could continue their game uninterrupted, a newspaper versified:

> *We are lost! the Captain shouted*
> *As he staggered down the stairs.*
> *"I've got a tip," he faltered*
> *"Straight by wireless from the aunt*
> *Of a fellow who's related*
> *To a cousin of Durant."*
> *At these awful words we shuddered*
> *And the stoutest bull grew sick*
> *While the brokers cried "More margin!"*
> *And the ticker ceased to tick.*[72]

The more committed Durant became to the boom, however, the more desperately he resisted a growing caution about the direction of the market which was being expressed by the board of governors of the Federal Reserve System. The board was charged with the regulation of the national credit supply through its control of the "rediscount rate," the interest it charged the system's member banks. And the board was visibly worried at the beginning of the year over certain disturbing figures. The volume of brokers' loans to customers had reached nearly $6 billion at the end of 1928. It had jumped by a quarter of a billion in January; it would go to $8.5 billion by a date late in the year. Most of these loans were accommodations to the 600,000-odd margin customers. The brokers could afford to make them, because they themselves had little trouble borrowing from the banks (except in certain brief periods of high demand for short-term "call loans"), and the banks were unstinting because the rediscount rate stood at a mere 3 percent.

What the board saw was a situation in which billions of dollars in debt rested on securities which could, in dropping only a few points, lose most of their collateral value, leading to a mounting demand for more margin, an avalanche of selling, an epidemic of default, and a collapse inconceivable in its dimensions—precisely what was to happen. The board's suggested remedy, which political pressure kept it from applying, was to raise the rediscount rate, tighten the money market, bring about a rise in margin requirements, and discourage speculative buying. Perhaps even to force some selling and bring stock prices down to realistic levels in terms of prospective earnings. To deflate the balloon slightly and slowly, and prevent the ultimate explosion. Board members and other fiscal conservatives and realists were convinced that, for example, when a stock like RCA shot from 85 to over 500 in a ten-day period in March, there could be no industrial cause. Instead, they reasoned, there was a buying pool that would shortly turn its attention to other issues and leave a good many people behind to be hurt in the following decline. And they were right— there was just such a pool, whose members included the Fisher brothers, John J. Raskob, Charles Schwab, Percy Rockefeller, Herbert Bayard Swope, Mrs. David Sarnoff, Walter Chrysler, and William C. Durant, who, in that week and a half, put up $400,000 and earned $145,855 on it.[73]

To Durant, the board's logic was not only wrong but dangerous. He became frantic in his public opposition to any restriction of the flow of loans. In part his reaction was prompted by the threat of personal loss; even a controlled fall in prices could not fail to be damaging to a man with millions of dollars in buying contracts awaiting fulfillment. In part, too, it was a predictable kindling of old embers. Only bears and bankers gained when the cost of money rose. Echoes of his grandfather's and his own perennial struggles for working cash were easily set to ringing by even a hint of contraction.

But it would not have been hard for anyone familiar with Durant's past to see deeper mechanisms at work. Another failure was unthinkable after the loss of General Motors, the miscarriage of Durant Motors. And in his own mind he had come to see those defeats as due to an engineered destruction of the vital element of confidence. Even if the Morgans had not conspired to drive down the price of GM in 1921, their refusal to join him in supporting the market then was the killing stroke of faintheartedness. And Forbes and Barron, raising their unfounded suspicions of his methods early in the twenties—they had let out the lifeblood of his last motor empire, which was trust in him. So this time there must be no faltering, no self-executing hint that things might go wrong. Belief in the natural tendency of stocks to rise must remain unspotted, so that he might recoup his losses and be able once more to bestow rewards and earn love.

And there was an even more fundamental need of Durant's ego. In 1929 he could have closed out his market activities and retired comfortably, as he might have done in 1921 with what was left to him. But that was an inconceivable choice. William Durant believed, like Gatsby, like an entire American generation, in the orgiastic future, the green light, the morning toward which one ran with arms ever outstretched in expectation. To live only for the existing moment was, for him, to confront vacancy. When the board talked, even theoretically, of curbing the power to invest in new self-sellers for later development, it denied the meaning of his life. It threatened not only his paper wealth but his illusions, indispensable to the survival of a positive thinker and a gambler.

So he fought the board with what energy was left to him, repeating to whatever audience he could gather that the constriction of credit would bring on the very collapse that the board claimed to fear, and that speculation could be controlled by the good sense of the business community. Late in February he issued the first of many statements to come, warning that:

Any group of eight men vested with or assuming power which, by careless or intentional action, succeeds in destroying credit and confidence—the basis of our great prosperity—will be subject to criticism by every sensible business man. . . . Businessmen generally resent the lack of tact and judgment displayed in the campaign now being conducted.[74]

On April 2, he got a news story out of one of his quixotic inspirations, the despatch of a wire to one hundred "executives of our representative industrial, railroad and public utility corporations," asking them to respond to the question of whether or not, based on "present conditions, prospects and plans for the future," they thought the existing market price of their common stock too high. Most of the answers were in the form of a monosyllabic and unsurprising "no," though there were a few exceptions, most notably Gerard Swope, the president of General Electric, who stood alone among them all in thinking that the head of a company was "the poorest person in the world to say anything about the market price of his stock," adding: "Personally, I have always been wrong in my guess."[75]

On the night of April 3, Durant stepped unnoticed from a train in Washington's Union Station, got into a taxi, and was driven to the White House for a 9:30 P.M. appointment with Herbert Hoover, then in his fifth week of office. The late hour and the anonymous cab protected a privacy that both the President and the millionaire desired. Durant's purpose was to implore Hoover to bridle the Federal Reserve Board. Neither man ever offered a detailed account of the brief conversation, but when the story of the meeting became public in the following year, reporters asked Durant if it was true that he had predicted a "financial disaster of unprecedented proportions."

"I intimated as much to him," was the reply.[76]

Durant's fears were disproportionate. The board and the President alike were inclined to no more than occasional verbal expressions of concern over the rampaging market, though the rediscount rate was raised in midsummer by a modest 3 percent. Conservative bankers were in fact worried that an untimely prediction of trouble ahead would trigger a selling landslide. They spoke with a wariness that did not tie the tongues of wholehearted believers in the gospel of prosperity through willpower, like Durant, who kept up his singleminded crusade with a zest no longer absorbed by work. On April 14 he bought time for a fifteen-minute radio address over New York's station WABC, and got the front-page headline that he expected in the next morning's *Times*: "W. C. Durant Demands Reserve Board Keep Its Hands off Business." Three days later he was off with Catherine on the *Aquitania* for the yearly European vacation. As always he would spend much of the late afternoon and evening in his hotel room on an overseas telephone line, paying hundreds of dollars each day for reports from the New York Exchange, where it was five hours earlier and flurries of trading traced out the curves of his destiny.

On the last day of May he was invited to give a speech at the American Club in Paris. It was a perfect setting for a full articulation of his credo, since the well-fed listeners had, for the most part, reached the city of light by courtesy of successful investments on their behalf. They were responsive to a message which mingled the clashing elements of their own national character in prosperity's high noon—exuberance and smugness; electric awareness of technology's potential for human happiness—and blindness to waste, injustice, and poverty. Durant told them that their prosperity rested on three props: the "efficient, low-priced motor-car; the high value we place on labor, and our ability to raise enormous sums of money for industrial development." "Where does this money come from, and why is it available for this purpose?" he asked.

A goodly portion of these funds represent[s] the surplus wealth which is being accumulated each year by an intelligent and energetic people and is being invested in our industrial institutions because of confidence in our country. Say what you will, confidence — not half-way confidence, but 100 per cent confidence (with a small portion of conservative optimism) is the real basis of our prosperity. With all the wealth in the world, confidence lacking, we never could have reached the position we occupy today, and this great asset, confidence, should not be destroyed. That is the reason why the business men of America are almost a unit against the present policy of the Federal Reserve Board.

He went on to explain, in elementary textbook language, the importance of stock issues in raising capital, and explained how the cloud-capped towers of prosperity were reared with the help of brokers. Margin buying was simply a way of capitalizing the future, and a high volume of brokers' loans was only "an evidence of prosperity." The securities that the brokers themselves held, or pledged as collateral to their banks, were carefully screened by knowing experts, and if "at times, by reason of overenthusiasm, certain securities sell above their proper value, it takes but a short time for this situation to correct itself, because in the long run in industrial undertakings, character of product, management and earnings are the determining factors."

The threat to the bonanza came from the eight men of the Federal Reserve Board who had taken it into their heads, "for reasons which no business men seem to understand," that brokers' loans were too high and that steps must be taken to curtail them.

As a result, hundreds of thousands of people, who have contributed to the prosperity of America, have lost hundreds of millions of dollars, while the Federal Reserve Board, in control of the life blood of the nation, Credit, sits idly by, unwilling to admit its error and not having the courage to reverse its decision. Result: Fear, trembling and destruction of confidence, so essential to our prosperity. The incapacity of these men in matters of finance, in which they are supposed to excel, has made the financial policy of America the laughing stock of the civilized world.[77]

Still charged with a sense of armed righteousness that was never part of his posture back in the early days, he returned on the *Majestic* on June 18 and gave the board more brimstone, but managed at the same time to avoid the dangerous prediction that its policies would actually cause a panic. While it was true, his homecoming interview conceded, that the board had weakened confidence by "lining up with the destructive forces of Wall Street, discriminating against our choicest securities, curtailing money and credit . . . fussing about brokers' loans, and interfering with business generally," the end result would be a triumph over negativism.

> We can and will have a "bull" market as soon as this question is settled and when it is settled, seasoned securities of merit and those having possibilities will sell much higher than ever before.[78]

The salesman in Durant had the necessary reassuring last word. The salvation he expected would come from a political curtailment of the board. On the August day when the rediscount rate went up, too little and too late, he uttered what was almost his last statement of the good times. "The day of reckoning is approaching. The business interests of this country are determined and will demand congressional investigation and proper control of this group of men."[79]

To speed along that demand, he continued to mail out free reprints of his Paris speech to a long list of corporation presidents. But the day of reckoning that he had anticipated was actually closer than he knew, and when it came, it was not the Federal Reserve Board that would be buried in the ruins. Once again, a falling market was to crush the fortunes of William C. Durant. This time, however, if he could extract any consolation from it, he would have the company in collapse of the entire nation.

On September 1, 1929, the total market value of the securities listed on the New York Stock Exchange stood at $89,668,276,854. On November 1, after waves of selling had sporadically washed through Wall Street, including the deluge of October 24, Black Thursday, the figure stood at $71,759,485,710. From nearly ninety billions to just over seventy, prices had toppled in sixty days, wiping out eighteen billions in paper fortunes. The stunned public was unaware that the worst was yet in store. There would be no more single catastrophic shocks, but the piecemeal crumbling would continue until, by July 1, 1932, the overall worth of the stocks handled on the Exchange would be down to approximately $15.6 billion.

More than money was lost. An entire view of life was changed for two ensuing decades at the least. Matthew Josephson said that the contrast between the twenties and thirties could be epitomized in the observation that "before October 1929 Americans lived from day to day . . . believing themselves well favored by fortune."[80] It was in that state of assumed grace that Durant had functioned best. But depression and war would put the notion of the purity of the American experience at least temporarily out of fashion. The master booster was obsolete. And broke.

The process of his impoverishment was deliberate but inexorable. Rumors would float through memoirs of the disaster, saying that he had sold his holdings before the bottom fell out of things, and then reentered the game too soon and unwisely. His records failed to give a precise answer, but in the end it did not matter whether he drowned in the first tidal wave or in succeeding breakers. The enormous size of his holdings delayed, but did not defer, the end.

In 1929, he bought some $210 millions' worth of stock, and received another $108 millions' worth from various sources such as splits, borrowings, reimbursements for services, and dividends paid in securities rather than in cash. He sold an approximate $244 millions in shares, and delivered others valued at $100 million in fulfillment of obligations. Though on paper this left him "ahead" by $26 million, the telltale indicator of trouble in his books was the set of figures revealing that his debit balance had been reduced from some $32.6 million to $6.9 million. In the curious economy of margin buying, year-end debts to brokers were normal. Durant had no more need to worry about them than a prospering merchant had to be concerned with his mortgage, or with unpaid balances on the goods filling his shelves.

The drop in debit balances, however, meant that Durant's brokers were no longer carrying him, but selling out his holdings for cash. In the mercantile analogy, the store owner was now facing demands for immediate payment to his creditors, which he was meeting by cleaning out his inventory at distress prices. He had fewer debts, and fewer prospects.

The 1930 books told a grimmer story. Durant had purchases and receipts of some 2.06 million shares valued at $86 million, and he sold and delivered 2.1 million, whose worth was recorded at $90 million. Once more, his $4 million "gain" went to pay off his debts. And a breakdown of the numbers showed how frantically he was cleaning his shelves. The shares that he bought came to 1.127 million with a value of $68.27 million, an average price of $60 to $61 per share. He sold 1.65 million shares for $72.5 million, an average of under $44 per share. He came out "ahead" by selling more, at lower prices, than he bought, and by handing over stock from other sources, at pitiful fractions of its original value, to pay off what he owed. His inventories dropped from 241,313 at the end of 1929 to 169,345 shares at the conclusion of 1930. He borrowed, never to return, 187,000 shares of GM from Catherine, and 157,500 shares which may or may not have been returned from Cliff and from his privately owned holding company, the Whittier Corporation. He received, "free," 180,000 shares of Durant

Motors stock from accounts that he had set up for Catherine and his children — and his creditors allowed him an approximate $1.50 a share for them. The overall average price for the 938,000 shares he received from sources other than purchases was $18. On the average, he was credited with about $38 a share for those that he delivered other than by sale. But the shares, both received and delivered, had originally cost sums running into the hundreds.

And the drain went remorselessly on. The great industrial names that had once sounded the cadences of prosperity were now crowded columns on a casualty list. In one three-month period he lost $80,000 on a single 3,000-share transaction in International Combustion Engineering, and $284,000 on 13,100 of National Cash Register, handled through five brokers — bought at an average price between $50 and $60, sold hopelessly and helplessly in ninety days at a little over $30.

And the man who believed that there was no ceiling on prosperity surveyed the year-end books and saw $140,000 lost on some 54,000 shares of U.S. Steel, $260,000 wiped out on a turnover of just under 11,000 of Vanadium Corporation, a $75,000 trimming on 4,000 General Electrics, and a stunning $3.36 million wipeout on 265,400 shares of Loew's. And then there were the huge deliveries, for pennies on the dollar, of shares with which he was well supplied. Nearly 64,000 Industrial Rayon delivered at $7 a share. A block of 182,000 GM turned over at the same figure, plus another 368,475 sold at a pallid $50. And 390,000 shares of Durant Motors unloaded for under $4 each on the average — in a year that saw the company sell all of 26,000 cars.[81]

Durant kept smiling throughout the endless weeks and months, while the whispers and the tales went from one financial columnist, one inside tipster to another. But John Thomas Smith's son recalled his father telling a story that probably dated from the end of 1930. The Durants and the Smiths had spent an evening on the town, celebrating some occasion. They were driving back to 907 Fifth, the two women seated in the back, the two men in jump seats just in front of them. In the darkness, broken only occasionally as they passed under a streetlight, something encouraged Durant to a moment of confession. He leaned over and put his hand gently on his old friend's knee.

"John Thomas," he said, "I'm wiped out."[82]

But that was private purgation. With the public, he maintained his own code — show no pessimism, and try to convert retreat into advance by setting the example of hope. One day late in the year a Wall Street reporter queried him about a rumor that he had been asked for $5 million in margin, failed to come up with it, and been sold out at a loss of over $20 million, "chiefly in his pet personal stocks, Industrial Rayon and International Combustion."

It was a rumor, said Durant, his mouth curved in a slight smile. "Some people like to spread harsh tales when it is just as easy to spread friendly ones." Then he leaned forward suddenly, and announced. "I'm the richest man in America"—pause, smile of impish pleasure.

"In friends," he finished.[83]

He was to learn how fast that capital would be eroded, too. What remained now was to be educated in reality. And, slowly, to die.

10)

Old Man in a

Dry Season

I When he opened his birthday mail on December 8, 1930, he found a greeting from Howard Clifford in the form of a poem, not claimed as original, for "my good friend, WILLIAM CRAPO DURANT,

> *the man*
> *Who has suffered and seen and knows,*
> *Who has measured his pace on the battle line*
> *And given and taken the blows,*
> *Who has never whined when the scheme went wrong*
> *Nor scoffed at the failing plan,*
> *But taken his dose with a heart of trust*
> *And the faith of a gentleman. . . .*
>
> *Who has gritted his teeth and clenched his fist*
> *And gone on doing his best,*
> *Because of his love for his fellow man*
> *And the faith in his manly breast.*
>
> Wishing with every good wish,
> Many years of happiness and health[1]

(335)

So he began his seventieth year under a new unwelcome sign, the valiant loser. With a flatterer's well-intentioned innocence, Clifford underscored that more had changed in Durant's life than his bank balance. The world saw him differently and ungraciously. There are no honored failures in American life. Towns like Flint did not have a role for brave but penniless ex-benefactors. The only way for a gentleman who had "taken his dose" was down.

As a sometime multimillionaire, Durant had only one advantage over men who lost on a smaller scale. It would take him longer to reach the approaches to destitution. But the road would lead through the same shadows and be just as steep and unretraceable.

He took a long time to travel it. There were to be seventeen years of absorbing those lessons of defeat that came especially hard to one who had given little of his mind to weighing alternatives to success. "He needed a challenge,"[2] a friend said of him, and in his old age he found his most exacting one, first in the struggle to make restitution, and then, failing in that, only to survive with dignity.

First there was anger, the rage of Lear still unable to believe himself shorn of his power. Throughout 1931 and 1932 Durant fought a series of small, uncoordinated public skirmishes with old enemies, darting from position to position on the unfamiliar terrain of politics where his naïveté was at its greenest. In the first postcrash year, when his opinions were still sought, he attacked Hoover for not arresting the movement toward higher interest rates, and predicted that the country would see "longer bread lines, more soup kitchens, continued uneasiness and distress, and a more pronounced tendency to socialism and communism" until such time as there was "a leadership that has the confidence of the people." In the long run, conditions would improve because Americans were "naturally . . . progressive and optimistic," and were living in "an age of big things." But the administration's mistake had been in letting the Federal Reserve Board interfere in the natural tidal rhythms of market confidence; it should "have left the business and industries of the United States to regulate themselves by the laws of supply and demand, and all would have been well today."[3]

But from this classical Republican laissez-faire position he jumped to the support of government guarantees of safe savings. He became the head and sponsor of an organization called the Bank Depositors' League, which, in the third winter of discontent after Black Thursday, solicited one-dollar contributions for a lobbying effort "to secure legislation to give depositors in national and state banks absolute protection . . . [and] provide safe and convenient places where people can put their money, with a United States government guarantee that it will be returned any time they ask for it." He drew, most probably, on his own dwindling funds to rent a Washington office and hire a secretary and a stenographer—the total outlay, with printing, telephone, and postage bills coming to a thousand dollars a month—and he paid an additional $6,000 a year to a retired Senator, Robert L. Owen of Oklahoma, to lead the effort on Capitol Hill. Owen was seventy-five years old, had a remote Cherokee ancestry, and was a veteran of Progressive fights against the "bank monopoly." He had been a drafts-man of the original Federal Reserve Act that created the erring Board of Governors, but Durant convinced himself that it was a "magnificent piece of legislation" that had suffered "damnable" abuse. The alliance itself was not so strange in those rudderless days, but Durant's desperation produced a brief flash of heresy in a postscript to one of his letters to Owen: "The capitalistic (so-called) system is a dismal failure."[4]

He did not linger long in the environs of eccentric radicalism, though he made a minor news item in the autumn of 1932 by announcing his intention to vote for Roosevelt. Meanwhile, he repeated his favorite device of the circular telegram, a quixotic gesture that he was prone to undertake whenever he was not profitably busy. On behalf of his league he wired an alleged ten thousand "leading statesmen, educators, economists and businessmen" a request for a yes-or-no answer to the query: "Are you in favor of providing safe and convenient places where the people of this country can deposit their money?" Only Will Rogers saw anything funny in the simplistic phrasing. "Dear Bill Durant," he responded, "I am going to answer 'No.' Has anybody else done that? You philosophers are always thinking up hard questions."[5]

As the election approached, Durant asked vainly for five hundred "prominent manufacturers and businessmen" to join him in a statement decrying "reckless preaching of the gospel of fear by thoughtless partisan politicians."[6] Four months later, on the eve of Roosevelt's inauguration, he was again questioning a list of luminaries as to what they thought of as the most important problem confronting the nation—the one which, given hypothetical absolute power, they would favor with "immediate and undivided attention." (The answers that survived in his files almost all singled out the banking crisis.)[7] And in mid-March of 1933 he implored Richard Whitney, then president of the New York Stock Exchange, to prohibit short selling as a necessary prop to confidence. Considering the state of things, he said in one of his final salvos against the bears,

the word TRAITOR is the only term that properly applies to the gam-blers who, without let or hindrance, and with the approval of your organization, are taking advantage of the weak and helpless and adding greatly to the demoralization now existing.[8]

None of these forays into opinion making had any consequence except for whatever help his lobby lent to the virtually uncontested passage of federal bank deposit insurance legislation in the spring of 1933. Moreover, he was soon back in his Republican moorings. But his thrusts at the public enemies whom he saw encircling his shrinking perimeter of optimism were delivered with a spasmodic, unfocused irritability that showed pain and fear breaking through his private defenses.

Still, even in rage, he could rise from time to time to the old grandeur of scale. In January of 1930 he suddenly became the target of a lurid charge. He was a partner with a friend and broker named Samuel Ungerleider in the Ungerleider Financial Corporation, an investment trust. Shares worth some $700,000 had been held by a wealthy divorcée, Mrs. P. K. Hudson. When they collapsed in value after the crash, she was asked to put up more margin on them, failed to do so, and was sold out. This had taken place while she was out of the country, and on her return she claimed in the press to have learned that Durant and Ungerleider were guilty of a criminal conspiracy. They had let the stock fall to 50, sold quantities of it to a dummy buyer at that price, then repurchased them at 52 with company funds and split the take with their confederates.

Durant's answer was to announce a libel suit against the six newspapers, one newsreel company, and two wire services involved in playing the story. The collective sum he was asking was $40,000,000, the largest claim for libel damages in history. Mrs. Hudson's attorney and the offending editors, discovering that the accusation was entirely groundless, backed away in profuse, apologetic horror. Durant, contented with the glow of one retrospective moment of his former style, dropped the matter there.[9]

Other litigations, however, did not go so well for him. He was sued by one of his brokers, Sailing W. Baruch, for a past due balance of $4,681 and lost. He filed a counterclaim for $70,000, alleging that a member of the Baruch firm had knowingly given him a false tip that caused him to buy 3,000 shares of International Combustion Engineering, which instantly dived 25 points.[10] He lost that case, too, and in the process made a forlorn admission of how little he resembled any longer the great seer to whom others went begging for an unveiling of the market future. At the end of 1930 another action was begun against him that stirred especially painful recall. The plaintiff was Ben Block, his old ally, whose firm had once, in the bright years of Durant's being the primal father bull, carried sixteen Durant accounts — four in his own name, six for his Whittier Corporation, one each for Catherine, Randolph Hicks, and Eddie Rickenbacker (who had married Cliff's divorced first wife), and three for associates from Durant Motors and other enterprises. In October of 1930, Durant owed Block a full $2.4 million, secured by stocks of considerably smaller value. Block was in the process of liquidating this debt by selling the collateral, when Durant tried, from New Jersey, to enjoin him. It was then that Block countersued to bring the matter into what he believed to be the friendlier courts of New York. So old acquaintance yielded to both parties' struggle for existence. Durant, after three years of legal delays, lost that one, too.[11]

And even where he was a winner in the courts, the extremity of his situation turned success rancid in the cup. As 1932 closed, Satterlee and Canfield informed him that they had persuaded the government to compromise with him in a dispute over the size of his income taxes for 1923 through 1927, and for 1929. He had a refund of $116,431 coming to him. But, they explained, submitting neatly supportive tables and charts, the amounts they had actually saved him, counting penalties and interest, amounted to upward of $1.75 million, for which a fee of more than $300,000 would normally be considered reasonable. In view of "present conditions," however, they would in kindness take only his refund, leaving him with a net gain of zero.

The dethroned tycoon pleaded with them, offered a larger fee if they would give him only $31,000 in instant cash and take his note for another $109,000. The answer was sheathed in Wall Street iron. Satterlee himself replied, the same Satterlee who had turned down his first appeal for the financial midwifery of General Motors twenty-five years earlier. "I trust that upon further reflection you will realize that our firm has made all the concession that can reasonably be asked of it."[12]

Along with anger and in its train came humiliation, and following humiliation, awareness of how bad things were. All of the elements of wealth were disappearing one by one, snuffed out like a row of candles, and often after an embarrassing sequence of protests and entreaties. Durant Motors first and foremost. In the summer of 1930 Durant discharged three of his four manager-morticians, resumed control, juggled, and promised. Once again he announced plans for manufacturing an American version of a small foreign auto, the Mathis, but they were dead before the echo of his voice had faded. He cut loose affiliates, sold off some parts companies and merged others. In vain, and in February of 1931, he placed a small order for supplies with several of the parts manufacturers who had once stood in line for his favors. They looked at his preceding year's balance sheet, shook their heads and denied him credit. He had overlooked certain obligations in listing liabilities, and among "assets" he had included such tragicomic items as an option to repurchase the collateral of an unpaid note, which the lender had seized. It was the kind of bubble-blowing that had been brilliant in the early days of expansion. Now it simply led to refusals and rejoinders of shabby dignity:

I understand that at the conference not only was the statement questioned, but there was (to be perfectly frank) a reflection upon my honesty
and integrity. While I have no objection, and you have a perfect right to
discuss Durant Motors, I cannot permit the reflection upon my honor
and integrity to go unchallenged.[13]

It was no use. Neither apologies nor further accommodation followed his
indignant explanation that the company was "worth every dollar" he
claimed for it, and that in any case he had merely intended to help the
suppliers through his order, by relieving them of "the burden of high
pressure production if by chance a seasonable spring business might
develop." And so he walked away from the encounter, keeping his back
straight and shutting his ears to the laughter, and by April the receivers
were having the fixtures removed from the Durant Motors New York
offices, and the company's attorney, Henry Herbermann, was fighting
foredoomed delaying actions against the creditors whom he aptly described
in one note as "after us."[14] It was not long before the final remaining
properties were sold or forfeited.

Liberty National Bank gasped its last around the same time. Durant
himself owed it $402,000 in March of 1931, and in turn it was behind
$50,000 in its rent. Its average deposit was a mere $1,600. Durant turned
the skills he had once used to purchase entire corporations into the
fabrication of intricate deals for changing collateral, shifting notes, and
purchasing stocks at arbitrarily set values, all to save a few thousand
dollars in cash. The end result was the same as with the shards of his motor
empire — forced sale of Liberty's remaining assets for a fraction of their
value.[15]

He dropped out of the other corporations in which he had taken some
interest, one by one and reason by reason, but always against the same
dark background of inability to continue his investment. Something went
wrong early at International Combustion Engineering, for in the immediate
aftermath of the 1929 collapse he wired an old friend who had asked about
buying some of its stock at bargain rates: "Would not buy International
Combustion. Have been misled regarding financial position of company.
Management has proved to be incompetent." He correctly predicted a
receivership soon after.[16]

He stayed with Industrial Rayon until early in 1933, then resigned
abruptly as a director over a mysterious disagreement on some new policy.
His departure was possibly hastened by the sale of the company to the Du
Ponts.[17]

American Cottonpicker had held the greatest possibility for becoming
another Frigidaire. In one of his moments of uncanny prognostication,
Durant had foreseen the drift to agribusiness, writing in a prospectus of the

1920s that "eventually men will understand farming at wholesale, fight pests with flying machines scattering poison, and pick cotton by machinery." The machine itself, pictured in a brochure, possessed a folksy charm that seemed appropriate to the South, and, like the Iron Horse, was intended to provide for a gradual transition from the old ways to the new. It was a kind of hand-drawn vacuum cleaner, from which multiple hoses stretched like octopus tentacles. Field workers applied them to the bolls, which were gently sucked into the collecting tank. One expert thought that it needed only a mule to pull it to make it a certain hit among cotton farmers, who did not want to do "a mule's work" in hauling it along the rows.[18]

But whether it would have become the nucleus of a modernized cotton-growing industry or not would never be known. Durant had put approximately $175,000 into Frederick Stukenborg's invention in the twenties, but in 1930 he no longer had money to continue paying salesmen and demonstrators.[19] The company was stranded in mid-development, staggered into a reorganization, and then collapsed into bankruptcy. It was one of his losing bets on the future, and this time he had no stake left with which to return to the table. He and the American public had marched through panics and setbacks together before, shaking them off, knowing that they were God's chosen and that all roadblocks were temporary. Now they seemed unable to rid themselves of the paralysis whose grip grew tighter with each month of the Depression.

Of the hundreds of thousands of shares that had once stuffed his stock portfolio, a few crumbs remained. He reported small holdings to the Internal Revenue Service, many of them stocks that would one day recover—GM, Chrysler, Curtiss Wright, American Telephone and Telegraph, Montgomery Ward, and others. But some were under liens, some not in his own name, none were then paying dividends to speak of, and all went eventually to meet the debts that never stopped mounting. In 1933 he reported a gross income of $9,478 and a net of only $3,731. He did slightly better in 1934, grossing $15,171, then dropped to $4,528. In 1936, the year that ended with his seventy-fifth birthday, his net income was $5,428.[20]

By that time the inevitable bankruptcy had been declared. The precise date was February 8, 1936, when the full dimensions of his ruin became a matter of record. His petition in bankruptcy, filed in New York's Federal District Court, was accompanied by a declaration that maintained a brave front.

My petition in bankruptcy, filed today, is due to frequent and repeated court proceedings instituted by a few creditors, representing less than 5 per cent of my total obligations, who have attempted to obtain a preferential position.

Action by the creditors referred to has prevented me from giving my best efforts to rebuilding my fortune, and I no longer propose to be harassed and annoyed. I wish to state that all creditors will be treated alike, and if fortune favors me all will be paid in full.[21]

That was his way, to go out with a promise that he was still at work, still planning to compensate those who trusted him. He had to cling to the life raft of an unchanged personal style insofar as he could manage it. No one ever saw him in anything but impeccable clothes, and when he traveled in the early thirties, he still stayed at the good hotels. "You'd never know he was broke," John Anderson said after seeing him in Detroit.[22]

But the courts knew and the newspaper-reading public knew after that winter day. His declared debts were $914,000, mostly in judgments to brokers and landlords. He owed $175,000 to Cusick, and $21,000 to Benjamin Block, $55,000 to Arthur Lipper and Company, $40,000 to Fenner, Beane and Ungerleider, and $118,000 to George Armsby of 44 Wall Street. There was a judgment of $105,000 to E. E. C. Mathias of Paris, the flotsam of the last-ditch effort to save Durant Motors with an imported design. There were $30,000 in arrears of rent owing to the company that owned 907 Fifth Avenue, from which he had moved into a smaller Park Avenue apartment, and a full $120,000 claimed by the 1767 Broadway Corporation for office rentals. There were sums that were the fruit of defaulted bank loans — about $30,000 claimed by the National City Bank of Cleveland, and another $20,000 due to the Guardian Trust Company of the same city. And a scattering of obligations to individuals.

To meet them all, he said, he had $250 worth of clothes left to him out of all that he had built and owned. Everything else was in Catherine's name, and going fast. There were notes in his neat handwriting, estimating what her jewels would bring. "1 pear emerald, 1 pear diamond, 3-4 round diamonds, paid 19,000, today's replacement, 15,000; marquise diamond, 60 round diamond, paid 55,000, today's replacement 40,000,"[23] and so on. What pledges of redemption he made to Catherine, what hopes of future luck he nursed, and what realities may have pierced through them can only be guessed.

The ultimate seal of defeat did not come until September of 1938, when the dream castle vanished into the past along with the lost factories, assembly lines, machines, warehouses, and showrooms. The Durants had stopped living at Raymere by the time of his bankruptcy, and could barely pay a caretaker to look after its untenanted chambers, filled with ghosts of extravagance past. When it proved impossible to find a single buyer in a time when splendor was no longer in fashion, Meredith Galleries of New

York was given the task of auctioning off the contents. It took five days, beginning on a Tuesday with the sale of the third-floor items. A Louis XVI suite in the master bedroom went for $350. Mrs. "Buddy" Clark, wife of a radio entertainer, bought a Sheraton bedroom suite for $250. With that beginning, the tone was set for the following days' scavenging. On Wednesday and Thursday, crowds of up to 300 paid tiny sums for the gold-rimmed goblets, the translucent porcelain, the cunningly woven rugs, the bronze statuettes, the carved chests, the china figurines, the centuries-old tapestries, one of which went for $375 and another for $200. On Friday the contents of the library, the billiard room, and the reception rooms were disposed of, for a total of $6,823, as against the $12,851 that the two preceding days had brought in.

Monday was a day of heavy rain, and fifty buyers pawed over what was left in the garage and the servants' quarters. Through it all, Durant stood at the front door, watching the files of men crossing and recrossing the lawn, staggering under the shape and weight of the boxes of books, the stone turtles, the gaming and billiard tables, the limp and trussed draperies and carpetings. Vans lined the yellow brick road, swallowing his and "Muddie's" showpieces. When the figures were totted up, he would find that with the $44,000 an unnamed purchaser's agent paid for the house and grounds, plus the receipts for the contents, he — or rather, the creditors — had garnered $111,778 for the property whose furnishings alone had been appraised a year earlier at over $300,000.[24]

Reporters for the local press gathered around him, shielding their notebooks from the drops, straining to catch the spoken words above the wet sounds of the morning. They were after the popular pathos of the fallen giant in farewell. But Durant spoke to them in the same softly positive tone that he had used when he was predicting a million cars on the road thirty years earlier. He said that he was relieved to be rid of Raymere. Its upkeep had been a burden on him, and he would now be free to use his resources for some projects he had in preparation.[25]

There was no snapping, this time, at the enemies of "confidence" in the business system. Durant was not merely making a brave exit. He was learning to smile again for the public.

II The bankruptcy declaration had been a bitter moment for Durant, and yet its sequel was a flow of spontaneous, comforting letters that reminded him of the existence of the hosts of ordinary friends who, it now turned out, cared about him still, even though he could no longer be a benefactor. Just as people identified themselves with him in his 1921 overthrow by "Wall Street," they saw him in 1936 as a fellow victim of the bitter times, and in reassuring him of the prospects of revival, they were heartening themselves. But mostly they were responding to a remembered warmth that he himself might have forgotten in the years of steadily ebbing fortunes. From Alfred Goebel, an elevator starter whose acquaintance with Durant went back to the takeoff days of Durant Motors, came a letter whose emotional value could not be measured on any numerical scale.

Dear Mr. Durant:

With sadness I read the article in the Sunday News of Feb. 9 and I do hope, and pray, that it isn't as serious as it reads.

It brought back to me, sweet memories of the Gotham Bank building, where I have spent many happy hours playing checkers with you, and although twelve years have passed, it can never be erased from my memory, not alone the playing of checkers, but your wonderful kindness to all the employees of the building, and on that Saturday, when the firm moved to the Fisk building, there was genuine sadness on the face of each, and every elevator operator.

Some years ago I tried ever so hard to see you at the Post Graduate Hospital, but was unable to get past the desk, but I kept myself posted on the progress of your condition through the daily papers, and words cannot explain how glad I was to read that you had fully recovered from your injuries. Please excuse me for writing this letter, and I do hope, Mr. Durant, that you are in the very best of health.[26]

Someone with the symbolic name of Jack Little wrote from Columbus, Ohio, that he hoped Durant kept "that 'million dollar smile.'" One, John Corcoran, of Cincinnati, sent a letter on the stationery of the Corcoran Manufacturing Company, Sheet Metal Products, and explained that the company itself was no longer in existence and he was in fact currently "bossing a W.P.A. gang." But, he added, "I am telling you this to let you know a man can take a good licking and still make good. Cheer up, Billy, and things will work out all right."

From the midwestern towns the words of consolation were unstinted. "I would make any sacrifice possible to assist you. . . . You always treated your friends like a prince, and I profited by such kindness. . . . You have the courage, honesty and the *guts* and friends to stage the *big come back.* . . . Whatever the future may bring forth for you, you have the satisfaction of great accomplishments. . . . The automobile and the electric refrigerator would not be what they are today except for your outstanding pioneer work."[27]

To all of them he replied with what was something of a form letter. "My coat is off and sleeves rolled up, and am working sixteen hours a day as usual, laying the foundation for a comeback, and if kind letters from my many friends mean anything I will surely make the grade."[28] Kindness was a restorative, but even as he rallied under its influence, he seemed to know that the best he could hope for thenceforward was to achieve small, essential gains that held the wolf at bay a short while longer. He could still outline ambitious projects, maintain the promoter's eloquence. But he spoke only infrequently for the record of any actual sums to be realized. The dreams of millions had finally yielded to the earthy recognition of the need for thousands — or only hundreds.

He foraged about for opportunities as undiscriminatingly as his Grandfather Crapo had done in his youthful days in New Bedford. His files testified to his willingness to try anything. He offered his old salesman's ability to a friend, Samuel Rosoff, a subway construction millionaire, who found himself the owner of a Brooklyn brewery. "My Dear Sam: In the event that I can work out a deal . . . on terms acceptable to you, will you allow me a commission of 5%?" And on the margins of his carbon copy of the letter he scrawled excitedly: "Located in Brooklyn near Wmsburg Bridge, central location for distribution to all points in Metro Dist. Selling 130,000 bbl. today; can expand to 300,000 within one year if management is efficient." But the arrangement was never reached; apparently, the sales talk delivered but no bargain struck. A year later he was writing to Rosoff at a Chicago address, enclosing a clipping that told of newly contemplated subway construction. "If you are interested in the contract, let me know and I will follow it up." The only response was a friendly but imprecise note offering, at some unstated time, to "discuss the matter."[29]

He also gave careful attention to mail that once would have gone into his wastebasket. Most of it came from inventors who still believed that Durant's powers could turn pebbles into diamonds and lift the pebble finders from the shadowy world of frustrated expectations that was the dwelling place of so many souls in the thirties. Someone wanted his help in financing the manufacture of a "remote control unit for radio," devised by "Radio-Vision Research Labs."[30] Someone wanted his assistance in furthering the fortunes of BOST toothpaste, a dentifrice of unparalleled power, named for its chemist creator, Dr. William Dale Bost, who had given the world "Orange Crush," and whose initials were also an acronym for Beware of Smokers' Teeth.[31] Someone held the patents to a power-driven scooter called the Motor Glide, and was certain that between himself and Mr. Durant they could turn it into a delivery vehicle called a "package car" that would have unlimited sales.[32] Someone controlled the Commonwealth Lead Mining Company, and besought the wizard to guide him to a "responsible banking house or a strong syndicate" that would provide a mere $200,000 of loan funds to make "large production" a possibility.[33]

The proposals for marketing new gadgets always received special care, often in the form of responses outlining elaborate schemes of incorporation and borrowing that would never quicken with life. Having risen to success on the thrust of the most successfully mass-marketed invention of all time, he kept a special place in his heart for anything novel. The mere discussion of such an item could kindle old sparks. John Thomas Smith's son recalled one moment around 1938 when Durant was describing to his father some coin-operated vending device in which he was interested. "It's so wonderful, John," he said. "You just take a quarter and put it in the machine . . ." and he reached into his pocket, took out a quarter and made the gesture of dropping it into a slot, his face alight and his eyes off on some distant vista as if he were speaking, thirty-five years earlier, of a new Buick model.[34]

The reality of his day-to-day economic plight only occasionally reached the daylight of publicity. When it did, it made colorful if misleading copy. In September of 1936 Durant leased to various concessionaires an abandoned Durant Motors showroom in Asbury Park, in which they established a food market and an adjacent lunchroom. On the eve of the grand opening, Durant had turned up to provide instructions to the employees on how to keep the surroundings spotless, as he always desired them. A newspaper photographer was present, and had an inspiration. Would Mr. Durant pose while demonstrating the best way to wash a dish? Mr. Durant was pleased to oblige, and readers the next day were presented with a picture of a man who had once been worth fifty to one hundred million dollars, a cloth in one hand, a saucer in the other, apparently reduced to the subbasement of the employment market.[35]

Follow-up stories soon dispelled the idea that Durant was a kitchen worker, but replaced it with an equally inaccurate conception that he was comfortably situated and enjoyed an adequate income from properties that had escaped the net of bankruptcy proceedings, or been restored to him after his discharge from them. He did have morsels of Michigan and New Jersey real estate left, but their yield was no more than token. The small houses of Deal Gables rented for only $65 or $75 monthly, the tenants were often in arrears, and Durant himself was unable to pay the real estate taxes. Though they were not large, even an assessment of approximately $100 a year multiplied by twenty or thirty lots proved too much to handle. By 1941, the tax delinquencies of the Deal Gables Corporation had mounted, with penalties and interest, to some $35,000 or more, and the remnants of the little domain that had clustered around Raymere went, like the mansion itself, under the hammer.[36]

For a time, Deal Gables had resembled the camp of an exiled monarch and the remnants of his entourage. Durant and Catherine occupied one of the houses in the summers that saw them unable any longer to finance the upkeep of Raymere. Winfred Murphy stayed on until the real estate work that he had undertaken carried him away to Kew Gardens, in the outskirts of New York. And one of the "cottages" was occupied, for part of the thirties, by a new and useful friend, Aristo Scrobogna.

Scrobogna was a twenty-five-year-old immigrant from Trieste when he first met the Durants in 1933. The youngest of eleven children, left fatherless in his youth, he had grown up in the turmoil of post-Versailles Europe, making a livelihood in whatever way he could, including a brief fling at professional boxing. Opportunity seemed to beckon from America when an uncle invited him over and promised help while Scrobogna fulfilled an ambition to study medicine. But the uncle died and the Depression struck almost at the same time, and the dark, curly-haired young immigrant found himself scraping for whatever odd jobs he could find in order to support a wife and infant daughter in a new world whose golden streets had turned to ashen alleys.

Scrobogna was well-read, energetic, and articulate. One of his friends in the Italian community of New York was a well-off woman who invited friends to parties at which Scrobogna provided a combination of entertainment and adult education. He would explain and describe various Italian operas while Signora Longori played passages from them. At one of these gatherings Mrs. Randolph Hicks showed up with Catherine Durant. Presently Scrobogna was invited to Raymere and met Durant himself. Before long, there was a ripening association based on a curious attraction between the older midwestern and the younger continental couple.

Durant liked the fact that Scrobogna undertook a vast variety of jobs with unflagging energy. He did translations, he managed properties, he handled real estate transactions, he was not too proud to be a chauffeur or a handyman when need seemed to demand those services. He may have reminded Durant of his own hustling youth of selling cigars, insurance, patent medicines, and the services of the gas and water companies of Flint. Eventually Durant put Scrobogna on the payroll of the Pomeroy-Day Company, the holding company for his Flint property, and Scrobogna cheerfully referred to him as "Boss" but continued, he reported later, to be "his own man on the side."

Mathilde Scrobogna, too, was furiously active, a clothing and fashion designer as well as a deft household manager. It was her habit to rise at six and begin working, and Durant, who also got up with the dawn, often dropped by at the cottage for breakfast. Catherine, who was shy and lonely, enjoyed the uncomplicated warmth of her hardworking neighbors, who bubbled with Mediterranean enthusiasm. Both Durants became quasi-grandparents to young Estelle. Catherine was known to her as Zia (aunt) and Durant referred to himself as her "Old Boy."

Scrobogna began his relationship to Durant, he afterward said, very conscious of the trappings of power that were still present in 1933, even thinking that there might one day be a restoration in which he could have some small share. But as loss followed loss, it became clear to him that the old man was past his greatness. Yet as the facade of sovereignty crumbled away, he saw an emerging gentleness and humanity that made him one of the last of a long line of men and women whom "Willie" had charmed. And he was stirred to admiration, too, at how the coals still glowed — how Durant's eyes would dart around a room, his quick and pointed questions fly, his mind leap to seize an idea even at seventy or seventy-five years of age.

So Scrobogna became friend, secretary, companion, nurse, helper, prop as the man went down into the valley. It was not an undemanding role, in Flint or in New York. Those who serve as agents and messengers of dethroned and dependent titans rarely travel an easy or popular path, and Scrobogna's actual credentials seem to have been now and again misunderstood. Moreover, he had to endure occasional bursts of imperial temper from Durant himself. Yet he carried on, loyal but not blinded, subordinate but not menial, keeping some private pact of fealty, not merely to Durant, but to whatever it was that Durant stood for in his mind — an ideal, a symbol, a folk-memory, a model, a missing piece of his life. He was the last of an array of different men to be close to Durant, or at least as close as Durant's nature allowed.[37]

Deal Gables struggled on toward its 1940 demise. The Asbury Park food center collapsed. The great inventions remained limp puppets, with no financial strings to make them dance. Oddly assorted enterprises led to nothing — and in one instance, to disgrace. Durant used some of what little was left to him in 1938 to buy a seat on the Chicago Board of Trade, where he became associated with a man named Joseph Buchhalter in what was known as the Buchhalter Plan of Trading. It was a curious kind of gambling in grain futures. Customers gave Buchhalter deposits and the power to make contracts in their name. He would then make agreements for them both to sell and to buy at existing prices. Whenever the price fluctuated up or down by a cent, he would execute that contract on which there was a profit, inform the customer of his winnings, deduct a commission, and leave the other, or losing position "open."

At a remove of many years, it is hard to see where the profit lay for the customer. In effect, he was betting both entries in a two-horse race, and what he won on the one he would lose on the other. But there was supposed to be a formula that would, in some mysterious, long-run fashion, return a small excess of gain over loss. On March 15, 1939, however, the Department of Agriculture's regulatory agency for the grain market stepped in with an accusation of criminal fraud against the operators of the Buchhalter Plan. The charge was that the method of operation deluded the customers, informing them of their profits and charging them, but leaving them unaware of counterbalancing losses until much later. After a year of hearings Buchhalter, Durant, Catherine, and another partner in the enterprise, were formally banned from the commodities market. It was in all respects a minor episode in Durant's final years, and if there was wrongdoing it seems almost a certainty that the seventy-seven-year-old man, tired and broke, was unaware of exactly where his sin lay.[38]

Nevertheless, it capped a melancholy decade with a crowning mortification. Each day his temperament, long confirmed in its resistance to images of death and decay and habituated to dwell on signs of strength and renewal, was tried with more of the cruelties that life knew how to inflict on the aging and the beaten. Yet amid the casualty reports and the steady disappearance of landmarks and powers, he kept up a front that showed nowhere so bravely as when he returned to face Flint.

III He came and went quietly, slipping almost unnoticed into the downtown hotel that General Motors had helped to build and had named for him in a gesture of appeasement to his city. Flint was no longer the dirt-alleyed nest of closely linked families, the shell out of which he had pecked his way. It was larger, less personal, cruelly stricken by the hard times, full of boarded windows and locked gates. There was a comradeship of mutual suffering, but the old paternalism had worn thin, and would disappear in January of 1937 in the shattering days and nights of the sit-down strike that forced General Motors to come to terms with the United Auto Workers.

For Durant it was full of ghosts, accusations, and properties that required his attention. Bert Pomeroy and Melzor Day had run them for him in the good times of the twenties, and brought in over $20,000 a year in profit—hardly enough to buy Catherine a bagatelle then, or justify his notice. But in his years of need he gradually moved back into full management of the Pomeroy-Day operation, and began, as with all his other possessions, to liquidate it, a task that ran on into the war decade.

In the beginning of 1935 he involved himself in another small undertaking that was a tacit acknowledgment of his reduced horizons. Three veterans of the early days of A.C. Spark Plug manufacture, A. R. Campbell, G. G. Somers, and R. B. Vessey, had gone into the business independently, styling themselves the C.V.S. Manufacturing Company. Who took the initiative was not spelled out, but they came to an agreement with Durant that reflected a trust in him not yet entirely dimmed. Among the numerous incorporations which Durant had spawned as profusely as frogs' eggs was an organization known as Crown Point Products, a distributing concern for automotive products. The three partners of C.V.S. laid joint plans with their long-ago employer (whom they now made a vice-president) to market their "Flint" plugs through Crown Point's extensive contacts.

The enterprise got under way with expansive hopes that were soon buried under disillusionment. "Arch" Campbell, who, as the company's treasurer, bore the major burden of dealing with Durant, found that the man, in his decline, was no easier to pin down than when he had held dozens of factories in his grasp. Durant, for his part, even with the utmost goodwill, could not focus his mind on the day-to-day commonplaces and miniature crises of routine business operations. Campbell wrote letter after letter, talking of accounts past due, of price changes, of raw materials that needed ordering, of difficulties on the technical side. And Durant, increasingly, sent replies through Murphy, who was an officer in the Crown Point concern. He kept Campbell waiting for his attention as he had once kept far more powerful men at General Motors dangling, and produced no results that would have justified the treatment. Although he kept ordering C.V.S. to produce more plugs in anticipation of great demand, there were few sales, despite Durant's preparation, with his own hand, of a pamphlet entitled: "Why the Crown Point Spark Plug Is a Perfect Plug and How It Is Made."

By mid-1937 Campbell was losing heart. Plugs with the Crown Point label were crowding the warehouse, receipts were down, and there seemed to be no way of capturing the errant vice-president for even a brief consideration of company problems. As 1938 started, Campbell pleaded with Murphy: "We have a serious problem confronting us here and can make no decision as to future activities until we know what Mr. Durant's plans are as to the future of Crown Point." Murphy could be consolatory, but he could not deliver Durant—not even for a February directors' meeting, which the onetime miracle worker skipped, at which it was decided to give up at last and go out of business.

Yet Campbell was not liberated for another two years from his futile pursuit. What he wanted was Crown Point's payment for 10,000 finished plugs that had sat on the shelves since 1936. The letters continued, respectful but in unmistakable pain: "We have been writing and talking about this subject for the past two years. . . . Disposition of your inventory . . . holding up entire company program. . . . You move around so fast that I do not know whether this will reach you in New York or not. . . . Had hoped to hear from you regarding the plan I first suggested to you last February and then again in April." And, finally, on June 6, 1941:

Am turning over all corporation affairs to be handled by auditor Mr. Hawes and attorney within ten days. . . .

There is no use reviewing the history of our loss thru Crown Point, and naturally the stockholders realize the fact that you were also an officer of C.V.S. during this period. Now I have done all I can to avoid unpleasant action, taking a personal loss. . . .

It seems you should give this your serious consideration and not sidetrack it for everything else — you said three weeks when I saw you last April. I too am busy, one reason for turning everything over to attorney, then too, I will be leaving Flint soon. So I am bringing this to your attention once more, and for the last time, as I am just about sick and tired of it after trying to clean up for the past two years.

Durant's answer came a full two months later, a royal gesture of forgiveness to a too-importunate follower. "Carrying out the spirit outlined in my letter of March 28," he announced, "I am assigning to the C.V.S. Manufacturing Co., in full settlement of Crown Point Products, Inc. account, the entire assets of the Crown Point Products, Inc."

The entire assets were a $112.68 cash balance in the Chemical Bank, minus a $50 legal fee. Total, $62.50. And three assigned accounts, one with an Italian firm cut off from imports since 1940.[39]

Yet what Arch Campbell remembered thirty-five years after that final communication was not the disappointment or the lost money, but the man's pathetic dignity and courage. "He was a lonely man in Flint," Campbell recollected. "Nobody had time for him, even men that he'd made millionaires." There were exceptions, like his grandnephew, Sidney Stewart, and a onetime Durant sales executive named Ralph Workman. But any time, evening or weekend, that Campbell wanted to see him on the occasions when Durant managed to come to town, he could count on finding him alone in his room. Howard Clifford would have had time for him, but Clifford was gone. He had surmounted the past and won election as mayor in 1934. On a May day in the following year, he collapsed in his office and was rushed to the hospital, suffering from a stroke that proved mortal. Durant happened to be in Flint at the time. He showed up at Clifford's bedside in Hurley Hospital and sat wordlessly alongside the family, until the anticipated end came. Then he walked heavily out into a city diminished for him by one more subtraction from the roster of faith.[40]

But forgotten or not, Durant kept the aura of command, and Campbell could do nothing but admire and obey. Durant would call early on a Sunday morning and ask Campbell to come down and write some letters for him, and it was unthinkable not to oblige. Once, on a Sunday, too — it was the autumn of 1939 — Durant thrust a bundle of flyers into Campbell's surprised hands and told him to distribute them outside several churches. Campbell glanced at the contents. Durant was, it appeared, on another political crusade. He was an isolationist, and the leaflets were an attack on Roosevelt's proposal to amend the nation's neutrality laws so as to permit the French and British to buy American munitions on a cash-and-carry basis. Campbell had neither a profound interest nor any abiding convictions on the subject, but "you didn't say no to Mr. Durant," and the petition against the amendments was duly circulated.

One of Campbell's final recollections was of a night on which Durant had fallen into a discussion with one of the partners on the subject of cheese, and promised to bring in some specimens for a tasting just before a management meeting. A bitter snowstorm was lashing the city, but Durant got Campbell to drive him to a dairy and wait in the car. Suddenly Campbell looked out to see the old man, staggering under the burden of packages with enough cheeses for "twenty or thirty people," fighting his way up a snowbank. He did nothing that was picayune; his plume remained as spotless as Cyrano's. "I never saw anybody like him," Campbell mused. "Even when he should have been despondent and down in the mouth the average person who had just met him wouldn't have known. He could take it."[41]

Late in 1939 a new conception took hold of Durant. Producing money from somewhere, he had a contractor turn one of Pomeroy-Day's properties, an empty garage near the Buick works, into an eighteen-lane bowling alley with deep blue and red appointments against cream-colored walls. He supervised every step of the preparation himself, enlisting Scrobogna to come out and paint, sweep, measure, load, and rearrange. Then, just prior to the grand opening, he spoke to reporters.

Was he a reduced figure? A man who had once been sovereign in Flint, now preparing to start a small business of entertaining the workers whom he had once hired by the thousands, collecting their dimes and quarters for shoe rentals and soft drinks? Not at all. Twirling a pince-nez on the end of a silk cord, he sketched out his project in its true dimensions — a wholesome flight into social self-improvement, a large-scale venture that would, like all the products he had sold in his long life, transform the user for the better. His plan was to lift bowling from its spit-and-sawdust atmosphere, and purge it of disrespectability. He would offer "bowling without beer." The enterprise was called North Flint Recreation, Inc., and was to be only "the first unit of a chain of recreational centers . . . for 'clean sports' in cities throughout the United States." Bowling had a "noble tradition," required "delicate co-ordination of brain and muscle," and belonged on a "morally wholesome plane." Soon there would be a second alley run on his new principles in Flint, and this would foreshadow the future by admitting women; more, would be owned and managed by them. Like the first one, it would encourage the participation of church groups — and have a parking lot.

It was a performance that rose to a final, curtain-lowering climax. "I haven't a dollar," the promoter beamed, "but I'm happy and I'm carrying on because I find I can't stop. . . . Many people value money too highly; I'm trying now to do good for as many people as possible. After all, money is only loaned to a man; he comes into the world with nothing, and he goes out with nothing."[42]

Style was all. A man might go out with nothing, but the flower in his lapel must be fresh. After the bowling alley had been in operation for a time, he opened a lunchroom adjacent to it, with counter service at a horseshoe-shaped bar, and a drive-in window. The floor had peach-colored carpeting, and a customer who showed up with dirty shoes was sometimes directed at the door to take his food at the outdoor wicket or not at all. The waitresses wore uniforms especially designed by Mathilde Scrobogna. And to a young married woman named Annabel Haskins whom he hired to help manage the place, he laid down strict rules. Inventories must always be kept high, malteds thick, dishes and silverware hot. He would, on occasion, demonstrate the making of a hamburger himself, much as he had created the 1910 Oldsmobile by sawing a Buick in quarters and enlarging its dimensions under the eyes of the engineers.

A man might go out with nothing, but the last dollar must be spent with the same carelessness as if there were thousands to follow it. Sometimes he would order Annabel Haskins to close the place to the public, and then he would hold a party for a few visiting friends from New York, with dinner cooked by a chef specially hired for the occasion. And when he paid he paid in cash from a briefcase full of bills that he carried, perhaps so that no one could question his credit.

But Annabel Haskins remembered moments when the bravado slipped. She and her husband, like Campbell, could always count on finding him alone in the Durant Hotel on Saturday nights or Sundays, when Flint bustled with family recreations. They fell into the habit of offering him a Sunday drive now and again, and his most frequent request was to be taken by what he still called "my plant." By that he meant the Flint Six factory, metamorphosed into a Fisher Body works by 1940. He would look out at the wire fences, the long sweep of wall, the orderly rows of windows, the symmetry of smokestacks, the gathered power to produce. "You know," he would say of it, "that cost me thirteen millions." And sometimes he would talk of the old days, his eyes wistful. "I used to spend a thousand dollars on a single phone call," he told them.

"He looked beautiful when he was talking like that," Annabel Haskins recollected. "Reminiscing and dreaming. Enthusiastic person, he was."[43]

So he went on, dreaming by the embers, keeping faith with his conception of himself and surrendering as little as possible to the years that demanded him to despair. As his life lengthened, both needs and losses continued their inexorable multiplication, and he was reduced many times to asking friends for "investments" that turned into "loans," and then into handouts. Mott lent him $30,000 in 1936, on which he defaulted. Sloan "contributed" $20,000 in the same way. There were persistent suspicions that Walter Chrysler provided money for various profitless final ventures, and Durant's repeated expressions of his affection for Chrysler, whom he described as "my best friend . . . the finest character and the greatest all-around man whom I have ever known," suggested that there was some truth to them. There may have been many letters to old associates that ran in the same vein as one sent to Kettering late in 1942. To "My dear Ket" Durant explained that an old friend, Ernest Moross, was developing a cinnabar mine in Nevada, which would produce mercury that was vital to the war effort. It was bound to receive government support as soon as production began, but needed priming to the extent of $2,100. In just the properly casual, offhanded tone, Durant concluded:

> To be brief, I would like to obtain $2100 for my friend and if you will make your check for that amount to the order of Ernest A. Moross I will appreciate it very much. This, of course, is in the nature of a loan and I will be responsible for its payment.

Durant was seeking only an indirect benefit for himself at that time. Moross, who had once managed the Buick racing team, had offered the old man a partnership in the mine if successful, and Durant saw once again a chance to make the vital lucky stroke that had been eluding him for a dozen years. The Nevada mine was not destined to fill the void. The answer came back, in a matter of days, from Kettering's Dayton bank:

> We know Mr. Kettering would personally like to comply with your request . . . but this cannot be done and be consistent with the financial program we have laid out. For this reason, we are overruling Mr. Kettering's wishes and requesting that you do not expect the check to be sent by Mr. Kettering.[44]

How many such rebuffs he received cannot be known from the fragmentary papers he left, but it is likely that there would have been many of them before he confronted the genuine shame, for him, of begging from Margery. He wrote to her in February of 1938, saying that it was "about the hardest thing [he] ever did in [his] life," and exposing the stark facts of that date. His income for the preceding five years had been $500 a month, his expenses $1,700 at a minimum. Catherine, he told her, had been "a wonderful pal," putting into his hands "every dollar she had saved before the great catastrophe." Sacrifice by sacrifice, she had written a lengthy story of divestiture. She had used up $9,000 left her as a legacy, $10,000 that were the proceeds of a ring worth $30,000, $1,900 received for gold cups, saucers, and spoons valued at $4,600 when new. He was asking for $1,200 a month until he could "get on [his] feet — a loan (not a gift) which [could] be written off" if he were not able to pay. He added the request that Margery ask her son, William Campbell, then about thirty, for some contribution as well, since "the great fortune he inherited did not come without effort."[45]

He had rarely spoken before about his "effort," and that he did so was a cruel exclamation point. Some help came, for sometime afterward he told Margery, "I am still unable to thank you for what you have done for me." But there was never enough for his exigencies.[46] He had to keep up the quest for money, not to assure his own comfort so much as to attempt the hopeless task of making things up to Catherine. So he went on brushing his cuffs, straightening his tie, looking for someone who would deal him into one more winning hand.

But he would not be able to turn to his own son for assistance. On the last Saturday in October, 1937, Russell Clifford Durant, not yet forty-seven, came back to dinner at his Beverly Hills home and complained to his third wife of feeling unwell. He went up to lie down for a while, and soon showed signs of such distress that a doctor was called. When he arrived, Cliff was dead of a heart attack. Durant described the news to John Anderson as a "crushing blow." Cliff was now gone to join the record book of bereavement — gone with Rosie and Rebecca and Dr. Campbell (who died in 1929), leaving of the old Flint family only Clara, still alive in California — she would go in 1940 — and Margery, now married to Fitzhugh Green and settled in New Canaan, Connecticut.

He saw her from time to time. There was time in full measure now; his hands were full of the one thing in which he had been niggardly, time for simple neighborliness. Time for playful notes to Murphy and Scrobogna and their children. Time for memories and small gestures that a New Jersey neighbor recorded:

More than once, while we were driving around through Monmouth County, he would have me stop at a candy store so he could buy a jar of hard candies; or at a bakery where he would emerge with a bag of lady fingers. Invariably he would say "Turner, I think I'll call up Mommie, and tell her about what time to expect me home."
Once, I said "How about coming to my house in Long Branch for dinner." He walked on through and said: "Let's eat out here in the kitchen." So we all did, and how he enjoyed it. . . . While Ernestine was preparing the meal, he and little Ernie, my daughter, would go right to

work on the checkerboard. Then afterwards we four would play bridge until it was time for me to drive him back to Asbury.

. . . One afternoon while he was with me, waiting for his train back to New York, I thanked him for his unusual interest in advising me on a certain matter. I mentioned . . . how deeply I appreciated his counsel and told him about my own father's being taken before I had ever seen him and that my mother had passed away when I was just a small boy. He said nothing but just took my hand in his and held it tightly for a while. I was so touched that it brought tears to my eyes and his were not dry either.[47]

"He was so nice, so kind," Scrobogna recollected. In his own extremity, he managed to find enough for small, regular gifts of money to Fred Hohensee, who had also lost his money and was enduring a lean old age. And once Scrobogna was with him in Asbury Park when they found a crowd of employees waiting outside the locked door of a skating rink that had gone into bankruptcy, stunned at the news that they would not be paid. Durant took out a wallet "which couldn't have contained more than fifty dollars and started to pay the help—ten dollars here, seven dollars there. And at this very time when driving to Flint he would deny himself a steak at a restaurant when stopping along the way . . . or a taxi."[48]

If there was a strange contradiction between the private self-denial and the flashy gestures before the public's scrutiny, it could only be ascribed to something which the man himself said to a reporter in his Flint bowling alley: "Nobody knows the real W. C. Durant."

In the abundance of empty hours he worked on a draft autobiography, sometimes in a little office that he kept in Manhattan's east Forties, and sometimes in his apartment. He was never to finish it, and the work went on fitfully as he dictated passages to Scrobogna or others, and wrote little notes to himself in the margin: "Presentation must be: clear, pleasant, not drag. Too full of Cliches. Make a proposition—Negotiate for control. . . . Select paper for book. Number of sheets, size, width of margin top, bottom and sides."

In a prefatory note which never saw the light of day there was a hint of bitterness: "I have had an eventful life, my work has been interesting, my friends legion. Naturally, I have suffered at times, as every man must suffer whose motives are misunderstood and whose confidence betrayed." And the suggested chapter headings raked over some of the long-buried battles with Stettinius, with Dwight Morrow, with Lee, Higginson. But the combative mood had yielded for the most part to one of resignation. What gentleness had been hidden in the years of strain resurfaced in a desire for reconciliation. He wrote to "My dear Charlie" Nash, asking to have his recollections confirmed on certain points, and concluded with an invitation to visit him either at his "pleasant little cottage down at Deal where we spend our summers," or at his new apartment at 45 Gramercy Park, fifty blocks south of, and $1,100 per month cheaper than, 907 Fifth Avenue. "My best to you and yours from a War-Scarred Veteran and Comrade," he ended. Nash replied with an amiable note. He was living in Los Angeles, complaining that his doctors had condemned him, in the aftermath of a heart attack, to a retirement during which he would "rust out." He hoped that they might get together sometime.[49]

He reopened the lines of communication with Sloan, too. When chapters of Sloan's autobiography, *White Collar Man,* appeared in the *Saturday Evening Post,* Durant read them and found an honest expression of Sloan's view that he had been a powerful visionary and a poor administrator. He took it pleasantly, writing:

I wish to thank you for the tactful way in which you handled the recent article in the Saturday Evening Post and the handsome compliments you paid me.

I do wish, Mr. Sloan, that you had known me when we were laying the foundation—when speed and action seemed necessary. You are absolutely right in your statement that General Motors justified an entirely different method of handling after the units had been enlisted. . . .

To sum up—the early history reminds me of the following story. General Wheeler, who came up from the ranks, met Major Bloomfield, a West Pointer, at the Chickamauga battlefield. . . . In speaking of the engagement General Wheeler said . . . "Right up on that hill there is where a company of infantry captured a troop of cavalry." Major Bloomfield said, "Why, General, you know that couldn't be, infantry cannot capture cavalry," to which General Wheeler replied, "but, you see, this infantry captain didn't have the disadvantage of a West Point education and he didn't know he couldn't do it, so he just went ahead and did it anyway."

Sloan responded with a stiff but genuine gratitude that Durant had not taken offense. "I would try, so far as I could, where personal references were made, to say nothing that would create unhappiness in the mind of any one, because there is plenty of unhappiness in the world today without adding more."[50] And he went on graciously to invite Durant to a preview of General Motors' 1941 line at the Waldorf. Overall, Sloan showed consideration for his predecessor. In January of 1940, when the twenty-five-millionth car produced by General Motors rolled off the line, Sloan had Durant brought out to a celebration in Detroit, and led him forward by the hand on the platform to introduce him to the crowd. On Durant's eightieth birthday he sent a bouquet of flowers and a note expressing "for myself personally and more particularly for the great organization of which I am a part, our appreciation and gratitude to you, our first leader."[51]

IV The eightieth birthday fell on the day after Pearl Harbor. There were hundreds of carefully preserved cards and messages, flowers, and gifts, which included subscriptions to a fund for publishing the autobiography, something arranged by his friends. Patiently and gratefully he tried to acknowledge them all with brief, standard messages. "Eighty cheers for eighty years." Or, "I notice the government did not make December 8th a holiday." In spite of the dreadful news crowding that morning's newspapers, there was a feature story in the Detroit *News* that brought him the kind of mail which every such occasion seemed to provoke. A forty-three-year-old woman who had been a hatcheck girl at the Detroit Athletic Club in 1916 wrote to say that his generous tips had helped her to raise her fatherless son, and she concluded: "God Bless you, Willie Crapo Durant . . . I shall say a prayer for you. . . . Some how, you are a symbol in my life."[52] A man who had worked in the Tarrytown Chevrolet plant remembered: "I got one of the greatest kicks out of life when one morning you came through the body plant and walked along holding my arm and giving us boys credit for putting over the 619 model at small cost." "So just thought," he concluded, "I would drop you a line congratulating you on being eighty years old, and hoping there are many more birthdays in store for you. . . . So just keep right up there swinging all the time."[53]

There were, in fact, to be no more birthdays in good health. In September of 1942, Durant went out with Scrobogna, to Goldfield, Nevada, to look at Ernest Moross's cinnabar mine. He scrambled up and down the side of a mountain as if it were a sand dune at Pentwater in his youth, pronounced the successful operation of the property as "possible," and then made his way back to Flint while Scrobogna proceeded home to Deal. On the night of October first, Durant lay in Room 544 of the hotel that bore his name, turning over in his mind the list of prospects who might be approached, the phrases that would need to be turned to raise the capital required. He finally drifted off to sleep. Then he woke to realize that something was terribly wrong. He tried to rise from the bed and toppled over to the floor, partially paralyzed. He managed to get to the telephone and reach Fred Aldrich, stammering out a garbled plea for help. The nimble brain had suffered a stroke; the persuasive tongue could scarcely frame coherent words.

Catherine and Aristo were summoned, and surmounted the tribulations of wartime travel to reach the bedside in Hurley Hospital. Durant lay there for eight weeks, slowly regaining some of his speech and motor functions, but also undergoing surgery for the removal of his prostate gland. On December 15, he left by ambulance for Detroit and the train ride home. He did not know it then, but he was never to return to Flint.[54]

The stroke was the felling blow of the ax, although it took the sturdy tree more than four years to topple. There were small, gradual supplementary strokes, each one a hemorrhage in the cunning, hairlike net of cerebral blood vessels, each one wiping out a tiny dot of consciousness, memory, control, organic capacity. He was reduced, bit by bit, to immobility. Scrobogna cleaned up the Pomeroy-Day work in Flint, and Durant wrote him letters that steadily became less like those of master to man and more like those of a grateful patient. "Dear Aristo, I am taking this opportunity for thanking you again and again for the many splendid things you have done for me while I have been on the 'sick list' and unable to do what I would like for myself. . . . Don't work too hard, and leave a few things for me to look after—otherwise, I will grow rusty. . . . Write often, as I enjoy your letters—that means make them short and frequent. Don't want you to sit up nights composing long ones."[55]

Sometimes he was playful still. Late in 1943 he informed Scrobogna that "Tillie" and Catherine were planning a shopping trip.

The girls, after thinking it over carefully, have decided to make a purchase today and have made up their minds that if they have enuf money between them they will buy out MACY'S. For some time it was a question between Saks' Fifth Avenue or Macy's. I hope to see them for a few minutes later in the day. This is all the good news I have at this time but think I have done pretty well even though I am half asleep.[56]

He was good-humored with old friends, too, muting his own complaints, cheering them up in their troubles. To Ralph Workman, seriously ill, he sent a mock warning:

It pleases me greatly to hear . . . that you are getting along fine after your setback of this winter . . . but take the "Old Man's" advice and go easy. I have been trying to recover my old form and have not succeeded exactly as I would like although have been on the retired list for eighteen months and the plan of winning the bowling championship of the State of Michigan is being postponed from day to day.

I am going to need some help when I get started and you and Aristo will have to assist me. Get yourself in shape because I've got a job for you. If Mrs. Workman doesn't like my plan the best thing for you to do is to get a good looking girl (blonde preferred) and that will make every-thing O.K.

The next time I come to Flint you can bet your life that I am going to apply for room and board with you on the catch as catch can plan. You can sass me all you like and you can be sure that I won't resent it — much.

Aristo is pretty strong and husky but I notice that he is getting tired of my worthless dictation. Behave yourself and mind the Lady of the House. . . .[57]

To Murphy on June 8, 1944, went a check with the notation of "a little something for your trouble . . . a 'Father's Day' present from one grand grandfather to another."[58] It was signed "Willie" Durant. The days of public petulance were behind him; a childlike gentleness settled in. "There was no harshness in him," his grandson-in-law, Grant Sanger, remembered.

Scrobogna said that as he descended into the final shadows amid his protective circle, he had moments of self-awareness. He had reached "those years when a man has a little time," and sometimes became dormant and pensive. To Scrobogna, who was a good listener, and regularly took his dictation, he came as close as it was possible for him to admit mistakes. "There are times," he said, "when I recognize that I have been a blundering fool." And once he wrote to Margery: "I have been extremely generous, but none too wise."[59]

Of all his regrets, the sharpest would be for the deprivations inflicted on Catherine. "My darling precious Muddie," he addressed her on her birthday in 1942,

To be able to write you this birthday letter is a thrilling experience — and I am thrilled.

I am not going to overdo it for reasons known to you because I am not very firm on my feet, which interferes with my writing — and by the way I have learned a lot of things in the last six months, the best of all that you are the dearest, most patient, most devoted, most unselfish, most adorable little woman in the world and without your wonderful care and constant attention I would not be here today. All this proves one thing — that you love me and I am happy to tell you (on the quiet of course) on your birthday that I love you.[60]

                                                            Willie Durant

His emotions were always near to the surface now. Tears came easily — at plays, when he could still get to them, on sentimental occasions, on visits of old friends. Sam McLaughlin came to see him one day and later reported to John Thomas Smith: "The tough part came when we were saying 'Goodbye,' as the dear old soul broke down." Once, when the

Durants and the Smiths were together, Durant began some reminiscence and his voice suddenly broke, his lips began to tremble. "Pinch yourself, Willie," Catherine whispered to him.[61]

By the spring of 1944 Durant needed steady nursing care. There was never enough money, even with occasional help from the grandchildren. The word got out to his oldest associates, and it was Sloan, of all people, who took the kindly initiative. He wrote to Mott, to Sam McLaughlin, and to John Thomas Smith, proposing that they take turns paying Catherine $2,500 each quarter for as long as Durant would live, in order to change "the closing years of Mr. Durant's life from one of anxiety to one of reasonable comfort." "Personally," Sloan continued in an odd style that suggested an imprisoned kindness struggling to escape its technocratic frame,

I don't know as I owe W. C. anything in one way, but in another way perhaps I owe him a great deal. He certainly was the pioneer who started the business as a result of which we have profited handsomely. J. T., Sam, you and others, of course, are in the same general position, although we are all different in degree. . . . I don't know as any of us mentioned could be called "Durant" men, so to speak, in relation to others that he had around him. But that is beside the point.

Mott replied somewhat guardedly, telling Sloan the story of his lost $30,000, and suggesting that he would join the pool when the others had already rendered an equal contribution. But then he added that he did not "propose to be a piker in this matter" and would "go along with [him] for Mr. Durant anyway, if that [was] what [Sloan wished]." Sloan's own answer was swift and precise. He had also made an unreturned loan to Durant, of $20,000, and in spite of it he was sure that all four of them would share the sentiments expressed by McLaughlin to Smith: "I am sure that Alfred, Stewart, you and I will never regret having done this little thing for our dearly beloved old friend."

Catherine's note of gratitude contained a pathetic summary. "Willie's condition is not at all good. . . . He has so little of interest these days."[62]

He went on downhill, except for final flickers. He would still rise at 7:30 each day, read a newspaper, and fidget if Scrobogna was late to take dictation. Once Catherine humorously reproached him for impatience. "Why don't you rest, Willie?"

"We are not given enough time, Mama," he answered.

He reached his eighty-fifth birthday on December 8, 1946, and there was one last interview. He sat in a wheelchair, still neat, dressed in a gray suit, with a red tie and a red carnation in his buttonhole. He was still, he said, "a bull of bulls."

His speech became more slurred, his functions harder to manage, the visits from old friends like Win Murphy briefer, and sometimes interrupted by moments of pain and nonlucidity. He sat in his wheelchair, slowly dying, on the edge of Gramercy Park, fifteen minutes by taxi and an entire lifetime as he had lived it from the Columbus Circle offices where he had kept the phones ringing to twenty brokers, and summoned men to action in Muncie and Flint, Detroit and Fort Worth, Jackson and Elizabeth, Flint and Bridgeport. He sat and listened to the sounds of traffic as part of the nearly forty million automobiles registered in the United States rolled past his windows — fragments of the cavalcade of wheels that he had set in motion to change the face of his country forever.

And on the morning of March 18, he heard nothing more. Catherine's message to Aristo, on the other end of the telephone was: "It's all over." "Billy's" mind would incubate no more schemes.

Condolence messages poured in from the friends of a lifetime of adventures in entrepreneurship. From Fred Aldrich and Della Bonbright and the Flint Chamber of Commerce; from Adelaide Frost Rickenbacker; from Benjamin Rosenthal, the real estate magnate of Deal, and from Arthur Lipper, one of the many brokers who had remained a friend; from Nathan Hofheimer's daughter-in-law and from Sam McLaughlin; from Ralph Dort and Samuel Ungerleider. From musicians whom Catherine had invited to Deal in the good days — Abram Chasins and Eubie Blake. From the barber four doors up from 45 Gramercy Park. From the Sloans and from Raymond Michel, whose father had manufactured the Mathis automobile. From Dr. Erdmann, and Thomas McTigue, the partner of Henry Herbermann, Durant Motors' attorney who had fought all the long retreats. From the Borough Commissioners of Deal. From all the people in showrooms and offices and shops whom he had managed, in some way, to touch in sixty years.[63]

The funeral was at the nearby Calvary Episcopal Church, and then they took his body to the family mausoleum in Woodlawn Cemetery, in the Bronx, the automotive caravan holding the narrow box and the file of mourners and moving slowly through the auto-dense avenues. He was placed on a shelf near Rebecca, and would finally never leave her side again.

His death was one of a series of them in the forties that took the generation of men who had made the automotive revolution. Walter Chrysler had passed in 1941, Ben Briscoe in 1945. Henry Ford died almost simultaneously with Durant himself. Nash went in 1948, and Ransom Olds in 1950. But Sloan, Mott, and McLaughlin lived on remarkably long — into their own eighties and nineties. McLaughlin lived to reach one hundred, active to the end.

Twelve years after Durant died, Margery's postcremation ashes were placed in the tomb occupied by her grandmother and "Pops." And in 1974, a long time later, Catherine finally joined them. Cliff was buried in California, but what remained of the family was together at last. The Yankee governor's daughter who had married badly. Her son, who had made his father's name famous in the land, and then caused it to evaporate. Her son's second wife, for whom he had built an Aladdin's palace that vanished in a puff. And the son's daughter, whose father-love had been a crippling load for her mind. They had loved each other, served each other in their separate fashions, and often failed each other in the fashion of families. And for them, finally, there were no more dreams.

Bibliography

I. MANUSCRIPTS

a. *In the General Motors Institute Alumni Foundation Collection of Industrial History, Flint, Michigan.*
    William C. Durant Papers
    Winfred W. Murphy Papers
    William S. Ballenger Papers
    George Willson Papers
    Charles Stewart Mott Papers
    Miscellaneous Durant materials in possession of Richard P. Scharchburg (cited as RPS File)
b. *In the Eleutherian Mills Historical Library, Greenville, Delaware*
    Pierre S. du Pont Papers
    John J. Raskob Papers
c. *In the Bentley Library, University of Michigan*
    Henry H. Crapo Papers
d. *In the Oral History Research Office, Columbia University*
    Nicholas Kelley Transcript
    Eugene Meyer Transcript
e. *In the Alfred P. Sloan Museum, Flint, Michigan*
    Minute Books, Durant-Dort Carriage Company
f. *In the possession of Aristo Scrobogna, Holmdel, New Jersey*
    Miscellaneous Durant materials

II. INTERVIEWS (all with the author, except as otherwise noted)

Annabel Haskins with Richard P. Scharchburg, July 12, 1973
Winfred W. Murphy with Richard P. Scharchburg, August 17, 1972
Winfred W. Murphy, December 5, 1975
Aristo Scrobogna, April 29, 1976
Arch Campbell, December 8, 1976
Conn Clifford, December 9, 1976
Arthur Sarvis, December 10, 1976
Edwina Sanger, June 21, 1977
John Anderson, January 22, 1978
John L. Bergen, January 12, 1978
Gregory Smith, March 21, 1978
David Sher, March 21, 1978

III. OFFICIAL DOCUMENTS

United States *v* E. I. du Pont de Nemours and Company, *et al.*, in U.S. District Court
for the Northern District of Illinois, Eastern Division, 1949, Testimony and
Exhibits. (Government exhibits are cited as GTX, followed by their number;
defense exhibits by name, followed by number.)
Stock Exchange Practices. Report of the Committee on Banking and Currency. *Senate
Reports,* 73d Congress, 2d Session, 1455. (Testimony before the committee is
contained in *Hearings,* 72d Congress, Part II, and cited as Pecora Committee
Hearings.)
Deed and Mortgage Books, Monmouth County Hall of Records, Freehold, New
Jersey

IV. UNPUBLISHED MANUSCRIPTS

In the General Motors Institute Alumni Foundation Collection of Industrial History.
Rodolf, Frank M., "An Industrial History of Flint."
Partridge, Bellamy, "Chevrolet in Peace and War."

V. PERIODICAL ARTICLES

John, A. P., "That Man, Durant," *Motor* (January 1923).
Kimes, Beverly Rae, "Wouldn't You Really Rather Be a Buick," *Automobile
Quarterly* (Summer 1968).
Newmark, Jacob H., "My Twenty-Five Years With W. C. Durant," *Commerce and
Finance* (May 16–Oct. 17, 1936).
Pound, Arthur, "General Motors' Old Home Town," *Michigan History* (March 1956).
Rae, John B., "The Fabulous Billy Durant," *Business History Review* (Autumn 1958).

VI. BOOKS

Allen, Frederick L. *Lords of Creation.* New York, 1935.
——— *The Great Pierpont Morgan.* New York, 1949.

Barnard, Harry. *Independent Man: The Life of James Couzens.* New York, 1958.

Barron, Clarence. *They Told Barron: Conversations and Revelations of an American Pepys in Wall Street.* New York, 1930.

Boyd, Thomas A. *Professional Amateur: The Biography of Charles F. Kettering.* New York, 1957.

Brooks, John. *Once in Golconda: A True Drama of Wall Street, 1920–1938.* New York, 1969.

Chandler, Alfred P., and Stephen Salsbury. *Pierre S. du Pont and the Making of the Modern Corporation.* New York, 1971.

Chrysler, Walter (with Boyden Sparkes). *Life of an American Workman.* New York, 1950.

Crabb, Richard. *Birth of a Giant.* Philadelphia, 1969.

Crow, Carl. *The City of Flint Grows Up.* New York, 1945.

Durant, Margery. *My Father.* New York, 1929.

Ellis, Franklin. *History of Genesee County, Michigan.* n.p., n.d.

Epstein, Ralph. *The Automobile Industry: Its Economic and Commercial Development.* Chicago, 1928.

Executive Committee, Golden Jubilee. *Golden Jubilee of Flint, Michigan, 1855–1905.* Flint, 1905.

Flink, James J. *America Adopts the Automobile.* Cambridge, Mass., 1970.

———— *The Car Culture.* Cambridge, Mass., 1975.

Fox, Jack C. *The Indianapolis 500.* Cleveland, 1967.

Galbraith, John K. *The Great Crash.* New York, 1954.

Garraty, John A. *Right-Hand Man: A Life of George W. Perkins.* New York, 1957.

Glasscock, C. B. *The Gasoline Age: The Story of the Men Who Made It.* Indianapolis, 1937.

Gustin, Lawrence R. *Billy Durant: Creator of General Motors.* Grand Rapids, 1973.

———— *A Pictorial History of Flint.* Grand Rapids, 1976.

Jardim, Anne. *The First Henry Ford: A Study in Personality and Business Leadership.* Cambridge, Mass., 1970.

Josephson, Matthew. *Infidel in the Temple.* New York, 1967.

———— *Life Among the Surrealists.* New York, 1962.

Leland, Mrs. Wilfred C. and Minnie D. Millbrook. *Master of Precision: Henry M. Leland.* Detroit, 1966.

Lewis, Eugene. *Motor Memories.* Detroit, 1947.

Lewis, Martin D. *Lumberman from Flint: The Michigan Career of Henry Howland Crapo.* Detroit, 1958.

McManus, Theodore, and Norman Beasley. *Men, Money and Motors.* New York, 1929.

Maines, George. *Men, A City and Buick.* Flint, 1953.

Maxim, Hiram P. *Horseless Carriage Days.* New York, 1962.

May, George. *A Most Unique Machine: The Michigan Beginnings of the Auto Industry.* Grand Rapids, 1975.

Nevins, Allan and Frank E. Hill. *Ford: The Times, the Man, the Company.* New York, 1954.

Pearson, Henry G. *Son of New England: James Jackson Storrow, 1846–1926.* Boston, 1932.

Pound, Arthur. *The Turning Wheel: The Story of General Motors through Twenty-five Years, 1908–1933.* New York, 1933.

Rae, John B. *The American Automobile.* Chicago, 1965.

——— *American Automobile Manufacturers: The First Forty Years.* Philadelphia, 1959.

Scharchburg, Richard P. *W. C. Durant, "The Boss."* Flint, 1973.

Seltzer, Lawrence H. *A Financial History of the American Automobile Industry.* Boston, 1928.

Sloan, Alfred P. (with Boyden Sparkes). *Adventures of a White Collar Man.* New York, 1941.

——— (with John McDonald and Catharine Stevens). *My Years With General Motors.* New York, 1963.

Sobel, Robert. *The Big Board: A History of the New York Stock Market.* New York, 1965.

Sparling, Earl. *Market Makers: Intimate Sketches of Wall Street Men and Their Millions.* New York, 1929.

Winkelman, Barnie F. *Ten Years of Wall Street.* Philadelphia, 1932.

Young, Clarence H. and William A. Quinn. *Foundation For Living: The Story of Charles Stewart Mott and Flint.* New York, 1963.

Notes

For full identification of sources cited, see the Bibliography. For the most part I have cited sources only for direct quotations or data not available in standard automotive histories, newspaper obituaries, and other easily accessible places. The abbreviation WCD always refers to William Crapo Durant. All references to his father, William Clark Durant, are spelled out in full.

1. DRUMMER FROM FLINT

1. Gustin, *Billy Durant*, p. 27.
2. *The Arrow*[missing], Flint, Aug. 31, 1913, RPS File.
3. W. W. Crapo to Rebecca Durant, July 17, 1917, Dec. 20, 1917, Durant Papers.
4. H. H. Crapo to WCD, June 4, 1864, Durant Papers.
5. Ibid., April 23, 1865.
6. Ibid., May 4, 1868.
7. Lewis, *Lumberman from Flint*, p. 50.
8. Ibid., p. 29.
9. Ibid., p. 49.
10. Ibid., p. 51.
11. Ibid., p. 55.
12. Ibid., p. 54.
13. Ibid., p. 109.
14. Ibid., p. 110.
15. Ibid., p. 152.

16. Ibid., p. 203.
17. Ibid., p. 230.
18. Ibid., p. 253.
19. Ibid., p. 84.
20. Ibid., p. 99.
21. W. W. Crapo to Rebecca Durant, Feb. 29, 1896, Durant Papers.
22. Handwritten genealogy, "John Durant of Billerica, Mass. and His Descendants," RPS File; Scharchburg, *W. C. Durant, "The Boss,"* pp.6–7.
23. William Clark Durant to H. H. Crapo, Feb. 8, 1854, H. H. Crapo Papers.
24. Marriage certificate in RPS File.
25. H. H. Crapo to William Clark Durant, Feb. 6, 1856; Durant to W. W. Crapo, Nov. 12, 1856; H. H. Crapo to Durant, Apr. 27, 1858; Durant to W. W. Crapo, undated; Durant to W. W. Crapo, July 24, 1858, H. H. Crapo Papers.
26. H. H. Crapo to Durant, June 26, May 25, 1861, H. H. Crapo Papers.
27. H. H. Crapo to W. W. Crapo, Aug. 13, 1863, H. H. Crapo Papers.
28. R. G. Dun (later Dun and Bradstreet) report, in manuscript, in Baker Library, Harvard Business School; copy in RPS File.
29. H. H. Crapo to W. W. Crapo, May 10, 1868, H. H. Crapo Papers.
30. H. H. Crapo Papers, various diary notes; H. H. Crapo to W. W. Crapo, July 30, 1868.
31. H. H. Crapo to W. W. Crapo, Aug. 18, 1868.
32. W. W. Crapo to William Clark Durant, Sept. 14, 1869, Durant Papers.
33. Rebecca Durant to Wilhelmina Clifford, undated but probably September, 1869, H. H. Crapo Papers.
34. W. W. Crapo to Rebecca Durant, Sept. 2, 1872, Durant Papers.
35. W. W. Crapo to William Clark Durant, Nov. 25, 1875, H. H. Crapo Papers.
36. Durant to W. W. Crapo, Oct. 8, 10, 1877, H. H. Crapo Papers.
37. Scharchburg, *W. C. Durant, "The Boss,"* p. 7; Gustin, *Billy Durant,* pp. 265–266.
38. Rebecca Durant to WCD, Sept. 18, 1916.
39. *Golden Jubilee of Flint,* pp. 111–113.
40. Rebecca to WCD, Sept. 18, 1916.
41. *Golden Jubilee of Flint,* p. 139.
42. Transcript of high school record, RPS File.
43. *Golden Jubilee of Flint,* p. 118.
44. Ibid., pp. 70–77.
45. Ibid., pp. 183, 193.
46. Ellis, *History of Genesee County,* p. 145.
47. Ibid.
48. *Golden Jubilee of Flint,* p. 183.
49. Ellis, *History of Genesee County.*
50. Lewis, *Lumberman from Flint,* p. 89.
51. Ellis, *History of Genesee County,* pp. 118–119, 132–138; Rodolf, "Industrial History of Flint," pp. 6–9.
52. Rodolf, "Industrial History of Flint," pp. 21, 36–46.
53. Ibid., pp. 48–58; Pound, "General Motors' Old Home Town," n.p.
54. Rodolf, "Industrial History of Flint," pp. 59–67.
55. Gustin, *Billy Durant,* p. 33.
56. Ibid., p. 34.
57. Ibid., p. 35.
58. Ibid., p. 41.
59. Unidentified clipping, RPS File.

2. THE MASTER CARRIAGE MAKER

1. WCD, "Autobiography." This brief and fragmentary manuscript, composed by Durant in his old age and never finished, must, of course, be used with care, particularly when it records verbatim conversations more than half a century old. Nonetheless, where the facts are not in dispute, or where there is no noticeable motive for distortion, I have not hesitated to accept Durant's version of his past, down to and including dialogue. See also May, *Unique Machine*, p. 186.

2. May, *Unique Machine*, p. 186.

3. Rodolf, "Industrial History of Flint," pp. 28, 56–58; WCD, "Autobiography." It is worth note that Rodolf's version of events, based in part on interviews with Durant in the latter part of the nineteen-thirties, coincides almost exactly with what Durant himself committed to writing sometime later.

4. WCD, "Autobiography."

5. Rodolf, "Industrial History of Flint," p. 78.

6. Ibid., pp. 81–82.

7. Glasscock, *Gasoline Age*, p. 151; Gustin, *Billy Durant*, p. 40; Chrysler, *American Workman*, p. 183; *New York Times*, June 7, 1948.

8. Gustin, *Billy Durant*, p. 42.

9. Rodolf, "Industrial History of Flint," pp. 79–94, 102–116.

10. F. A. Aldrich, transcript of speech given to "Old Timers'" dinner in Flint, April, 1946, Durant Papers.

11. Rodolf, "Industrial History of Flint," pp. 6, 27–29.

12. Ibid., p. 145; Aldrich speech.

13. Rodolf, "Industrial History of Flint," p. 120.

14. Minutes of Directors' Meeting, Durant-Dort Carriage Company, May, 1907.

15. Rodolf, "Industrial History of Flint," p. 138.

16. Gustin, *Billy Durant*, p. 56.

17. Records of divorce proceedings of WCD and Clara Pitt Durant, RPS File.

18. W. W. Crapo to Rebecca Durant, Nov. 10, 1902, Durant Papers; Rebecca to WCD, Nov. 4, 1902.

19. Rebecca to WCD, Nov. 4, 1902, Mar. 3, 1902, Durant Papers.

20. WCD to Rebecca Durant, Mar. 26, 1901, in possession of Aristo Scrobogna.

21. Rebecca Durant to WCD, Dec. 6, 1901; WCD to Rebecca Durant, Aug. 25, 1901.

22. W. W. Crapo to Rebecca Durant, Jan. 26, 1901, Durant Papers.

23. Rebecca Durant to Rosa Willett, May 8, 1903, Durant Papers.

24. Copy of death certificate from Bureau of Vital Records, New York City Department of Health, in possession of author.

25. Rebecca Durant to WCD, May 17, 1903, Durant Papers.

26. *Trow's Business Directory of Manhattan and Bronx*, 1901 and 1902.

3. THE AUTO COMES TO MICHIGAN

1. Robert Pirsig, *Zen and the Art of Motorcycle Maintenance*.

2. May, *Unique Machine*, pp. 83–87.

3. Ibid., pp. 30–34.

4. Nevins and Hill, *Ford*, I, 146.

5. May, *Unique Machine*, pp. 38–39.

6. Ibid., p. 99; Nevins and Hill, *Ford*, I, 171.

7. Nevins and Hill, *Ford*, I, 172–186; May, *Unique Machine*, pp. 91–108.

8. Nevins and Hill, *Ford*, I, 225–236.

9. May, *Unique Machine*, p. 63.

10. Ibid., p. 66.

11. May, *R. E. Olds*, p. 121. This full-dress life of Olds by Professor May appeared when my own work was substantially complete. I therefore rely heavily for the Olds material in this chapter on May's earlier and likewise excellent study, *A Most Unique Machine*.

12. May, *Unique Machine*, pp. 112–116.

13. Ibid.

14. Nevins and Hill, *Ford*, I, 223–224.

15. Gustin, *Billy Durant*, pp. 60–61.

16. Ibid., pp. 49–53.

17. May, *Unique Machine*, p. 194.

18. Gustin, *Billy Durant*, p. 48; Rodolf, "Industrial History of Flint," p. 88.

19. Rodolf, "Industrial History of Flint," pp. 173–184; Flink, *America Adopts the Automobile*, pp. 318–331.

20. Kimes, "Wouldn't You Really Rather Be a Buick," p. 80.

21. May, *Unique Machine*, p. 196.

22. Gustin, *Billy Durant*, pp. 59–60.

23. "History of the Original 1904 Buick," pamphlet, GMI Collection; Gustin, *Billy Durant*, pp. 62–63.

4. THE BUICK YEARS

1. Scrobogna interview.

2. Pound, *The Turning Wheel*, p. 79.

3. Margery Durant, *My Father*, pp. 78–97. It should be noted that this memoir is generally imprecise as to dates, and is contradicted on some points by other testimony.

4. Gustin, *Billy Durant*, p. 69.

5. Ibid., p. 76; May, *Unique Machine*, p. 212. May's account of early Buick financing is indispensable.

6. Pound, "General Motors' Old Home Town," n.p.

7. May, *Unique Machine*, p. 203.

8. Pound, *The Turning Wheel*, p. 85.

9. Pound, "General Motors' Old Home Town," n.p.

10. May 7, 1906, Durant Papers.

11. Kimes, "Wouldn't You Really Rather Be A Buick," p. 85.

12. WCD, "Autobiography."

13. Ibid.

14. Kimes, "Wouldn't You Really Rather Be A Buick," p. 85.

15. May, *Unique Machine*, p. 202.

16. Kimes, "Wouldn't You Really Rather Be A Buick," p. 86.

17. C. S. Mott, remarks on dedication of monument to WCD in Flint Cultural Center, Aug. 15, 1958; copy in possession of Aristo Scrobogna.

18. Rodolf, "Industrial History of Flint," pp. 230–233.

19. Sloan, *White Collar Man*, p. 49.

20. May, *Unique Machine*, p. 215.

21. Sloan, *White Collar Man*, p. 50; "History of Weston Mott Co.," typescript in Durant Papers; Memorandum by C. S. Mott, Mar. 19, 1951, Mott Papers.

22. WCD, "Autobiography"; May, *Unique Machine*, p. 217.
23. May 7, 1906, Durant Papers.
24. Sloan, *White Collar Man*, p. 86.
25. Gustin, *Billy Durant*, p. 125.
26. Margery Durant, *My Father*, p. 57.
27. Ibid., p. 157.
28. Ibid., p. 64.
29. May, *Unique Machine*, p. 177.
30. Ibid., p. 218.
31. Gustin, *Billy Durant*, p. 85.
32. Kimes, "Wouldn't You Really Rather Be A Buick," p. 87.
33. Flink, *America Adopts the Automobile*, pp. 328–331; Pound, *The Turning Wheel*, p. 90.
34. Rodolf, "Industrial History of Flint," pp. 147–149, 244–250; Gustin, *Billy Durant*, pp. 94–95.
35. Ibid., pp. 287–293.
36. WCD to Nash, Jan. 29, 1942; Nash to WCD, Mar. 5, 1942, Durant Papers. Other details of Flint's booming Buick years are in Maines, *Men, A City and Buick*.
37. Newmark, "Twenty-five Years with Durant."
38. Divorce proceedings, RPS File; Gustin, *Billy Durant*, p. 81.
39. Ibid., p. 78.
40. Rebecca Durant to WCD, Mar. 30, 1908, Durant Papers.
41. WCD, "Autobiography."

5. GENERAL MOTORS: CREATION AND CRISIS

1. "Flint Got His Dad's Buick Co.," Flint *Journal*, Nov. 19, 1972; copy in RPS File. Transcript of interview, John D. Briscoe and Richard P. Scharchburg, Nov. 15, 1972; copy in RPS File.
2. Seltzer, *Financial History of Auto Industry*, p. 21.
3. Flink, *America Adopts the Automobile*, pp. 310–311. Figures on mortality of companies are in Epstein, *Automobile Industry*, pp. 163–187.
4. May, *Most Unique Machine*, p. 23.
5. Ibid., pp. 295–299.
6. WCD, "Autobiography."
7. Eugene Meyer, interview, Oral History Research Office, Columbia University.
8. May, *Unique Machine*, p. 235; Barnard, *Independent Man*, pp. 72–75.
9. Garraty, *Right-Hand Man*, pp. 88, 185.
10. Ibid., pp. 132–133; WCD, "Autobiography"; McManus and Beasley, *Men, Money and Motors*, pp. 103–106; May, *Unique Machine*, pp. 310–313.
11. May, *Unique Machine*, pp. 313–314.
12. WCD to Hatheway, July 29, 31, Aug. 1, 1908, Durant Papers.
13. Briscoe to WCD, undated telegram, and letter, Aug. 1, 1908, Durant Papers.
14. WCD, "Autobiography."
15. Newmark, "Twenty-five Years with Durant."
16. Hatheway to WCD, Sept. 10, 1908, Durant Papers. There are several other claimants to the honor of suggesting the name, but this is the only one with documentation.
17. Pound, *The Turning Wheel*, pp. 114–118; May, *Unique Machine*, pp. 315–323.
18. Seltzer, *Financial History of Auto Industry*, pp. 156–157.
19. Kimes, "Wouldn't You Really Rather Be a Buick," p. 88.

20. WCD, "Autobiography"; Pound, *The Turning Wheel*, pp. 92–97.
21. Sloan, *White Collar Man*, pp. 37–40.
22. Leland, *Master of Precision*, p. 89.
23. Ibid., pp. 97–98; Newmark, "Twenty-five Years with Durant."
24. Newmark, "Twenty-five Years with Durant."
25. *Motor World*, November, 1910, copy in Murphy Papers.
26. Barnard, *Independent Man*, pp. 75–78. In another version, in Pound, *The Turning Wheel*, p. 121, Ford says: "All right — but gold on the table." The version drawn from the Couzens material used by his biographer seems more trustworthy.
27. May, *Unique Machine*, p. 325.
28. Seltzer, *Financial History of Auto Industry*, p. 157.
29. Flink, *The Car Culture*, p. 51.
30. Glasscock, *The Gasoline Age*, p. 193; Durant, "Autobiography."
31. McManus and Beasley, *Men, Money and Motors*, p. 109; Seltzer, *Financial History of the Auto Industry*, p. 159.
32. Pound, "General Motors' Old Home Town," n.p.
33. Seltzer, *Financial History of the Auto Industry*, pp. 160–163.
34. November, 1910.
35. Gustin, *Billy Durant*, p. 139. It is Margery's testimony that Durant complained that he hated cold weather.
36. Newmark, "Twenty-five Years with Durant."
37. W. W. Murphy, interview with RPS.
38. Crabb, *Birth of a Giant*, p. 244.
39. Pound, *The Turning Wheel*, p. 95.
40. WCD, "Autobiography."
41. Sloan, *White Collar Man*, p. 72.
42. W. W. Murphy, interview with RPS.
43. A. P. Sarvis, interview with author.
44. Gustin, *Billy Durant*, p. 125.
45. McManus and Beasley, *Men, Money and Motors*, p. 100.
46. W. W. Murphy, interview with author.
47. Flink, *America Adopts the Automobile*, pp. 64–72, 100–109.
48. May, *Unique Machine*, p. 176.
49. McManus and Beasley, *Men, Money and Motors*, pp. 116–122.
50. Pound, *The Turning Wheel*, pp. 125–126; Gustin, *Picture History of Flint*, pp. 107, 126.
51. WCD, "Autobiography"; WCD to Fidelity Trust Co., Kansas City, July 23, 1909, copy in possession of Aristo Scrobogna.
52. Aug. 15, 1910, Durant Papers.
53. Circular letter to stockholders, July 15, 1910, Willson Papers; another, Mar. 15, 1910, Ballenger Papers.
54. Pound, *The Turning Wheel*, pp. 125–126.
55. Ibid., p. 128.
56. Leland, *Master of Precision*, pp. 104–106.
57. WCD, "Autobiography"; Pound, *The Turning Wheel*, p. 131.
58. Willson Papers. The letter is undated.

6. THE COMEBACK

1. Pearson, *Son of New England*, p. 128.
2. WCD, "Autobiography."

3. Pearson, *Son of New England*, pp. 138–139.
4. McLaughlin, *Seventy-Five Years*, p. 25.
5. Gustin, *Billy Durant*, p. 146.
6. Sloan, *White Collar Man*, pp. 79–80.
7. May, *Unique Machine*, p. 178; Gustin, p. 148.
8. Pound, *The Turning Wheel*, p. 146.
9. Partridge, "Chevrolet in Peace and War."
10. Rebecca Durant to WCD, Dec. 25, 1911; Durant Papers.
11. Margery Durant Campbell to WCD, May 24, 1912, Durant Papers.
12. Gustin, *Billy Durant*, p. 152.
13. WCD, "Autobiography."
14. Gustin, *Billy Durant*, p. 159.
15. Ibid., p. 157.
16. W. W. Murphy, interview with RPS.
17. Pound, *The Turning Wheel*, p. 148.
18. Seltzer, *Financial History of Auto Industry*, p. 173.
19. Sloan, *White Collar Man*, p. 53.
20. W. W. Murphy, interview with author.
21. John L. Bergen, interview with author.
22. WCD to Arthur Bishop, May 2, 13, Dec. 4, 1914; Bishop to WCD, May 8, Dec. 8, 1914; Durant Papers.
23. WCD to Bishop, Nov. 21, 1914, Durant Papers.
24. WCD to Bishop, Nov. 3, 1914, Durant Papers.
25. McLaughlin, *Seventy-Five Years*, pp. 26–29.
26. W. W. Murphy, interview with RPS.
27. Partridge, "Chevrolet in Peace and War."
28. WCD, "Autobiography."
29. Barron, *They Told Barron*, pp. 100–101; Gustin, *Billy Durant*, p. 161; copy of agreement in Durant Papers.
30. U.S. *v* du Pont, GTX 115, and Irénée du Pont testimony, p. 866; Chandler and Salsbury, *Pierre S. du Pont*, p. 435. There is, of course, a problem of evaluation in using the record of this trial, which was an antitrust action, begun by the federal government in 1949, to force the Du Pont firm to divest itself of its controlling interest in General Motors. Eventually, the government won in the Supreme Court. A major prosecution contention was that the Du Ponts had, from a very early date, conceived the intention of dominating GM. It can be argued, therefore, that those surviving Du Pont executives who took the stand naturally shaped their testimony to refute this view. My own assessment, on the basis of all the evidence, is that the government was wrong, but I have used the testimony as judiciously as possible, and where I have reservations or questions, they appear in the text.
31. Pearson, *Son of New England*, pp. 130–131.
32. Ibid., p. 115.
33. Ibid., p. 132.
34. Ibid., p. 144.
35. Seltzer, *Financial History of Auto Industry*, p. 68.
36. Chrysler, *American Workman*.
37. Ibid., p. 105.
38. Ibid., p. 120.
39. Ibid., p. 127.
40. Ibid., pp. 140–142.
41. Seltzer, *Financial History of Auto Industry*, pp. 171–172.

42. Gustin, *Billy Durant*, pp. 165–168; WCD to George Willson, Aug. 22, Sept. 1, 1915, Willson Papers; WCD to William Ballenger, Sept. 9, 1915, Ballenger Papers.

43. Pound, *The Turning Wheel*, p. 156; Leland, *Master of Precision*, p. 117.

44. E. R. Campbell to WCD, undated, 1915, Durant Papers.

45. Campbell to WCD, undated, and Sept. 12, 1915; WCD to Campbell, Sept. 16, 1915, Durant Papers.

46. The two primary sources for the account of the meeting are a letter from Pierre du Pont to J. Amory Haskell written on the following day, available in the Du Pont Papers and also in U.S. *v* du Pont, GTX 116, and a long letter from McClement to Campbell, Sept. 16, 1915, which Campbell passed on to Durant and which is in the Durant Papers. Rodolf's "Industrial History of Flint," pp. 334–336, has an account apparently based on an interview with Durant some twenty or more years later.

47. Gustin, *Billy Durant*, p. 171.

48. Pierre du Pont to Haskell, Sept. 17, 1915, Du Pont Papers; Chandler and Salsbury, *Pierre S. du Pont*, pp. 436–437.

49. Chandler and Salsbury, *Pierre S. du Pont*, p. 437.

50. Ibid.

51. L. G. Kaufman to WCD, Oct. 27, 1915, Durant Papers.

52. Delos Fall to WCD, Sept. 22, 1915, Durant Papers.

53. Smith to WCD, Oct. 31, 1915, Durant Papers.

54. Hardy to WCD, Sept. 18, 1915, Durant Papers.

55. Arthur Mason and Harry Shiland to WCD, n.d., W. P. Cook to WCD, Sept. 18, 1915, and W. W. Mountain to WCD, Sept. 19, 1915, Durant Papers.

56. WCD from F. D. Lambie, Oct. 1, James Slocum, Oct. 2, W. S. Powell, Sept. 23, and Theodore Bird, Oct. 18, 1915, Durant Papers.

57. WCD to Hardy, Sept. 24, 1915, copy in Ballenger Papers.

58. WCD to Kaufman, Oct. 1, 1915; Kaufman to WCD, Dec. 7, 1916, Durant Papers.

59. William Ballenger to Curtis Hatheway, Dec. 21, 1915, Ballenger Papers.

60. *New York Times*, Dec. 22, 23, 1915.

61. Chandler and Salsbury, *Pierre S. du Pont*, p. 441.

62. Campbell to WCD, Dec. 31, 1915, Durant Papers.

63. Copies of both circulars in Durant Papers.

64. Pearson, *Son of New England*, p. 141.

65. WCD to Campbell, Mar. 26, 1916, Durant Papers.

66. WCD to Nash, Jan. 29, 1942, Durant Papers.

67. WCD to Nash, Mar. 13, 14, 1916; Nash to WCD, Mar. 14, 1916, Durant Papers.

68. WCD to Nash, Mar. 16; Nash to WCD, Mar. 17; S. G. Bayne to WCD, Mar. 14, 15, Durant Papers.

69. WCD to Campbell, Mar. 26; Nash to S. G. Bayne, Mar. 1; Nash to WCD, Apr. 7, Durant Papers.

70. Nash to Pierre du Pont, Apr. 18; WCD to Du Pont, undated, Du Pont Papers.

71. W. W. Murphy, interview with RPS.

72. Campbell to WCD, May 1, 1916, Durant Papers.

73. WCD to Campbell, May 4, 1916, Durant Papers.

74. Undated memorandum, Durant Papers.

75. Coleman du Pont to WCD, undated; Kaufman to WCD, May 16, 1916, Durant Papers.

76. From Durant Papers. There is no date on this letter, but along with the others cited it clearly dates from May, 1916.

77. Lewis, *Motor Memories*, p. 66.
78. John L. Bergen, interview with author.
79. Chrysler, *American Workman*, pp. 143–145; WCD, "Autobiography."
80. WCD to James Slocum, June 2, 1916, Durant Papers.
81. Gustin, *Billy Durant*, p. 180.
82. Sloan, *My Years With General Motors*, p. 13.

7. SECOND EMPIRE: THE BEST OF YEARS

1. Standish Backus to Pierre du Pont, July 15, 1916; Pierre du Pont to WCD, Aug. 25, 1916, Du Pont Papers.
2. WCD to L. G. Kaufman, Aug. 10, 1916, Durant Papers.
3. Sloan, *White Collar Man*, pp. 64–68.
4. Ibid., p. 57.
5. Ibid., pp. 91–101.
6. Durant tried to reconstruct this story for his autobiography almost thirty years later, and succeeded only in securing neither a denial nor an affirmation from Kettering and Deeds after a long, frustrating correspondence. See WCD to Deeds, Dec. 4, 1940, and June 9 and 28, 1943; Deeds to WCD, June 18, 1943; WCD to Kettering, undated and June 28, 1943; Kettering to WCD, two undated letters and one of July 10, 1943, Durant Papers. For information on Kettering's early life, Boyd, *Professional Amateur*, is the source.
7. Newmark, "Twenty-five Years with Durant."
8. David Sher and Gregory Smith, interview with author; Aristo Scrobogna, interview with author; Smith essays in possession of Aristo Scrobogna.
9. David Sher, interview with author.
10. Copies of Durant's tax returns for various years, in possession of Aristo Scrobogna.
11. The deed of sale is in the Monmouth County Hall of Records, Freehold, N.J., DB 1055, 47–49. See also Asbury Park [N.J.] *Press*, Feb. 11, 1940.
12. Pierre du Pont to J. Tracy, Mar. 6, 1917, Du Pont Papers.
13. Pierre du Pont to WCD, May 9, 1917. See also Du Pont to WCD, Oct. 23, 1916, and Mar. 4, 1918; likewise a cluster of letters among Du Pont, Durant, and Francis E. Whitten of the American Graphophone Company, dating from April 26 through May 1, 1917, all in Du Pont Papers. Also John Raskob to WCD, Aug. 16, 1916, Raskob Papers, and L. G. Kaufman to WCD, Jan. 27, 1916, Durant Papers.
14. Chandler and Salsbury, *Pierre S. du Pont*.
15. Young, "Raskob of General Motors," p. 489.
16. Sloan, *My Years With General Motors*, pp. 46–47.
17. Raskob to WCD, Mar. 10, Nov. 6, Dec. 7, 1917, Raskob Papers.
18. Raskob to WCD, Nov. 12, 1917, Sept. 9, 1918, Raskob Papers.
19. Aristo Scrobogna, interview with author.
20. Wilfred Leland to WCD, Mar. 17, 1917, Durant Papers. The complete file on the departure of the Lelands, containing about three dozen letters and several news-clips, is in Folder D74-2.40.
21. Raskob to WCD, Jan. 24, 1917, Du Pont Papers; Raskob to WCD, Mar. 6, 1917, Raskob Papers.
22. Chandler and Salsbury, *Pierre S. du Pont*, pp. 444, 456.
23. Ibid., p. 447; Newmark, "Twenty-five Years with Durant."

24. Chandler and Salsbury, *Pierre S. du Pont*, p. 448; Hayden, Stone *Weekly Market Letter*, Sept. 14, 1917, Du Pont Papers.

25. Unsigned circular letter, presumably Durant's, on stationery of General Motors, Office of the President, Dec. 23, 1917, Durant Papers.

26. Chandler and Salsbury, *Pierre S. du Pont*, pp. 449–450; J. H. McClement to "Members of the Finance Committee," Nov. 9, 1917, Du Pont Papers.

27. Chandler and Salsbury, *Pierre S. du Pont*, pp. 451–454.

28. U.S. *v* du Pont, GTX 124. In their testimony both Pierre and Irénée du Pont, questioned about this document, insisted that no matter what it said, they had never envisaged taking control of General Motors away from Durant; see pp. 673–683 and 923–926 in the testimony.

29. Chandler and Salsbury, *Pierre S. du Pont*, pp. 455.

30. L. G. Kaufman to Pierre du Pont, Jan. 15, 1918, Du Pont Papers.

31. Pierre du Pont to J. M. Earle, Mar. 17, 1918, Du Pont Papers.

32. *New York Times*, Mar. 3, 1918.

33. Gustin, *Billy Durant*, pp. 196–197.

34. Chandler and Salsbury, *Pierre S. du Pont*, p. 456; U.S. *v* du Pont, GTX 129; circular invitation, Feb. 5, 1918, Du Pont Papers.

8. SECOND EMPIRE: THE COLLAPSE

1. WCD, "Autobiography"; Sloan, *White Collar Man*, pp. 107–110.

2. Gustin, *Billy Durant*, pp. 185–188.

3. Eugene E. Husting, interview with author, and materials provided; "Samson's Iron Horse."

4. Newmark, "Twenty-five Years with Durant."

5. Ibid.

6. Ibid.

7. Pound, *The Turning Wheel*, p. 170.

8. U.S. *v* du Pont, GTX 133.

9. Pound, *The Turning Wheel*, pp. 171–175; Chandler and Salsbury, *Pierre S. du Pont*, pp. 462–464.

10. Gustin, *Billy Durant*, p. 191.

11. Ibid., p. 197.

12. Pound, *The Turning Wheel*, pp. 176–183; Chandler and Salsbury, *Pierre S. du Pont*, pp. 465–466.

13. Mason to WCD, Mar. 12, 1919, Durant Papers.

14. Raskob to WCD, Jan. 28, 1920, Durant Papers; *New York Times*, May 2, 1919.

15. Raskob to WCD, Sept. 10, 1918, Raskob Papers.

16. In February of 1921, stung by charges that he had extravagantly furthered work on the building, Durant wrote to every member of the executive committee for their recollections of his opposition. The file of responses is in the Durant Papers.

17. WCD to Raskob, Oct. 31, 1919, Durant Papers; Gustin, *Billy Durant*, p. 205; Sloan, *Years With General Motors*, pp. 31–34.

18. U.S. *v* du Pont, Sloan testimony, p. 1040; Sloan to WCD, Feb. 26, 1919, Durant Papers, in which Sloan suggests investigation of patents claimed by Heany with no apparent awareness of General Motors' previous involvement with him.

19. U.S. *v* du Pont, Pratt testimony, p. 1406.

20. E. L. Bergland to H. M. Pierce, Chief Engineer, Sept. 12, 1918, Du Pont Papers; Chandler and Salsbury, *Pierre S. du Pont*, pp. 468–474.

21. David Sher, interview with author.

22. U.S. *v* du Pont, Pratt testimony, pp. 1402–1406.

23. Ibid., General Motors Exhibit 195.

24. Ibid., Pratt testimony, pp. 1392–1396.

25. Ibid., p. 1406.

26. Newmark, "Twenty-five Years with Durant"; Margery Durant, *My Father*, p. 61.

27. Chrysler, *American Workman*, p. 156.

28. Newmark, "Twenty-Five Years With Durant."

29. Sloan, *White Collar Man*, pp. 113–114.

30. Chrysler, *American Workman*, p. 156; Sloan, *White Collar Man*, p. 118.

31. Chandler and Salsbury, *Pierre S. du Pont*, p. 475; Seward Prosser to Pierre du Pont, Jan. 20, 1920, Du Pont Papers.

32. Sloan, *Years With General Motors*, p. 34; Pound, *The Turning Wheel*, p. 184.

33. U.S. *v* du Pont, Pratt testimony, pp. 1408–1410.

34. *New York Times*, Mar. 21, 1920; Gustin, *Billy Durant*, p. 210.

35. U.S. *v* du Pont, Kettering testimony, pp. 1530–1531.

36. Chrysler, *American Workman*, pp. 146–160.

37. Chandler and Salsbury, *Pierre S. du Pont*, pp. 475–476.

38. Copy, Mar. 10, 1920, in Du Pont Papers; another, penciled in WCD's hand, in Durant Papers.

39. WCD to E. A. Watson, Mar. 22, 1920, Durant Papers.

40. Smith to WCD, Mar. 5, 1920, Durant Papers.

41. WCD to Mrs. L. T. Hollister, n.d., Durant Papers.

42. Press release dated June 3, 1920, Du Pont Papers; Chandler and Salsbury, *Pierre S. du Pont*, pp. 475–480.

43. Pierre du Pont to E. R. Stettinius, July 16, 1920, Du Pont Papers.

44. Pierre du Pont to Prosser, July 16, 1920; Stettinius to du Pont, July 20, 1920, Du Pont Papers.

45. The memorandum itself is in the Durant Papers. For Stettinius's side of the argument, see Chandler and Salsbury, *Pierre S. du Pont*, p. 483, and Barron, *They Told Barron*, pp. 105–106.

46. Sloan, *White Collar Man*, p. 119.

47. Pound, *The Turning Wheel*, pp. 185–186.

48. Leland, *Master of Precision*, p. 205.

49. Chandler and Salsbury, *Pierre S. du Pont*, pp. 480–482; U.S. *v* du Pont, Pratt testimony, p. 1404.

50. Sloan, *Years with General Motors*, pp. 36, 49, 57; Du Pont to Sloan, Sept. 15, 1920, Du Pont Papers.

51. WCD to Catherine, July 1, 1920, in possession of Aristo Scrobogna.

52. Edwina Sanger, interview with author.

53. Fox, *The Indianapolis 500*, appendix.

54. Barron, *They Told Barron*, pp. 100–110; John, "That Man Durant."

55. Arthur Bishop to WCD, Mar. 4, 1920, Durant Papers.

56. U.S. *v* du Pont, Pratt testimony, p. 1410.

57. Letter from manager, GM Stockholders Service Division, to J. G. Blaine, n.d. but fall, 1920, from internal evidence; *New York Times*, Oct. 8, 12, 1920.

58. Pierre du Pont to WCD, Nov. 8, 1920, Du Pont Papers.

59. Chandler and Salsbury, *Pierre S. du Pont*, p. 483.

60. The only known extant primary accounts of the Nov. 10–20, 1920, crisis — that is, written almost immediately after the event — are from the Du Pont–Morgan side. Pierre wrote a letter to brother Irénée on Nov. 26, 1920, in the Du Pont Papers and also printed in Sloan, *Years With General Motors*, pp. 37–44. Dwight Morrow

apparently dictated a letter to Pierre du Pont on Jan. 17, 1921, which he did not send, but which was unearthed and turned over to Du Pont in 1953 by one of the attorneys in the antitrust trial. Both are extensively drawn on in Chandler and Salsbury's account. Durant (and Morrow) told their versions later to Clarence Barron. The version presented here is my best synthesis, allowing for my opinions about the men involved. I have only footnoted direct quotations, and one or two interpolated facts.

61. Sept. 8, Sept. 12, 1919, Du Pont Papers.
62. Barron, *They Told Barron*, p. 106.
63. Ibid., p. 101.
64. A detailed accounting of the sums disbursed on Durant's account by the Morgan firm is in the Durant Papers.
65. Sloan, *White Collar Man*, pp. 125–126; Margery Durant, *My Father*, pp. 268–269.
66. U.S. *v* du Pont, Pratt testimony, p. 1411. Another version, by A. B. C. Hardy, is in Partridge, "Chevrolet in Peace and War."
67. *New York Times*, Nov. 26, 1920.
68. John, "That Man Durant."
69. Clip from *Evening Mail*, undated, Du Pont Papers.

9. KING OF THE BULLS

1. W. W. Murphy, interview with author; Newmark, "Twenty-five Years with Durant."
2. R. Clifford Durant to WCD, Rebecca Durant to WCD, E. R. Campbell to WCD, Dec. 8, 1920, in possession of Aristo Scrobogna.
3. W. W. Crapo to Rebecca Durant, Mar. 22, 1921, Durant Papers.
4. Memorandum dated Dec. 31, 1920, Durant Papers.
5. WCD to Pierre du Pont, Jan. 6, 1921, Durant Papers.
6. Chandler and Salsbury, *Pierre S. du Pont*, pp. 499–507.
7. Barron, *They Told Barron*, p. 108.
8. WCD to Irénée du Pont, Mar. 16, 1921, Durant Papers.
9. Irénée du Pont to WCD, Mar. 30, 1921, Durant Papers.
10. WCD to various subscribers to Syndicate #5, Dec. 24, 1920, Durant Papers.
11. WCD to H. K. Noyes, Dec. 28, 1920, Durant Papers.
12. Pierre du Pont to WCD, Mar. 16, 1921; WCD to Pierre du Pont, Mar. 18, 1921, Durant Papers.
13. Gustin, *Billy Durant*, p. 224.
14. WCD to L. A. Young, Aug. 27, 1921, Durant Papers. There is a complete file of similar letters.
15. Lansing *State Journal*, May 21, 1921.
16. New York *Curb*, Nov. 19, 1921.
17. Undated newsclip in Durant Papers, early 1921 by internal evidence.
18. Quoted in *New York Times*, Aug. 10, 1921.
19. John, "That Man Durant."
20. Newmark, "Twenty-five Years with Durant"; *New York Times*, Jan. 26, 1923.
21. Newmark, "Twenty-five Years with Durant."
22. *New York Times*, Apr. 2, May 3, 7, 1921.
23. U.S. *v* du Pont, Pratt testimony, p. 1413.
24. Pamphlet, "Durant Breaks World Records," in Durant Papers; Gustin, *Billy Durant*, p. 229.

25. Gustin, *Billy Durant*, p. 228; Nicholas Kelley, interview, Oral History Research Office, Columbia University; *New York Times*, June 10, 1922; Chrysler, *American Workman*.

26. WCD to Pierre S. du Pont, Jan. 18, 1921, Durant Papers.

27. Flint *Journal*, July 25, 1922, and Detroit *Free Press*, undated, clipped in Durant Papers; *New York Times*, July 25, 1922.

28. Newmark, "Twenty-five Years with Durant"; *New York Times*, July 23, Oct. 4, 17, 1922.

29. Newmark, "Twenty-five Years with Durant"; *New York Times*, Apr. 20, Aug. 30, 1923.

30. Newmark, "Twenty-five Years with Durant."

31. WCD to Forbes, May 28, 1923; Forbes to WCD, May 29, 1923, Durant Papers; Gustin, *Billy Durant*, p. 233.

32. *New York Times*, Oct. 2, 1921.

33. WCD to S. S. Fontaine, May 15, 1923; Fontaine to WCD, May 16, 1923; J. T. Collins to WCD, May 10, 1923, Durant Papers.

34. Barron, *They Told Barron*, p. 110.

35. Gustin, *Billy Durant*, p. 230.

36. Newmark, "Twenty-five Years with Durant."

37. *New York Times*, Jan. 25, 26, 27, 1923, Sept. 9, 1924.

38. Ibid., Dec. 11, 1924, Feb. 11, 1925, Apr. 10, 1927.

39. Ledger, "Brokers and Securities Analysis, 1927," Durant Papers.

40. Gustin, *Billy Durant*, p. 246.

41. New York *Herald*, European edition [Paris], June 1, 1929.

42. *New York Times*, Feb. 12, 1927.

43. Josephson, *Infidel in the Temple*, p. 19.

44. Sparling, *Market Makers*, pp. 4–8, 17–19, 22–27.

45. The *Sketch* was edited by M. Mustin; a file of clippings on Deal is to be found in the Long Branch, N.J., Public Library; see stories in the Asbury Park *Press*, Feb. 11, 1940, Mar. 19, 1961, Nov. 11, 1966, Apr. 21, 1967, and June 1, 1969.

46. Sale catalog by Meredith Galleries (indexed in New York Public Library under Durant, Mrs. William C.); W. W. Murphy, interviews with RPS and author; Gregory Smith, Aristo Scrobogna, interviews with author.

47. Chrysler, *American Workman*, p. 143.

48. "Journal of Personal and Business Expenses," Durant Papers (covering years 1923 through 1928); "Durant Motor Co. of N.J., Branch Payrolls, Compiled Apr. 5, 1928," Durant Papers.

49. WCD to Catherine L. Durant, Feb. 7, 1924, Durant Papers; Margery Durant, *My Father*, p. 296.

50. W. W. Crapo to WCD, Feb. 9, 1924, Durant Papers.

51. Edwin Atwood to WCD, Aug. 12, 1925, Durant Papers.

52. Edwina Sanger, interview with author; obituary of R. W. Daniel, *New York Times*, Dec. 21, 1940; obituary of Fitzhugh Green, *New York Times*, Dec. 3, 1947; clip from magazine, *The Sphinx*, May 30, 1931, Durant Papers.

53. R. Clifford Durant to WCD, May 8, 1927; WCD to R. Clifford Durant, May 9, 1927, Durant Papers.

54. John Anderson, interview with author; *New York Times* (obituary), Nov. 1, 1937; Flint *Journal*, Nov. 1, 1937; miscellaneous material in RPS File; Fox, *The Indy 500*; Houghton Lake [Mich.] *Resorter* Summer Guide, 1973.

55. Gustin, *Billy Durant*, p. 239; Margery Durant, *My Father*, pp. 297–300; W. W. Murphy, interview with author; *New York Times*, Jan. 11, 12, 1926.

56. *New York Times*, Jan. 13, 14, 15, 17, 21, 1926.
57. Ibid., Feb. 19, 1926.
58. Epstein, *Auto Industry*, pp. 163–187; Rae, *American Auto Manufacturers*, p. 133.
59. Letter to stockholders, Jan. 7, 1926, in possession of Aristo Scrobogna.
60. *New York Times*, June 2, 1928.
61. W. W. Murphy, interview with RPS.
62. "Schedule of Assets and Liabilities, Durant Motors, June 30, 1926"; "Production Schedules, 1927-1, Durant Motors of New Jersey and Durant Motors of Michigan," Durant Papers; Flint *Journal*, Jan. 11, 1929.
63. *New York Times*, Mar. 22, 1927.
64. Ibid., Mar. 23, 24, 26, 27, 29, Apr. 6, 7, 8, 20, 1927.
65. Ibid., Nov. 15, Dec. 1, 1927.
66. Ibid., Mar. 2, 1928.
67. Copy of the contract, signed at Paris, Oct. 6, 1928, Durant Papers.
68. *New York Times*, Jan. 11, 12, 1929.
69. Jan. 23, 1929, in possession of Aristo Scrobogna.
70. Gustin, *Billy Durant*, pp. 241–243.
71. WCD to P. Cusick, Feb. 5, 1928, Durant Papers.
72. Galbraith, *Great Crash*, pp. 86–87.
73. *Stock Exchange Practices*; Pecora Committee *Hearings*, pp. 469, 765; Winkelman, *Ten Years of Wall Street*, p. 288.
74. *New York Times*, Feb. 28, 1929.
75. Telegram and replies in Durant Papers; *New York Times*, Apr. 2, 1929.
76. Sparling, *Market Makers*; *New York Times*, Dec. 14, 1929.
77. New York *Herald*, European edition [Paris], June 1, 1929.
78. *New York Times*, June 19, 1929.
79. Memorandum, Aug. 9, 1929, Durant Papers, presumably a press release.
80. Josephson, *Infidel in the Temple*, p. ix.
81. "Brokers and Securities Analysis, 1929" and "Ledger," 1930, Durant Papers.
82. Gregory Smith, interview with author.
83. Sparling, *Market Makers*.

10. OLD MAN IN A DRY SEASON

1. Letter in possession of Aristo Scrobogna.
2. Aristo Scrobogna, interview with author.
3. *New York Times*, Apr. 23, June 30, 1930.
4. Circular; undated budget; WCD to R. L. Owen, Jan. 7, 1932, Durant Papers.
5. Copies of the telegram in Durant Papers. Several bear the date of Feb. 8, 1932. Rogers's answer was written directly on the telegram itself, which he returned.
6. A surviving copy in the file is addressed to M. L. Pulcher, Nov. 2, 1932, Durant Papers.
7. Mar. 1, 1933; several copies in possession of Aristo Scrobogna.
8. WCD to R. Whitney, Mar. 15, 1933, Durant Papers.
9. A complete file of correspondence on the case is in the Durant Papers; included are newsclips from the New York *Telegram*, Jan. 23, 1930, and New York *World*, Feb. 4, 1930. There are stories in the *New York Times*, Feb. 9 and Mar. 2, 1930.
10. Winkelman, *Ten Years of Wall Street*, p. 303.
11. *New York Times*, Dec. 7, 1930, June 3, 1932, Jan. 21, Dec. 30, 1933, May 19, 1934.

12. H. Satterlee to WCD, Jan. 5, 1933; WCD to Satterlee, Jan. 6, 10, 1933, Durant Papers.

13. Report of Durant Motors, Inc., Dec. 12, 1930; *New York Times*, Aug. 20, 1930; WCD to W. R. Angell, C. A. Dana, A. A. Henninger and C. O. Miniger, Feb. 13, 1931, Durant Papers.

14. H. Herbermann to WCD, June 15, 1931, Durant Papers.

15. WCD to Ralph Poucher, Mar. 25, 1931; "Proposed Settlement of WCD-Fisk Building Account, May 8, 1931"; R. W. Daniel to WCD, June 25, 1931, Durant Papers.

16. WCD to A. H. Sarver, Nov. 4, 1929, Durant Papers.

17. WCD to W. S. Ballenger, Dec. 30, 1929, Mar. 21, 1930, Mar. 30, 1933, Ballenger Papers; "Memorandum of Activities," Nov. 4, 1931, Durant Papers; *New York Times*, Mar. 29, 1933.

18. Undated newsclip in file, "American Cottonpicker," Durant Papers.

19. "Advances to American Cottonpicker Corp.," July 29, 1927; E. J. Silvers to WCD, Jan. 22, 1930, Durant Papers.

20. Tax returns in possession of Aristo Scrobogna.

21. *New York Times*, Feb. 9, 1936.

22. John Anderson, interview with author.

23. Undated, handwritten note, in possession of Aristo Scrobogna.

24. *New York Times*, Sept. 5, 14, 15, 16, 17, 20, 1938.

25. Asbury Park *Press*, Feb. 11, 1940.

26. A. Goebel to WCD, Feb. 9, 1936, Durant Papers.

27. J. Little to WCD, Feb. 9, 1936; John Corcoran to WCD, n.d.; Thad B. Preston and W. L. Kellogg to WCD, n.d.; J. P. B. Fiske to WCD, Feb. 21, 1936, Durant Papers.

28. Durant Papers, various dates.

29. WCD to S. Rosoff, Feb. 10, 1936, June 14, 1937; Rosoff to WCD, June 15, 1937, Durant Papers.

30. Memorandum of no date, but apparently 1932.

31. "Report on Accounts of BOST Corp., Sept. 30, 1934," Durant Papers.

32. Memorandum, July 16, 1940, Durant Papers.

33. C. B. Little to WCD, July 29, 1934, Durant Papers.

34. Gregory Smith, interview with author.

35. "Durant's Dishes," *Time*, Sept. 28, 1936.

36. "Financial Statement of Pomeroy-Day Land Co., Dec. 31, 1926"; "Trial Balance, Deal Gables, 1932"; WCD to A. Scrobogna, Dec. 22, 1941, all in possession of Aristo Scrobogna. Foreclosures on Deal Gables properties in Monmouth County Hall of Records under various dates as the properties were sold off; see Oct. 22, 1940, Nov. 2, 1940, and Dec. 3, 1941, for examples.

37. Aristo Scrobogna, interview with author.

38. Ibid.; *New York Times*, Mar. 16, 17, 29, Apr. 30, May 3, 1939, Mar. 19, 1940.

39. Complete, or at least very full, files of the entire Crown Point Products correspondence are in the Durant Papers. Arch Campbell, interview with author.

40. Conn Clifford, interview with author.

41. Arch Campbell, interview with author. The leaflet involved is in the Durant Papers with other material on a short-lived creation of that period, the World Peace League.

42. Newsclips in W. W. Murphy Papers, "Bowling For All," Detroit *News*, Apr. 27, 1941; "Once GM Head Now Runs Bowling Alley," identifiable only as an Associated Press story of Dec. 8, 1941; another Associated Press story, "Durant Tries Again for Fortune," June 8, 1940.

43. Annabel Haskins, interview with RPS; A. Scrobogna and A. Campbell, interviews with author; Flint *Journal*, Nov. 12, 1941.

44. WCD to Kettering, Nov. 11, 1942; R. H. Brundrett to WCD, Nov. 14, 1942, Durant Papers.

45. WCD to Margery, Feb. 1, 1938, in possession of Aristo Scrobogna.

46. WCD to Margery, Dec. 15, 1941, Durant Papers.

47. W. Mason Turner to Catherine Durant, Mar., 1947, in possession of Aristo Scrobogna.

48. Aristo Scrobogna, interview with author.

49. WCD to Nash, Jan. 29, 1942; Nash to WCD, Mar. 5, 1942, Durant Papers.

50. WCD to Sloan, Sept. 13, 1940; Sloan to WCD, Sept. 24, 1940, Durant Papers.

51. Gustin, *Billy Durant*, p. 252; Sloan to WCD, Dec. 8, 1941, Durant Papers.

52. Anna Langdon to WCD, Dec. 14, 1941, Durant Papers.

53. Clarence [Kaye?] to WCD, Dec. 7, 1941, Durant Papers.

54. Gustin, *Billy Durant*, pp. 253–255.

55. WCD to Scrobogna, n.d., and July 18, 1944, in possession of Scrobogna.

56. WCD to Scrobogna, Oct. 30, 1943, in possession of Scrobogna.

57. "Durant Few Knew," Flint *Journal*, May 12, 1974.

58. W. W. Murphy Papers.

59. Aristo Scrobogna, interview with RPS.

60. Letter in possession of Scrobogna.

61. Gregory Smith, interview with author; R. S. McLaughlin to J. T. Smith, Sept. 7, 1944, Mott Papers.

62. Sloan to Mott, Feb. 2, May 19, 1944; Mott to Sloan, May 24, 1944; Sloan to Mott, June 3, 1944; Mott to Sloan, Sept. 23, 1944; Catherine Durant to Sloan, May 17, 1944; R. S. McLaughlin to J. T. Smith, Sept. 7, 1944. All in Mott Papers; there is additional correspondence between Mott and his accountant relating to the defaulted debt of 1936.

63. Gustin, *Billy Durant*, p. 257; messages of condolence in possession of Aristo Scrobogna.

Acknowledgments

First of all, I would like to render special thanks to Professor Richard P. Scharchburg, of the General Motors Institute, teacher, curator, collector, author, and enthusiast. His generosity and energy were indispensable to this book and are appreciated beyond words.

Aristo Scrobogna likewise shared his irreplaceable memories and memorabilia of William C. Durant with warmth and encouragement that sped and lightened my work.

Roger van Bolt, the now-retired director of the Alfred P. Sloan Museum in Flint, was an infallible guide to needed materials and likewise made possible a brief and exhilarating spin in a 1910 Buick, the high point of the research.

I would like to say a special word of thanks for the effort of Winfred W. Murphy, ninety-two when I interviewed him in 1975, to recall his years with Durant, particularly those early ones for which he was the only living source.

I thank the Eleutherian Mills Historical Library, the General Motors Institute Alumni Foundation, the Bentley Library of the University of Michigan, and the Oral History Research Office of Columbia University for permission to use the materials in their control which I have cited in the book. Thanks are also due the Baker Library of the Harvard Business School for permission to quote the R. G. Dun (later Dun & Bradstreet) report on William Clark Durant.

Needless to say, I am especially grateful to the people who permitted me to interview them, and whose names appear in the bibliography. Mrs. Sanger and Mr. John Anderson were especially helpful in providing photographs or clues to the location of photographs, for which I happily render extra thanks. I am additionally indebted to Mr. Eugene E. Husting for similar aid.

Superlative research assistance was provided by Mrs. Eugene T. Anderson. During a brief research stint, Ms. Celia Hartmann was also prompt, complete, and thoroughly helpful.

For suggestions and answers to queries, I would also like to thank the following people: Martha Briscoe, Lawrence Gustin, Janet McGill, George May, John B. Rae, Pam Sheridan, the late Thomas Storrow, Mrs. Jay Thompson.

I tender special thanks to Dr. Gordon I. Kaye, a longtime and valued friend, who not only photographed documents and locations in Flint for my benefit but provided stimulating suggestions and questions from the book's inception to its conclusion.

In addition, I would like to express my debt to the staffs of the Flint Public Library, the Public Library of Long Branch, New Jersey, the Monmouth County Historical Association, and the Alexander Library of Rutgers University. Particular thanks are due to Ms. Elsalyn Drucker, Ms. Miriam Scholes, and Mr. Ron Becker.

Two institutional acknowledgments are a special pleasure. The Frederick Lewis Allen Room of the New York Public Library is a place where a few lucky writers, for temporary periods, are given relative seclusion and a desk at which they can use the library's collections, gathered at their request by a helpful staff. I feel privileged to have used it. The MacDowell Colony, in Peterborough, New Hampshire, offered two months of unbroken privacy and attentive care, for which there is no adequate recompense, but I offer my heartfelt thanks in token.

For all of these helpers, the conventional disclaimer applies: they are not responsible either for my interpretations or my errors.

A final word. Ned Bradford, a senior editor at Little, Brown and Company, died on May 12, 1979. He had been my editor and my friend for nearly twenty-nine years, and his encouragement, patience, and helpful criticism were always deeply important to me, particularly so in the case of this book. Though he is gone, I want to express here my thanks for all that he did on my behalf.

B. A. W.

Index

B—Durant

Weisberger, Bernard
A.

The dream maker

DATE DUE

AUG 12 1998			